Curiouser

Curiouser

On the Queerness of Children

Steven Bruhm and Natasha Hurley, Editors

University of Minnesota Press • Minneapolis • London

See pages 321–22 for copyright information for previously published material in this book.

Copyright 2004 by the Regents of the University of Minnesota

All rights reserved. No part of this publication may be reproduced, stored in a retrieval system, or transmitted, in any form or by any means, electronic, mechanical, photocopying, recording, or otherwise, without the prior written permission of the publisher.

Published by the University of Minnesota Press
111 Third Avenue South, Suite 290
Minneapolis, MN 55401-2520
http://www.upress.umn.edu

Library of Congress Cataloging-in-Publication Data

Curiouser : on the queerness of children / Steven Bruhm and Natasha Hurley, editors.
    p. cm.
Includes bibliographical references and index.
ISBN 0-8166-4201-X (hc : alk. paper) — ISBN 0-8166-4202-8 (pb : alk. paper)
    1. Children and sex.   2. Homosexuality.   3. Children in literature.
4. Children in popular culture.   5. Sex in popular culture.   I. Bruhm, Steven.   II. Hurley, Natasha.
    HQ784.S45C87 2004
    305.23—dc22

                                                                2003027197

Printed in the United States of America on acid-free paper

The University of Minnesota is an equal-opportunity educator and employer.

12 11 10 09 08 07 06 05 04   10 9 8 7 6 5 4 3 2 1

Contents

Acknowledgments

For their insights, suggestions, resistances, and inspiration in various forms, we thank the following people: Andrea Baldwin, Maggie Berg, Elizabeth Freeman, Emily Givner, Susanne Luhmann, Barbara Markovits, Robert K. Martin, Robin Metcalfe, Maurice Michaud, Shawn Miner, Dan O'Neill, Adèle Poirier, Melea Seward, Peter Schwenger, Heidi Ship, Theresa Smalec, Edie Snook, Goran Stanivukovic, the Sexuality Studies Working Group at Rutgers University, as well as family and friends.

For putting their money where our mouths were, we are grateful to the Social Sciences and Humanities Research Council of Canada, Mount St. Vincent University, and Rutgers University, all of whom funded our research.

For support as research assistants and jills of all trades, we thank Peggy MacKinnon and Lori MacDonald. Debbie Fewer, secretary of Mount St. Vincent's English Department, never tired of giving us extra computer paper. And speaking of computers, many thanks to Alvin Comiter.

For commending us on the good things and taking us to task on the worst ones, we would like to thank our readers, including Carol Mavor, and our editor, Richard Morrison, who never lost his sense of humor.

Finally, for agreeing to be part of this project and then being such wonderful people to work with, we thank our contributors, without whom this *Curiouser* collection could not exist.

Curiouser: On the Queerness of Children

Steven Bruhm and Natasha Hurley

A Simple Story

This book is about stories: stories we tell to children, stories we tell about children, stories we tell about ourselves as children. It's also about sex and queerness as they relate to the contemporary and historical field of such stories. There is currently a dominant narrative about children: children are (and should stay) innocent of sexual desires and intentions. At the same time, however, children are also officially, tacitly, assumed to be heterosexual. Cute boy-girl romance reads as evidence for the mature sexuality that awaits them, and any homoerotic behavior reads as harmless play among friends or as a mistake that can later be corrected by marriage. In the apparent simplicity of this story, child sexual life persists in its most benign forms: it pervades the happily-ever-after of fairy tales and Disney films; it circulates in diaper ads; it permeates the scientific discourses of university curricula. North America welcomes this story, as long as it remains a *particular* one. People panic when that sexuality takes on a life outside the sanctioned scripts of child's play. And nowhere is this panic more explosive than in the field of the *queer* child, the child whose play confirms neither the comfortable stories of child (a)sexuality nor the supposedly blissful promises of adult heteronormativity. It is the effort to examine the complex stories that arise from the field of child sexuality, and in particular their relation to the queer, that unites the essays in this volume. At the heart of these complexities are some fairly basic narrative questions: Who tells the story, to whom, and how?

Who tells the story matters because the storyteller defines what can exist in the field of representation. Whether that storyteller is a novelist, a filmmaker, a researcher, a photographer, a day-care leader, or a parent, he or she decides what is inside and outside the narrative world, which is also, implicitly, a decision about what is inside or outside a world whose language tries to normalize some behaviors at the expense of others. How the story is conveyed—who is rendered visible, what language they use, the narrative or cinematic biases that frame them, the fate of their sexual innocence or dissidence—carries the moral weight of creating the statistically "normal" child. How there has come to be a language of the "normal child" itself poses a curious question that requires a more detailed historical analysis than we can provide here. What we can observe, however, is that the representative field of that child has certainly expanded in the past thirty years. According to Nettie Pollard, we now hold it as "indisputable that everyone is sexual, even before birth."[1] As a result, we religiously school our children in bodily awareness, in "good touch versus bad touch," and in the kinds of physical—even sexual—expression that bestow upon them the "at-homeness" in their bodies so crucial to that holy state of "self-esteem." As historian of sexuality Michel Foucault cautions us, reveling in this proliferation of stories about the sexual child does not guarantee a new, free world. This proliferation may herald new ways of expressing sexuality, especially for children, but according to Foucault it also invents new regimes for controlling and regulating the sexuality we think we are affirming—regimes that have a long history in modern thought and culture. In telling stories about children and sex, our culture's storytellers have long gestured to the stories that ought not feature children: stories that make children "queer" in a number of distinct ways and therefore are rarely told. In this collection, as in much contemporary criticism, the term *queer* is intended to be spacious. The authors (ourselves included) use the term *queer* in its more traditional sense, to indicate a deviation from the "normal." In this sense the queer child is, generally, both defined by and outside of what is "normal." But the term *queer* derives also from its association with specifically sexual alterity. In this collection, the figure of the queer child is that which doesn't quite conform to the wished-for way that children are supposed to be in terms of gender and sexual roles. In other circumstances, it is also the child who displays interest in sex generally, in same-sex erotic attachments, or in cross-generational attachments. The essays in this volume approach these stories and tease out the range of possibilities for child sexuality. These essays look to the dominant heteronarrative to see how normalizing language itself both produces and resists queer stories of childhood sexual desire—stories that often appear to be beyond the narrative pale.

Architects of the child in culture have developed elaborate means of editing out or avoiding the kinds of sexuality children aren't supposed to have—all in an effort to simplify what is, in fact, not at all a simple story. Consider the following:

Exhibit A: Queerness in Wonderland

Throughout her journey, Alice is quite fond of identifying things in Wonderland as "queer" and awakes excitedly to tell her sister about these episodes, thus using a story to link the dreamworld to the framing narrative world. One of those queer episodes is Alice's adventure in babysitting, during which the infant for whom she is forced to care transforms into a pig. Alice releases the pig into the forest with horrifying nonchalance: "It would have made a dreadfully ugly child," she reasons, "but it makes a rather handsome pig, I think."[2] At this moment, Alice rejects the role of motherhood that golden-age Victorian literature sees as inevitable for little girls. But the rejection is lost on her sister, who sees in the episode only an occasion for Alice's maternal performance. She imagines Alice as a grown woman repeating her adventures to the "other little children" whom "she would gather about her."[3] As the sister sees Alice's role of storyteller as a particularly *maternal* one, she transposes the queer into the domestic pastoral. Alice's confusion, bewilderment, and anger—culminating in the final rejection of her culture as "nothing but a deck of [playing] cards"[4]—are transmogrified into a blissful domestic scene where Alice, her audience, her sister, and we as readers curl up with a childhood that has been re-created as "simple sorrows" and "simple joys,"[5] void of the "curiouser and curiouser" quality by which Alice had continually defined it. It becomes a "child's story," bereft of any pleasures other than what the sister may want to imagine childhood to be. By the novel's end, desire belongs to the sister alone, as she superimposes the banalizing *form* of the child-story over the *content* of what that child is telling.

Exhibit B: The "Real" Queer Child

When Robert Owens decided to write *Queer Kids*, his aim was to "let [gay, lesbian, and bisexual] youth speak for themselves," to "disclose" something very personal about their lives and experiences. And yet the project of recording authenticity quickly became a problem for Owens:

> Originally, I had intended to interview lesbian, gay, and bisexual teens and to quote them extensively in this book. I have talked with many across the country. A problem arises, not from talking but from quoting in print. It is difficult to get permission to quote . . . underaged teens, especially when they are in the closet. On advice from an editor friend, I decided to paraphrase teens with whom I talked and to supplement this with appropriate

quotes from other authors. I believe the combination provides more varied and lively reading.[6]

As Owens attempts to liberate the voices of queer youth, he is faced with a number of narrative problems: first, he meets the limits of print culture when he encounters the legal difficulty of quoting teens; second, he must deal with the challenges of being a writer himself (how can he write a book that makes for "lively reading"?). Like Alice's sister, Owens recasts these voices for the story he wants. He then insists that he is still "letting youth speak for themselves," just as Alice is seen to be telling *her* own story to other children. Compounding this further is a layer of narrativizing that Owens does not account for. He says that his problems arise from quoting, not talking, which assumes that what his teenagers say is a transparent presentation of experience. But as Hayden White has argued, all discourses claiming to present the historical "truth" are themselves confined by the conventions of narrative.[7] In the act of telling their lives to Owens, the youths have already made their realities into stories. Owens uses pieces of these stories, adds pieces of other authors' stories, and sutures them all together using his own voice. The effect is a queer kid whose monologue is really editorial pastiche—all in the effort to make "more lively and varied reading."

Exhibit C: The Progeny of Homos

The fictional children of gay and lesbian parents, by contrast, are children without many desires at all. In books like *Heather Has Two Mommies, Daddy's Roommate, Uncle What-Is-It Is Coming to Visit!!,* and *Gloria Goes to Gay Pride,* we find sanitized middle-class worlds where the children are evacuated of any desires but those of creature comforts—Who will pick me up from my politically correct day care? or Why do I have to eat brussels sprouts?[8] These children do express some anxiety about their queer domestic configurations—Why don't I have a daddy like other kids? What does it mean that my uncle is "gay"?—but these anxieties are quelled by the assurance that they are just like everyone else, that love makes a home, and that Uncle What-Is-It is not a drag queen but a Princeton letterman. These children live perfect lives, evidence of homosexual respectability. They exhibit a pronounced absence of sexual curiosity: they don't play at imitating their homosexual elders in the way typical of "dolls-and-trucks" children's culture, and they *never* wonder about their own sexual tastes or consider their own erotic identities. Granted, the authors of these books are writing in a climate where panic about (at best) recruitment and (at worst) pedophilia in gay and lesbian culture is rampant. But their bland children throw into high relief the truism that sexuality is otherwise omnipresent in children's

▼ Steven Bruhm and Natasha Hurley

culture. These books write the child's desire out of existence, eradicating the sexual child in the process. Jacqueline Rose has argued that "childhood innocence [is] . . . a portion of adult desire,"[9] and in these books the child becomes a cipher into which adult desires and anxieties are poured.

In all of these ostensibly simple stories—about Alice, queer teens, the children of gay and lesbian parents—the story of the child shifts almost imperceptibly to the story of the adult at a key moment: the ending. If writing is an act of world making, writing about the child is doubly so: not only do writers control the terms of the worlds they present, they also invent, over and over again, the very idea of inventing humanity, of training it and watching it evolve. This inscription makes the child into a metaphor, a kind of ground zero for the edifice that is adult life and around which narratives of sexuality get organized. As long as there is a sister to contain Alice, an editor to organize the voices of queer youth, and a squeaky-clean uncle to make being gay all right, the fantasy of a preferred future that the child embodies is secure.

Utopianism follows the child around like a family pet. The child exists as a site of almost limitless potential (its future not yet written and therefore unblemished). But because the utopian fantasy is the property of adults, not necessarily of children, it is accompanied by its doppelgänger, nostalgia. Nostalgia is the fantasy of a preferred past (past pleasures, past desires for the future). Caught between these two worlds, one dead, the other powerless to be born, the child becomes the bearer of heteronormativity, appearing to render ideology invisible by cloaking it in simple stories, euphemisms, and platitudes. The child is the product of physical reproduction, but functions just as surely as a figure of cultural reproduction. Thus both the utopianism and the nostalgia invoked by the figure of the child are, in turn, the preferred form of the future.

Lee Edelman has considered the significance of the child *as* future. In his 1998 essay "The Future Is Kid Stuff," Edelman reads the child as the anti-queer, claiming that the future is figured by the ubiquitous icon of the innocent child and that this child is often invoked as a symbol of family values, especially by the political right in the United States today. "The cult of the child permits no shrines to the queerness of boys or girls," he asserts, and draws from this absence the following conclusion about queer politics:

Choosing to stand, as many of us do, outside the cycles of reproduction, choosing to stand, as we also do, by the side of those living and dying each day from the complications of AIDS, we know the deception of the societal lie that endlessly looks toward a future whose promise is always a day away. We can tell ourselves that with patience, with work, with generous contributions to lobbying groups, or generous participation in activist groups, or general doses of political savvy and electoral sophistication, the future will hold a place for us—a place at the table that won't have to come, as it were, at the cost of our place in the bed or the bar, or the baths. But there are no queers in that future as there can be no future for queers.[10]

Edelman resists the coherence and reason of liberal political discourse, arguing that we need to embrace the negativity of queerness, not what he sees as the heterosexual narrativity of liberalism and its commitment to reproduction as the basis of social continuity.[11]

What is the effect of projecting the child into a heteronormative future? One effect is that we accept the teleology of the child (and narrative itself) as heterosexually determined. Whatever might be said about the viability of this telos for queer politics more generally, it is also worth pointing out that the narrative pressure on producing the proper ending of the story (the heterosexual adult) allows a little more play for the child prior to the moment of ascension into that heterosexual future. The very effort to flatten the narrative of the child into a story of innocence has some queer effects. Childhood itself is afforded a modicum of queerness when the people worry more about how the child turns out than about how the child exists as child. Alice, for instance, can be as queer as she likes in her dreams and in her childhood sorrows and joys, as long as she can be imagined telling her stories to other children around her when she is an adult. The utopian projection of the child into the future actually opens up a space for childhood queerness—creating space for the figure of the child to be queer as long as the queerness can be rationalized as a series of mistakes or misplaced desires. In this sense the figure of the child is not the anti-queer at all. Its queerness inheres instead in innocence run amok.

The contributors to this volume agree that there is no constituency in Western culture as susceptible to narratives of simplification as children. They also agree that the seemingly invisible processes that distill the child into an image and a story are anything but simple. As the contributors to this collection expose these narrative strategies, they present us with a very queer child indeed—queer in the sense of being odd or peculiar and queer in the sense of being outside the usual and accepted parameters of the sexual child. In short, this collection suggests that the children who populate the stories our culture tells about them are, in fact, *curiouser* than they've been given credit for.

Little Queer, Who Made Thee?

The modern-day queer is unthinkable without the modern child. In the past fifteen years, queer theory has traded liberally in Foucault's famous pronouncement in *The History of Sexuality* that, before the late nineteenth century, "the sodomite had been a temporary aberration; the homosexual was now a species."[12] What goes relatively unmarked is that the construction of this species depends to a great degree upon the child. As Foucault writes, "The nineteenth-century homosexual became a personage, a past, a case history, and a childhood"; "all around the child, indefinite lines of penetration were disposed."[13] What Foucault calls the "Repressive Hypothesis" *needs* the child: "Educators and doctors combatted children's onanism like an epidemic that needed to be eradicated."[14] "Throughout this whole secular campaign that mobilized the adult world around the sex of children," Foucault continues, educational and medical authorities used "these tenuous pleasures as a prop, constituting them as secrets (that is, forcing them into hiding so as to make possible their discovery), tracing them back to their source, tracking them from their origins to their effects, searching out everything that might cause them or simply enable them to exist."[15] The initial policing of child sexuality thus enabled the persecution of perversions that would eventually earn the sodomite his certified homosexuality. And the key example Foucault cites is the way institutions endeavored to separate boys from each other at school for fear that they would engage in sexual contact. In this way, the homosexual subject is possible to history only by way of the homoerotic, sexually performing child.

However, the problematic status of childhood sexual desire precedes the end of the nineteenth century; it is built into the Cult of the Child at its inception as it comes to structure the dialogue between innocence and experience. This dialogue itself is a peculiarly modern problem, one that is inherently tied to any discussion of liberal thought and the evolution of the individual. Most readers are probably familiar with John Locke's idea of the child as blank slate. In his 1690 *An Essay Concerning Human Understanding*, he wrested the figure of the child from original sin and posited it as tabula rasa, which represented for Locke's developing bourgeois culture the almost infinite possibilities of the individual. Furthermore, recent scholarship such as Thomas Laqueur's *Solitary Sex: A Cultural History of Masturbation* points us to a wealth of evidence for the idea that the child was no less susceptible than adults to being sexually policed. Laqueur outlines numerous examples of the extent to which "the eighteenth-century tradition that mixed medicine with moral pedagogy also grew cancerously; word of the solitary vice's peculiarly insidious threat metastasized everywhere." "Modern masturbation," he claims, "can be pinpointed with a precision rare in cultural history[:] ... sometime between 1708 and 1716—'in or around 1712'" with the publication and circulation of *Onania; or The Heinous Sin of Self Pollution, and all its Frightful consequences, in both SEXES Considered, with Spiritual and Physical Advice to those who have already injured themselves by this abominable practice. And seasonal Admonition to the Youth of the nation of Both SEXES.*[16] The fact that "youth" feature so prominently in the title of a book designed to influence all citizens gestures to the moral imperative to school the desires of the young in particular.[17] As Laqueur tells us, women and children, long ignored as subjects in sexual ethics, have become in modern masturbation "sexual beings whose development might be stunted or further, degraded and refined."[18] It is hard to tell whether texts like *Onania* presumed to prolong an innocence somehow presumed to have already existed. However, one interesting fact about the text's evolution stands out: the more *Onania* circulated, the longer it became, because letters of testimonials from women and men, young and old, were continually added to it. If youth could testify to their having been cured of masturbation in such letters, their newly found innocence often looked back awkwardly at a prior state of sexual experience.

By the end of the eighteenth century, this state of innocence or Lockean blank slate apotheosized into Jean-Jacques Rousseau's Emile, the romantic child of essential goodness and innocence. William Blake's *Songs of Innocence* is often trotted out as evidence for this angelic, prelapsarian child. His 1789 "Cradle Song" presents a parent gazing "o'er my lovely infants head" where the child is defined by its "sweet moans, sweeter smiles," "dovelike moans," and the representation of a holy and wholly innocent Christlike image.[19] However, Blake will not let us get away with such an uncomplicated Rousseauistic innocence: in a correlative poem to his "Cradle Song," the poet has the parent observing "little sorrows," "soft desires," and "cunning wiles" in the sleeping child.[20] Significantly, Blake did not include this in the original *Songs of Innocence and of Experience*; rather, it appeared in collections of Blake's *Songs* only later in the nineteenth century. Blake's desirous and cunning child operates as a kind of necessary other for the angelic, pristine infant (the way Dickens's Nancy may be that other for the unfailingly innocent Oliver Twist [1837–38]). To make the child innocent is to suppress the disruptive alternative to innocence—which, in fine binary logic, makes that "other" essential to our understanding of innocence itself.

The "soft desires" and "cunning wiles" of this child-in-bed foreground what became in the nineteenth century the fundamental nexus of theorizing about sexuality: the relation of desire to behavior, or sexual psychology to sexual acts.[21] As Michael Moon shows in his essay reprinted here, the nineteenth century often deployed images of the erotic child—in Moon's example, Horatio Alger's ragged boys—as conduits for an adult's accession to spiritual and social goodness. Whereas Moon uses this intergenerational engagement to expose the pedophilic nature of American capitalism (Richard Mohr makes a similar point), other critics, such as Gillian Avery and Karen Sánchez-Eppler, point out the prevalence of the erotic child in

Christian temperance who saves the wayward adult from sin. In contrast to Moon and Mohr, who emphasize same-sex, boy-man relations, Avery and Sánchez-Eppler focus on young girls saving older men. In much nineteenth-century fiction about children, these "chastely erotic" figures can expect one of two fates: marriage to the reconstructed male they have saved, or death.[22] What is remarkable for these sexual children is that their fates amount to the same thing. The chastely erotic girls of Susan Warner's *The Wide, Wide World* (1850) and Maria Susanna Cummins's *The Lamplighter* (1854) become paradigms of bourgeois heteronormativity, whereas the dead girls— Elizabeth Oakes-Smith's "Sinless Child" Eva (1846), Dickens's Little Nell (1841), Harriet Beecher Stowe's Little Eva (1852), and Louisa May Alcott's Beth March (1868–69)—are fetishized as martyrs. Their virtue and sinlessness are protected from the inherently sin*ful* culture they have transcended through their deaths, their eroticism producing a disembodied sexlessness. In all of these narratives, childhood sexuality is exploited so that it can be dismissed, sacrificed on the altar of secular gender normativity.

So what of the child who does not fit this ideal, and whose desires cannot be plotted along this straight narrative line? Take the example of Constance Fenimore Woolson's character Felipa (from the story of the same name, published in 1876). A young Minorcan girl in rural Florida, the masculinely clad Felipa is discovered by the narrator, Catherine, and her "friend" Christine. Felipa is captivated by Christine, whose figure the narrator describes in sumptuous detail (providing an explanation for both her own and Felipa's attraction to her). Later, when Christine has become engaged to a man named Edward, Felipa attempts suicide by encouraging a snake to bite her neck, in large part for love of Christine. Christine recognizes what's happened right away:

> Christine smiled. "Jealousy," she said in a low voice. "I am not surprised." But at the first sound of her voice Felipa had started up, and wrenching herself from old Dominga's [her grandmother's] arms, threw herself at Christine's feet. "Look at *me* so," she cried—"me too; do not look at him. He has forgotten poor Felipa; he does not love her any more. But *you* do not forget, señora; *you* love me. Say you do, or I shall die!"[23]

Although she is racked with pain from the poison, Felipa does not die. The visitors go away "to leave her to her kind," but not before the following exchange between the narrator and the girl's grandfather:

> I said: "It will pass; she is but a child."
> "She is nearly twelve, señora. Her mother was married at thirteen."
> "But she loved them both [Christine and Edward] alike, Bartolo. It is nothing; she does not know."

"You are right lady; she does not know," replied the old man slowly; "but *I* know. It was two loves, and the stronger thrust the knife."[24]

Catherine and the grandfather agree that Felipa has two loves. This is taken as evidence that "she does not know" the nature of her own desire, as Felipa seems to be afforded only one "nature." Felipa's mother was married at thirteen, but, only a year shy of that age, Felipa remains a "child"—designated so by her grandfather's speech act. Being Minorcan, Felipa is already outside white American culture. But her status as outsider is compounded by her desire for Christine and cemented when Catherine, Christine, and Edward leave for home. She is isolated from them in both time and space. The grandfather "knows" that "the stronger [love] thrust the knife" (her love for Christine) and that Felipa's desires, which she herself presumably does not understand, are legible to the knowing adult. As comforting as it may be to both the grandfather and the narrator that Felipa does not know as they do, Felipa clearly *does* know something. And that something is strong enough to make her want to die, even though the narrator is sure that "it will pass." It may be the adults for whom this will pass, as they leave Felipa to "her kind" and the amnesia the narrator wishes for her.

In the grammar of this story's adults, Felipa's sexuality is caught between the future and the future anterior: like Lewis Carroll's Alice, Felipa will have been a queer child. "It *will* pass," the adults insist. Felipa can be imagined into a more proper domestic role, as the specter of her thirteen-year-old married mother hints. The "stronger love" that the grandfather identifies will exist *in the past*. For Catherine and the grandfather alike, Felipa's sexuality is not to exist ("she doesn't know"; "she is a child") *and* to exist in only one form ("her mother was married at thirteen"). They can imagine her two loves but they can't imagine her acting on them. Again like Alice, Felipa must let her childhood experience outside of accepted flirtations and crushes fade into the background of a domestic life yet to come. And yet, Felipa's grammar is not one of the future, repressed or otherwise. Her cry is for something immediate, in the present: "Look at *me* so." What makes Woolson's "Felipa" so remarkable (and so representative of child queerness) is less the fact that it discusses sexuality at all (although this is important in itself) than the fact that the language of child sexuality is so strictly governed by the language of temporality. Felipa's queerness is assumed to be incompatible with her future, but it will be okay for it to be part of the past. It can be acknowledged in the present among adults only with the reassuring proviso that "she does not know."

Verbs matter to the configuration of child sexuality in that they displace sexuality from the present to the future or the past (that is, the future anterior). This forked grammar comes to constitute the narrative status of the queer child. This temporal displacement can be seen not just in the future anterior state of sexuality imagined by Alice's sister (in Carroll's story) or Felipa's grandfather (in Woolson's). A similar movement is identified in Ellis Hanson's discussion of Regan MacNeil's forgotten demonic possession and in Eric Savoy's discussion of Miles's missing behind. In all of these examples the child's primary caretakers and storytellers insist on making child queerness into a story that will not *be,* but will only *have been.* In this sense, the queer child gets displaced grammatically into a different temporal register, a register that will allow the dominant narrative to consign the child to a cultural unconscious. But the queer child is also schooled by this narrative structure, no less the product of modern history and grammar for being the less elevated in discursive status. And so, another unconscious: the part of Felipa that she "does not know" is the part that Freud, in another odd configuration of the future anterior, will have been waiting for.

The Use and Abuse of Psychoanalysis for Child Life

Multiple sexual natures, parental recognitions and misrecognitions, amnesia both personal and cultural, origins and futures: the story of Felipa forecasts the world of Sigmund Freud, its heroine the typical stuff of a psychoanalytic case history. In Freud the twentieth century would find its fullest articulation of the psychogenesis of adult homosexuality in the child. Freud's now famous letter of April 1935 to the American mother of a homosexual son designates homosexuality not as a perversion but as "a certain arrest in sexual development."[25] Throughout his oeuvre, Freud comes at the problem of children and homosexuality from a number of angles, but nowhere more clearly than in his work on narcissism.[26] For Freud, the male homosexual finds his genesis in the original cathexis to the mother. At a certain point in his development, the child refuses to direct his love for his mother onto another object (that is, another woman). "Things take a sudden turn," writes Freud in "Group Psychology and the Analysis of the Ego" (1921), "the young man does not abandon his mother, but identifies himself with her; he transforms himself into her, and now looks about for objects which can replace his ego for him, and on which he can bestow such love and care as he has experienced from his mother."[27]

Although this arrested development is not so clear in the female homosexual, it is equally palpable. In "The Psychogenesis of a Case of Homosexuality in a Woman" (1921), Freud posits the etiology of his patient's lesbianism as the product of disappointment in her father, whose child she is not allowed to bear. Thus, argues Freud, "she changed into a man and took her mother in place of her father as the object of her love," a process Freud describes in a footnote as "equivalent to a kind of regression to narcissism."[28] This schema suggests not only that certain experiences in childhood produce homosexuality in the adult, but that the concepts of childhood and homosexuality are also homological: homosexuality *is* childhood, played out in another place but still enacting the desires generated in infancy.

However, Freud argues many times in his work that homoerotic infantile attachments can be the *basis* of normal social and sexual life. In "Totem and Taboo" (1913) and "Group Psychology and the Analysis of the Ego," Freud posits homophilic attraction as the fundamental glue of a Western, masculinist culture, a glue that Eve Kosofsky Sedgwick identifies as the "homosocial bond" in her early work.[29] Leo Bersani extends the implications of such childhood homophilia by analyzing its importance in the production of art. Bersani argues that, for Freud, the self-shattering matrix of heterosexual passions grounded in homosexual ones produces the artistic and scientific genius of a Leonardo da Vinci.[30] If childhood erotics—and their specifically queer engagements—underlie so much of the world, as psychoanalysis imagines it, why then the debilitating equation between the kid and the queer? Why does psychoanalysis (and a Western culture influenced by it) equate the queer with the child as a way of containing them both? Moreover, how might psychoanalysis provide us with some ways through the paralyzing equations it has helped to establish?

According to prominent child psychologist Adam Phillips, psychoanalysis is a story like all others, one in which the child "usually has only two genres available to him: romantic comedy or tragedy."[31] Like so many other stories, psychoanalysis idealizes a particular version of the child and looks to that child, as William Wordsworth does, to see how he fathers the man. The trouble is that psychoanalysis concerns itself far more with disavowal and lack than it does with affirmation and world making:

> There is a Freudian child who has been mislaid. This child is not merely the satisfied child. . . . The child I am referring to that psychoanalysis has mislaid—who is rarely the subject of psychoanalytic theory—is the child with an astonishing capacity for pleasure, and indeed the pleasures of interest, with an unwilled relish for sensuous experience which often unsettles the adults, who like to call it affection. This child who can be deranged by hope and anticipation—by ice cream—seems to have a passionate love of life, a curiosity about life, which for some reason isn't always easy to sustain.[32]

For Phillips, the psychoanalytic emphasis on lack and privation is also a disavowal of pleasure, fantasy, and desire in their more positive aspects.[33] Children, he asserts, are far more interested in making stories and pursuing pleasure than in fitting into previously established parental, therapeutic, or academic templates; after all, "it is not the child who believes in something called development."[34] If there is anything "natural" about children it is their curiosity about bodies and pleasure, their desire to make stories that are not the colonizing narratives of heteronormativity. From this perspective, the story generated by Phillips's psychoanalytic child has the ring of polymorphous perversity, more Susie Bright than Susie Homemaker. And this is certainly not the story that most parents—or the psychoanalytic industry—have in mind as the preferred one.

Leaving aside the issue of whether children "naturally" have the curiosities and pleasures that Phillips ascribes to them, we want to emphasize what he says about the possible uses of psychoanalysis in the representation of queer kids. Undoubtedly, the therapeutic practice of psychoanalysis has helped to create the image of the traumatized and battered child (to whom we shall return), but as a theoretical hermeneutic, psychoanalysis—with its emphasis on the unconscious, on the play of fantasy, and on the vicissitudes of desire—can help to complicate the stories that circulate as "truth" in the therapeutic enterprise. Psychoanalysis, says Phillips, "is the art of making interest out of interest that is stuck."[35] The art of making interest is nothing less than an act of story making. And the art of psychoanalysis, in its best form, is the art of exploring the unconscious of narrative itself.

The contributors to this volume seek to understand how our cultural stories have gotten stuck on children. While a number of the authors implicitly or explicitly detail the violent disavowals conducted under the name of therapy (see Kincaid, Mohr, Berlant, Ohi, Hanson, and Sedgwick), others return us to the more spacious possibilities that Freud himself afforded. Following Leo Bersani, Paul Kelleher emphasizes the ways in which Freud attempted to impose a teleological narrative on psychoanalytic insights while exposing the degree to which those insights were themselves antinarrative. The "perversion of adults," he quotes Bersani as saying, is really "the sickness of *uncompleted narratives*."[36] It is precisely in incompletion that some of our contributors find queerly productive moments. For Eric Savoy, Henry James's reveling in the linguistic tropes of aposiopoesis (the unfinished sentence), preterition (that which is omitted or refused speech), and prosopopoeia (the giving of voice to the dead) marks a child who is unknowable, and whom we assume to be the victim of a trauma the child cannot narrate. Yet this is also the child whose refusal to speak is ultimately a refusal of allegory, of the diagnostic game of identification where desires can be made to read monolithically. For Kathryn Bond Stockton, a similar effect is produced by *metaphor*, a "this is that" that isn't. Stockton's queer child is always "estranged" from the adult it is to become, and in that estrangement we can detect other possibilities for nonnormative growth, what Stockton calls a growth "sideways." In these essays, a more Lacanian vision of language exploits the possibilities of uncolonized, nonnormative desire, the unsettled and unsettling range of erotic possibilities that psychoanalysis has helped to articulate. The letter has an agency in the unconscious, and Stockton wants us to know that that letter is *q*.

For the Love of the Child; or, Sticking It to the Kid

Whatever paradoxes may present themselves in the cultural and psychoanalytic fantasies surrounding children and their sexuality, there is one aspect of this fantasy that officially brooks no exceptions whatsoever: that sex between a child and an adult, regardless of the gender of either party, is inevitably traumatic and debilitating for the child. This aspect, perhaps more than any other, may represent what Phillips calls a narrative interest that is "stuck." In some of the earliest attempts to afford positive political space to child sexuality, Kate Millett and Nettie Pollard argued that any sexual contact between adults and children is bound to be exploitative because children are weaker than adults in physical, emotional, and financial resources. Whereas sex between children has a democratic air around it,[37] according to Millett, "conditions between adults and children preclude any sexual relationship that is not in some way exploitative."[38] In the realm of public policy making, allegiances between gay/lesbian constituencies and anyone sympathetic to child sex have been brittle, to say the least. Activists for intergenerational sex have been more or less consistently shown the door by queer activist groups who see their credibility as too thoroughly compromised by their admittance of child-lovers (including same-sex child-lovers) to their ranks.[39] Andrea Dworkin and Catharine MacKinnon's famous drafting of a constitutional amendment on pornography as violence against women not only served a certain branch of radical lesbian feminism in the 1980s but also significantly partnered with Ronald Reagan's Meese Commission on Child Pornography in 1986. In Dworkin and MacKinnon's account, seeing the child as sexual was completely at odds with any kind of program for protecting children (and women) from harm.

This protectionism has become the cornerstone of law in many Western countries. In Canada, the federal government's passing of a child-pornography law was tied to the issue of lesbian and gay rights, although in inverse relation to it. As Stan Persky and John Dixon detail in their book *On Kiddie Porn*, the impetus behind the drafting of a tough and narrow kiddie-porn law for Canada in the 1990s was a melodrama whose key players were Justice Minister Kim Campbell (who later became prime minister), gay and lesbian interest groups, and the right-wing Family Caucus of Campbell's Progressive Conservative Party.[40] According to Persky and Dixon, Campbell had committed herself publicly to entrenching nondiscrimination protection for gays and lesbians in the Canada Human Rights Act during her tenure as justice minister. She was eventually successful, but knew that such a move risked alienating the conservative Family Caucus, whose support and dollars she needed as much as she needed those of the gay and lesbian population of her hometown, Vancouver. While admirably refusing to renege on her commitment to gays and lesbians, Campbell very publicly pursued the drafting of a child-pornography bill—despite the warnings of her advisers and the sheer lack of evidence that Canada needed legislation on the issue—thus placating the right. What Campbell ultimately achieved was a further entrenchment of the perceived division between the sexually queer adult and the sexual—and queer—child. On this issue, queer liberatory practices are less in conflict with the political right than they are in concert. Little wonder, then, that Eve Sedgwick should observe in her essay reprinted here, "The gay movement has never been quick to attend to issues of effeminate boys." Discussions of queerness and child sexuality all too quickly invoke the specter of the pedophile, which all too quickly destroys one's political credibility.

Adam Phillips has written, "One can, and should, disapprove of the sexual abuse of children without denying that it raises some unsettling questions about its uncertain measure in our lives."[41] More than ever, the phenomenon of child sexual abuse finds its way into news programs, glossy magazines, talk shows—as James Kincaid has argued, it is everywhere. The persistence of stories about this trauma indicates the extent to which our culture is both repulsed by and fascinated with the traumas attributed to the sexual abuse of children. Rarely do we consider that both trauma and intergenerational sex themselves have historical dimensions. Trauma is historical in the sense that it has been configured differently at different moments in time and historical in the sense that it throws a wrench into the very idea of telling history. What now counts as trauma has not always been counted as such (or not counted as such in the same ways). And trauma points to the problem of knowing a past that constitutes a gap in, or a threat to, life narrative as we know it. Similarly, intergenerational sex has not always been reducible to trauma as we know it. In other words, the history of ideas about intergenerational sex and the idea of remembering one's personal experiences of intergenerational sex are often much more complicated than we have allowed ourselves to think.

If we look, for instance, at Greek history, we can see that shame functions much differently in considerations of intergenerational sex than it does for our contemporary ideas about the phenomenon. In his second volume of *The History of Sexuality,* Michel Foucault outlines the elaborate choreography by which erotic relations were conducted between the adult male suitor (the *erastes*) and his beloved youth (the *eromenes*) in ancient Greek culture. Contrary to our simplifying narratives about Greek pederastic love, Foucault asserts, the Greeks were indeed worried about the boy's participation in sexual relations with an adult. But the terms of that concern were very different from those of our historical moment. The preadolescent body—that which did not yet show signs of a beard—was characteristically represented as the "right object," the proper ethical model for a man's erotic attraction;[42] the boy's body approximated the ideal of beauty to which the adult freeborn male should continually aspire, as long as he did so openly and noncoercively. The problem in this relationship was that, in being the object of erotic pleasure, the adored boy risked being seen as "passive," a suspect and denigrated ethical position: "The boy . . . could not and should not identify with that role [of *eromenes*]. . . . [To] be an object of pleasure and to acknowledge oneself as such caused a major difficulty for the boy."[43] However, the role of (potentially passive) beloved could induce feelings of shame and disgrace in the *eromenes* only if he bestowed his sexual favors too readily or too liberally, or if he did so for money or other dishonorable types of social advancement. Thus the *eromenes* "was supposed to yield only if he had feelings of admiration, gratitude, or affection for his lover, which made him want to please the latter"[44]—but he *was* supposed to yield. And this yielding was not to be a simple surrender: the boy "complied" or "granted his favors" in what appears to have been a very active passivity.[45] According to Foucault (and to historians such as Kenneth Dover before him and David Halperin following), pederastic behavior properly conducted was the boy's means to social and philosophical accession. The age disparity between the parties did not make the relationship a priori exploitative; rather, it "was at the heart of the relationship; in fact, it was what made it valuable and conceivable."[46]

While Foucault spells out a positive and mutually beneficial pedophilia in the Greeks, no such optimism is possible in our contemporary moment. What always emerges as the site of contestation in discussions of man-boy relationships is the way hierarchies become central to the psychologies involved. The controversy inevitably surrounds the extent to which the boy member of an intergenerational relationship can consent to the perceived power imbalance of such a relationship. Whatever one may think of how "ideal" or "beautiful" love between men and boys may be, the discursive treatment of "consent" is itself problematic. First, discussions of intergenerational sexual contact seem always to invoke the blank, innocent child who is free from the very desire he or she often seeks in the body of the adult other (in marked contrast to the Greek model—the *eromenes*, remember, was not to be a passive victim nabbed by some philosophical pedophile hiding in the Athenian bushes). To the degree that a child consents to sexual contact, he or she simply allows or endures it; the child does not, in our cultural imagination, seek it out. Second, such consent is, in therapeutic and medical discourses, always temporally troubled: any consent a child may express easily can (nay, inevitably *will*) become trauma later on, when the "full impact" of intergenerational sex makes itself felt on the older, wiser adult. In this narrative of child sexuality any consent that is not coerced is nonetheless misguided and will produce dire effects down the road. The grammar of the future anterior remains firmly in place: regardless of what the child feels at the time, he or she will have been traumatized.

But who, one might ask, *is* this "child" who will have been traumatized? What is the magic age of childhood? Those who discuss age-of-consent laws seem to consider anyone under that age (usually sixteen) to be a child: teenagers are "children" (indistinguishable from toddlers, it seems) if they are involved in the making of pornography. Yet teens who rape or murder are tried as "adults," as if the concept of childhood were dependent entirely on the magnitude of the crime. Still other people mark sexual awakening by a person's ability to reproduce—a stunning index of the heteronormativity that infuses theories of human development (operating with a fairy-tale logic of Sleeping Beauties with pricked fingers). As in the other narratives of the child we have been tracking here, the juridical child appears to get defined by whoever is talking on behalf of that child. Thus laws get manufactured despite—or perhaps because of—the murkiness surrounding child sexuality and children's nebulous ability to consent. While no one would suggest that there is no such thing as a child, there may very well be no definition of "child" that applies to all situations, as defining the child is itself often the source of debate in any legally contested form of sexuality: prostitution, pornography, and any sexually explicit mode of expression. Our culture affords itself a sliding scale of "appropriate" childhood sexuality and sexual expression, but for all its vexations it is still a very comfortable scale within which to work: it invites parents, therapists, social workers, and the police to determine and revise continually what counts as "enough" and "too much" physicality while never having to abandon the axis of the scale itself.

So how might the antihomophobic project approach the historical, political, psychological, and epistemic pressures that have come together to construct the thesis of child-loving as exploitation, or intergenerational sex as trauma? As Eve Kosofsky Sedgwick contemplates how we might bring our kids up gay in her essay in this volume, she catalogs the brutal and hopeless information on teen suicide as a particularly queer-kid problem. Where, she asks, are the helping professions in all of this? Where is psychoanalysis? To Sedgwick's list of questions we also want to add: Where is queer theory?[47] Where can we look to find a paradigm for the psychic investments of child-adult sexual contact? On this score, our intellectual history is incomplete.

The best work that has been done on child sexuality comes from writers such as Gayle Rubin and Pat Califia, who argue that sexual dissidents have often acquired experience with people who are significantly older than they are. When the sexuality wanting to be expressed is homoerotic, they contend, there are no imitable socially approved models: queer children often have their initial sexual experiences with older men or women, experiences they will probably not define as traumatic or exploitative as they reflect on them later. For Rubin and Califia, depth psychology is at odds with a political program that tries to afford some place for sex among/with children, for clinical psychoanalysis—like contemporary popular wisdom—sees the violation of the ego that comes with pedophilic sex as necessarily engendering a posttraumatic stress disorder. And Rubin, for one, will have none of it: "Psychology," she avers, "is the last resort of those who refuse to acknowledge that sexual dissidents are as conscious and free as any other group of sexual actors."[48] These sexual dissidents include children who, presumably, can find in their sexual expression a consciousness and freedom.

Rubin's and Califia's work is important in its historical context, for it invites us to move beyond the stuck story of clinical psychology. However, their work precedes the psychoanalytically inflected queer discourse of the late 1980s and the 1990s, a discourse that insists that there is an unconscious and that it matters. In Rubin's and Califia's arguments we find no psychoanalytic residue: there are none of the psychic aggressions and conflicts to which psychoanalysis has made us sensitive. The older "partner" is loving and gentle, and there is no whiff of anything but utopia: the women's healing circle closes around, or Walt Whitman rushes in where Jean Genet might have been. Indeed, apologists for queer childhood sexuality are often vehemently anti-Freudian, finding in psychoanalysis no useful rubric for discussing their experiences. But we can no longer take at face value the comforting assertion that "sexual dissidents are . . . conscious and free." Rather, we need to ask how the premises of psychoanalysis might help us to imagine the queer child.

Certain branches of queer theory see the smashed ego—that tragic and inevitable condition of children who have sex with adults—in very different ways from the official versions of American ego psychology. One of the major premises of poststructural thinking has been that the ego, described by Freud as a bodily ego, delimits the bourgeois subject in the humanist illusion of self-control. For queer theory, this bourgeois subject is the straight subject, its ego the straight ego. Shattering the boundaries of that ego through sexual *jouissance* is a way past the self-protectiveness and xenophobia of the bourgeois subject. One of the most famous articulations of this for queer theory is Leo Bersani's "Is the Rectum a Grave?" Here Bersani argues that only a "radical disintegration and humiliation of the self" can open the subject to desire, to a form of powerlessness in which sexuality can be enjoyed qua sexuality.[49] He concludes the essay by asserting that "gay men's 'obsession' with sex . . . never stops re-presenting the internalized phallic male as an infinitely loved object of sacrifice. Male homosexuality advertises the risk of the sexual itself as the risk of self-dismissal, of *losing sight* of the self, and in so doing it proposes and dangerously represents *jouissance* as a mode of ascesis."[50] Nor would Bersani deny that privileged *jouissance* to the child. In *The Freudian Body*, he suggests that "the distinguishing feature of infancy would be its *susceptibility to the sexual*. The polymorphously perverse nature of infantile sexuality would be a function of the child's vulnerability to being shattered into sexuality."[51] For Bersani, masochism, properly understood, *"serves life."*[52]

Bersani's theoretical ruminations offer some way of thinking beyond the straight ego in a way that respects different dynamics for queer children. The possibility of being "shattered into sexuality" might help to reconfigure that child in intergenerational relations. Shattering the ego may serve the queer child's life to the degree that it resists the development of the normatively straight ego. But Bersani will not go there. His treatment of masochism and "susceptibility" becomes problematic in "Is the Rectum a Grave?" when Bersani gets to the question of sex between adults and children. He is wary of the fantasies that might accompany such practices. For him, fantasy games that enact power—SM, camp and drag, leather machismo—all proceed from a politicized unconscious of the straight world. Searching for daddy—what those children who *seek out* sex with adults are presumably up to—is for Bersani a dangerous replication of the Oedipal struggle to please daddy. He contends that the male imagination cannot get past that power struggle unless the ego sacrifices itself on the penis (the male sexual organ) rather than paying homage to the phallus (the signifier of masculine power). But once again the child is caught coming and going; his "susceptibility to the sexual" is a mixed blessing. Should he smash his ego on the older man's penis, he risks replicating a phallic subservience to the Father. Bersani's version of psychoanalysis endorses the pleasures of *jouissance* in the child as long as those pleasures are not contaminated by adult fantasy life. And so the child who wants sex with an adult is back where he started, with no theoretical pegs to hang his hat on, no homo to go home to.

But what if there were a different story to tell about kids, sex, power, and fantasy? Or the same story but with a different ending? The story we have in mind is Peter Straub's "The Juniper Tree," published in his collection *Houses without Doors*. As the title suggests, "The Juniper Tree" is a revision of the Grimm brothers' version of a folktale about a child who is dismembered by his mother but who is miraculously resurrected, whole and joyful, at the end of the story.[53] "The Juniper Tree" recounts the childhood experiences of a now adult writer who frequented a movie theater in his youth. As a seven-year-old, he was drawn there by his fixation on the movie idol Alan Ladd and stayed because of a molesting wino named Jimmy. During the daily performances of Ladd's films noir, Jimmy tried to earn the boy's love and trust as a way of keeping open sexual access, but he eventually disappeared, afraid the boy had reported him to the police. The result of this coercion is exactly what we might expect: confused fear in the child produces an adult narrator who is incapable of emotional depth and happiness (read: heterosexual fulfillment); he is prone to bouts of depression, vomiting, and suicidal thoughts; and at one moment, remembering himself entering the movie theater, he proclaims, "I thought that I was having a stroke."[54] Straub has read his Freud, or Freud as the late twentieth century remembered him: in psychoanalytic terms, the narrator's ego has been smashed, so that the boundaries that would constitute the safe space of identity have dissolved and rendered the self vulnerable. The powerful adult figure supplants the child's identity with his own, so that at one point in the story the child looks into the mirror and sees the face of Jimmy instead of his own reflection. Memory, that narrative link to his childhood experience, disrupts into fragments. So "stuck" is the narrator in this pedophilic past that his adult life is all but destroyed: he can find his history only in fits and starts, his "child within" having become the mere strobe effects of a film on a screen.

For all of its horror, "The Juniper Tree" is comforting because it fits precisely with what we all know about children, and about the effects of sex with children. But the story is not so sure of the tight narrative that sees the child as by definition devastated. It interposes the narrator's analysis of what happened in the movie theater with a somewhat different category of narrative memory, one that is less symptomatic of the trauma he understands himself to have experienced. There seems to be a difference between the narrator's official recounting of the experience and the actual *emotional* memories that surround that experience, as if the very telling of the story resurrected the child who lived it rather than pronouncing on the child that adult imagines being there. For example, there is the following line, written in the present tense of a remembered *now:* "I am certain of only one thing: tomorrow I am again going to see my newest, scariest, most interesting friend" (Jimmy).[55] And there is this candid admission, which seems to contradict the major thrust of the story the narrator wants to tell: "I suddenly realized that part of me was glad to be in this place [the movie theater], and I shocked myself with the knowledge that all morning I had been looking forward to this moment as much as I had been dreading it."[56] Gone is that sense of the future anterior we saw earlier in Felipa and Alice, the queer child whose queerness disappears as childhood disappears; this child *likes* the experience that is meant to terrify him, or at least likes it more than the

▼ Steven Bruhm and Natasha Hurley

adult narrator who remembers it. Defense mechanism, we might wonder? Dissociation as a means of handling the horror? Perhaps, but such a slick diagnosis hardly leaves room for those gay men and lesbians (and, as this collection shows, they are legion) who got their starts in movie theaters, at church camps, or in locker rooms, initiated into sex by older figures who were not necessarily exploitative or harsh. Clearly, remembered childhood sexual experiences can be traumatic *or* pleasant; the problem that interests us most here is how to make sense of the child's pleasure without pathologizing it or reducing it to "trauma."

If intergenerational desire carries the specter of playing for daddy, such Oedipal hangover doesn't seem to bother our narrator at crucial moments in his story. Let's remember that what took the child to the movie theater every day was not just the threat of violence should he disappoint Jimmy but the positive desire to see Alan Ladd films. Ladd is not simply a father figure or ego ideal, he is also the erotically desired object. The boy basks in his beauty, masculinity, and physicality; he wants to *have* Alan Ladd as much as he wants to *be* him. Little wonder, then, that the boy should be so forthcoming with Jimmy, who "looked like Alan Ladd's twin brother."[57] Both have dirty-blond hair, both have a certain handsomeness and the same facial type, and both use the mise-en-scène of the theater to engage their eros. This erotic triangle takes us some distance to calming Bersani's concerns about the role of fantasized power imbalance in configurations of queer desire. While it gets played out within material scenes of power (Jimmy, after all, *is* committing a crime and the boy *will* grow up to have psychological "problems"), it also engages differences in age and power to figure homoerotic pleasure in the boy.

And perhaps here is where psychoanalysis may speak with queerness about the vexed realm of trauma. Straub's postmodern tale insists on returning to the child's psyche and teasing out the effects of same-sex erotic experiences in youth. There is a sense of trauma, but trauma as Freud describes it, where the meaning lies not in the experience but in the memory, that temporally displaced nexus of narratives that cannot help but pathologize the event. The adult narrator overlays his own remembered experience with another narrative, one that renders him victim. Significantly, that victim narrative is the only one available to him—and to us, in our culture. We lack the possibility to narrate a pedophilia that will have been benign (let alone benevolent, in the Greek way). And the product of this is another kind of violence done to the narrative child: if we condemn Jimmy the pedophile for trying to destroy the boy in the theater, then we must also condemn the narrator for doing the same thing. To the degree that the remembered child is the child who liked the sexual contact, that child is killed off; the narrative brought to define him is one of fear, power abuse, and shame.

This particular narrative produces the terms of trauma as much as it claims to represent them. If Jimmy tried to kill "the child," the narrator tries to kill "the child within," that agent of queer identifications and desires for whom unequal power relations can be as erotically pleasurable as they are traumatizing and oppressive.

Jimmy: the name of this Father is queerly resonant, for the narrator is "jimmied" in two dictionary senses of that verb. On the one hand, he is jimmied open so that a crime can be committed against him. In the worst-case scenario his experience in the theater is an assault, an act of psychological and emotional murder. On the other hand, he is jimmied open in the sense that different kinds of entrances and exits are created, passageways that, in this story, move from disembodied homoerotic fantasy to actual sexual performance. And these passageways of ingress and egress are ultimately the lines of *story*, the warp and woof of *narrative*. As the narrator deals with the childhood sexual experience that he *now* understands to be traumatic (an understanding that narrative time has created more than reflected), he deploys strategies for his survival. And surviving trauma, as Cathy Caruth has shown, is itself an act of storytelling.[58] What is perhaps most unsettling—or most promising—in "The Juniper Tree" is that the smashing of the child's ego in the movie theater is not (only) the death of his childhood and his future; it is, as Leo Bersani and Judith Butler might argue, the opening of the subject into desire, into otherness, into a more formal engagement with storytelling. At a conference, the narrator is asked to give advice to someone who wants to be a writer, and his response is something that we can only read as overdetermined: "Go to a lot of movies."[59] This queer child-adult is a prolific writer in spite of—*or perhaps because of*—the smashing of his ego in pedophilic sex. The point is not that if you want to be a writer you should get yourself molested early in life. The point is that we cannot and must not try to predict in advance what psychological, emotional, and political stories will arise from childhood sexual engagement.[60]

On the Queerness of Children: A User's Manual

We opened these remarks by expressing our suspicions about storytelling as it relates—or refuses to relate—to the queer child. Storytelling, we have argued, removes the queer child from its present desires and projects it into a future where those desires will not have been. But in this volume we want to resist that displacement by submitting childhood to another kind of story. We see this story as dividing itself (shamelessly but conveniently) into two sections that reflect the central tension between child sexuality and/as child queerness. The first, "Sexing the Child," comprises essays on child sexuality generally, and begins with the work of a scholar who has been instrumental in defining the fields of inquiry about child sexuality: James R. Kincaid.

Kincaid makes us aware above all of the *usefulness* to which childhood sexuality, whether real or fantasized, can be put, as he demonstrates the range of definitions that encircle the erotic child. Richard D. Mohr's essay follows and, in some ways, extends the points that Kincaid makes about our culture's need for the proliferation of panicked discourse about the child. Both writers are interested in the media's portrayals of childhood innocence and sexuality, and both concern themselves with our investment in perpetuating, exploiting, and fetishizing the innocent child, but whereas Kincaid discusses a figure such as Michael Jackson as our culture's panicked invention of the pedophile, Mohr shows us how Jackson actually exploits that pedophilic scandal to figure his own innocence. Michael Moon then demonstrates the long shelf life of this connection between the protected and the eroticized; in fact, he takes the analysis one step further when he points to how pedophilic class relations structure the narrative of upward mobility in Horatio Alger's classic nineteenth-century American texts. Moon's focus on America's mythology of the rags-to-riches child bearing the trace of pedophilic desire segues into Lauren Berlant's essay on infantile citizenship. Like Moon, she points to the status of the child in the national imaginary, but whereas Moon sees that child status as founding a certain definition of the nineteenth-century American citizen, Berlant highlights how the protection of that child curtails adult citizenship. Connecting also to the work of Kincaid and Mohr, Berlant demonstrates how innocence is marshaled to instill panic around the figure of the girl-child (for Mohr, it's the boy-child and same-sex desire). Rounding out this section are Kevin Ohi and Ellis Hanson, whose essays delve into particular cultural texts (Henry James's *What Maisie Knew* and William Friedkin's film *The Exorcist,* respectively) that draw on and contribute to the status the child has achieved in our cultural imaginary and its forms. Each of these authors locates a child at the center of adult interpretive strategies: Maisie in the drawing room of Henry James's late-nineteenth-century London and Regan in the bedroom of late-twentieth-century religious and medical consciousness. What each of these essays makes deliciously clear is the way in which the excesses and overdeterminations of juvenile sexual desire escape the limited diagnosis and blind projections of more "knowing" adults. As Ellis Hanson's title suggests, "knowing desire" is an oxymoron when it comes to children.

Where the essays in the first section illustrate what's at stake in thinking about children and sexuality at all, the essays in the second section, "The Queers We Might Have Been," up the ante by focusing on the queer significations—both within and without genital homoeroticism—that we have been discussing here. In Eve Kosofsky Sedgwick's essay, we find ourselves confronted with the problem of psychology and the way it has "disciplined" the proto-gay kid. This work has initiated a great deal of discourse about queer kids and has made many of the other essays in this section possible. In his consideration of childhood sexuality and its relation to the criminal, Paul Kelleher outlines psychiatry's wish for the terminal and terminable queer child, yet points to the way Freud's original texts locate all sexuality in childhood's perverse possibilities. Like Kelleher, Kathryn R. Kent is also interested in the institutionalization of the queer child, but whereas Kelleher finds his subject on the psychoanalytic couch, Kent takes as her archive the Girl Scout camp, in all its white-bread-and-mayonnaise splendor. Replete with snippets of memoir, Kent's essay calls attention to how regimes of the normal often breed and shelter gender and sexual deviance through childhood homosocialization—the girl becomes a Scout by eating her first Brownie, to continue the gustatory metaphor. Through her recollection of her own childhood, Kent introduces a theme that binds the next two essays in the collection as well. Collectively, they constitute a genre that we might call the "theoretical memoir." Kent, Judith Halberstam, and Michael Warner all return to moments of their own childhoods for ways of understanding the infusion of queer culture by all sorts of childhood influences: the class implications of one's upbringing, the relationship of gender deviance to sexuality, and the way religion and the Girl Scouts inflect and even nurture queer desires. Thus we find Halberstam outlining a theory of punk tomboyism and Warner examining the cast-off life of religious fundamentalism, demonstrating from very different vantage points how queer political adults can resonate with their remembered childhood experiences.

Each of these memoirs alerts us to the form of autobiography and the difficulties of telling one's own childhood. Yet each richly suggests the interplay between queer adults and their queer—or queered?—childhoods. This problematic historiography becomes the central concern for the final three contributors. A treasure trove of intertextual references to the classical pastoral, Andre Furlani's essay argues that the "radical innocence" of the pastoral child makes that child's sexuality possible. In the postmodern novels of Guy Davenport, such innocence grounds no simple telos; rather, the innocence is shaped and informed by the history of writing on child sex. This problem of absent origins is further thematized in Eric Savoy's reading of *The Turn of the Screw*, where childhood queerness is figured as something "behind"—both a temporal experience and a topos. This behindness (the primal scene, the rectum) is, in James, an absence whose presence continually signifies the scandalously homoerotic child. All of this sets us up for Kathryn Bond Stockton's finale, which argues that "growing sideways" is the central ontology of the queer child. Stockton's analysis looks to fiction's uses of narrative time as a way of presenting, representing, and misrepre-

▼ Steven Bruhm and Natasha Hurley

senting queer child sexuality to show how queerness is superimposed on the very innocence out of which it flows.

Scandal, homoeros, children—as James Kincaid tells us in his essay here, the word *scandal* originally connoted a trap through which one was kept from receiving divine law. And in it, Kincaid finds the possibility of "hope," of discovering new paths by which we might find more open fields for queer kids, queer adults, queer representations. Few people know scandal better than Kincaid: his now famous 1992 book *Child-Loving: The Erotic Child and Victorian Culture* met with outrage in England, where Tory members of Parliament tried to have the book banned, citing as a particular problem that Kincaid refused to fess up to what he does sexually in his spare time. Moreover, he runs with a scandalous set: Eve Sedgwick found herself in the headlines for her work on Jane Austen and the masturbating girl—or rather, she became infamous for the title alone; the brouhaha over connecting Austen, masturbation, and girls arose well before Sedgwick had written her essay. Her argument, according to one critic, evidenced the very "idiocy" that used to be attributed to the compulsive masturbator herself.[61] Richard Mohr gathered a stack of rejection letters from publishing houses for his *Gay Ideas* on the grounds that it was seen to "promote" pedophilia and was a work of kiddie porn (it doesn't and it isn't). Ellis Hanson's dean at Cornell received some one thousand letters of protest demanding that he be fired for teaching a seminar titled "The Sexual Child." And as we sit down to write this introduction, we can still smell the lingering smoke from witch burning as numerous fundamentalist Christian and "family-focused" groups try to consign to the ash bin Judith Levine and her 2002 *Harmful to Minors: The Perils of Protecting Children from Sex*. The conflagration led some of our authors to wonder whether the University of Minnesota Press would be able to honor its contract for our book, or whether the policy review called for by the university administration would result in a silencing of intellectual exchange. Obviously it did not—you are holding this book in your hands—but one cannot underestimate the explosive potential of conjoining discourses of childhood with the discourses of a sex that does not trade in the same-age, same-class, same-race, same-sexuality, other-gender marketplace or contribute to the therapeutically sanctioned idol of self-esteem. To talk about child sex outside of sweeping generalizations is tantamount to invading the innocent, pristine body of the child. (After all, Levine had the temerity to wonder whether every sexual relation between a priest and a boy is *prima facie* exploitative and destructive.)

For some people, the scandals noted above are evidence of the sad state of affairs in North America at the current moment—evidence that it really *is* open season on innocent children. But for others, these scandals jimmy open the possibility of both *identifying* and *articulating* queer child life.

Identifying because, as the essays in this collection illustrate, the stories of queer child life are not just ones we have to invent. These stories exist already. Queer children populate the stories that have already been told about children and even the stories we tell to children in a Wizard of Oz sense: they've been there all along if we'd only known where to look. *Articulating* because in the act of identifying, we tell a new story about stories themselves—in turn making it possible to tell other stories. A discussion of the narrative constraints of the queer child encourages us to take stock of the temporality of normative life narrative, to investigate and isolate our investments in a past and a future where the child is a placeholder for adult desire. Ultimately the scandals and panics about children, and the authors who create them, can, if we recast the conclusions they draw, force us to imagine where the desire of the adult and the desire of the child might diverge. Only then can we conceive of children as desiring creatures who, although tough to access in theory, exist and make stories beyond the simple ones adults see in them. To unearth the queer child of narrative may well be to make the child as utopian as do discussions of childhood innocence, but in doing so, it complicates the story of innocence itself as a foundational narrative. It enables us to analyze our own nostalgia and to begin relinquishing our idealized stranglehold on innocence and children alike. The figure of the child is not the anti-queer, but its future is one we might do well not to predict.

Notes

1. Nettie Pollard, "The Small Matter of Children," in *Bad Girls and Dirty Pictures: The Challenge to Reclaim Feminism,* ed. Alison Assiter and Avedon Carol (London: Pluto, 1993), 108. The context of Pollard's claim is as follows: "Far from being 'innocent' and becoming sexual at puberty, as was once the common belief, it is now indisputable that everyone is sexual, even before birth. Erection in males is detected in the womb from 29 weeks; erection in females, of course, is harder to detect. But baby boys are born with erections and girls with genitals swelling and vaginal lubrication. The vagina is responsive sexually from birth in cyclic lubrication. Masters and Johnson found that lubrication resulted from sexual stimulation in baby girls. Clearly, birth contains elements of sexual arousal for babies. Babies often react sexually when being held, or in other moments of physical pleasure. Reaction akin to orgasm has been detected in babies only a few months old" (108).

2. Lewis Carroll, *Alice's Adventures in Wonderland and Through the Looking-Glass and What Alice Found There* (London: Everyman, 1993), 56.

3. Ibid., 103.

4. Ibid., 101.

5. Ibid., 103.

6. Robert E. Owens Jr., *Queer Kids: The Challenges and Promise for Lesbian, Gay, and Bisexual Youth* (New York: Harrington Park, 1998), xiii.

7. Hayden White, "The Value of Narrativity in the Representation of Reality," in *On Narrative*, ed. W. J. T. Mitchell (Chicago: University of Chicago Press, 1981), 1–23.

8. Lesléa Newman, *Heather Has Two Mommies* (Los Angeles: Alyson Wonderland, 1989); Michael Willhoite, *Daddy's Roommate* (Boston: Alyson Wonderland, 1991); Michael Willhoite, *Uncle What-Is-It Is Coming to Visit!!* (Boston: Alyson Wonderland, 1993); Lesléa Newman, *Gloria Goes to Gay Pride* (Boston: Alyson Wonderland, 1993).

9. Jacqueline Rose, *The Case of Peter Pan, or The Impossibility of Children's Fiction* (Philadelphia: University of Pennsylvania Press, 1994), xii.

10. Lee Edelman, "The Future Is Kid Stuff: Queer Theory, Disidentification, and the Death Drive," *Narrative* 6, no. 1 (1998): 25, 29.

11. Ibid., 29. In a heated debate that followed the publication of Edelman's article, John Brenkman resisted the psychoanalytic, deconstructive politics by which Edelman comes to embrace negativity over the cultural construction of child-centered futurity. See John Brenkman, "Queer Post-politics"; Lee Edelman, "Post-partum"; and Brenkman, "Politics, Mortal and Natal: An Arendtian Rejoinder," all in *Narrative* 10, no. 2 (2002): 171–92.

12. Michel Foucault, *The History of Sexuality*, vol. 1, *An Introduction*, trans. Robert Hurley (New York: Vintage, 1980), 43.

13. Ibid., 43, 42.

14. Ibid., 42.

15. Ibid.

16. Thomas W. Laqueur, *Solitary Sex: A Cultural History of Masturbation* (New York: Zone, 2003), 47, 13.

17. The anonymously published French text *L'école des filles* also points to the significance of the figure of the youth and the staging of pedagogical dialogue in the rise of modern pornography. See Joan DeJean, *The Reinvention of Obscenity: Sex, Lies, and Tabloids in Early Modern France* (Chicago: University of Chicago Press, 2002). For pre-nineteenth-century treatment of this subject, see James Grantham Turner, *Schooling Sex: Libertine Education in Italy, France, and England, 1534–1685* (Oxford: Oxford University Press, 2003).

18. Laqueur, *Solitary Sex*, 82.

19. William Blake, "A Cradle Song," in *Blake's Poetry and Designs*, ed. Mary Lynn Johnson and John E. Grant (New York: W. W. Norton, 1979), 28–29.

20. William Blake, "A Cradle Song," in *Blake's Poetry and Designs* (see note 19), 194.

21. The persecution of desire came earlier than the nineteenth century. According to G. S. Rousseau, Richard Spencer was hanged in 1749 "for merely *hoping* 'to commit the Crime of Sodomy.'" G. S. Rousseau, "The Pursuit of Homosexuality in the Eighteenth Century: 'Utterly Confused Category' and/or 'Rich Repository'?" in *'Tis Nature's Fault: Unauthorized Sexuality during the Enlightenment*, ed. Robert P. Maccubbin (New York: Cambridge University Press, 1987), 147.

22. Gillian Avery, *Behold the Child: American Children and Their Books, 1621–1922* (Baltimore: Johns Hopkins University Press, 1994), 114–18; Karen Sánchez-Eppler,

"Temperance in the Bed of the Child: Incest and Social Order in Nineteenth-Century America," in *The Serpent in the Cup: Temperance in American Literature,* ed. David S. Reynolds and Debra J. Rosenthal (Amherst: University of Massachusetts Press, 1997), 60–92.

23. Constance Fenimore Woolson, "Felipa," in *Two Friends and Other Nineteenth-Century Lesbian Stories by American Women Writers,* ed. Susan Koppelman (New York: Meridian, 1994), 75.

24. Ibid., 76.

25. Sigmund Freud, "A Letter from Sigmund Freud," *American Journal of Psychiatry* 107 (April 1951): 786.

26. For a more complete discussion of Freud and narcissism, see Steven Bruhm, *Reflecting Narcissus: A Queer Aesthetic* (Minneapolis: University of Minnesota Press, 2001).

27. Sigmund Freud, "Group Psychology and the Analysis of the Ego," in *The Standard Edition of the Complete Works of Sigmund Freud,* vol. 18, ed. and trans. James Strachey (London: Hogarth, 1921), 108.

28. Sigmund Freud, "The Psychogenesis of a Case of Homosexuality in a Woman," in *The Standard Edition,* vol. 18 (see note 27), 158.

29. See Eve Kosofsky Sedgwick, *Between Men: English Literature and Male Homosocial Desire* (New York: Columbia University Press, 1985); Eve Kosofsky Sedgwick, *Epistemology of the Closet* (Berkeley: University of California Press, 1990).

30. Leo Bersani, *The Freudian Body: Psychoanalysis and Art* (New York: Columbia University Press, 1986), 43–44.

31. Adam Phillips, *The Beast in the Nursery: On Curiosity and Other Appetites* (New York: Vintage, 1999), 19.

32. Ibid., 18.

33. Phillips is not the only writer to be dissatisfied with the fixation on *lack* in psychoanalysis. For another discussion of the problem, see Gilles Deleuze and Félix Guattari, *Anti-Oedipus: Capitalism and Schizophrenia,* trans. Robert Hurley, Mark Seem, and Helen R. Lane (Minneapolis: University of Minnesota Press, 1983).

34. Phillips, *The Beast in the Nursery,* 17.

35. Ibid., 8.

36. Kelleher's source is Bersani, *The Freudian Body,* 32.

37. We have certainly lost faith in such democracy. The popular press is now flooded with stories about children exploiting and murdering other children, and this has become the stuff of fiction as well. Simona Vinci's provocative title for her novel, *What We Don't Know about Children* (New York: Knopf, 2000), turns out to be not that provocative at all, for in her imagination what we don't know about children seems to be precious little: they are rampantly sexual beings, polymorphously perverse little creatures whose sexual appetites are limitless. The novel also suggests that such sexual dalliance is as dangerous as it is universal. According to this painful book, what we also know about children is that sex in their orbit is always exploitative and damaging, bound to produce bent adults, assuming they survive the experience.

38. Kate Millett, "Beyond Politics? Children and Sexuality," in *Pleasure and*

Danger: Exploring Female Sexuality, ed. Carole S. Vance (London: Pandora, 1989), 222.

39. For more on this, see Gayle Rubin, "Thinking Sex: Notes for a Radical Theory of the Politics of Sexuality," in *Pleasure and Danger* (see note 38), 267–319; Pat Califia, *Public Sex: The Culture of Radical Sex* (San Francisco: Cleis, 1994).

40. Stan Persky and John Dixon, *On Kiddie Porn: Sexual Representation, Free Speech, and the Robin Sharpe Case* (Vancouver: New Star, 2001).

41. Adam Phillips, *Promises, Promises: Essays on Literature and Psychoanalysis* (London: Faber and Faber, 2002), 101.

42. Michel Foucault, *The History of Sexuality*, vol. 2, *The Use of Pleasure*, trans. Robert Hurley (New York: Vintage, 1985), 200.

43. Ibid., 221.

44. Ibid., 223.

45. Ibid., 224. Earlier in his discussion, Foucault outlines in more detail the elements of the negotiation between boy and man. The boy, he says, "had to be careful not to yield too easily; he also had to keep from accepting too many tokens of love, and from granting his favors heedlessly and out of self-interest, without testing the worth of his partner; he must also show gratitude for what the lover had done for him" (196). Thus, says Foucault, the sexual relationship was highly complex, "accompanied by conventions, rules of conduct, ways of going about it, by a whole game of delays and obstacles designed to put off the moment of closure, and to integrate it into a series of subsidiary activities and relations" (196–97).

46. Ibid., 195.

47. The field is beginning to open up. We direct interested readers to other important collections, such as Matthew Rottnek, ed., *Sissies and Tomboys: Gender Nonconformity and Homosexual Childhood* (New York: New York University Press, 1999), and Henry Jenkins, ed., *The Children's Culture Reader* (New York: New York University Press, 1998), and to significant books such as Judith Levine's *Harmful to Minors: The Perils of Protecting Children from Sex* (Minneapolis: University of Minnesota Press, 2002) and Ursula Kelly's *Schooling Desire: Literacy, Cultural Politics, and Pedagogy* (New York: Routledge, 1997). Although these books are crucial to any consideration of queerness and sexuality in children, they make gender their particular focus. The focus of this volume, in contrast, is the particular queer resonance of child sexuality. For a consideration of the relations between homosexuality and pedophilia, see Harris Mirkin, "The Pattern of Sexual Politics: Feminism, Homosexuality, and Pedophilia," *Journal of Homosexuality* 32, no. 2 (1999): 1–24.

48. Rubin, "Thinking Sex," 306.

49. Leo Bersani, "Is the Rectum a Grave?" in *AIDS: Cultural Analysis/Cultural Activism*, ed. Douglas Crimp (Cambridge: MIT Press, 1988), 217.

50. Ibid., 222.

51. Bersani, *The Freudian Body*, 38.

52. Ibid., 39.

53. Peter Straub, "The Juniper Tree," in *Houses without Doors* (New York: Signet, 1991). Beyond the folktale source is an homage to Tennessee Williams, whose story

"The Mysteries of the Joy Rio" is about intergenerational sex in the confines of a seedy movie theater.

54. Ibid., 107.

55. Ibid., 93.

56. Ibid., 101.

57. Ibid.

58. Cathy Caruth, "Trauma and Experience: Introduction," in *Trauma: Explorations in Memory,* ed. Cathy Caruth (Baltimore: Johns Hopkins University Press, 1995), 10.

59. Straub, "The Juniper Tree," 109.

60. But predict in advance is exactly what Straub seems to do when he rewrites this story ten years later, as "Bunny Is Good Bread," in his collection *Magic Terror: Seven Tales* (New York: Random House, 2000), 98–153. Here the child who is molested in the theater understands his experience to be nothing but traumatic. Gone is the ambivalence of "The Juniper Tree"; gone is the connection between sex in the theater and the protagonist's becoming a writer. Straub's later version of the same narrative surely marks a decade of panic around childhood and sex as he writes out the richness that his earlier story contained.

61. For Sedgwick's characteristically urbane treatment of this issue, see Eve Kosofsky Sedgwick, *Tendencies* (Durham, NC: Duke University Press, 1993), 16.

Part I
Sexing the Child

Producing Erotic Children

James R. Kincaid

This essay is divided into eleven parts, eleven being a prime number. The eleven parts are not equal in length or weight, and they do not carry the same importance; nonetheless, they are exactly symmetrical and harmonious.

These are the parts:

1. Ellie Nesler's Son
2. Michael Jackson's Driveway
3. McMartin-Menendez
4. The Coppertone Child Home Alone
5. Questions We Love to Ask
6. My Thesis
7. Resisting the Obvious
8. Recovered Memory
9. Scandal—That's What We Need
10. Me
11. You

1. Ellie Nesler's Son

Ellie Nesler's son is named Willy, Willy Nesler. He is now [in 1996] about thirteen years old, living, I think, in Jamestown, California, where, in 1993, in April, he was in a courtroom waiting to testify in the preliminary hearing of one Daniel Driver, accused of seven counts of child molesting. The papers say Willy Nesler was one of the alleged victims; they also say that, according to his mother, he was vomiting wildly the morning he was scheduled to tell his story. Anyway, before he got the chance to speak, his mother took control, silencing her boy and the accused forever. When Daniel Driver looked at that mother with what she took to be a smirk, Ellie, goaded beyond her limits, bolted from the courtroom, filched a .22 semiautomatic from her sister's purse, charged back in, and plugged the guarded and manacled Driver in the head and neck five times at close range, proclaiming, "Maybe I'm not God, but I'll tell you what: I'm the closest damn thing to it."[1] I mention Willy Nesler because at this point he becomes invisible, silent and empty, a vacancy at the center of the story—filled up and written on by his mother, and the press, and the nation's outrage, our own included. Willy Nesler becomes our principal citizen, the empty and violated child, whose story we need so badly we take it into ourselves. No one wants Willy Nesler testifying, taking on substance: the erotic child is mute, under our control. Once the accused is out of the way, and the child is rendered speechless and helpless, we can proceed to our usual business: the righteous, guilt-free constructions of violent pornographic fantasies about child sexuality.

In this case, Willy Nesler's mother thrusts herself between us and the speaking child, blocking his words just in time, and giving us the screen we need. In the scores of accounts I read of the trial, Willy appears only as "Ellie's boy," "Nesler's son."[2] Ellie Nesler herself forms the displaced, disowned, and finally discarded projection we can use for a while to contemplate with impunity her thoroughly sexualized boy. For a moment, Ellie grabs the headlines, becomes a vigilante June Cleaver, the American Mom of the fifties, reborn snarling, protecting her chick. Defense funds spring up, fueled by spaghetti suppers; schoolchildren are forced to write thank-you notes; T-shirts and bumper stickers scream, "Nice Shootin' Ellie"; *Hard Copy* and Charles Kurault descend on Jamestown. All this so we can do as we like with our image of Willy Nesler. We can sentimentalize him erotically, as a townsperson does by saying, "His little soul died the day he was molested";[3] we can indulge in the full-scale fantasies scripted by Ellie's attorney, who asked the jury to "pick a child you know and look at their innocence and sweetness," and then imagine it being violated.[4]

This does not last very long. For a while, Ellie gave us a story so compelling in its gothic simplicities that it was irresistible: drive a stake through the heart of the pedophile and bourgeois America will be safe, along with our illusions about childhood, the family, sexuality, and our own rectitude. But Ellie's story never sold. The crowds of media talent that drew into Jamestown from Los Angeles and New York, like vultures to roadkill, fled even more quickly. All of a sudden, Ellie was abandoned—left to fend for herself in the trial and reduced to claiming that she was insane at the time of the killing. In a last-ditch, double-barreled bid for sympathy, she claimed that she had been molested herself as a child, and also that she had a fatal disease; but the insanity defense failed, and nobody cared by then whether Ellie had cancer or not, or even whether those she named—her father's poker buddies and a state senator[5]—had sexually abused her.

What had happened was that Ellie turned out to be complicated, not the simple heroine we needed for gothic, but a woman with a history, a history we did not want. She had a minor criminal record; she had taken drugs, perhaps on the morning of the shooting; she had threatened to kill Daniel Driver months earlier. We no longer had the clean-cut simplicity that would allow us the screen of outrage between us and our object of interest, which had never been Ellie or Driver but Willy Nesler, the breached, silent child. Without the screen story, we were left to face the music ourselves, or go and find other stories. Since the stories are not hard to find, we hesitated not a second in getting out of Jamestown and leaving Ellie to her sentencing— ten years—while we hustled to locate more guilt-free eroticism.

2. Michael Jackson's Driveway

In the joke, Michael Jackson's driveway is as erotic as our construction of Willy Nesler. The joke is this: How do you know Michael Jackson is having a party? By all the Big Wheels parked in his driveway. The other Michael Jackson joke has him visiting O. J. Simpson and offering to look after the children, should things go badly for Simpson. It's the same joke. Simpson's children, Willy Nesler, the drivers of all those Big Wheels: they take their parts in the narratives we manufacture, the narratives of innocence protected and pure, that is, lost and sullied. It does not matter much what line we take on the issues we can pretend these cases contain. Issues are there simply to give us, as they say, deniability, psychic deniability.

Take the fun in being outraged with Michael Jackson as boy-lover, and telling our friends how outraged we are. And not just with Jackson either, but with the failure of others to be as loving to children as we are: "Can you imagine anyone letting a son sleep with that man?" Actually, imagining is what we are all good at; otherwise such stories would not find ready listeners such as me and you. Had Michael Jackson not existed, we would have been forced to invent him, which is, of course, what we did.

Or take the way we can use the Jackson story to blow off steam about "the media," as if "the media" were an independent agent, an outsider whose desires and energies are foisted on us against our will. "The media," then, becomes a little like "the pedophile," a handy fabrication and focus for our passions that we can abuse and pretend to disown.

The hounding of Michael Jackson is a spectacular case in point. Michael Jackson, to whose music we have sent our children and our soft-drink companies with record piles of dollars, is superchild and now super-child-molester. Michael Jordan would have done as well, or Barney. Jackson as a construction of our eroticism and our guilt, of our lavish, capitalist fantasies and generosities, and our frightened, repression-driven paranoia: he can hardly be said to exist outside our needs. Once he was a child himself, and it is commonly said that he still is; but we can make him play the part of the *guilty* child, absolving us from guilt. Jackson is reduced to his bed and his relationships, to the "sharing" of that bed. That's all he is, as he and dozens of boys (including our star boy, Macaulay Culkin) pose for our collective scrapbooks. Even Jackson's recent marriage is openly construed as a reason for getting not Lisa Marie [Presley] but her children into that bed.

Not mentioned in my eleven-point outline, and offered as an undeserved bonus: Woody Allen forms a more troubled, sophisticated version of this cultural drama. His story and his role shift before our eyes, as he bounces from child to child (younger and younger all the time), from villain to victim, from comedian to ogre. Allen becomes, like Oscar Wilde, the repository of a fair number of hatreds—of artists, Jews, New Yorkers, cosmopolitans generally, short guys, redheads, Knicks fans—but primarily he becomes (as in Chaucer's "Prioress's Tale") the monster who threatens the child, and thus gives us exactly what we want.

3. McMartin-Menendez

The McMartin trial, dealing with allegations of child molesting and ritual satanic abuse at a Southern California preschool, began with charges in the summer of 1983 and did not end until the summer of 1990, the trial itself running, with one short break, from April 1987 until July 1990. This, the longest criminal trial in American history, ended mostly with acquittals, along with some deadlocks and inconsequential declarations of mistrials, all signaling that we had other spectacles to attend to and could finally let this one go. Along the way, though, we had provided ourselves with seven rich years of titillating narratives about animal sacrifice and demonic possession, about games of Tickle and Naked Movie Star, about Raymond Buckey's underwear and his collection of *Playboy* magazines, about children and sex.

Menendez is McMartin II, an artful variation on what has become our favorite public entertainment: staged dramas of child molesting, masked as exercises in justice. Lyle Menendez, who has been compared to Judy Garland and Montgomery Clift as a "great neurotic actor,"[6] testifies, with a tough-guy sob we have all become attached to, "He raped me." Not only that—he testifies the very next day that he had, as an eight-year-old, molested his fellow defendant, Erik, then six, with a toothbrush. "I'm sorry," Lyle says to his brother, right there in the courtroom, not omitting the sob.

According to most spectators, Erik is not so gifted, despite his acting ambitions, and really pours out too many details without anything like his brother's mastery of narrative pace and flow. Erik talks, all in a rush, about the taste of his father's semen, sweetened with cinnamon; he speaks of his mother squeezing blisters on his penis; he mentions categories of incestuous activities and the names each had—Knees, Nice, Rough, and Sex— respectively, oral, hand, needles and tacks, and anal. He is in too much of a bustle to add flourishes from bad novels: his father lighting candles and slowly placing them about the room before saying to the boy, like an X-rated Vincent Price, "One last fuck before I kill you." Still, even Erik manages to do the job. One alternate juror confesses on the *Donahue* show, "Phil . . . it was sickening. . . . I could *visualize* this pedophile father—he's down the hall in the bedroom, he is sodomizing his six-year-old child."[7]

What is being visualized so clearly is a child, a figure in this drama so important that it seems to replace the actual bodies of the grown-up and athletically bulky Lyle and Erik. Both are referred to, not only by their attorneys but by many of our deputies in the press, as children, kids, boys, sometimes prefixed by "little." It is this image of the child that we are paying for in the trial, and we use the besweatered young men as transparent agencies, peering back through them to the child within, down the hall in the bedroom.

4. The Coppertone Child Home Alone

But what about Macaulay Culkin? What about the adorable child? The adorable child is not our only child-species, as Lyle and Erik demonstrate, but adoration is still dear to our erotic centering of the child. The vacantly androgynous Culkin on the beach, his swimming trunks being pulled down behind cutely by a cute little dog: that's the national pinup.[8] I grant you that Culkin is fast losing his hold on this role, and his ability to present himself to us with no face and no body, as a blankness we can fill in. Still, the desire that once rushed into his emptiness lingers on, and he is still the ghost of a cultural wish-fulfillment dream to find the perfectly evacuated child, isolated and suitably domesticated, at home in bourgeois familiarity.

The film *Home Alone* covers its own appeals just barely, using Three Stooges comedy and loading the child with sadistic potency in the make-believe layering of "fun" that allows us to enjoy the erotic formulations without beginning to acknowledge them: the child alone, defenseless, needing us. The sequel is a lot less smooth about all this, coarsening itself to the point of having Culkin make comments about seeing naked butts, and forcing him to jump into a swimming pool with a suit so many sizes too big that it peels off when he hits the water—surprise, surprise.

As Culkin reluctantly acquires a body of his own, and thus fades from our fantasies, others are found to take his place, in films like *The Client* or *The Little Rascals,* where adorable children inherit Culkin's position, one he took over in turn from a long line of culturally mandated cuties: Ricky Schroeder, Henry Thomas, Jay North, Tatum O'Neal, Jodie Foster, Brooke Shields, Mark Lester, Shirley Temple, Freddie Bartholomew, and on into the night.

Last year's Clint Eastwood film, *A Perfect World,* offers a darker, less obviously "cute" version of Culkin: a small boy played by T. J. Lowther, in a role that is actually given some substance, thus reducing his potential as a target for our usual erotic adoring. All the same, he plays out explicitly a variety of our most distressing and titillating narratives about child sexuality, in scenes that either reproduce or parody (depending on one's position) the child as object of sexual attention. He spends the first half of the movie in his briefs and the last half in a Halloween costume that gets torn so as, again, to expose his underpants. At one point, the vicious convict, commenting on the boy's "cute underwears," inserts his hand into them to examine the penis, pronouncing it "puny." Later the good convict (Kevin Costner), sensing that the boy is reluctant to undress before him, and learning that it is all because he is ashamed of his "puny" penis, says, "Let me see it," takes a long look, and tells him it's okay, thus reassuring us that our own voyeurism here is also absolutely okay. The film works over again the erotic pedagogical territory tromped on in *The Earthling, Treasure Island, Searching for Bobby Fischer, Kidnapped, Redneck, Willy Wonka, The Man without a Face, The Champ, Shane,* and *The Client.*

5. Questions We Love to Ask

But first: questions we don't love to ask. Let us take the stories of Ellie Nesler, Menendez, Woody Allen, Michael Jackson, the day-care trial du jour, and ask about the source, the nature, and the size of the pleasures we take from such stories. What are these stories, where do they come from, and why do we tell them with such relish? What kind of relish is it? Why do we want to hear these feverish tales about the sexuality of children, and why do we listen to them so eagerly? What is it about the child and its eroticism that so magnetizes us? In short, Why do we tell the stories we tell? Why do we need to hear them? These are plain sorts of questions, but we don't often attend to them. We prefer others:

1. How can we spot the pedophiles and get rid of them?
2. Meanwhile, how can we protect our children?
3. How can we induce our children to tell us the truth, and all of it, about their sexual lives?
4. How can we get the courts to believe children who say they have been sexually molested?
5. How can we get the courts to believe adults who suddenly remember they were sexually molested as children?
6. How can we get ourselves to believe others when they say they remember being sexually molested years ago?
7. How can we know if maybe some people are not making these things up, misremembering?
8. How can we know if bumbling parents, cops, and (especially) therapists are not implanting false memories?

Though some of these questions seem to take revenge on other questions, they all have one thing in common: they demand the same answer, "We can't."

I think that is why both the standard and the backlash stories are so popular: they have about them an urgency and a self-flattering righteous oomph. Asking them, I can get the feeling that I care very much, and that I am really on the right side in these vital issues of our time. Even better, these open-ended, unanswerable questions generate variations on themselves, and allow us to keep them going, circulating them among ourselves without ever experiencing fatigue, never getting enough of what they are offering.

And what they are offering is a nicely protected way of talking about the subject of child sexuality. I do not deny that we are also talking about detection and danger. Certainly we care about the poor, hurt children. But we care also about maintaining the particular erotic vision of children that is putting them in this position in the first place.

6. My Thesis

You have already beat me to it, but here it is anyway, blunt and persuasive. My argument is that erotic children are manufactured—in the sense that we produce them in our cultural factories, the ones that make meanings for us. They tell us what "the child" is, and also what "the erotic" *is*. I argue that for the last two hundred years or so, they have confused us, have failed to distinguish the two categories, have allowed them dangerously to overlap. And the result of all that is the examples I've mentioned to this point. All these are public spectacles of child eroticism, an eroticism that can be flaunted and also screened, exploited and denied, enjoyed and cast off, made central and made criminal.

This new thing, the postromantic child, has been deployed as, among other things, a political and philosophical agent, a weapon used to assault substance and substitute in its place a set of negative inversions: innocence, purity, emptiness. Childhood in our culture has come to be largely a co-ordinate set of *have nots:* the child is that which *does not have.* Its liberty, however much prized, is a negative attribute, as is its innocence and purity. Moreover, all these, throughout the nineteenth century, became more and more firmly attached to what was characterized as sexually desirable, innocence in particular becoming a fulcrum for the nineteenth and twentieth centuries' ambiguous construction of sexuality and sexual behavior. Innocence was what came to you in heaven, or in marriage, as a kind of prize. Innocence was that which we have been trained to adore and covet, to preserve and despoil, to speak of in hushed tones and in bawdy songs.

The same goes for purity, of course, another empty figure that allows the admirer to read just about anything he likes into that vacancy, including a flattering image of his very self. The construction of the modern "child" is very largely an evacuation, the ruthless sending out of eviction notices. Correspondingly, the instructions we receive on what to regard as sexually arousing tell us to look for (and often create) this emptiness, to discover the erotic in that which is most susceptible to inscription, the blank page. On that page we can write what we like, write it and then long for it, love it, have it. Children are defined, and longed for, according to what *they* do not have.

Bodies are made to conform to this set of cultural demands. Heathcliff and Cathy (aged twelve) are symbols of titanic passion; Shirley Temple was enticing until puberty, when she instantly became a Republican frump; Rick Schroeder lost our interest when he stopped calling himself "Ricky"; Macaulay Culkin teeters on the brink of unerotic oblivion; Tom Sawyer's later adventures do not interest us. Baby-smooth skin is capable of making us pant with desire, while unsmooth, or contoured, skin is not: Is this because flatness is innately more titillating than texture, or because flatness signifies nothing at all and thus does not interfere with our projections? In the same way, desirable faces must be blank, washed out of color, eyes big and round and expressionless, hair blond or colorless altogether, waists, hips, feet, and minds small. The physical makeup of the child has been translated into mainstream images of the sexually and materially alluring.

We are told to look like children, if we can and for as long as we can, to pine for that look. (These cultural directives equating the erotic with eternal youth operate, perhaps, with special ferocity on women, but not only on women: think of Tom Cruise, Marky Mark, John Kennedy Jr., Matthew Broderick, Prince Charles, David Letterman, Jimmy Connors, Tom Brokaw, Mick Jagger, Jack Nicholson, George Burns—all cute little boys forever.)

It is worth noting that these various narratives of the child not only focus and allow desire, but also erase various social and political complications, performing essential cultural work that is not simply erotic. By formulating the image of the alluring child as inevitably bleached, bourgeois, and androgynous, these stories mystify material reality and render nearly invisible, certainly irrelevant, questions we might raise about race, class, and even gender. Such categories are scrubbed away in this state, laved and snuggled into the grade-A homogeneity we might call Shirley Shroeder Culkin/Macaulay Ricky Temple. When poor children are allowed, as they sometimes are, to play this part, they are elevated (helped) into the class above them; boys and girls leave gender markers behind and meld together; children of color find themselves blanched to ungodly sallowness, Moby-Dicked, we might say. In all our stories, there is but one erotic child, and his name is Purity: neither rich nor poor, neither male nor female, neither black nor brown (yellow and red being out of the question). These swirling tales of desire allow nothing that would distract us from the primary fantasy.

In any case, the major point and dilemma is that we are instructed to crave that which is forbidden, a crisis we face by not facing it, by becoming hysterical, and by writing a kind of pious pornography, a self-righteous doublespeak that demands both lavish public spectacle and constant guilt-denying projections onto scapegoats. Child molesting becomes the virus that nourishes us, that empty point of ignorance about which we are most knowing. It is the semiotic shorthand that explains everything, that tells us to look no further: having been on either side of the child-molesting scene defines us completely. Lawyers know this, as do politicians and storytellers. In *Forrest Gump*, for instance, as in a hundred other recent narratives, the fact that the heroine was abused by her father, who was also drunk and lower-class, explains to our full satisfaction why she is suicidal, drug infested, looking for love in all the wrong places, and willing to settle for the dim-witted hero.

It is not a pretty landscape we have constructed, nor one with clearly marked exits. We think we know a great deal about this subject of child molesting; we are told that many things connected with it are obvious. But it is possible that this obviousness is the glue that cements the double bind.

7. Resisting the Obvious

So we might try to avoid the stupefyingly obvious: common and natural assumptions that seem to be continuous with the problem of child molesting. We might even resist the most compelling ritual gesture of all: acknowledging that, of course, sexual child abuse does exist, and exists on a very large scale. We need not deny it; we just do not want to begin the discussion in the territory left to us once we offer that disclaimer. I suspect that this disclaimer is a vital part of the discourse that eroticizes the child and keeps us blind to what we are doing. It forces the discussion into channels of diagnosis and cure, mandates certain assumptions about what is and is not important, allows us to see some things and blinds us to others. It traps us into offering one more set of tips on how to determine whether or not child molesting "happened." But what if we explored another set of happenings: What is happening to us and to our children as we tell our customary stories of the child and of sexuality?

It is not rewarding to keep acknowledging that "molestation happens." One notices that every debunker of every salacious popular myth (even brilliant debunkers like Elizabeth Loftus and Paul McHugh) begins by saying, in effect, "Now, don't misunderstand me; I know that millions of children are sexually abused." I think we need to fly past that net. That we are compelled to say that molestation happens is an insistence that it must. Where would we be without it? Its material presence is guaranteed by our usual stories, stories of displacement and denial, stories that act to keep alive the images that guarantee the molesting itself or at least our belief in it. Now, it is true that the stories themselves are based on a cultural inheritance that is very deep and complex. I do not claim that if we outlawed the stories, then the attraction to children would end. Censorship would not help us. It is just that the molesting and the stories protesting the molesting walk the same beat. When we seek to adjust the protesting stories by saying, "Yeah, but let's take recovered memory out of the plot," we do nothing to disrupt the circuitry, only to further remove from investigation its generating sources. Why do we talk about sex with children as if it were an isolated physical catastrophe, divorced from our talk? Maybe the child-molesting problem is married to the way we think about "the child-molesting problem."

8. Recovered Memory

But haven't we already recognized our position, and aren't we moving even now to correct it? The pendulum is swinging, we might say, and we now are starting to see that things are more complicated than we supposed, that not absolutely everyone mentioned in connection with child molesting may be guilty. We are now willing to grant that there are neurotics out there, and misrememberers, and clumsy therapists, and even liars. In our zeal, we may have falsely convicted some and driven others to suicide; we may have been so eager to hear children make accusations that we were not critical enough of what they were saying; we may even have implanted those accusations by being so insistent; we may have victimized ourselves, some of us, by asking ourselves to remember molesting scenes of years ago, asking in such an expectant way that we remembered in detail things that never happened.

We like to think we see all this now, with a clarity that is perhaps not unflinching, but growing in sharpness and focus. And the result of this creditable advance, we suppose, is that we have abandoned the old, melodramatic, gothic way of seeing intergenerational sex, the simple plot wherein there were grotesque villains, easy to spot, attacking a pure, uncomplicated virtue.

Or *maybe* all this complicating in reference to the dubiousness of recovered memory and of children's testimony about sexual issues is really just a matter of keeping the talk going by slightly rejiggling the terms. Maybe it's not so much a complication as a reversal, a way of maintaining the same structure of titillating talk and effective self-protection. Turning the accuser into the accused, swapping villain and victim, does not, when you look at it, seem like that much of a change. Demonizing Freud and psychoanalysis can be done without a paradigm leap. It is still a gothic melodrama, filled with self-protective name-calling. The game stays as it was; we all just switch sides: the accused now deserves sympathy and the accuser condemnation. But the primary discourse stays. In fact, these new twists are so intriguing they demand even more talk, serving the same old needs.

9. Scandal—That's What We Need

Scandal: the *Oxford English Dictionary (OED)* says it is, at root, a trap; it is believed to be from the Indo-Germanic *skand,* to spring or leap. Early on, *scandal* meant to cause perplexity of conscience, to hinder the reception of faith or obedience to Divine Law, to present a stumbling block. Ignoring all the alternate meanings given by the *OED,* let us settle on this cluster. Scandal is a trap sprung on the main bullies of any culture: faith, law, and submission to them. Scandal is the enemy of cultural hegemony; it is the offense that frees us from piety; it is the gross material fact that thumbs its nose at all metaphysical policemen. We are drawn to scandal by a hope to trip up the cultural censors, by a dream of escaping culture or transforming it. Compliance, we sense, will get us nowhere, great as the rewards for compliance may be. Let me prove all this to everyone's satisfaction.

Take the most banal of all scandals, political scandal—and ask yourself what draws you to it. Why are the erotic doings of, say, Bill Clinton so much more interesting than his policies? Not, let me suggest, because he is himself erotic; like most politicians, where he is, eros is not. Most of us would do a great deal to avoid imagining the actual doings of Clinton's body. Let me assume, then, that what draws us to scandal is the energy and promise of scandal itself, not the particulars of any one scandal. It is the offense that matters, that holds out promise, that gives us hope.

10. Me

I caused a scandal myself, but it was a comic miniscandal, altogether insufficient for the job I have in mind. Still, how would you like it if you got a review, a prominent review, by an Oxford don in the *London Times* (albeit the *Sunday Times*) and the best thing in that review was the following: "It is astonishing that a Professor of English could be so poorly informed." The review goes on to call my book, *Child-Loving: The Erotic Child and Victorian Culture,*[9] "fatally flawed," but that amounts almost to praise compared to the allegation that, although I do not exactly "recommend the practice or admit to it myself," being annoyingly "evasive" on what I really do in my spare time, the book I have written makes it clear that I am "a passionate champion of pedophilia."[10] In a separate article in the same edition, the *Sunday Times* said, "Kincaid's theories support those of the infamous Paedophile Information Exchange, or PIE," banned in Britain several years ago for allegedly dealing in child pornography. To cement the connection between me and PIE, the *Sunday Times* contacted Lord Bernard Braine, Tory MP for Castle Point and crusader for sexual decency, who said he was sending a copy of my book to the home secretary so he could ban it. "I simply cannot believe," said Lord Braine, "a reputable publisher could consider printing a book with such views. For any rational human being to give currency to what the vast majority of people regard as the vilest crime possible is deeply shocking." This article was headlined, "Anger over US Don's Support for Paedophiles."[11]

This was nothing compared to the coverage in the *Daily Mail*, which was more forthright in its headline: "Paedophile Book 'Should Be Banned.'" The *Daily Mail* said my book portrays pedophiles as "kindly people who cause no ill-effects," and they sought out Lord Braine again, who says, "We have enough social problems in this country without encouraging publications of this kind." Ann Winterton, Conservative MP for Congleton, agrees—"I am appalled that this book is being published in Britain"—and so does Dame Jill Knight, Tory MP for Edgbaston: "It is crucial for the normal development of children that their innocence be preserved." The *Daily Mail* also quoted some experts in the field as saying that "child sexual abuse can have very damaging effects," suggesting, I guess, that I was the passionate champion of the reverse view. Michael Hames, head of Scotland Yard's Obscene Publications Squad, gave the judicious overview: "People will be rightly outraged. This book won't offend against the law, but it will give comfort to paedophiles."[12]

11. You

But my book only tapped, predictably, a small feeder line of outrage and caused hardly more than a belch. For the truly scandalous, I look to you readers, the leaders of our profession. The *OED* tells us that being scandalous means being willing to take on big-time opprobrium, and that takes big shoulders, and many of them. The only way, though, to rewrite the script is, I think, first to jar loose the present one, to drain its power by drawing it into the trap that scandal can set and then spring.

Disgrace can do that, can revise the narrative, perhaps into one kinder to us and to children as well. For one thing is clear: our present gothic scapegoating stories, our stories of denial and projected desire, are doing few of us any good. Perhaps we can write ourselves into the plot directly, give up our immunity. We might then be anxious to find narratives other than the gothic, to cast about for other genres so we can avoid playing the monster part. Such alternate genres, I think, would be mixed, modulated, abandoning, for instance, stark essentialist notions of sexuality and sexual behavior in favor of the idea of a range of erotic feelings even within and toward children. Such scandalous narratives, finally, might see more calmly the way children and eroticism have been constructed for us, and might help us decide that the problems involved in facing these things are much smaller than those that come down on us when we evade them. We know that a child's memory is developed not simply from data but from learning a canonical narrative; we know that what we are and have been comes to us from narrative forms that take on so much authority they start looking like nature. We suspect that events themselves are complicit with the narrative authority that forms and licenses them. Why not snub the authority and change the stories? We might find that, all along, we have been afraid of the wrong things. We might even find stories that are not fueled by fear.

But none of this is going to happen without a fuss, without a most distressing and ignominious set of scandals—which is where you come in.

Notes

1. Quoted in *Los Angeles Times*, July 23, 1993, A26.

2. It was not until *Redbook* published Beverly Lowry's account of the imprisoned Ellie Nesler's struggle with cancer, "Should Ellie Nesler Go Free?" (August 1994, 82–85, 114–17), that Willy's name surfaced. It is possible, of course, that his name was withheld from the newspaper accounts out of consideration for his age (though this is by no means a universal practice); but such erasures still have the effect of eroticizing the emptiness. They also fold the child into the adult, as a possession or

an extension: "Ellie's boy" is really a part of Ellie (Ellie's foot), a function of Ellie (Ellie's job), and an object (Ellie's afghan).

3. Frankie Tinkle, "mother of three" and lifelong resident, quoted in the *San Francisco Chronicle*, August 13, 1993, A17.

4. Tony Serra, San Francisco attorney and Nesler's lawyer, quoted in the *San Francisco Chronicle*, August 12, 1993, A18.

5. According to the *Los Angeles Times* (September 10, 1993, A32), Nesler blurted out this accusation during the sanity phase of her trial, charging that psychiatrists covered up for a probation officer she says molested her when she was fourteen, the cover-up being arranged, she yelled, "because he's a state senator." She named no names, but State Senator Patrick Johnston issued a statement acknowledging that he had been Nesler's probation officer and denying the allegation.

6. Dominick Dunne, "Menendez Justice," *Vanity Fair*, March 1994, 111. Other details are drawn from this article, from television news coverage and Court TV, and from newspaper accounts that ran in the *Los Angeles Times*.

7. Transcript from *The Phil Donahue Show*, February 2, 1994, 9; concerning the statements of Judy Zamos, identified as "Jury Alternate in Lyle's Trial."

8. Interestingly (I guess), a prominent child actor, Culkin's costar in *The Good Son* and his rival for the big bucks, Elijah Wood, serves as the model for a Coppertone kid in Rob Reiner's *North*. The child is used in a scene as the model for a tourist billboard, where his trunks are pulled down repeatedly by a dog, causing Wood to protest, repeatedly, about having his "crack," "the most private crevice on my body," shown. Nonetheless, shown it is, albeit as a representation (graphic).

9. James R. Kincaid, *Child-Loving: The Erotic Child and Victorian Culture* (New York: Routledge, 1992).

10. John Carey, "The Age of Innocents," *Sunday Times* (London), March 7, 1993, "Features," 9–11.

11. James Dalrymple, "Anger over US Don's Support for Paedophiles," *Sunday Times* (London), March 7, 1993, n.p.

12. Edward Verity, "Paedophile Book 'Should Be Banned,'" *Daily Mail* (London), March 8, 1994, n.p.

The Pedophilia of Everyday Life

Richard D. Mohr

Nearly every week for more than a decade, the Partnership for a Drug-Free America has placed a full-page display ad in the business section of the *New York Times*. The often gorgeous designs of the ads are as subtle as their overt messages are blunt: Drugs Scramble Your Brain. Fire Employees Suspected of Drug Use—It's for Their Own Good. Drug Use Cuts Corporate Profits. That sort of thing. In their iconography, however, the ads roam over a much wider social field and frequently convey insidious messages—messages no less powerful for their indirection.

An easy case: a disproportionately high percentage of these ads picture professional women as the drug users in need of social disciplining. Frequently these women are the only women to be seen anywhere in the *Times* business section. The ads freight these pages with the message that women do not belong in business—they belong somewhere else. The ad campaign uses America's demonization of drugs as both an energy source and vehicle for advancing an agenda of "traditional family values."

It should not then come as much of a surprise that the ad campaign also includes iconography that links—indeed, virtually identifies—demon drug use with being gay. Numerous times, Drug-Free America has run an ad that features a nearly life-size portrait of a sylphlike boy (Figure 1). You have to look twice to tell that it is a boy, for he is coded all over with signs of

IT USED TO BE, AT 13, LITTLE BOYS BECAME INTERESTED IN LITTLE GIRLS.

Boys and girls used to use straws to sip sodas at the drug store. Now they cut the straws in half and use them to snort drugs deep into their nostrils.

Times have changed. Our children need our help. We need to talk with our children. And talk. And talk. This way, we'll learn what they think about drugs. What they know about them. What they don't know.

Then, once we understand their perspective, we'll be in a better

position to offer our own. Then we'll be able to talk about the dangers of various drugs. And about what our children can do to avoid them.

It takes courage to talk to them like this. And to do it effectively, it takes homework—like reading articles, attending meetings and talking to other parents. Otherwise, our children won't see us as informed sources. And they'll get their answers elsewhere.

As a parent, you can get answers to your own questions by contacting your local agency on drug abuse.

PARTNERSHIP FOR A DRUG-FREE AMERICA

Figure 1. Full-page advertisement for Drug-Free America in the "Business Day" section of the *New York Times*, September 21, 1992; January 7, 1994; February 6, 1995; et al.

femininity. His lips are slightly glossed, slightly pursed. His posture is coy. His head tilts forward over a unisex sweater, causing luscious and illuminated blond tresses to cascade over one eye. The other looks seductively at the camera—square at you. The arc formed by his neck and hair continues on to a plastic tube that he holds toward cocaine lined on a mirror, which in turn reflects his image. Indulgent and languorous, Narcissus invites you to drown with—in—him.

The caption's huge sans serif headline reads: "It used to be, at 13, little boys became interested in little girls." What is the unstated antistrophe? One obvious possibility is "But now little boys are becoming interested in drugs." The copy, dripping with nostalgia and, like the caption, cast in the Norman Rockwell tense—the imperfect—continues: "Boys and girls used to use straws to sip sodas at the drug store." Our world is out of kilter, things are somewhat queer. At a minimum, drug use is billed as arresting hetero-sexual development. It deflects youth from the culturally proper object of erotic choice (coke replaces "woman"). And it disrupts the social rituals by which culture prods youth along nature's path (snorting replaces courting). But this verbal flag of deviance is not entirely queer, for it fails to establish for the youth a positively limned perverted identity. The ad's iconography takes up this chore. It layers over the boy both of the tropes by which our civilization marks out perverted male sexuality: sexual inversion (being a woman trapped in a man's body) and bad object choice (desiring a man rather than a woman).

The codes of femininity that engulf the boy iconographically suggest that a feminine essence is seeping through the shell, the pores, of his mar-ginally male body. The boy—really, deep down—*is* a girl. So the caption's cadences invite us to another possible antistrophic horror: "It used to be that little boys became interested in little girls, but now—with drugs—little boys become little girls." The ad would have us believe that more than cor-rupting the body, drugs corrupt, pervert, the soul.

But what of the lad's enticing glance? This provides him with a bad object choice—you, the viewer. It is practically an axiom of contemporary art theory that the gaze of the viewer is presumptively a male gaze. But even without theory, we know that overwhelmingly the readership of the *Times* business pages is male. The boy's come-hither glance is for a man. He invites the man to become absorbed in his gaze. As a consequence, the boy's association with drugs makes him doubly homosexual—having both inverted gender and improper object choice.

The ad uses homosexuality and drugs to mutually demonize each other. But the ad achieves this identification only at a high and surprising price: the ad is so thickly laden with codes and subterfuges that, top-heavy, it inadvertently trips over its own intentions. Through the very glamour and lure that the ad uses to homosexualize its subject, it turns its viewer into a pedophile. The sumptuous layout gives the boy a sensuous, enticing star quality. Paradoxically, the very medium of its antigay message makes the boy sexy to men.

Perhaps we have here an example of what Foucault hints at in the *History of Sexuality* when he repeatedly but vaguely refers to "perverse implantations," those means by which culture instills or invokes sexual desires rather than represses or punishes them. The ad gives its viewer ideas, ones that he might very well not have had otherwise. If not exactly nudging him toward action, the ideas at least open his mind to new possibilities for action, and they do so even though they are put forth in a context of condemnation and suppression. Thus for Foucault, psychiatrists create perversions even as they are ostensibly trying to suppress them. Insane asylums make their inhabitants crazy, and prisons produce, rather than rehabilitate, the criminal type. Similarly, the ad, even as it demonizes sexual perversion, implants the idea of the most condemned perversion of all in the mind of its beholder.

Pedophilic images are ones in which youthfulness sexualizes the image and in turn the image enhances the sexiness of youth. These images are surprisingly common in society—surprising given that society careers from hysteria to hysteria over the possible sexiness of children. Society seems to need these images. And the images are allowed to the extent that they are buffered, not read in the first instance as sexual representations, and do not develop beyond mere suggestive idea into a pedophilic discourse, a context of meaning for the pedophile. Indeed, the social requirement that the pedophile's existence be shadowy helps society make sure that sexy images of children will not be read as such. Society needs the pedophile: his existence allows everyone else to view sexy children innocently. But his conceptualization by society must not be allowed to be rich enough to be interesting, to constitute a life. Sexy images of children abound, but NAMBLA remains a universal whipping boy.

The death threats and pundit carping that were targeted at director Todd Solondz for his 1998 movie *Happiness* were prompted not so much by its admitting that children have sexual drives, some directed to adults, as by its giving the pedophile a platform on which to give an account of himself. Admittedly the account is drenched in the same self-hatred one finds awash in speeches by that character The Homosexual who is finally permitted to speak in the films of the 1960s (one thinks of William Wilder's *The Children's Hour*), but it is an account nonetheless. And the source of anxiety expressed by the Billy Sundays of Cyberland over pedophilic immigrés to the Internet is not so much that they will find children there as that they will find each other, and so achieve (as the December 23, 2001, *New York Times* put it in an article on Japanese pedophiles) "the 'validation' that comes with meeting other pedophiles on-line and sharing interests and experiences"—to wit, form a discursive community of the sort that gay youth have created on the Internet in response to forces in the noncyber world (parents, friends, schools, churches) that will not let them speak there.

The pedophile must exist, but in an immature, if germinal, phantom, if fearsome, form. Society's panicked worry over kiddie pics, then, is not chiefly about their sexiness—either as something inherently dirty or as having aesthetic, erotic, and moral effects on people in general. Rather, social conventions simultaneously insist on and convulse over the existence of a certain type of *mind*, one that—quite independent of what it sees and does—can be branded as perverted. This becomes even clearer if one sorts through the tangle of statutes, regulations, administrative interpretations, and judicial decisions that makes up current kiddie-porn law.

What makes a picture of a kid into kiddie porn? For starters, the child's being naked, even partially naked, is not a necessary condition for kiddie porn. Since the *Knox* case of 1994, the child pictured may be completely clothed and the picture may still be considered indictable kiddie porn. Further, the child need not be performing any act that would be socially counted as sexual in order for the picture to be treated legally as kiddie porn. Nor need the child even be posed provocatively, lewdly, or seductively. But then what's left? What distinguishes kiddie porn from Christmas snapshots? The mind of the beholder. The image is kiddie porn if it is possessed by someone who, quite independent of the image's content, can be considered perverted. And whether or not parents find themselves incarcerated for bear-rug and bathtub shots of their kids turns on what prosecutors and juries think was in the parents' minds when they took the photos, rather than on anything distinctive about the pictures themselves.

Toni Marie Angeli found this out when, in 1996, she was arrested for photographs she had taken of her four-year-old son for a photography class, "Innocence in Nudity," at Harvard University. Charges were dropped when her mind was declared clean. The Massachusetts Department of Social Services and the local district attorney agreed that "the mother's photos were not done with lascivious or harmful intent." Not so lucky was Ejlat Feuer, a student at the International Center for Photography in New York City. In 1994, he was coerced into pleading guilty to child abuse in order to secure a probationary sentence for photographs he had taken of his six-year-old daughter. His district attorney found his mind to be unclean. It is the mind, not the image, that is dispositive.

That the law typically gives longer sentences to possessors of "kiddie porn" than to adults who have sex with kids shows the contortions and absurdity of culture's anxious construal of pedosexuality. Imagine making the possession of an image of a murder a more serious crime than murder itself.

We would do this only if we thought, first, that the mere existence of the murderous mind constitutes treason pure and simple; second, that the act of murder is chiefly a representation or extension of this mind rather than something culpable because harmful; and finally, that, as a representation or extension, the act is less robust than the image. We see this configuration of values as bizarre in the counterfactual murder case, but our culture replicates this absurdity precisely in its configuration of the pedophilic mind, images of children, and sex acts with children.

But, then, isolate this pedophilic mind from the rest of culture, label it perverted, derive the unacceptability of image and act from it, and, then, hey presto, sexy children are all right for viewing by everyone else. We see them—virginal and alluring—in mainstream clothing ads. Havana Joe Boots punningly invites the straight male yuppie readers of *Details* magazine to "Save Your Sole," even as you lose it (your soul, that is) in the bare butt of a naked, ambiguously sexed child, tush thrust camera-ward (Figure 2).

The Sunday *New York Times Magazine* is a regular source for pedophilic

Figure 2. Havana Joe Boots advertisement from *Details* magazine, November 1995.

images. Here on February 21, 1999, appeared the glossiest version of an advertisement that ignited the second Calvin Klein underwear scandal—the designer's inauguration of a national display ad campaign in which two little boys frolic on a sofa, wearing underpants and nothing else. Smiley and radiant, with right hands clutched—half in shake, half in grapple—the boys and their crotches reenact in unwitting mockery that grown man's psychic tussle between briefs and boxers (Figure 3). In the first Calvin Klein underwear scandal, of 1995, the designer had run an ad campaign featuring scantily clad fifteen-year-old boys decked out in heroin chic and posed "provocatively" (the press's adverb of choice) in settings of cheap paneling "suggestive" of amateur porn production. The FBI threatened to investigate the 1995 ads as child porn on the ground that they were "lascivious," but

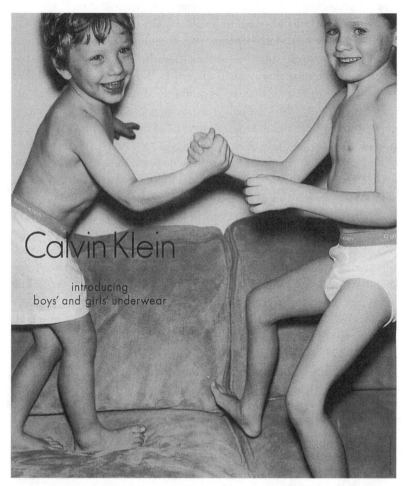

Figure 3. A glossy black-and-white advertisement for the Calvin Klein children's underwear campaign as it appeared in the Sunday *New York Times Magazine*, February 21, 1999, four days after the campaign's one-day run.

ultimately the Justice Department punted. It realized that any attempt to apply its own need-not-show-genitals standard to a major corporation would likely prove just too embarrassing for Justice.

Even without the assistance of FBI threats, a storm of criticism scotched the 1999 boys' underwear campaign—in just one day. The ad first ran, at full page, in the *New York Times* and some other urban papers on Wednesday February 17, announcing for the next day free in-store distributions of artist-signed posters of the boys and the unveiling of a billboard of them above Times Square. But the next day did not come for the campaign. On Thursday, the posters remained crated, the billboard furled. But by this time, the *Times Magazine* issue carrying the ad had been printed up, and so, come Sunday, it launched the already terminated campaign into an existence at once showy and spectral. The image sublated into icon.

Critics, although successful in squelching the campaign, had difficulty putting their fingers on exactly what was objectionable about the ad. In an Associated Press wire story on the flap, Morality in Media was quoted as confidently claiming that it could discern in the crotch of the battler in briefs "the outline of the little boy's genitals." Morality in Media then inferred that, given Klein's use of a professional photographer, this flaunting of boy cock could not have been accidental: "At Calvin Klein nothing is innocent." Reassuring traces of requisitely perverted mind had been found— but only, so it seems, with the help of a Sherlock Holmes–sized magnifying glass, a hungry eye, and some imagination. The lady protests too much—or at least for the wrong reasons.

The sexiness of the ad has nothing to do with genitals and perversion. It has everything to do with the glamour, framing, and cropping by which the ad links the radiance, intimacy, physicality, and joy of the boys, a linkage that is made all the more taut and tense by the ad's deft allusion to a trope of outlaw sexuality and of Thomas Eakins's and George Luks's wrestling paintings—fighting as a front for fucking.

Nonetheless, like Morality in Media, with its cock-seeking mind, all America got to indulge in the ad, for the AP wire story was accompanied by the ad itself. In the heartland of the homeland, millions of solid citizens who had never read the *New York Times* received from their paperboys what nearly everyone was willing to call kiddie porn (Figure 4).

The *New York Times Magazine*'s weekly fashion section is a particularly rich site for pedophilic images. Take the March 2, 1997, spread titled "Endless Summer" promoting children's swimwear. The shot shows five five-year-olds in swimsuits—four girls symmetrically flanking a boy. The kids are at the beach, but the beach is also a discotheque—sand below, mirrored ball above. The boy and three of the girls face camera-ward and are captured with hips in mid-gyration and arms flinging their hands ball-

Figure 4. The Associated Press's wire story announcing the quick demise of the Calvin Klein children's underwear campaign, Thursday, February 18, 1999.

ward in bacchanalian abandon. Tucked knees and spread legs complete each child as a contrapposto ecstasy. The fourth girl, with arms akimbo, wiggles her behind at the camera. When the endlessness of summer draws clothing that would be ordinary at the beach into the sexual hothouse of the disco, that clothing—like a stiletto-heeled shoe hanging pendulously off a polished toe—becomes a sign of pheromone-drenched nakedness, which in child form the fashion spread serves up for adult delectation.

On the back page of the *Times Magazine*'s October 9, 1995, issue devoted entirely to children's issues and on billboards of the time up and down the Metro-North commuter lines, a Tommy Hilfiger ad displayed a naked-tummied, adultly dressed boy of about six dangling insouciantly from a branch (Figure 5). His tongue slurps the air. His boxer shorts scoot up above his belt loops just as underwear does in adult jean ads, which everyone acknowledges as sexy in the main because of this joint peekaboo revelation of torso and boxers. A cliché of cultural studies holds that wearing briefs says, "I have a penis," whereas wearing boxers says, "I am the penis." Nevertheless, stamp the ad, with its child phallus, "not kiddie porn," for it incidentally serves as a promotion for the *Times*' child-oriented charity, the Fresh Air Fund.

Please support the fresh air fund. Call 800-367-0003

Figure 5. Tommy Hilfiger and the *New York Times* team up to sell clothes and charity for kids on the back page of the Sunday *New York Times Magazine*, October 9, 1995.

Using social concern as a pedophilic medium is also the lucky gambit of photographer Larry Clark's 1995 movie *Kids*. The hugely successful media blitz attending the movie's release carefully avoided any reference to, let alone an examination of, Clark's history of obviously pedophilic photographs—*Teenage Lust* (1983, 1987), *1992* (1992), and *The Perfect Childhood* (1993). The German publisher of the last collection of photos, fearing customs seizures, never released the book in the United States. The collections include photos of Clark himself cavorting naked with naked boys in fountains. Indeed Clark himself—an ex-con—was nowhere in evidence during the media blitzes. Instead, the morning TV shows offered a parade of latter-day Officer Krupkes—Krupkes with Ph.D.s—to discuss what the hell's the matter with kids today, to bemoan their "social diseases," and to praise the pseudodocumentary's realism and grit in facing or at least showing these problems. Drug taking, cat kicking, petty thievery, unsafe sex, public urination, assault—you name it—Clark has carefully larded his film with kids' naughty doings in order to distract the critics' view from the cinemagraphic point of the movie, which is to linger on naked boys—naked boys spritzing each other, naked boys relaxing in hustler poses, naked boys shooting the macho breeze, naked boys showing off their cocks. Moralizing becomes, like the Fresh Air Fund, both a vehicle and a buffer for prurient interest.

The film's pseudodocumentary style complements the effects of its moralizing content. The documentary style makes the pretense of simply "presenting the facts"—a would-be charitable and disinterested act. But this posturing simply serves to insulate both director and viewer from taking responsibility for the movie's voyeurism, its visual lusting for kids.

The movie's final scene, the sleepy aftermath to a teenage orgy of sex and drugs, is a takeoff on Michelangelo's 1492 sculpture *Battle of the Lapiths and Centaurs,* with its swarm of naked male flesh deployed for a good moral cause—saving women, who, however, are conveniently absent from the sculpture. With Clark, the swarm of naked male flesh hugged and caressed by the roving camera is kiddie flesh, all deployed for a good cause. The gorgeous supporting actor awakens shocked to the glistening carnage and, the movie's last line, queries for the Krupkes, "What happened?!" This ending is laughable, but the critics ate it up like talk-show fodder.

Everyday pedophilic iconography can even be used as a force for innocence. Such is Michael Jackson's 1995 videographic appropriation of Maxfield Parrish's 1922 pedophilic painting *Daybreak* as part of Jackson's return and rehabilitation from charges of child molestation. Despite its central image of a pubis-exposed ten-year-old in the pose of a succubus, the Parrish painting has stood as a cultural icon on a par with Dürer's *Praying Hands.* Today, in the afterglow of Norman Rockwell, it seems hard to imagine, but by the end of the 1920s, one in every four American households had purchased a print of the Parrish painting, with its treacly depiction of a wholly naked sylph, hands to knees, leaning over a supine awakening woman clad in flowing robes, framed by Grecian columns, all set against flowering trees, a peaceful lake, and purple misty mountains.

Jackson remakes this image to accompany the first love song released as a single, "You Are Not Alone," from his double album *HIStory: Book I.* A convincing love song from Michael is going to be a tough sell given the cultural backdrop of the molestation charges. In August 1993, a twelve-year-old boy accused Jackson in a civil suit of sexually molesting him over a four-month period the previous year. Jackson denied the accusations, but settled out of court for an undisclosed sum estimated by the *New York Times* and others to be between ten and twenty million dollars. What to do? Well, the thirty-seven-year-old black man recasts himself in the role of Parrish's ten-year-old white all-but-genderless sylph. Iconographically he regains for himself his earlier status as child star and sends the recuperative messages: How can I be a child molester when I am a child myself? How can I even be sexual, since I do not have a sex? I'm not a sexual threat: I'm white.

He reconfigures and neutralizes the picture's succubus overtones by substituting for the reclining Arcadian the woman whom he married after the molestation charges broke into the general press, Lisa Marie Presley, Elvis's only child. In contrast to Jackson, she looks in the video like a beached whale. Here artistic effect is sacrificed in order to heterosexualize the video's hero. Jackson deploys Parrish's pedophilic image to make himself over to appear as innocent as a child bride while also pressing the view that if there are any pedophiles around—and there may well be—they are in the audience, not in the frame.

Who needs an All Party Congress to restore one to grace when one can use images homeopathically? Jackson is cured by a dose of the very poison that ailed him. He has brilliantly recycled and teased America with a pedophilic image, which he has stunned and altered so that it can serve as a live-virus vaccine against the very charges of pedophilia laid against him. And it worked. By contrast, during the week that I drafted this article, a journalism professor at Toronto's Ryerson Polytechnic University was suspended for having suggested in class that not all acts of intergenerational sex should be counted as child abuse. Looking is okay, thinking about these issues is not.

Why does the American national psyche need the pedophilia of everyday life? What drive does it stoke, even as the nation condemns any mention or thought of it? Following the lead of some other social critics, such as Kenneth Plummer and James Kincaid, and before them Philippe Ariès, the late Walter Kendrick argued in a brave piece for the Sunday *New York Times Magazine*'s all-kids issue that our contemporary understanding of childhood as a period of innocence and purity solidified only in the Victorian era, and that before then, going back to the Middle Ages, children were viewed simply as little adults. Childhood took all its cues from adulthood. It did not constitute an independent, freestanding style of living or mode of existence. Until 1900, the age of consent in half of the United States was ten.

Apparently having gone about as far as he felt he dared in the *Times,* Kendrick concluded by pointedly reducing the anxiety that these revelations no doubt stir in the average reader: "Today's hysteria over child pornography springs mainly from adults' fear of themselves, the guilty knowledge that you don't have to be a pedophile to get an occasional frisson from looking at children." But guilty self-knowledge does not hysterical witch hunts make; one simply lies low. True: today's hysteria springs mainly from adults' fear of themselves, but this fear issues from their half recognition that to admit explicitly, as pornography does, that children are sexy would mean that virtually everyone is a pedophile. In light of the current cultural view that sexual interest in children flows only from, is contingent solely on, the mind of the pedophile, for anyone to admit that he or she has any frisson at all from looking at children is necessarily to be branded as deviant. Were society to allow itself to articulate that it does have sexual interests in children—little adults are not sexy, but innocence and purity are—society would have met the enemy and seen that he is us.

In another article on the young, the *New York Times Magazine* itself came surprisingly close to admitting that Americans want to have kids in more ways than one. A feature article on America's 1996 female Olympic gymnasts is all atwitter with the national adoration of these medal winners (October 20, 1996). They are touring the country's arena circuit like rock stars. Some will even continue to tour with gymnasts from the 2000 Olympics. But it's not their medals that Americans are flocking to see. The article compares the female gymnasts to women in "modeling and pornography," and contrasts them with their male counterparts, who lack "mystery" and just seem like "friendly jocks." In the female athletes, we are told, America "glorifies a hyper-niche body type." And what type is that? Well, it falls in a "specific lacuna between girl and woman." And what are the specifics of this lacuna and what is the source of the "mystery" that gives these females a porn-star quality? Well, petite bodies are part of it, but the main explanation—and here the *Times* cites the authority of the *New England Journal of Medicine*—is that in these females' bodies "years of intense training suppress estrogen production, delaying puberty and causing 18- and 19-year-olds to look and sound like 12-year-olds." In other words, these petite females are "street legal" prepubescent girls. America could have sex with these girls. America could take sexual delight in viewing these girls, and it would be all right, even science says so. One could even pay for such prepubescent eye candy. And America does by the stadium full, night after night.

America's hysteria over kiddie porn, then, is not simply the result of the country's epicyclical prudishness about matters sexual. Rather, it is the result of our general worries about purity, innocence, and identity—who we are. Childhood—the social concept—cannot do the moral work society has created it to do. In an era whose distinguishing marks are depression and the Depression, genocide and the prospect of omnicide, life can look pretty damn nasty, brutish, and short. And so to serve both as ethical prop and security blanket, we have created a moral museum of innocence and purity—our Eden—and we have labeled it *childhood*. But then the paradox of everyday pedophilia is this: once we have made over childhood into purity and innocence, we naturally enough want to have it, but to have it would make it what we no longer want.

Note

This essay was originally written in the fall of 1995 as a meditation on charges laid by university presses, book printers, book distributors, and Canada Customs that my book *Gay Ideas: Outing and Other Controversies* (Boston: Beacon, 1992) was, in part, a work of kiddie porn. The essay originally appeared in *Art Issues* 42 (March 1996), without whose editor, Gary Kornblau, the piece never would have come into being. He has my thanks and esteem. The essay has been updated and expanded for this volume.

"The Gentle Boy from the Dangerous Classes": Pederasty, Domesticity, and Capitalism in Horatio Alger

Michael Moon

hrongs of ragged children bent on earning or cadging small sums of money filled the streets of mid-nineteenth-century New York, if we are to credit the testimony of a large number of chroniclers of city life of the period. These genteel observers—journalists, novelists, social reformers, early criminologists—professed to be alternately appalled and enchanted by the spectacle of street children noisily and energetically playing, begging, and hawking a multitude of services and goods: shoeshines, matches, newspapers, fruit. In considering the accounts of this scene made by those who first concerned themselves with it, one soon becomes aware that a significant number of writers respond to it with strong ambivalence. For many of them, there is an undeniable charm or beauty, strongly tinged with pathos, in the spectacle of the pauper children: the high style with which they collectively wage their struggle for subsistence exerts a powerful appeal. For some of the same observers, however, the charm of the street urchins is a

31

siren song: beneath their affecting exteriors many of them are prematurely criminal, expert manipulators of the responses of naive and sentimental adults.

George Matsell, New York's first chief of police, initiated the vogue for writing "sketches" of the city's street children with his sensationalistic and strongly unfavorable report of 1849 on "the constantly increasing number of vagrants, idle and vicious children of both sexes, who infest our public thoroughfares."[1] The extensive testimony of minister and reformer Charles Loring Brace, who devoted a long career to "saving" street children, is more ambiguous, and consequently more representative of genteel response in general. While professing to detest the criminal tendencies that he believes street life encourages in poor children—indeed, the "philanthropic" plans for them that he and his colleagues in the Children's Aid Society (founded in 1853) framed and enacted involved systematically removing them from the city—Brace nevertheless often confesses to feeling a powerful attraction toward the children themselves, especially the boys. Brace seems to have possessed a remarkable capacity for "activat[ing] male sympathies," to borrow a phrase historian Christine Stansell has used to characterize his program:[2] both the middle-class, reform-minded men who funded and worked in his programs and many of the ragged boys whom they housed, counseled, educated, and sent away to work seem to have found compelling the particular version of male community institutionalized in his charities.

One often hears in the language Brace and his colleagues directed toward their boy charges the familiar intensities of evangelical piety, hortatory and emotionally charged. Unsurprisingly to readers familiar with the rhetoric of nineteenth-century American Protestant revivalism, Brace's language frequently exhibits a markedly homoerotic character, as when in one of his "sermons to news boys" he appeals to his boy auditors' longings for an "older and wiser" male friend who would love and support them unreservedly:

> Though you are half men in some ways, you are mere children in others. You hunger as much as other children for affection, but you would never tell of it, and hardly understand it yourselves.
>
> You miss a friend; somebody to care for you. It is true you are becoming rapidly toughened to friendlessness; still you would be very, very glad, if you could have one true and warm friend.[3]

Although the "friendship" Brace is urging the street boys to accept here is ostensibly that of Christ, one can readily see how closely congruent a rhetoric of seduction could be with discourses of middle-class philanthropy like his, as when the adult male avows his willingness to recognize and respond (in various institutionally mediated ways) to adolescent male desires for dependency on an older, more powerful man for affection and support. The genteel gaze of Gilded Age New Yorkers seems always to descry disturbingly mixed qualities in pauper children, and the boundaries these imputed mixtures disturb are often ones of age and gender, as witness the ambiguous "half men" (adult males)/"mere children" (minors of indeterminate gender) to whom Brace addresses his exhortations.

Despite the pederastic overtones of some of their discourse, Brace and his fellow reformers seem to have been primarily interested in seducing poor children away from their underclass environments rather than actually engaging in sexual activity with them. However, at least one man who long associated himself with Brace's boy charities—Horatio Alger Jr.—is known to have seduced boys sexually during at least one period of his career as well as to have participated actively in the reform movement to "seduce" New York street boys away from their milieu into an at least minimally genteel way of life. Alger has long been recognized as (in Hugh Kenner's phrase) "the laureate of the paradigms of ascent" in early corporate capitalist America; since 1971, his expulsion from the Unitarian ministry for pederasty in 1866 has been a matter of public record.[4]

In this essay, I propose to explore how Alger's reformulation of domestic fiction as a particular brand of male homoerotic romance functions as a support for capitalism. Alger's writing provides a program cast in moralistic and didactic terms for maximizing a narrow but powerfully appealing range of specifically male pleasures: certain forms of social respectability and domesticity, the accumulation of modest wealth, and the practice of a similarly modest philanthropy toward younger needy boys. As a number of critics have noted, Alger's tales generally prove on inspection to be quite different from what the "Alger myth"—"rags to riches" for industrious poor boys—has prepared readers to expect. Rather than promising riches to boy readers, they hold out merely the prospect of respectability; also, rather than presenting examples of "rugged" and competitive individualism, they show boys "rising" through a combination of genteel patronage and sheer luck. As Michael Zuckerman has perceptively observed, "Beneath [Alger's] paeans to manly vigor" one can discern "a lust for effeminate indulgence; beneath his celebrations of self-reliance, a craving to be taken care of and a yearning to surrender the terrible burden of independence."[5] Alongside the apparent support of such capitalist ideals of the period as the self-made man and the cult of success, notions to which Alger's writing pays lip service but fails to narrativize or thematize effectively, another agenda inconspicuously plays itself out in tale after tale—one that would appear to be the antithesis of the idea commonly associated with Alger that any reasonably bright boy can rely on his own hard work and "pluck" to catapult him to a place near the top of the Gilded heap. Actually, Alger's tales hold out a considerably less grandiose prospect for boy readers: that any boy who is reasonably willing to please his potential employers can attain a life of modest comfort. Only a character as programmatically resistant to this prospect as Bartleby the Scrivener stands to lose out entirely in the new modest-demand, modest-reward ethos of the rapidly expanding corporate/clerical workplace. A characteristic authorial aside in Alger's 1873 *Bound to Rise; or, Up the Ladder* makes apparent in unmistakable terms the large part that patient passivity, rather than competitive aggression, plays in the scheme of his stories:

> Waiting passively for something to turn up is bad policy and likely to lead to disappointment; but waiting actively, ready to seize any chance that may offer, is quite different. The world is full of chances, and from such chances so seized has been based many a prosperous career.[6]

"Rising" for Alger's heroes always remains a waiting game; within this pervasive passivity, there is an active and a passive position, but there is no way for a boy to take a more direct approach to the world of work and achievement in Alger's books.

How does one explain the gap that yawns between the reputation of Alger's books as heroic fables of ascents from the gutter to the pinnacle of power and wealth with their actual narrative contents: the achievement—with the benefit of considerable "luck" and patronage—of a mild form of white-collar respectability that releases the boy hero from the competitive struggle he has had to wage on the street? I propose that the answer lies not in some quirk in Alger's personality but in some basic contradictions in his culture that the tales engage. Alger's books can be read—and were by generations of young readers, albeit probably largely unwittingly—as primers in some of the prevailing modes of relationship between males in corporate/capitalist culture. I will argue further that the pederastic character of much of the "philanthropic" discourse about boys in this period is particularly marked in Alger's texts, and that what this sexual undercurrent reveals is not so much that the leading proponents of this discourse were motivated in large part by conscious or unconscious pederastic impulses—some, like Alger, no doubt were; perhaps others were not—but that there are determinate relations between social forms engendered by the emergent Gilded Age culture and some of the quasi-sexual ties and domestic arrangements between males that impel Alger's fiction.[7]

"Gentle-but-Dangerous" Horatio Alger

Alger arrived in New York City in 1866, eager to put his disgrace in Brewster, Massachusetts, behind him and to establish himself as a professional writer for boys (he had combined careers as a divinity student and fledgling juvenile author for a few years before his exposure). In one of the first pieces he published after moving to New York, Alger expresses the kind of fascination with the precocity of street boys familiar from other genteel writing:

> The boys looked bright and intelligent; their faces were marked by a certain sharpness produced by the circumstances of their condition. Thrown upon the world almost in infancy, compelled to depend upon their own energy for a living, there was about them an air of self-reliance and calculation which usually comes much later. But this advantage had been gained at the expense of exposure to temptations of various kinds.[8]

Struggling to establish himself as a popular writer in a competitive and demanding market, Alger may well have envied the ragged boys of Brace's Newsboys' Lodging House the "self-reliance" they had acquired not from reading Emerson (who is said to have once visited the home of Alger's parents) but from premature and extensive "exposure to temptations." The element of glamour he attributes to the street boy heroes of the books that followed *Ragged Dick; or, Street Life in New York* (1867) for a decade or so after is a quality that arises (as I shall try to show) from the way the figure embodies certain sexual and class tensions that were markedly present in the culture of Alger's period, tensions that had forcefully asserted themselves at critical points in his own life. Unlike most of his genteel contemporaries, Alger shared with the street boys he began writing about in New York the experience of having been deemed outcast and "dangerous" to the community. That the boy ideal in his fiction should magically combine both "gentle" (genteel) and "dangerous" (underclass) qualities is the generative contra-action in Alger's work, but it bears closely on significant contradictions in his culture. Gentility and public disgrace, respectability and criminality were states that were not supposed to interact closely in mid-nineteenth-century America, but they did so with notable violence at several points for Alger, as when his Unitarian minister father, plagued with debt throughout Alger's childhood, was forced to declare bankruptcy in 1844, or when Alger himself was ejected from the ministry for (in the words of the report of the church's committee of inquiry) "the abominable and revolting crime of unnatural familiarity with boys."[9]

The Discourse of the "Dangerous Classes"

Alger's pederasty was an act that simultaneously transgressed a number of fundamental proscriptions in his culture: its object was male rather than female and a child rather than an adult. Although apparently the boys with whom he was sexually involved during his days as a Unitarian minister were themselves middle-class, Alger may have added a third form of transgression— sex across class lines—to his offenses against the dominant morality with some of the numerous underclass boys he fostered during his thirty years' residence in New York.[10]

Although there is no lack of documentary evidence to support the assertion that feelings of guilt and anxiety over real and imaginary wrongdoing were felt by many of Alger's middle-class contemporaries, a considerable amount of literary energy in the United States as well as in Europe in the two decades before he began producing his books was devoted to representing the actual states of being deemed outcast or criminal as conditions that properly happened only to the denizens of a segment of the urban world somehow fundamentally disjunct from the one middle-class readers inhabited—despite the physical proximity of the two worlds. Some of the most popular writing of the day served to provide these readers with vicarious experiences of the supposed color and romance of underclass life while reassuring them not only that the "honest" or "deserving" poor could readily transcend the worst effects of poverty but also that the squalor and violence of their lives could be readily contained—in slums, workhouses, charity wards, and prisons. Such experiences were likewise contained (and placed on exhibit, as it were) on the fictive level in such voluminous and widely read works as Eugene Sue's *Les Mystères de Paris* (1842), G. W. M. Reynolds's *Mysteries of London* (1845–48), George Lippard's *The Quaker City* (1845), and Ned Buntline's *Mysteries and Miseries of New York* (1848). In the late 1850s, *Godey's Lady's Book* opined that the vogue for books like these, which depicted the lives of "rag-pickers, lamplighters, foundlings, beggars . . . murderers, etc.," was having the undesirable effect of "widen[ing] the social breach between honest wealth and honest poverty."[11] In 1867, Alger began pursuing his own literary method of bringing the "gentle" and the "dangerous" back into touch with one another—by locating these supposedly mutually exclusive qualities in the person of the same boy character.

An abundance of stimulating scholarship published in recent years has established the interdependence of the discourse of "the dangerous classes" in mid- to late-nineteenth-century fiction with the forensic forms of the same discourse, in government reports, police dossiers, and sociological studies.[12] One of the most notable characteristics of this massive body of discourse is its frequent placement of the figure of the child in the foreground. From its inception, writing of all kinds about the "dangerous classes" took as its special concern the peril to the social order that the children of the urban poor allegedly posed.[13] Writing about the children of the "dangerous classes" frequently exceeded the ostensible purpose of alerting a middle-class readership to the minatory aspects of these "dangerous" children to celebrate their beauty or charm. This conflicting tendency reaches a culmination of sorts in the heroes of Alger's street-boy fictions, in which the child of the "dangerous classes" is presented as being an estimable and even desirable figure.

The Discourse of the "Gentle Boy"

The particular means by which the boy of the "dangerous classes" is idealized in Alger's texts involves his being conflated with another, older writerly construction, the "gentle boy." This figure was itself a hybrid, two of its principal antecedents being the exemplary "good little boy" (sometimes middle-class, sometimes not) of evangelical tract literature for children and (coming out of a quite different discursive formation) the boy version of the "natural aristocrat" central to Jeffersonian social mythology. This latter figure, the "natural little gentleman," the boy of lowly origins who manifests from early childhood the virtues and graces associated with "true gentility," was a staple of "democratic" writing for children. Alger's boy heroes are both a belated and an extreme version of him.[14]

One need not look far in the discourse of the "gentle boy" in nineteenth-century America to appreciate that the terms *gentle* and *gentleman* were extremely unstable markers of a broad spectrum of attributes ranging from purely moral qualities, such as chivalrousness and benevolence, to purely economic ones, such as the source of one's income. Given the constantly shifting meanings that *gentleman* is given in the nineteenth century, one of the few generalizations about its usage it seems safe to hazard is that the term's exclusionary powers are usually more important than its inclusionary ones. That is, establishing who is a gentleman is usually secondary in importance to establishing who is *not; gentleman* often is not so much a description of a type of person as an attempt to draw a line between two levels of social status. This yields widely various definitions of *gentle* and *gentleman,* such as the "high" or "aristocratic" sense of the term, "a man of 'good' family and independent financial means who does not engage in any occupation or profession for gain"—a sense of the term quite different from what one might call the "bourgeois" one, "a man who does not engage in a menial occupation or in manual labor to earn his living." By the first definition, to be a "true" gentleman one must be rich, leisured, and a member of an upper-class family; by the second, one need only not be a working man to qualify—that is, it excludes from its compass only lower-class men.[15]

Aside from signifying rigid divisions and invidious distinctions between social classes, *gentle* and *gentleman* bore a number of other meanings. "Soft" definitions of *gentleman* were based not on the source of a man's income or on the lowest level of work that it was necessary for him to do, but on an unstable set of moral qualities that commonly included courtesy, chivalry, benevolence to "inferiors," and a lively sense of personal "honor." The range was even wider (and must have been even more confusing) for boys who aspired to be "gentlemen": to be considered "gentle," boys, in addition to possessing various combinations of the foregoing qualities, were expected to be (in certain relations) tractable, docile, and mild—types of behavior neither required of nor even particularly admired in adult males. At the extreme of the "soft" end of the spectrum, we arrive at a stretch of potentially hazardous meanings for males living in a society in which gender roles were becoming ever more polarized, elaborated, and rigidly prescribed: "sweet," "delicate," "tender," "fond," "loving," "affectionate." Embodying such qualities, even when they were part of behaving in a "gentle" or "gentlemanly" manner, could be a treacherous business for nineteenth-century boys, especially if these qualities came into play not between the boy and an infant or female family member, where they might seem appropriate, but between one boy and another or between a boy and a man. At the "soft" end of the "gentle" spectrum, disgrace by (alleged) feminization threatened the unwary boy.[16] Social constructions of such matters as what success and security, manliness and "gentle" behavior are, as well as what is truly "dangerous" about the urban poor, are some of the basic elements of which Alger's tales are composed. His attempts to stabilize in didactic narratives the volatile field of meanings these terms represented in his culture remain instructive in ways he could not have anticipated.

Ragged Dick and Tattered Tom

Perhaps the master trope, insofar as there is one, for nineteenth-century attitudes toward the urban poor is the figure common to pictorial representations of the proletarian uprisings in Paris in 1830: that of the young or mature man, usually depicted half naked, who is possessed of a beautiful, muscular torso and a bestial face.[17] Middle-class facial beauty, lower-class muscle; middle-class mentality, lower-class bodiliness; middle-class refinement, lower-class brutality; lower-class vigor and middle-class malaise; an overbred middle class and an overbreeding lower class—these are some of the constants in the shifting spectrum of stereotypical paradigms of social class in which nineteenth-century sociologists, journalists, novelists, and illustrators traded. Ragged Dick, the prototypical Alger hero, is not composed of ugly face and muscular torso as a thoroughly "dangerous" youth in popular representation might be; other qualities are mixed in him. As the hero-to-be of Alger's particular brand of male homoerotic domestic romance, he conspicuously combines, to begin with, the qualities of appearing both dirty and handsome:[18]

> But in spite of his dirt and rags there was something about Dick that was attractive. It was easy to see if he had been clean and well dressed he would have been decidedly good looking. (*Ragged Dick*, 40)

Sexual attractiveness is the one characteristic Alger's heroes all have in common. "Luck" comes to them, and "pluck" they exhibit when it is required, but their really defining attribute is good looks. Statements such as the following occur ritualistically on the opening pages of the books:

> Both [boys] had bright and attractive faces. . . . [Dick] had a fresh color which spoke of good health, and was well-formed and strong. (*Fame and Fortune*, 53)

> In spite of the dirt, his face was strikingly handsome. (*Phil the Fiddler*, 283)

> He was a strongly-made and well-knit boy of nearly sixteen, but he was poorly dressed. . . . Yet his face was attractive. (*Jed the Poorhouse Boy*, 401)

The narrators of Alger's tales are fierce discriminators of good looks in boys, which they suggest might be obscured for other spectators by shabbiness and grime. The boy's initially mixed appearance, the good looks revealing themselves despite the physical evidence of poverty—dirt and rags—is the infallible sign that one of Alger's boy characters is likely to emerge from his outcast condition to become a "gentle/dangerous" boy.

In additon to the handsome faces and comely bodies visible despite their shabby coverings, another strikingly homoerotic characteristic of Alger's writing is the element of seduction involved in the first steps of the ragged hero's conversion to respectability through his chance street encounters with genteel boys and men. Here the mixing is not figured on the hero's person (handsome/dirty) but on the social level: "dangerous" (street boy) and "gentle" (genteel boy or man) not only meet but make lasting impressions on one another. This impression making takes the form of a mutual seduction of sorts, as in the following representative episode from early on in *Ragged Dick*. When Dick puts himself forward for hire as a guide for a rich boy who is visiting the city, the boy's businessman uncle hesitates to entrust his nephew to Dick. After a moment's reflection, the older man decides to take the risk: "He isn't exactly the sort of guide I would have picked out for you," the man says. "Still, he looks honest. He has an open face, and I think he can be depended upon" (55). The man's quick physiognomic assessment of Dick is amply borne out by the rest of the story: the ragged boy is not only honest, open, and dependable, his contact with Frank (the rich boy) is decisive in his transformation from "street pigeon" to young gentleman. It is Ragged Dick's looks that initially allay the older man's anxieties about him; on the rich boy's side, young Frank does some seducing of his own. Amid the plethora of advice and encouragement Dick receives from Frank and his uncle in the course of the single day of their acquaintance, it is possible to overlook the significance that direct physical contact has in Frank's ability to convince Dick that he is capable of "rising." The first instance of this occurs when Dick lapses for a short time from his usual jocular tone to tell Frank about his occasional "blue spells" over the hard and lonely life he lives on the street. Frank replies, "'Don't say you have no one to care for you, Dick,' . . . lightly laying his hand on Dick's shoulder. 'I will care for you'" (99). There is another laying on of hands by Frank when the two boys part and Frank persuades Dick to give up his unthrifty (and, by Frank's lights, immoral) street-boy amusements: "'You won't gamble any more,—will you, Dick?' said Frank, laying his hand persuasively on his companion's shoulder" (110). "A feeling of loneliness" is said to overwhelm Dick after Frank leaves the city, as a result of the "strong attachment" he has rapidly formed for the rich boy, but this feeling of loneliness soon gives way to Dick's overriding desire to be fully "gentle" (genteel), rather than merely Frank's "gentle" (sweet, fond, affectionate) ragamuffin.

A modest suit of new clothes is almost always the symbolic gift that enables the Alger hero to begin rising (Dick's is a "hand-me-down" from Frank), just as the gift of a pocket watch is often ritually made at a later point in his ascent. It is as a part of the ritual of donning his first suit that the matter of the boy's still-mixed nature frequently arises for a second time: "He now looked quite handsome," the narrator says of Dick when he has put on Frank's gift, "and might readily have been taken for a young gentleman, except that his hands were red and grimy" (58). Alger's hero's face can simply be washed clean, and most of his body encased in suit and shoes, but his hands are the last part of his person to be divested of signs of hard toil and "dangerous" living.

A particularly interesting example of the mixed Alger hero is Tattered Tom, hero of a book of that title (1871) that inaugurated the Tattered Tom series, which soon followed the successful Ragged Dick series. The appropriately named Tom, a girl who has taken to living on the streets disguised as a boy, is the only "girl hero" in all of Alger's books for boys. She competes on an equal basis with other boys, selling newspapers and carrying heavy luggage for nickels. Although the narrator makes passing gestures toward women's rights ("There seemed a popular sentiment in favor of employing boys, and Tom, like others of her sex, found herself shut out from an employment for which she considered herself 'fitted'; 71), the book, far from being a feminist fable, thoroughly endorses the privileging of the figure of the attractive boy that impels all of Alger's books. Of all of his heroes, only Tom does not "rise" as a consequence of her demonstrably enterprising and honest behavior; she is finally rescued from her plight on the street and restored to her mother, a rich Philadelphia lady from whom she had been abducted years earlier, whereupon she resumes her long-lost genteel, feminine identity as "Jane Lindsay."

Alongside this conventional story of a tomboy who attempts to live as a street boy but is rescued and reclaimed for genteel femininity it is possible to perceive a highly unconventional story of a partially feminized street boy who is drawn upward into genteel femininity by the irresistible magnetic force of Alger's model. This tale represents a twist on the standard one because its hero ends up becoming entirely feminine, instead of the mixed composite of putatively masculine and feminine qualities that Alger's heroes usually represent. *Tattered Tom* can be read not as a story of a literal sex change but of the "rise" from the street to the parlor usual in Alger combined with an unusually complete reversal of gender roles from street boy to young lady.

While it might be difficult to support such a reading of *Tattered Tom* on the basis of that text alone, it is possible to do so by interpreting the tale in the context of the series it follows (the Ragged Dick series and the first three volumes of the Luck and Pluck series) and the one it introduces and to which it gives its name. One of the characteristics of a proliferating multiple series like Alger's street-boy stories is that repetitions and variations in the writing from volume to volume can produce meanings that are not readily available to the reader of any single volume in the series. The unique degree to which Tattered Tom in its course completely refigures Alger's typical boy hero as a genteel young lady provides a good example of the way formulaic and apparently tautological and repetitious writing like that in Alger's serials can generate unexpected meanings. By inaugurating a major series of boys' books with the story of a "female street boy" and by frequently employing gender-related formulas from the other stories of the series with the gender signifier reversed, *Tattered Tom* represents a point in Alger's writing where the dynamic interactions of the relative age, gender, and class positions of child and adult characters are revealed with particular clarity. When, for example, the narrator says that Tattered Tom's face is dirty but that if it were clean, "Tom would certainly have been considered pretty" (80), his use of the normative feminine-gender term *pretty* recalls at the same time that it momentarily reverses other descriptions of the boy heroes of the previous tales in the series who have been said to have dirty but *handsome* faces. Similarly, when the narrator says of the benevolent gentleman who takes an interest in Tattered Tom, "There was something in this strange creature—half boy in appearance—that excited his interest and curiosity" (42–43), the text exhibits with exceptional directness the primary role that ambiguities of age and gender play in the appeal of Alger's heroes (one thinks of Brace's "half men"/"mere children") to their genteel benefactors.

"The Fashionable Newsboy at Home":
Alger's Reformulation of the Domestic Ideal

> The idea of a fashionable newsboy! It's ridiculous!
> —*Horatio Alger Jr.*, Herbert Charter's Legacy, *1875*

Having attracted the attention and favor of a genteel man with his un-mistakable good looks, and having in turn been "seduced" by the warm concern of a rich boy into embracing genteel aspirations, Alger's prototypi-cal hero begins his transformation from "dangerous" child/vagrant into "gentle" youth. That Alger's books are not only homoerotic romances but also represent a genuine reformulation of popular domestic fiction is made evident by the regularity and narrative intensity with which the tales high-light the boy hero's moving from the street or from a transitional charity shelter into his own modest little home (usually a boardinghouse room).[19] That this transition is perhaps the most crucial in the boy's development is manifested in the elaborate care that Alger expends on discriminating the fine points of comparative domestic amenities at this point in his narra-tives. Once his boy hero reaches the point of setting up a little home of his own, Alger, otherwise often vague about "realistic" detail, shows himself to be as astute a recorder of the differences between the four or five lowest grades of boardinghouses as Balzac could have wished to be.

Having negotiated shifting one type of social construction of themselves ("dangerous") for another ("gentle"), Alger's heroes, in their culminat-ing move into private lodgings, undertake the project of shifting another set of social constructions—those of gender identity and family role. As I have discussed above, gender confusion is thematized extensively in the street phases of Alger's tales only in the case of the female street boy, Tat-tered Tom. As long as he remains a poor boy on the streets, the Alger hero remains fairly conventionally gender bound in his behavior. But once the "gentle boy" is removed from the street and street occupations and is placed in a private, at least minimally genteel domestic setting, he and his boy friends begin to differentiate themselves along (for boys of Alger's day, or of our own) highly unconventional gender-role lines. For example, as soon as fifteen-year-old (formerly Ragged) Dick can manage it, he moves his twelve-year-old friend Henry Fosdick (their very names suggesting they somehow belong together) into his lodgings with him. The two boys share a cult of domestic comfort and respectability that in many ways conforms to the standards of simplicity, cleanliness, and efficiency set in Alger's time by ideologues of "scientific" domesticity such as Catharine Beecher.[20] As it is in her work, the Alger hero's first real home, like the poor but decent lodgings Dick and Fosdick take on Mott Street, is a man's refuge from the demands of the marketplace and an appropriately ordered decor in which he can pursue self-improvement.[21]

Dick and his friend and roommate Fosdick inaugurate the second major phase of their joint ascent by moving from their extremely modest digs on Mott Street to a more pleasant place uptown on Bleecker Street. These are the opening lines of the sequel to *Ragged Dick:*

> "Well, Fosdick, this is a little better than our old room in Mott St.," said Richard Hunter, looking complacently about him.
>
> "You're right, Dick," said his friend. "This carpet's rather nicer than the ragged one Mrs. Mooney supplied us with. The beds are neat and comfortable, and I feel better satisfied, even if we do have to pay twice as much for it."
>
> The room which yielded so much satisfaction to the two boys was on the fourth floor of a boarding-house in Bleecker St. No doubt many of my young readers, who are accustomed to elegant homes, would think it very plain; but neither Richard nor his friend had been used to anything as good. They had been thrown upon their own exertions at an early age, and [had] had a hard battle to fight with poverty and ignorance. Those of my readers who are familiar with Richard Hunter's experiences when he was "Ragged Dick" will easily understand what a great rise in the world it was for him to have a really respectable home. (*Fame and Fortune,* 9–10)

The Bleecker Street boardinghouse that is the boys' second home together is relatively luxurious; the narrator contrasts it with the minimal, unfastidious amenities that have been available to them back on Mott Street: "There once a fortnight was thought sufficient to change the sheets, while both boys were expected to use the same towel, and make that last a week" (52).

The practical, quotidian ideals of the domestic ideology in its "scientific" and privatizing aspect (a clean and comfortable home that serves as both a haven from the world and a suitable environment for continuous self-improvement) seem entirely congenial to Alger. Other aspects of the conventional domestic ideal that had come into being in the two or three decades preceding, such as its rigid polarization of gender roles, seem considerably less congenial to him. In order to consider how Alger represents these matters, one must attend not to those attitudes that Dick and Fosdick share, such as their desire to live as "respectably" as they possibly can afford to, but those characteristics of either boy by means of which the text differentiates, and indeed to some degree dichotomizes (although not nearly as far as other domestic definers of gender roles would have done), their respective personalities.

Alger characterizes the younger boy, Fosdick, as a sweet, timid, quiet, and clever boy, obviously the stereotypically feminine version of the "gentle boy" type, in contrast with the stereotypically masculine Dick, who is thoroughly "gentle" in Alger's ambiguous sense (handsome, kind, nurturant, and, to all appearances, born with embryonic genteel values despite his actual origins in poverty) but is also self-confident, "handy," and generally competent in the realm of what Alger's culture defined as masculine affairs. The significant twist on the gender-role stereotypes in this representative tale of Alger's is that it is Dick, the "dominant" type of these two gentle boys, who plays the maternal role in Alger's version of domesticity, and not, as one might expect, the "feminine" character Fosdick.

The relationship between the dominant boy in the maternal role and his partner (for example, Dick and Fosdick, respectively, in the first three volumes of the Ragged Dick series) is thoroughly familial; so much so, in fact, that Alger specifies (another significant example of his uncharacteristic precision about detail) that nine months after the two boys move in together ("at the end of nine months, therefore, or thirty-nine weeks"; chapter 20, "Nine Months Later," *Ragged Dick,* 166), Dick is said to bring forth a little bundle—a nest egg of $117 that has accumulated in his new savings account. But fascinating as the nursing of this nest egg is depicted as being for both boys, they eventually acquire a real human child: in the third volume of the series they adopt a small beggar boy to round out their family, and they make available to him in his turn the experiences—primarily domestic ones—that have aided their own earlier transformations from "dangerous but gentle" street boys to young gentlemen and members of an ideal, genteel, all-boy family.

This fantasmatic family serves as a lingering ideal in Alger's books, but, as he depicts it, it is a far from stable unit.[22] For example, Mark the Match Boy, the adopted "son" of Dick and Fosdick, is revealed at novel's end to be the missing and long-searched-for grandson of a rich merchant from Milwaukee. The old man rewards Dick and Fosdick handsomely for fostering the boy, who is then removed to Milwaukee to enjoy the life of the grandson of a rich gentleman. Dick and Fosdick revert to nursing a now considerably enlarged nest egg. Dick's intermittent maternity toward his nest egg and his temporary ward, Mark, and the essential interchangeability of "baby" and capital in this scheme—the last in the series of transformations I have been describing—requires consideration in relation to one final aspect of domesticity in Alger, and that is the all-important habit of "saving." Good looks combined with other virtues—honesty, enterprise, male homosociability—are all qualifications for "good fortune" in the forms this takes in Alger. But once the hero begins to "rise" and achieves a modicum of domestic stability, the activity or habit that is represented as being indispensable to maintaining his personal ascendancy is that of "saving." It is by saving—that is, thriftily and systematically accumulating bits of capital—that Dick produces his nest egg; it is by virtue of these habits that he shows himself to be a fit parent (mother) for Mark; and it is his "saving"—by rescuing from dead-end poverty—first Fosdick and then Mark that the cycle of ascent is renewed in the series. Just as Dick has been saved in order to learn to "save" himself, so will he save younger boys and provide them a model of "saving" both money and still more boys. This religion of accumulating (saving) both money and other boys is ubiquitous in Alger:

> The disposition to save is generally the first encouraging symptom in a street boy, and shows that he has really a desire to rise above his circumstances, and gain a respectable position in the world. (*Mark the Match Boy*, 293)

> Of greater value than the [monetary] sum . . . was the habit of self-denial and saving which our hero had formed. (*Risen from the Ranks*, 141)

> Boys who have formed so good a habit of saving can be depended upon. (*Fame and Fortune*, 11)

> "All labor is respectable, my lad, and you have no cause to be ashamed of any honest business; yet when you can get something to do that promises better for your future prospects, I advise you to do so. Till then earn your living in the way you are accustomed to, avoid extravagance, and save up a little money if you can." (*Ragged Dick*, 109)

It is in the "saving" (i.e., salvific) habit of "saving" money and other boys that Alger's work represents its cycle of transformations—street boy into "gentle" boy, newly "gentle" boy into domestic partner and foster parent (mother), capital into baby and baby back into further capital—reaching a state of equilibrium: at the end of the narrative, there lies ahead for Alger's heroes a static future of endlessly pursuing the two "saving" projects (i.e., of money and other boys). I want now to consider the question of what is being "saved" in Alger's fantasmatic no-loss chain of transformations and exchanges, the process that begins at the lowest end of his society—at an isolated ragged boy—and extracts from this supposedly unpromising figure the particular combination of virtues and powers normally ascribed to his remote social superiors: gentility, domesticity, wealth, philanthropy.

"Taking an Interest": The Art of Saving Boys

As the preceding discussion has shown, the salvaging operation ongoing in Alger's writing is a complex one. In each book, a boy is "saved from ruin," from possibly becoming a criminal or a derelict, by being fostered as a candidate for recruitment into the petty bourgeoisie. Furthermore, an outmoded model of virtue (thrift, probity, self-restraint, ambition, hard work—"the Protestant work ethic") is reformulated to correspond more closely to the requirements of changed social and economic conditions: aspiring to and finally reaching the kind of low-level clerical position that brings "respectable" social status as well as access to a modest array of consumer "goodies" to its holder is presented as being a high moral achievement. What is ultimately being saved or recuperated in Alger's writing, however, is something more primal than the notion of the worldly efficacy of a certain combination of virtues: it is a belief that a kind of "magic" acts to secure his boy heroes in the corporate/capitalist network. As I have discussed earlier in this essay, critics of Alger have often decried the regularity with which experiences of sheer "luck" set his boy heroes on their way, rather than something like the recognition of the workings in their world of some consistent notion of "character" or "self-making." It is crucial to notice in this regard that the ritualistic "lucky break" that initiates the boy's rising usually takes the form of his attracting the attention of a well-to-do male patron, usually through some spontaneous exhibition of his physical strength and daring. The "magic trick" that the Alger text ultimately performs is to recuperate the possibility of a man's taking an intense interest in an attractive boy without risking being vilified or persecuted for doing so—indeed, this "interest" is taken in a manner that is made thoroughly congruent with the social requirements of corporate capitalism for both parties: boy and potential employer alike "profit" from it.

Alger's 1876 *Sam's Chance, and How He Improved It,* in the second Tattered Tom series, provides a representative example of this in the interactions of fifteen-year-old Henry, a clerk in a shipping company, and his employer, James Hamilton. Although Henry is said not to be aware that Hamilton favors him or is even aware of his presence in the firm, the narrator relates that the older man has been "observing him [Henry] carefully, fully determined to serve him in the future if he should deserve it" (89). One day, after four years in the firm, Henry is called into Hamilton's office, where his employer interviews him about how he manages his life and his small income, and then, pleased with what he learns, invites the boy to make a substantial investment in a shipping venture the firm is about to undertake:

> Henry stared at his employer in surprise. How could he, a boy with thirty-five dollars capital, join in such an enterprise?
> "I don't see how I can," he replied. "I am afraid you take me for a capitalist." "So you are," said his employer. "Have you not money in the bank?" Henry smiled. (93)

Hamilton encourages Henry to participate in the venture, saying he will take the boy's savings bank book (with thirty-five dollars in the account) as security. "Thirty-five dollars will pay a year's interest on the five hundred dollars I lend you; so my interest is secure," Hamilton tells him. "I am willing to take the risk," the older man tells him (twice) to counter Henry's anxieties about becoming his "partner" (94–95). Henry finally happily agrees to the transaction and rises to leave Hamilton's office with the words, "Thank you, sir. I am very grateful to you for your kind interest in me."

With Hamilton's "interest" in Henry thus firmly secured, three months come and go, during which period nothing passes between man and boy except frequent "pleasant word[s] or smile[s]" (107). Henry is then called back into Hamilton's office, and their talk immediately turns to their mutual "interest": "I have just received a statement of [the outcome of the shipping venture]," Hamilton tells Henry, "and as you are interested, I have called you in to let you know how it has turned out." Henry is delighted to learn his investment has earned him a hundred dollars. The following conversation ensues:

"I shall charge you interest on the five hundred dollars you borrowed of me, at the rate of seven per cent. You have had the use of the money for three months."

"Then the interest will amount to eight dollars and three quarters," said Henry, promptly.

"Quite right; you are very quick at reckoning," said Mr. Hamilton, looking pleased.

"That is not a difficult sum," answered Henry, modestly.

"I did not suppose you knew much about computing interest. You left school very young, did you not?"

"At twelve, sir."

"You had not studied interest then, had you?"

"No, sir; I have studied it since."

"At evening school?"

"No, sir; I study by myself in the evening."

"How long have you done that?"

"For two years."

"And you keep it up regularly?"

"Yes, sir; occasionally I take an evening for myself, but I average five evenings a week at studying."

"You are a remarkable boy," said the merchant, looking surprised.

"If you flatter me, sir, I may grow self-conceited." said Henry, smiling.

(108–9)

Once again, a mutually "profitable" encounter leaves Henry "smiling" and Hamilton looking "surprised" and "pleased," their "partnership" fulfilled. The boy has proven himself to be as quick and expert a computer of "interest" as his merchant employer; with a little further education in calculating "risk," one suspects, he will have little more to learn from Hamilton. (In their crucial first nine months together, Ragged Dick is said to learn everything from Fosdick that he has to teach, which includes reading, writing, and "arithmetic as far as Interest"; 167.)

The recognition and avowal of "interest"—one's own in other men and theirs in oneself—and the close study of calculation and risk in pursuing these "interests" are matters that have figured as highly problematic and emotionally charged concerns in male homosexual behavior in homophobic capitalist culture. As Michael Pollak has written of the institutions of the "sexual market" of the gay ghetto (bars, baths, cinemas, and so on), as these functioned between the time of the emergence of gay liberation in Western metropolises at the beginning of the 1970s and the decline of "casual sex" practices among many gay men in recent years in response to the AIDS epidemic, "Of all the different types of masculine sexual behavior, homosexuality is undoubtedly the one whose functioning is most strongly suggestive of a market, in which in the last analysis one orgasm is bartered for another."[23]

As is evident from passages such as the dialogue from *Sam's Chance* quoted above, the network of calculation, risk, and interest that binds males together in Alger's work is a complex one; the economic workings of the quasi-sexual marketplace of these "boys' books" leaves the crude barter system described by Pollak far behind. At a representative moment in an earlier entry in the Tattered Tom series, *Paul the Peddler,* distinctions between the boy hero or his body and corporate economic forms vanish; as Paul considers how to come up with thirty-five dollars to buy out another boy's necktie stand, the narrator observes:

> If Paul had been a railroad corporation, he might have issued first mortgage bonds at a high rate of interest, payable in gold, and negotiated them through some leading banker. But he was not much versed in financial schemes, and therefore was at a loss. (164)

Paul's being "at a loss" is a circumstance that "gets worse before it gets better"; his case provides a typical example of the way in which the networks of interest between males in Alger's fiction can be disrupted by the incursion of the feminine—a quality that is frequently represented in these stories as being equivalent to (in readily recognizable infantile-fantasy form) the quality of anality. Paul becomes involved in a series of misadventures when he attempts to sell a valuable "ring" his mother has found and given him to provide the capital for his "rise." A con man named Montgomery who poses as "a jeweler from Syracuse" is said to overhear "with evident interest" a conversation between Paul and another boy about this ring. The man steps forward and avows his "interest in examining" and possibly buying Paul's ring; permitted to do so, he pronounces it "handsome" and valuable, and invites the boy to his hotel room to complete the transaction (199–200). Once at the hotel (called "Lovejoy's"), Montgomery grabs Paul and applies a sponge soaked in chloroform to the boy's nose until he passes out. "Eyeing the insensible boy with satisfaction," he seizes the ring and flees (208–9).

Alger's fiction never allows such disruption of the networks of male interest by the incursion of what it represents as the feminine/anal—a position of jeopardy into which every "gentle boy" can at least potentially be forced—to become more than temporary: Paul recovers his ring and completes his sale of it, then deposits most of the proceeds with his gentleman patron, who promises him "interest" on it (295). When the con man is sent off to Sing Sing after being convicted of assaulting and robbing Paul, according to the narrative, even the man's wife is said to be indifferent: "As the compact between her and her husband was one of interest rather than of affection, her grief at his confinement is not very deep" (304). Compacts of interest between man and wife, the narrative leads us to assume, are ignoble, but between man and boy "on the market," there is no comparably invidious distinction to be drawn between mutual "interest" and "affection": they come to the same thing, and both qualities are estimable.

Older men who might (but actually do not) stand in relation to Alger's boy heroes as fathers may "take an interest" in them that may eventuate (as we have seen) in actions as various as respectful advancement or rape, but none of these interactions with older men on the boys' part leaves any permanent trace in the lives of the boy characters except in the form of yet another accession of capital. Domestic arrangements are formed between boy and boy, but relations between man and boy remain casual, intermittent, and extradomestic: the "rise" of Alger's hero is fostered by "interested" older patrons, but (the informing, contradictory fantasy runs) the boy remains entirely self-fathering.

Alger's particular version of the "self-made man" takes the form of this "self-made" all-boy family that the boy protagonist generates with his money. This version of domesticity, as I have suggested above, derives from the infantile-fantasy equivalence that the stories propose between femininity and anality. Drawing on the succinct psychoanalysis of the "magic-dirt" complex that Norman O. Brown makes in *Life against Death*, I would argue that Alger's writing denies sexual difference—and privileges the figure of the formerly "dirty" boy-turned-gentle over figures of other age, gender, and class positions—"in the interest" of promoting this particular notion of self-making, of simultaneous self-mothering and self-fathering, that it takes over from capitalist culture:

The infantile fantasy of becoming father of oneself first moves out to make magic use of objects instead of its own body when it gets attached to that object which both is and is not part of its own body, the feces. Money inherits the infantile magic of excrement and then is able to breed and have children: interest is an increment.[24]

Alger's all-boy families merely imitate the extraordinary propensities for self-reproduction, for apparently asexual breeding, that they are represented as discovering already ongoing in their first accumulations of capital. The chain of "magical" transformations I have charted in Alger's writing from ragged to gentle boy by way of a series of negotiations of capital into baby and then back into capital conforms entirely to Brown's Freudian reading of the fantasy of transformation of bodily excrement into capital increment by way of the metamorphosis of feces into baby and subsequently into "magical," self-engendering money.

Alger's tales sometimes manifest a modicum of self-awareness on the author's part with regard to his role of purveyor of a "magical thinking" that effectively links infantile fantasies of self-fathering with some of the fundamental formations of capitalist culture. In his recent study of forms of popular narrative in nineteenth-century America, Michael Denning has likened the function of Alger's street-boy heroes—"dangerous" figures drawn from contemporary popular, nongenteel fiction (story papers, dime novels) who enact what Denning (correctly) reads as unequivocally genteel moralistic fables—to the use of "a ventriloquist's dummy to recapture and reorganize working class culture."[25] I would supplement Denning's characterization of Alger as a ventriloquist across class lines (as well as, I would add, across lines of prohibited sexuality between man and boy) with a brief analysis of Alger's representation of himself in the figure of Professor Henderson, a magician/ventriloquist who figures as a patron/employer of the boy hero of *Bound to Rise*. Henderson first deceives the boy Harry Walton, who has come to work as his assistant, by throwing his voice into a trunk, from which emerges a child's voice pathetically pleading, "Oh, let me out! Don't keep me locked up in here!" Harry is said merely to "smile" when he realizes Henderson has tricked him with ventriloquism (102). Shortly thereafter, Henderson repeats the trick in the boy's presence, this time at the expense of an elderly woman character; Henderson and Harry have a good laugh at her chagrin. The trick is more elaborate the second time: Henderson throws his voice into the boy's body and increases their mirth by making Harry seem to lie to the woman to the effect that the professor does indeed have someone locked away in the trunk; this time Henderson specifies (ventriloqually) that the child is female—in fact, his little daughter. The climax of the trick comes when the professor throws open the trunk and shows the woman that there is no one there (114–15).

The reader may share some of the woman character's discomfort over the "little girl in the trunk" trick that at a critical point in the episode turns into the "vanishing daughter" trick. Not much imagination is required to produce the biographical speculation that the little girl locked in the trunk, crying to be released, is a figure from Alger's psychological past who survived in encrypted and rejected form in his unconscious and whose ultimate fate was to be pressed into service as comic relief in texts like *Bound to Rise.* Even more thoroughly than the ambiguously feminine Tattered Tom, this fantasmatic "little girl" vanishes almost without a trace from the magical network of male interests through which she is passed in this text—leaving the reader to suspect, at this and other points in the Alger corpus, that the "dangerous" figures in his writing are not really at any point the ragged street boys whose labile qualities it celebrates but the little girls it almost totally excludes—along with the femininity they embody, a "threatening" quality insofar as it might permanently disrupt the smooth unfolding in the America of the time of the exclusively male homosocial institutions of corporate capitalism.

It was in the decade or so after Alger's death in 1899 that Lewis Hine began to produce his extraordinary photographs of the new, turn-of-the-century generation of urban street boys at their work of peddling, shining shoes, selling newspapers, and delivering parcels. What is striking about Hine's photographs is their self-conscious refusal to "gentle" their underclass subjects in the way that Alger and his philanthropist colleagues had done: Hine's boy subjects are not represented as picturesque ragamuffins or charming but dangerous "animals" or "savages," some of whom will inevitably make their way to affluence and respectability. Rather, his images of these boys reveal their sufferings as real, lasting deformations rather than as transient experiential way stations on the road to untroubled security and success: the child subjects of Hine's photographs characteristically look weary, depressed, and even bitter. In association with the Progressivist reform organization the National Child Labor Committee (NCLC), Hine wrote and lectured extensively on the need for legislation prohibiting the exploitation of poor children as laborers by either their parents or their employers: his photographs, he insisted, were his incontrovertible documentary evidence that children forced to support themselves by full-time employment at low-paying labor were generally destroyed physically and morally in the process. Hine supplemented his photographic record of street-boy life with his own antisentimental testimony about their plight: for example, apropos of his 1909 photograph of a Hartford, Connecticut, newsboy named Tony Casale, Hine records that the boy had recently shown his boss the marks on his arm where his father had bitten him "for not selling more papers"; Hine also mentions that the boy said he disliked being the object of verbal abuse from the drunken men with whom he constantly came in contact on the city streets.[26]

Hine and the NCLC encountered strong popular resistance to their movement; politicians and other members of their audiences vociferously denied that conditions for street-child laborers were as grim and brutalizing as Hine represented them as being. Hine's street boys, his opponents often argued, were Horatio Alger heroes, toiling their way up from paupery to comfortable, respectable lives.

It was during these years, between the turn of the century and the beginning of World War I, at the height of the Progressive Era, that Alger's books, republished in cheap reprints that suppressed substantial amounts of the books' didactic moralizing, sold in the millions of copies.[27] During his lifetime, Alger had had only one genuine best seller, the early *Ragged Dick;* only posthumously did he achieve true mass popularity. It was also during the early years of the twentieth century that the term "a Horatio Alger story" became fixed in the language to mean a tale of a man's "rise" from boyhood poverty to a position of great wealth and power. The myth that Alger's are male-capitalist Cinderella tales has had an astonishing success of its own. How can one account for the ubiquity of this inaccurate characterization of the content of Alger's stories? With the benefit of hindsight, we can see that one thing that was being "saved" in Alger's writing was a notion of "virtuous poverty rewarded" that was already archaic when his first street-boy series appeared in the decade after the Civil War. The Alger mania of readers in the first fifteen years of the twentieth century might be said to have served as a reinoculation of American readers with the myth of "virtuous poverty rewarded," an article of faith that was being vociferously combatted from Progressivist, socialist, and organized-labor quarters during those years. I would attribute some of the popularity of Alger's stories with boy readers during and after his lifetime to their propensity for combining a not inaccurate representation of the conditions, requirements, and mild rewards to be expected on the extensive lower reaches of the corporate workplace with a version of boy life—idyllic, domestic, self-perpetuating, untroubled by direct intervention from parents or other adult figures of authority or by the "threat" (to male supremacy) of female enfranchisement—that may strike us as highly unrealistic at first glance but that is (again) a not inaccurate version of some of corporate culture's favorite modes of self-presentation (i.e., as fraternal, financially rewarding, benevolently hierarchical, open to individual talent or "merit").

I would attribute the extraordinary tenacity of the "rags-to-riches" misreading of Alger to corporate/capitalist culture's need for a serviceable mythology of "success" like Alger's—but one that entirely represses (as Alger's does not) the determinate relations perceptible in his stories between the achievement and maintenance of white-collar "lifestyles" and particular, exclusive modes of relationship between males. I first began to read Alger's writing out of an interest in thinking about ways in which his pederasty might have determined it, but I have come to think that the far more interesting way his work manifests male homosexuality is not as indirect autobiographical data for a single figure (i.e., Alger) but as an encapsulation of corporate/capitalist America's long-cherished myth, its male homoerotic foundations fiercely repressed, that the white males who control wealth and power have their eye out for that exceptional, "deserving," "attractive" underclass youth who defies his statistical fate to become (with the benefit of limited paternalistic "interest") yet another "gentle boy from the dangerous classes."

Notes

I wish to thank Jane Tompkins and Larzer Ziff for thoughtful readings of an earlier draft of this essay, and Jonathan Goldberg and Michael Warner for helpful advice on subsequent versions of it. I also wish to thank Michael Rogin for making valuable editorial suggestions.

1. Quoted in Christine Stansell, *City of Women: Sex and Class in New York, 1789–1860* (New York: Knopf, 1986), 194. I have depended on the chapter of Stansell's book in which this report is quoted ("The Use of the Streets," 193–216) for my brief opening account in this essay of genteel response to street children in New York City in the years just before Alger's arrival on the scene.

2. Ibid., 212.

3. Charles Loring Brace, *Short Sermons to News Boys* (New York, 1866), 140–41.

4. Hugh Kenner's phrase occurs in his "The Promised Land," in *A Homemade World: The American Modernist Writers* (New York: Knopf, 1975), 20. Richard Huber, who rediscovered the documentary material on Alger's pederasty, discusses it in his book *The American Idea of Success* (New York: McGraw-Hill, 1971).

5. Michael Zuckerman, "The Nursery Tales of Horatio Alger," *American Quarterly* 24, no. 2 (May 1972): 209.

6. Horatio Alger Jr., *Bound to Rise; or, Up the Ladder* (New York: New York Book Company, 1909), 101 (in a chapter significantly titled "The Coming of the Magician").

7. My thinking about homoeroticism, homophobia, social class, and capitalism in this essay is indebted to Eve Kosofsky Sedgwick, *Between Men: English Literature and Male Homosocial Desire* (New York: Columbia University Press, 1985), especially her chapter "Homophobia, Misogyny, and Capital: The Example of *Our Mutual Friend*," 161–79. I am also indebted to Luce Irigaray, "Commodities among Themselves," in *This Sex Which Is Not One*, trans. Catherine Porter with Carolyn

Burke (Ithaca, NY: Cornell University Press, 1985), for her analysis of the determinate relation between homophobia and the foundations of patriarchal economics: "Why is masculine homosexuality considered exceptional, then, when in fact the economy as a whole is based upon it? Why are homosexuals ostracized, when society postulates homosexuality?" (192). In considering the profound effects of the requirements of the forms of corporate capitalism emergent in Alger's time on his culture, I have also profited from Alan Trachtenberg's treatment of this matter in *The Incorporation of America: Culture and Society in the Gilded Age* (New York: Hill & Wang, 1982).

8. Alger's sketch of the boy residents of the Newsboys' Lodging House of the Children's Aid Society (Brace's organization) originally appeared in the pages of the *Liberal Christian*. It is reprinted in Gary Scharnhorst with Jack Bales, *The Lost Life of Horatio Alger, Jr.* (Bloomington: Indiana University Press, 1985), 79. The appearance at long last of a factually reliable biography of Alger such as this one makes writing about his work substantially easier.

9. Quoted in ibid., 67.

10. The boys involved were apparently all members of Alger's Unitarian congregation in the small Cape Cod community of Brewster. If Alger did cross class lines "for sex" in his later years in New York, where, according to Scharnhorst, he entertained hundreds of street-boy friends in his rooms (ibid., 77) and semiofficially adopted three of them (124–25), it was of course only the official version of the morality of his time and place that he was violating: the casual sexual exploitation of the poor by those who were economically and socially better-off than they was of course a pervasive feature of nineteenth-century urban life. For the example of New York City in the decade before the Civil War, see Christine Stansell, "Women on the Town: Sexual Exchange and Prostitution," in *City of Women*, 171–92.

11. Quoted in Nina Baym, *Novels, Readers, and Reviewers: Responses to Fiction in Antebellum America* (Ithaca, NY: Cornell University Press, 1984), 210–11.

12. Stansell gives a brief and useful history of the "sketch" of scenes, especially street scenes, of urban poverty in New York in the three decades before the Civil War in *City of Women*, 195–97, demonstrating as she does so how much what genteel observers of the time "saw" depended on expectations that writing about "the problem" had helped to form. Stansell writes, "Although the *problems* of the streets— the fights, the crowds, the crime, the children—were nothing new, the 'problem' itself represented altered bourgeois perception and a broadened political initiative." She goes on to say, "Matsell's report and the writing Brace undertook in the 1850s distilled the particular way the genteel had designated themselves arbiters of the city's everyday life" (197). Louis Chevalier, *Laboring Classes and Dangerous Classes in Paris during the First Half of the Nineteenth Century,* trans. Frank Jellinek (New York: Howard Fertig, 1973), gives extensive documentation of the interdependence of the depictions of the urban poor to be found in Sue, Balzac, and Hugo with contemporary forensic writing. D. A. Miller has analyzed similar interdependences between contemporary "policing" techniques and the fiction of Wilkie Collins, Dickens, and Trollope in such articles as "From *Roman policier* to *Roman-police*: Wilkie Collins's *The Moonstone*," *Novel* 13 (winter 1980): 153–70; "The Novel and

the Police," *Glyph* 8 (1981): 127–47; "Discipline in Different Voices: Bureaucracy, Police, Family, and Bleak House," *Representations* 1 (February 1983): 59–89; and "The Novel as Usual: Trollope's *Barchester Towers*," in *Sex, Politics, and Science in the Nineteenth-Century Novel: Selected Papers from the English Institute, 1983–84,* ed. Ruth Bernard Yeazell (Baltimore: Johns Hopkins University Press, 1986), 1–38. Mark Seltzer has explored the relation of the forensic discourse of surveillance to Henry James's writing in "*The Princess Casamassima*: Realism and the Fantasy of Surveillance," in *American Realism: New Essays,* ed. Eric J. Sundquist (Baltimore: Johns Hopkins University Press, 1982), 95–118.

13. Louis Chevalier has called M. A. Fregier's influential 1840 study *Des Classes dangereuses de la population dans les grandes villes* "a close study of the process by which the course of the lower-class child's life was shaped toward crime." Chevalier, *Laboring Classes,* 120.

14. John G. Cawelti traces the lines of descent of this "democratic" boy hero in his chapter on Alger in *Apostles of the Self-Made Man: Changing Concepts of Success in America* (Chicago: University of Chicago Press, 1965). See also, in the same volume, "Natural Aristocracy and the New Republic: The Idea of Mobility in the Thought of Franklin and Jefferson," 1–36.

15. For comparative purposes, see the discussions of the shifting parameters of gentility in nineteenth-century England in the respective introductory chapters of the following two works: Robhi Gilmour, *The Idea of the Gentleman in the English Novel* (London: George Allen & Unwin, 1981), 1–15; Shirley Robin Letwin, *The Gentleman in Trollope: Individuality and Moral Conduct* (Cambridge: Harvard University Press, 1982), 3–21.

16. All these senses of the term, and all these potential occasions of social unease, ranging from simple embarrassment to disgrace and persecution, are alive in American Renaissance writing about the "gentle" and "gentlemen." The figure of the "gentle boy" reached an apogee of sorts in Hawthorne's 1832 tale of that name. A second key text for this figure as it appears in American Renaissance writing is Thoreau's poem "Lately, alas, I knew a gentle boy . . . ," which he published in the "Wednesday" section of *A Week on the Concord and Merrimack Rivers* (1849).

17. See Chevalier, *Laboring Classes,* 414.

18. Alger's novels are cited by short titles in the text. The editions cited are *Ragged Dick* (New York: Collier, 1962); *Fame and Fortune* (Boston: A. K. Loring, 1868); *Phil the Fiddler,* in *Struggling Upwards and Other Works* (New York: Project Trinigy, 1945); *Jed the Poorhouse Boy,* in *Struggling Upwards; Tattered Tom* (Boston: Loring, 1871); *Mark the Match Boy* (New York: Collier, 1962); *Risen from the Ranks* (Boston: A. K. Loring, 1874); *Sam's Chance, and How He Improved It* (Chicago: A. K. Loring, n.d.); *Paul the Peddler: The Fortunes of a Young Street Merchant* (New York: n.d.); *Bound to Rise; or, Up the Ladder* (New York: New York Book Company, 1909).

19. Nina Baym briefly but perspicaciously classifies Alger as a domestic writer in *Woman's Fiction: A Guide to Novels by and about Women in America, 1820–1870* (Ithaca, NY: Cornell University Press, 1978), 261.

20. For an informative account of Beecher's theory of domesticity, see Kathryn

Kish Sklar, *Catharine Beecher: A Study in American Domesticity* (New Haven, CT: Yale University Press, 1973), 158ff.

21. See Mary P. Ryan, "Varieties of Social Retreat: Domesticity, Privacy, and the Self-Made Man," in *Cradle of the Middle Class: The Family in Oneida County, New York, 1790–1865* (Cambridge: Cambridge University Press, 1981), 146–55, for a discussion of the compatibility and indeed the congruence of the cult of the "self-made man" with the cult of (feminine) domesticity.

22. Fredric Jameson, *The Political Unconscious: Narrative as a Socially Symbolic Act* (Ithaca, NY: Cornell University Press, 1981), employs the term *fantasm* to denote "the traces and symptoms of a fundamental family situation which is at one and the same time a fantasy master narrative" that "is an unstable and contradictory structure, whose persistent actantial functions and events . . . demand repetition, permutation, and the ceaseless generation of various structural 'resolutions'" (180). If, as Jameson suggests, a residue of fantasmatic thinking about "a fundamental family situation" is characteristic of all bourgeois narratives, then it becomes possible to perceive many more narratives as being fundamentally "domestic"—or antidomestic—in their emphases than most of us are probably used to doing.

23. Michael Pollak, "Male Homosexuality; or, Happiness in the Ghetto," in *Western Sexuality: Practice and Precept in Past and Present Times,* ed. Philippe Ariès and André Bejin, trans. Anthony Forster (Oxford: Blackwell, 1985), 44.

24. Norman O. Brown, *Life against Death: The Psychoanalytical Meaning of History* (Middletown, CT: Wesleyan University Press, 1959), 279.

25. Michael Denning, "Cheap Stories: Notes on Popular Fiction and Working-Class Culture in Nineteenth-Century America," *History Workshop* 22 (autumn 1986): 6.

26. Quoted in the catalog entry for Lewis Hine's photograph titled "Bologna, Hartford, Connecticut, 1909," in Julie R. Myers et al., *Of Time and Place: American Figurative Art from the Corcoran Gallery* (Washington: Smithsonian and the Corcoran Gallery, 1981), 92.

27. Scharnhorst, *Lost Life,* 149–56, provides an illuminating account of the "editorial reinvention" of Alger's work (often by silent abridgment) in the years after his death.

Live Sex Acts
(Parental Advisory: Explicit Material)

Lauren Berlant

> I am a citizen of the United States, and in this country where I live,
> every year millions of pictures are being made of women with our legs
> spread. We are called beaver, we are called pussy, our genitals are tied
> up, they are pasted, makeup is put on them to make them pop out of a
> page at a male viewer. . . . I live in a country where if you film any act
> of humiliation or torture, and if the victim is a woman, the film is both
> entertainment and it is protected speech. Now that tells me something
> about being a woman in this country.
>
> *—Andrea Dworkin*[1]

I open with this passage not simply to produce in advance the resistances,
ambivalences, and concords that inevitably arise when someone speaks
with passion and authority about sex and identity, but also to foreground
here the centrality, to any public-sphere politics of sexuality, of coming to
terms with the conjunction of making love and making law, of fucking and
talking, of acts and identities, of cameras and police, and of pleasure in the
text and patriarchal privilege, insofar as in these couplings can be found
fantasies of citizenship and longings for freedom made in the name of national culture.

I'm going to tell you a story about this, a story about citizenship in the
United States. It is about live sex acts, and a book called *Live Sex Acts,* and a
thing called national culture that, in reference to the United States, I mean
to bring into representation here—which is hard, because the modality of
national culture in the United States that I will describe exists mainly as

a negative projection, an endangered species, the shadow of a fetish called normalcy, which is currently under a perceived attack by sex radicals, queers, pornographers, and pop-music culture. This perceived attack on national morals raises a number of questions. What kinds of forces in national life are being both marked and veiled by the culturally defensive demonization of atypical sexualities? And if sex and sensuality radicals were really circulating a kind of pleasure acid that could corrode the American Way of Life, what about it exactly would they be attacking?

Some vulnerable spots on the national terrain should be flagged from the very outset. The first is the national future. Because the only thing the nation form is able to assure for itself is its past, its archive of official memory, it must develop in the present ways of establishing its dominion over the future. This is one reason reproductive heterosexuality and the family always present such sensitive political issues. Reproduction and generationality are the main vehicles by which the national future can be figured, made visible, and made personal to citizens otherwise oblivious to the claims of a history that does not seem to be about them individually. The anxieties surrounding the process of making people into national subjects confirm that the hegemonic form of national culture is fragile and always in the process of being defined, even when it appears as a thing with an essential character that can be taken prisoner like the soul in fierce battles between rival gangs of angels and devils.

Once it is established that national culture demands a continuous pedagogical project for making people into "private citizens" who understand their privacy to be a mirror and a source for nationality itself, it becomes equally important that the national culture industry generate a mode of political discourse in which the nation form trumps all other images of collective sociality and power. However, the content of the nation's utopian project has been complicated during the rise of the Reaganite right. One axiom of this ideology has been to destroy an image of the federal state that places its practice at the center of nation formation. The right's attempt to shrink domestic government and thereby to hack away at the hyphen between the nation and the state has required the development of new technologies of patriotism that keep the nation at the center of the public's identification while shrinking the field of what can be expected from the state.[2]

During the last twenty years as well, the sexual minorities of the United States—heterosexual women and gays and lesbians—have developed sexual publics that not only demand expanded protections from the state and the law but also challenge the practices, procedures, and contents of what counts as politics, including questioning whether the nation form as such should continue to organize utopian drives for collective social life. Additionally, using the forms of publicity that capitalist culture makes available for collective identifications, some of these sex publics have exposed contradictions in the free-market economics of the right, which names nonmarital sex relations as immoral while relations of economic inequality, dangerous workplaces, and disloyalty to employees amount to business as usual, not provoking any ethical questions about the privileges only some citizens enjoy. These complex challenges, posed by a diverse set of politically embodied publics, are therefore both central to how citizenship must be thought as a question of sexuality and convenient distractions from the conservative project of installing a sanitized image of normal culture as the nation's utopian aspiration.

One result is that the national culture industry is also in the business of generating paramnesias, images that organize consciousness, not by way of explicit propaganda, but by replacing and simplifying memories people actually have with image traces of political experience about which people can have political feelings that link them to other citizens and to patriotism. This process veils, without simply suppressing knowledge of, the means by which the nation's hegemonic contradictions and contingencies are constructed, consented to, displaced, and replaced by images of normal culture that "the people" are said already to accept. The political fantasy of the infantile citizen is an image of extremist and hypersexualized citizens recently generated in the public struggle over what will count as the core national culture. Most of the time, political discourse about sex in this modality is a way of creating instant panic about the fragility of people's intimate lives; most of the time, extravagant sex is a figure for general social disorder and not a site for serious thinking and criticism about sexuality, morality, or anything. But the relation between nationalized knowledge and amnesia is not one of mutual negation. Instead, we never really know whether the forms of intelligibility that give citizens access to political culture are monuments to false consciousness or the inevitable partial truths of publicly held information. Michael Taussig argues that state knowledge is a site of the full "coming together of reason and violence" that generates paradoxes of knowing and unknowing, such that ordinary pragmatic detail, good-enough comprehensions of national activity, and traumatized pseudoknowledges together can be said to constitute the ongoing lived relations among states, national ideology, and citizens.[3] Along with drawing attention to sexuality and its place in the contemporary construction of U.S. citizenship, the sex culture wars I investigate here provide a way of exploring what different kinds of national world are brought into being by different conceptions of sex.

This essay began as a review of some recent feminist work on pornography.[4] In it I take no position on "pornography" as such, but discuss pornography in terms of how, more broadly, the U.S. citizen's vulnerability and aspiration to a nationally protected identity has been orchestrated by a national culture industry that emphasizes sexuality as the fundamental index of a person's political legitimacy. In this regard I refocus the discussion of sex and representation away from the domain of the politics of sexual difference and toward the conjunction of sexuality, mass culture, and mass nationality.

In particular, I am interested in tracing some meanings of privacy, a category of law and a condition of property that constitutes a boundary between proper and improper bodies, and a horizon of aspiration vital to the imagination of what counts as legitimate U.S. citizenship. *Privacy* here describes, simultaneously, a theoretical space imagined by U.S. constitutional and statutory law; a scene of taxonomic violence that devolves privilege on certain actual spaces of practical life; a juridical substance that comes to be synonymous with secure domestic inferiority; and a structure of protection and identity that sanctions, by analogy, other spaces that surround, secure, and frame the bodies whose acts, identities, identifications, and social value are the booty over which national culture wages its struggle to exist as a struggle to dominate sex.

Thus this story indeed contains graphic images, parental advisories, and magical thinking—that is to say, the usual dialectic between crassness and sublimity that has long dressed the ghosts of national culture in monumental forms and made it available for anxious citizens who need to invoke it on behalf of stabilizing one or another perceived social norm. This story has real and fictive characters, too—John Frohnmayer, Andrea Dworkin, Tipper Gore, and some fat, queer Nazis who try to join the military—but its main players are a little girl and an adult, both Americans. The little girl stands in this chapter as a condensation of many (infantile) citizenship fantasies. It is in her name as future citizen that state and federal governments have long policed morality around sex and other transgressive representation; the psychological and political vulnerability she represents has provided a model for other struggles to transform minority experience in the United States. And it is in her name that something Other to her, called, let's say, "adult culture," has been defined and privileged in many national domains. Although not without its contradictions: we have the adult by whose name pornography is marked, as in "adult books," and, on the other hand, the adult who can join with other adults to protect the still unhistorical little girl whose citizenship, if the adults act as good parents, might pass boringly from its minority to what has been called the "zone of privacy" or national heterosexuality "adult" Americans generally seek to inhabit.

"Zone of privacy" is a technical phrase, invented in a Supreme Court opinion of 1965. It was Justice William O. Douglas's opinion in *Griswold v. Connecticut* that designated for the first time the heterosexual act of intercourse in marital bedrooms as protected by a zone of privacy into which courts must not peer and with which they must not interfere. Justice Douglas's rezoning of the bedroom into a nationally protected space of privacy allowed married citizens of Connecticut for the first time to purchase birth control. It sought to make national a relation that it says precedes the Bill of Rights. It consolidated the kind of thinking that happened when the justices recently, in *Bowers v. Hardwick,* confirmed the irreducible heterosexuality of the national bedroom, as it established once again that homosexuality has no constitutionally supported privacy protections in the United States. It could have been otherwise. Writing a memo to be circulated among Supreme Court justices, Daniel Richman, a clerk for Thurgood Marshall, sought to instruct the Court about oral and anal sex. He wrote to the justices, in capital letters, "THIS IS NOT A CASE ABOUT ONLY HOMO-SEXUALS. ALL SORTS OF PEOPLE DO THIS KIND OF THING."[5] He did not name the "sorts" of people. But in almost referring to heterosexuality, that sacred national identity that happens in the neutral territory of national culture, Richman almost made the "sex" of heterosexuality imaginable, corporeal, visible, public.

Thus I mean to oppose a story about live sex acts to a story about "dead citizenship." Dead citizenship, which haunts the shadowland of national culture, takes place in a privacy zone and epitomizes an almost Edenic conjunction of act and identity, sacred and secular history. It involves a theory of national identity that equates identity with iconicity. It requires that I tell you a secret history of acts that are not experienced as acts, because they take place in the abstract idealized time and space of citizenship. I use the word *dead,* then, in the rhetorical sense designated by the phrase *dead metaphor.* A metaphor is dead when, by repetition, the unlikeness risked in the analogy the metaphor makes becomes so conventionalized as to no longer seem figural, no longer open to history; the leg of a table is the most famous dead metaphor. In the fantasy world of national culture, citizens aspire to dead identities—constitutional personhood in its public-sphere abstraction and suprahistoricity, reproductive heterosexuality in the zone of privacy. Identities not live, or in play, but dead, frozen, fixed, or at rest.

The fear of ripping away the privacy protections of heteronational culture has led to a national crisis over the political meanings of imaginable, live, and therefore transgressive sex acts, acts that take place in public by virtue of either a state optic or a subcultural style. By bringing more fully into relief the politics of securing the right to privacy in the construction of a sexuality that bears the definitional burden of national culture, I am in part telling a story about preserving a boundary between what can be done and said in public, what can be done in private but not spoken of in public, and what can, patriotically speaking, be neither done nor legitimately spoken of at all in the United States. Thus there is nothing new about the new national anthem, "Don't Ask, Don't Tell, Don't Pursue." I am also telling a story about transformations of the body in mass national society and thinking about a structure of political feeling that characterizes the history of national sentimentality, in which, at moments of crisis, persons violate the zones of privacy that give them privilege and protection in order to fix something social that feels threatening: they practice politics, they generate publicity, they act in public, but in the name of privacy. I mean to bring into representation these forms of citizenship structured in dominance, in scenes where adults act on behalf of the little-girl form that represents totemically and fetishistically the unhumiliated citizen.[6] She is the custodian of the promise of zones of privacy that national culture relies on for its magic and its reproduction.

Looking for Love in All the Wrong Places: Live Sex Acts in America

When John Frohnmayer made his pilgrimage to serve the National Endowment for the Arts in Washington, he was a "babe in the woods" of politics who hoped to "rekindl[e]" the "free spirit" of the nation, a spirit now endangered by television and other mass-mediated forms of alienation in the United States.[7] He initially imagined using the NEA to re-produce the nation through its localities—emphasizing not cities (which are, apparently, not localities) but the rural and provincial cultures whose neglected "vitality" might help return the mass nation to a non-mass-mediated sense of tribal intimacy. In his autobiography, *Leaving Town Alive: Confessions of an Arts Warrior,* Frohnmayer describes in great detail the deep roots of the nation in aesthetic genealogies of an organic citizenry. For example, he tells of the gospel roots of rap, the spirit of fiddling in an age of "overamplified electronic music," Native American weaving, ballet, and other arts that make "no mention of homosexuality, foul words, or nudity"[8]—which, according to this logic, become phenomena of cities and of mass culture.

Yet his ambitions for cultural reformation did not protect Frohnmayer's tenure at the NEA, which was so riddled by the competition between a certain metropolitan and an uncertain national culture that he was driven out of office. The cases of the X, Y, and Z portfolios of Robert Mapplethorpe, of the NEA Four, and of *Tongues Untied* are famous examples of how sex-radical performance aesthetics were unassimilable to the homophobic and mock-populist official national culture-making machine that currently dominates Washington. But what actually got Frohnmayer fired was the NEA's support of a *literary* publication project in New York City that dragged the nation into the dirt, the waste, and the muck of sex and other gross particularities. This project, managed by a press called "the portable lower east side," produced two texts in 1991: *Live Sex Acts* and *Queer City.*

The Reverend Donald Wildmon made these texts available to every member of Congress, President George Bush, and Vice President Dan Quayle. He also wrote a letter to them citing an excerpt from a poem as evidence for the virtually treasonous use of taxpayer money to support art that besmirches national culture.

My first exhibit—or, should I say, my first "inhibit"—is the poem "Wild Thing," written by the poet Sapphire (Ramona Lofton) and published in *Queer City*. "Wild Thing" is written in the fictive voice of one of the boys whose wilding expedition in 1989 resulted in the rape and beating of the woman called "the Central Park jogger." Here is the excerpt from the poem that Wildmon sent to Congress:

> I remember when
> Christ sucked my dick
> behind the pulpit
> I was 6 years old
> he made me promise
> not to tell no one.[9]

I will return to this poem anon. But first, let me characterize the scandalous magazines that were the context for it. Frohnmayer describes *Queer City* accurately: "Although some of the pieces were sexual in tone and content, they were clearly meant to be artful rather than prurient."[10] *Queer City* is a collective work of local culture, positing New York as a vibrant site of global sexual identity, a multinational place where people come to traverse the streets, live the scene, have sex, write stories and poems about it, and take pictures of the people who live it with pleasure and impunity. It is an almost entirely apolitical book, except in the important sense that the title *Queer City* remaps New York by way of the spaces where queer sex takes place, such that sexual identities are generated in *public,* in a metropolitan public constituted by a culture of experience and a nourish of publicity.

In contrast, and although *Live Sex Acts* is equally situated in New York City, a marked majority of its texts explain sex in terms of the national context and the political public sphere; indeed, many of the essays in *Live Sex Acts* are explicit responses to the right-wing cultural agenda of the Reagan revolution. They demonstrate that it is not sexual identity as such that threatens America, which is liberal as long as sex aspires to iconicity or deadness, and suggest rather that the threat to national culture derives from what we might call sex acts on the live margin, sex acts that threaten because they do not aspire to the privacy protection of national culture, or to the narrative containment of sex into one of the conventional romantic forms of modern consumer heterosexuality. This assertion of a sexual public sphere is also striking because *Live Sex Acts* closes by moving beyond a sexual performance ethic and toward other live margins. Two final segments, Krzysztof Wodiczko's "Poliscar: A Homeless Vehicle" and a portfolio of poems by patients at Creedmoor Psychiatric Hospital, explicitly seek to redefine citizenship by naming who lives on the live margins, and how.[11] They show how the waste products of America must generate a national public sphere and a civic voice. To do this, the live margin must find its own media. A radically redefined category of live sex acts here becomes a mass medium for addressing and redressing the official national culture industry.

In any case, as Frohnmayer says, the scandal these two magazines created had nothing to do with what kinds of subversive effect their small circulation might conceivably have had or aspired to, with respect to either sexual convention or national identity. He describes the uproar as an effect of bad reading. Donald Wildmon has spent much time in the last decade policing sexual subcultures. He does this by attempting to humiliate state and federal arts councils that use taxpayer money to support transgressions of norms a putative ordinary American holds sacred. To christen the national as a locale with discernible standards of propriety, he uses the logic of obscenity law, which since the 1970s has offered local zones the opportunity to specify local standards with respect to which federal law might determine the obscenity of a text.

Wildmon is unconcerned with the referential context of both the wild thing and the poem about it. This lack of concern is central to the story of the Central Park jogger: many have noted how a serious discussion of the wilding event—in terms of the politics of public spaces, of housing projects, of city parks as homes and public property, of gender, of race, of classes and underclasses, of sexuality, of mass media, and of the law—was deflected into a melodrama of the elite. Here, Wildmon seeks to make irrelevant any full exploration of the wilding poem by deploying the anti-live-sex terms of the "true" national culture he claims to represent. Already on record accusing the NEA of promoting "blasphemy" and "the homosexual lifestyle," Wildmon grasped the passage "Christ sucked my dick" and brought it to the attention of Jesse Helms, who shortly thereafter got Frohnmayer, whom Pat Robertson had nicknamed "Satan," fired.[12]

Frohnmayer claims to know nothing about homosexuality in the United States, and I believe he is right, though he knows something about homoeroticism. For example, in arguing against the Helms amendment he suggests the difficulty of telling "whether homoeroticism differed from garden-variety eroticism, whether it applied to females as well as males, whether it would pass muster under the Fourteenth Amendment tests of rational classifications and equal protection, or whether it was illegal for two persons of the same gender to hold hands, kiss, or do something more in deep shadow."[13] Of course, we know there is no deep shadow for gay sex in America: deep shadow is the protected zone of heterosexuality, or dead citizenship, and meanwhile all queers have is that closet. But if Frohnmayer does not know sex law, he knows what art is and also knows that when the NEA funds works of art it effectively protects them from obscenity prosecution.[14] Thus he legitimates this poem and *Queer City* in toto by reference to the standard of what art *attempts*. If the aspiration to art makes sexual representation protected by the national imprimatur, it is the content of "Wild Thing" that secures the success of its aspiration. Frohnmayer writes:

> These lines have been taken out of context and sensationalized. The poem, in its entirety, is emotional, intense and serious. . . . [It] deals with an actual event—the violent rape of a female jogger in Central Park—and must be read in its entirety in order to receive a fair appraisal. . . . It's not meant to make us feel good. It's not meant as an apology for a violent act. And it's certainly not meant to be sacrilegious, unless pedophilia is part of religious dogma. The poem is meant to make us think and to reflect on an incredibly brutal act in an allegedly civilized society.[15]

Again, there is much to say about wilding, the wild thing, the poem about it, the song it refers to, and the wild incitement to govern expression that this unfinished event has generated, which results in the contest over national meaning and value. First of all, Wildmon reads the poem as a direct indictment of the church for its alleged implied support of homosexual child molestation. Frohnmayer contests this reading with one that focuses on the purported failure of the black family to guide youth toward disciplined obedience to patriarchal authority. In Frohnmayer's description, the fate of the white woman represents what will happen to America when undersocialized boys abused by life in the projects and failed by parents leave their degenerate natal locales. They will terrorize property, women, and the nation: they will be bad men.

Frohnmayer's version of the poem cuts out entirely the poet's image of the fun, the pleasure, indeed the death-driven *jouissance* of the wilding man, his relation to mass culture, to his own body, to his rage at white women and men, his pleasure in his mastery over language and over the racist conventions he knows he inspires. Clearly that isn't the stuff of art or America. Most important, Frohnmayer parentalizes the nation by locating the virtue of art in its disclosure that the source of sexual violence and social decay (the end of American civilization) is in absent fathers and failed mothers. He ventriloquizes the poet's ventriloquized poem about wayward youth to prophesy about the future of national culture, which is in danger of collective acts of wilding. This hybrid official image—of the nation as a vicious youth, and as a formerly innocent youth betrayed by bad parenting, and as a child who might be saved by good official parents—is at the heart of contemporary citizenship policy. Here is a story about the attempt to construct a national culture that resists an aesthetic of live sex in the name of youth, heterosexuality, and the national future.

What "Adults" Do to "Little Girls": Minor Citizens in the Modern Nation

When Anthony Comstock made his pilgrimage to Washington in 1873 to show the Congress what kinds of literature, information, and advertisements about sex, contraception, and abortion were being distributed through the U.S. mails, he initiated a process of nationalizing the discipline of sexual representation in the United States in the name of protecting national culture. Comstock installed this regime of anxiety and textual terror by invoking the image of youth and, in particular, the stipulated standard of the little girl whose morals, mind, acts, body, and identity would certainly be corrupted by contact with adult immorality.[16] Until the 1957 *Roth v. United States* and the 1964 rulings on the novel *The Tropic of Cancer* and the film *Les Amants,* the Comstockian standard of the seducible little girl reigned prominently in court decisions about the obscenity of texts; indeed, as Edward de Grazia describes in *Girls Lean Back Everywhere: The Law of Obscenity and the Assault on Genius,* this putative little girl who might come into harmful contact with unsafe sexual knowledge and thus be induced by reading into performing harmful live sex acts (at least of interpretation) has been central to defining minor and full citizenship in the United States. She has come to represent the standard from which the privileged "adult" culture of the nation has fallen. Protecting her, while privileging him, establishing therein the conditions of minor and full citizenship, has thus been a project of pornographic modernity in the United States.

To certify obscenity legally, a three-pronged standard must be met: the material must appeal to a prurient interest in sex, be patently offensive to contemporary community standards, and be "utterly without redeeming social value."[17] The *Roth* and *Miller* decisions nationalized obscenity law for the first time, thus defining the adult who consumes pornography as an American in the way that the Fourteenth Amendment enfranchised African Americans as full citizens by locating citizenship primarily in the nation and only secondarily in states. Speaking of pornography's consumers, Dworkin and MacKinnon put succinctly this conjuncture of what we might call pornographic personhood, an amalgam of nation, nurture, and sacred patriarchy: "Pornography is their Dr. Spock, their Bible, their Constitution."[18] De Grazia's history of obscenity in the United States, along with his anthology *Censorship Landmarks,* reveals how the pressure to define obscenity has all along involved a struggle to define the relative power of national, state, and local cultures to control the contact the public might have with prurient materials. For example, in *Jacobellis v. Ohio,* the Ohio case concerning *Les Amants,* Justice Brennan argued: "We recognize the legitimate and indeed exigent interest of States and localities throughout the Nation in preventing the dissemination of material deemed harmful to children. But that interest does not justify a total suppression of such material, the effect of which would be to reduce the adult population . . . to reading only what is fit for children."[19] This tendency to nationalize the obscene, the child, and the adult has been checked by the "community standards" doctrine embraced by Chief Justice Warren Burger in 1973. This doctrine empowers local police, judges, prosecutors, juries, and citizen interest groups to determine the standards of local morality from which the nation should protect them. The Burger Court thus dissolved a major blockage to promoting a conservative cultural agenda, at least from the vantage point of Supreme Court precedent; one could avoid the constitutional protection of free speech against the "chilling effect" of censorship, which sought to avert the terroristic effects of political repression on speech, by localizing the relevant "context" according to the most local community standards. Central to establishing and maintaining these standards is the figure of the vulnerable little girl, a figure for minors in general. The situation of protected minor citizenship is thus a privilege for protection from adult heterosexual exploitation that national culture confers on its youth, its little girls and boys; paradoxically, the aura of the little girl provides a rationale for protecting the heterosexual privacy zones of "adult" national culture.

Sometimes, when the little girl, the child, or youth is invoked in discussions of pornography, obscenity, or the administration of morality in U.S. mass culture, actually endangered living beings are being imagined. Frequently, however, we should understand that these disturbing figures are fetishes, effigies that condense, displace, and stand in for arguments about who "the people" are, what they can bear, and when, if ever. The purpose of this excursus into the history of obscenity law has been to recast it within an assembly of parental gestures in which adult citizens are protected as children are protected from representations of violence and sex and violent sex, for fear that those representations are in effect understood as doctrine or as documentary fantasy. Even the most liberal obscenity law concedes that children must neither see nor hear immoral sex/text acts: they must neither know them nor see them, at least until they reach that ever more unlikely moment of majority when they can freely consent to reading with a kind of full competence they must first be protected from having.

Nowhere is this infantilizing confluence of media, citizenship, and sex more apparent and symptomatically American than in the work of Andrea Dworkin and Catharine MacKinnon, and the 1986 report on obscenity popularly called the Meese Commission report. Much has been written on the paradoxical effects of this collaboration between these radical feminists and the conservative cultural activity of the Republican-dominated state: Carole Vance and Edward de Grazia give scathing detailed accounts of the ideological excesses and incoherences of this collaboration, and MacKinnon and Dworkin write eloquently about why the sexual harms women experience must be mended by law.[20] I am not interested in adjudicating this debate here in its usual terms (civil rights/harm speech/antipatriarchal versus First Amendment/free speech/sex radical), but I mean to enter it obliquely, by examining the logics of its citizenship politics. I am interested in how it has helped to consolidate an image of the citizen as a minor, female, youthful victim who requires civil protection by the state whose adult citizens, especially adult men, seem mobilized by a sex- and capital-driven compulsion to foul their own national culture.

This story can be told in many ways. The first step of the argument by which pornography represents harm speech that fundamentally compromises women's citizenship in the United States establishes that pornography is a live sex act. It is live partly because, as the Milwaukee ordinance avows, "Pornography is what pornography *does*." There is a sense here, shared by many textual critics (not just of pornography), that texts are muscular active persons in some sense of the legal fiction that makes corporations into persons: texts can and do impose their will on consumers, innocent or consenting.[21] Second, this notion of textual activity, of the harm pornographic texts perform as a desired direct effect on their consumers, has become intensified and made more personal by the visual character of contemporary pornography.

The optical unconscious dominates the scene of citizenship and pornographic exploitation the Meese Commission report conjures. I quote at length the opening to the chapter titled "The Use of Performers in Commercial Pornography." This chapter opens with a passage from André Bazin's "The Ontology of the Photographic Image": "The objective nature of photography confers on it a quality of credibility absent from all other picture-making. . . . The photographic image is the object itself, the object freed from the conditions of time and space that govern it."[22] The text glosses this representation of the image:

> The leap from "picture making" to photography was . . . the single most important event in the history of pornography: images of the human body could be captured and preserved in exact, vivid detail. As with every other visible activity, sex could now, by the miraculous power of the camera, be "freed from the conditions of time and space." "Sex" in the abstract, of course, remains invisible to the camera; it is particular acts of sex between individual people which photographs, films, and video tapes can record.[23]

By equating the violence that photography performs on history and person-hood with the citizenship harms of pornography, the commission locates the solution to sexual violence in a return to the scene and the mode of production, and, indeed, in her own work, MacKinnon sees herself as a materialist feminist for this reason. This powerful view has incited a fundamental shift in the focus of assessments of pornography's effects. While social scientists are still trying to determine whether seeing violence leads to violence, and how, this antipornography view also insists on engaging with the backstory of the porn, taking its effect on performers and on the businessmen who control the condition of the performers as an important measure of its meaning. Furthermore, as we shall see, the exploitation of the pornographic performer becomes the model for the exploitation and violence to all women involved in the path of pornography's circulation.

> Unlike literature or drawing, sexually explicit photography cannot be made by one person. . . . No study of filmed pornography can thus be complete without careful attention to the circumstances under which individual people decide to appear in it, and the effects of that appearance on their lives. Nor is this an academic or trivial exercise. The evidence before us suggests that a substantial minority of women will at some time in their lives be asked to pose for or perform in sexually-explicit materials. It appears, too, that the proportion of women receiving such requests has increased steadily over the past several decades. If our society's appetite for sexually-explicit material continues to grow, or even if it remains at current levels, the decision whether to have sex in front of a camera will confront thousands of Americans.[24]

The ordinary woman and the pornographic model will experience second-class citizenship in U.S. society, the argument goes, because sexualization constructs every woman as a potential performer of live sex acts that get photographed. The Meese Commission supports this by showing how even models in pornographic films insist that "acting" in pornography is a fiction: it is sex work euphemized as acting; it is public euphemized as private and personal; it is coerced and exploitative, euphemized as consensual and part of a simple business exchange.

To find a precedent for protecting actors in pornography from experiencing in their jobs the unfreedom U.S. women experience in everyday heterosexual life, the Meese Commission, MacKinnon, and Dworkin turn to the model of child pornography, both to psychologize the vulnerability of women and to justify the prosecution of all pornographers. "Perhaps the single most common feature of models is their relative, and in the vast majority of cases, absolute youth." By definition, pornographers are exploiting young girls when they pay women to perform sex acts in front of cameras.

Exploiting women-as-young-girls, they are performing a class action against women's full citizenship in the U.S. public sphere.

> Pornographers promote an image of free consent because it is good for business. But most women in pornography are poor, were sexually abused as children, and have reached the end of this society's options for them, options that were biased against them as women in the first place. This alone does not make them coerced for purposes of the Ordinance; but the fact that some women may "choose" pornography from a stacked deck of life pursuits (if you call a loaded choice a choice, like the "choice" of those with brown skin to pick cabbages or the "choice" of those with black skin to clean toilets) and the fact that some women in pornography say they made a free choice does not mean that women who are coerced into pornography are *not coerced*. Pimps roam bus stations to entrap young girls who left incestuous homes thinking nothing could be worse. . . . Young women are tricked or pressured into posing for boyfriends and told that the pictures are just "for us," only to find themselves in this month's *Hustler*. . . . Women in pornography are bound, battered, tortured, harassed, raped, and some- times killed. . . . Children are presented as adult women; adult women are presented as children, fusing the vulnerability of a child with the sluttish eagerness to be fucked said to be natural to the female of every age.[25]

Leo Bersani has argued that the big secret about sex is that most people don't like it, but also that the fundamental transgressiveness and irrationali- ty of sex makes its enactment a crucial opportunity to resist the dead identi- ties of the social.[26] We see in the antipornographic polemic of MacKinnon and Dworkin a fundamental agreement with Bersani's position, although they reach antithetical conclusions: they would argue, more dramatically, that the little girl too sexualized to be a citizen has no privilege, no "adult" advantages, that would allow her to shuttle between legitimated sociality and a sexual resistance to it. Rather, she is the opposite of "someone who matters, someone with rights, a full human being, and a full citizen."[27] The sentimental logic of this antipornography argument thus links women and children to the nation in a variety of ways. In terms of the public contexts where civil rights are experienced as a matter of everyday life, women are paradoxically both the bearers of the value of privacy and always exposed and available to be killed into identity, which is to say into photography, into a sexual optic, and into heterosexuality, but not the sacred kind. Thus the cycle of pornography: it makes men child abusers who sentimentalize and degrade their objects; meanwhile, because young girls and women need to survive both materially and psychically in a culture of abuse, they become addicted to the stereotypical structure of sexual value and exploitation, forced to become subjects either in or to pornography. In this way the child's, the young girl's, vulnerability is the scene merely covered over and displaced by the older woman's pseudoautonomy; the young girl's minority is the true scene of arrested development of all American women's second-class citizenship. For this reason, this logic of infantile second-class citizenship has become both a moral dominant in the public sphere and a precedent in court prosecution of pornography.

Court prosecution of pornography found its excuse to rescue adult women from pornographic performance by taking the image of the vulnerable child performer of sex acts as the auratic truth of the adult. The Supreme Court decision in *New York v. Ferber* in 1982 for the first time extended the Court's analysis of such material to encompass the "privacy interests" of the performers—in this case, children. Filming children in the midst of explicit sexual activity harmed them not only because of the sexual abuse involved, but also because "the materials produced are a permanent record of the children's participation and the harm to the child is exacerbated by their circulation." In addition, the continued existence of a market for such materials was bound to make it more likely that children would be abused in the future, thus justifying a ban on distribution.[28] We have seen this argument before—that child abuse begets itself, that child porn begets both abuse and porn, and that these beget the damaged inner children of adult women, who therefore must be saved from the child pornography that is the truth of their submission to the sex apparatus that befouls the national culture whose privileges women have either no access to or access to only by virtue of proximity to heterosexual genital intercourse. The stakes of this vision of juridical deliverance therefore are not just personal to some American women, but reveal fundamental conditions of national identity for all women in the United States.

Even more striking is how vital a horizon of fantasy national culture remains, even to some radicals, in its promise of corporeal safety and the privacy of deep shadow. When Dworkin asserts that women's everyday experience of sexual degradation in the United States is both a condition of their second-class citizenship and the most fundamental betrayal of them all, she also seeks to occupy the most politically privileged privacy protections of the very national sexuality whose toxic violence defines the lives of American women. Here America's promise to release its citizens from having a body to humiliate trumps the feminist or materialist visionary politics Dworkin might have espoused, politics that would continue to imagine a female body as a citizen's body that remains vulnerable because public and alive, engaged in the ongoing struggles of making history.

How to Raise PG Kids in an X-Rated Nation

We have seen that in Washington the nationalist aspirations to iconicity of the high arts and the ars erotica play out a wish to dissolve the body. They reveal a desire for identity categories to be ontological, dead to history, not in any play or danger of representation, anxiety, improvisation, desire, or panic. This sentimentality suggests how fully the alarm generated around identity politics in the United States issues from a nostalgia or desire for a suprahistorical nationally secured personhood that does not look to acts of history or the body for its identifications. Recently, the education of the American into these fantasy norms of citizenship has become an obsession about pedagogy. My third inhibit in this argument about how the moral domination of live sex works in contemporary U.S. culture takes the form of a book report on Tipper Gore's *Raising PG Kids in an X-Rated Society.*[29]

It would be very easy to cite passages from this book in order to humiliate it. It is full of bad mixed metaphors, pseudoscience, and rickety thinking. But I want to take seriously its images of the citizen as a minor. The mirror that Gore looks into shows a terrible national present and foretells a frightening future for what she calls our national character. Her representation of the inner child of national culture repeats precisely the icon of feminized infantile vulnerability I have described as the scene of national anxiety in the previous two sections of this essay; she assumes as well the absolute value of the implicit, private, sacred, heterofamilial fetish of national culture. But my main interest is to trace the logic and social theory of citizen action that emerges here, which has become dominant in the contemporary U.S. public sphere, for reasons I have tried to suggest. The book's very reference to "PG kids" in its title suggests a theory of national personhood in which each person is an undeveloped film whose encounters with traumatic images and narratives might well make him or her a traumatized person who repeats the trauma the way a film repeats scenes. It suggests that a rating system for such persons might reveal their identities to each other and protect us all from the mere repetition of violence that is the social text of the United States, an X-rated place with X-rated adult citizens begetting a generation of monsters (someone might call it "Generation X").

Raising PG Kids in an X-Rated Society opens like a slasher film, with a scene of Tipper Gore fleeing New York City to the "familiarity, love, and comfort of home" in bucolic Washington, D.C.[30] Yet she finds that the sin of the big city has invaded Washington through the infectious circuits of mass culture. At home Gore faces what she has purchased for her eleven-year-old daughter: a record, *Purple Rain,* which contains "Darling Nikki," a song that glamorizes masturbation. With MTV, Gore realizes Prince and his ilk make sexual trouble for her daughters: "These images frightened my children; they frightened *me!*"[31] Gore then sets out on a pilgrimage from her living room, through Washington, to the nation, to defend youth from premature contact with sex. By "sex" she means the practice of violent liveness the antipornography activists described above also imagine, as portrayed here in lyrics, on album covers, in rock concerts, and on MTV. Meanwhile, what she means by "youth" is similarly elastic, as the vulnerable little-girl citizen of American culture ranges in this book from age one to her early twenties, the time when, Gore admits, kids are finally competent to enter "sexual relationships."[32] However, she also uses the consumer bromide "youth of all ages" to describe the ongoing surprise, hurt, humiliation, and upset even adults experience when having unwonted encounters with all kinds of "excess," including sex, alcohol, drugs, suicide, and satanism.

Under the pressure of this youth crisis, which also generalizes to all ages and is therefore in her view a crisis of national character and national culture, Gore joined with other concerned wives of men powerful in the U.S. state apparatus to engender a counterpublic sphere—via the Parents Music Resource Center (PMRC)—whose purpose is to make the profit-driven sexually suffused popular-music industry nationally accountable for terrorizing a generation of American youths through premature exposure to a world of live sex acts. Gore claims her arguments are antimarket but not anticapitalist, anti–sexual explicitness but not pro-censorship, "pro-morality" but not antisex. She notes acutely that there seems to be a lyric/narrative hierarchy in obscenity law. Although children are indeed not permitted access to adult films, books, and magazines, they are permitted access to equally explicit record covers, live-performance rock concerts and videos of songs, as well as lyrics that perform the same acts minors are not allowed to consume when they are not the market population designated by capitalists. "If no one under eighteen can *buy Penthouse* magazine," she writes, "why should children be subjected to . . . hard-core porn in the local record shop? A recent album from the Dead Kennedys band contained a graphic poster of multiple erect penises penetrating vaginas. Where's the difference? In the hands of a few warped artists, their brand of rock music has become a Trojan Horse, rolling explicit sex and violence into our homes."[33]

In addition to pointing out the intemperance of the record industry and the artists who produce what she calls "porn rock," and in addition to exposing the contradictions in the law's stated intention to protect children, two other issues dominate Gore's reading of the general crisis in national culture. They do not involve critiques of the immorality of capitalism and law. They involve the failure of American adults to be competent parents and a passionate argument to extend the model of infantile citizenship to nonminor U.S. citizens through an image of the adult citizen as social parent. In particular, Gore depicts the devastating effects of adults' general

▼ Live Sex Acts

73

refusal to acknowledge the specifically limited capacities of children, such that proper boundaries between children and adults are no longer being drawn. She also testifies to the failure of the family to compensate for the escalating norms of sexual and corporeal violence in everyday life, mass culture, and the public sphere at large.

Gore turns to social scientists and psychologists to mourn the loss of childhood in America: not only in families with latchkey children whose mothers work, not only in broken families (that is, ones without fathers), but even in the 7 percent of families with intact originary parental couples, stay-at-home mothers, and fully genetically related children, parents have begun to mistake the eloquence of children for "mature reasoning powers and critical skills."[34] She argues that "anyone who attempts to debate the porn rock issue as if young people are in the same intellectual and emotional category as adults does them a terrible injustice. We need to let children be children. Children think differently from adults, and process information according to their own stages of development."[35]

If the cognitive difference between children and adults were not enough to require special adult wisdom with respect to superintending the lives of children, Gore goes on to show that the dissolution of the "smiling nuclear family," increases in family violence, spouse abuse, and child abuse, and, most dramatically, the "violent world" of life in the United States have resulted simultaneously in the saturation of children's minds with scenes of terror and the desensitization of their minds toward terror, through its transformation into pleasure and entertainment.[36] Gore argues that adults have ruined American society with their excesses, with their will to make public intimate and complicated relations, like sex, and with their negligent complacence about the violence, annihilation, exploitation, and neglect into which children are thrust daily. This sacrifice to the indulgences of U.S. adulthood is the distinguishing mark of the generation of children that currently exists. In contrast, Gore distinguishes (and, one must say, misremembers) her own generation, which we might call the generation of 1968, by its relation to two key texts: "Twist and Shout" and *I Love Lucy*.[37]

Thus when Tipper Gore places the words "Explicit material—parental advisory" on the title page of her book, we are to understand that her project is to train incompetent American adults to be parents, as a matter of civic and nationalist pedagogy. Although all Americans are youths in her view—in other words, incompetent to encounter live sex acts or any sex in public—she also desperately tries to redefine "adult" into a category of social decay more negative than any national category since the "delinquent" of the 1950s. The new virtuous category of majority is "parent." The new activist citizenship Tipper Gore imagines to express the true morality of U.S. national culture refuses the contradictions of traditional patriarchal privilege that both moralizes against and promotes the erotic terrorizing of women and children. (No sympathetic mention is made of the sexually terrorized Others on the live margins of national heterosexuality.) In every chapter Gore advises parents to think of parenting as a public profession, like being a lawyer or a politician, and she encourages what she calls "parental solidarity" groups to take the private activity of nurturing children away from mass-media-induced but home-circulated materials that promote sex and violence. She imagines a nation controlled by a local, public, community matrix of parental public spheres.[38] Above all, she characterizes this grassroots model of citizenship on behalf of the "rights" parents have to control what they and their children encounter as a model for national political agency itself. Here are the last words of Gore's conclusion: "It's not easy being a parent these days. It's even tougher being a kid. Perhaps together we can help our society grow up."[39]

Wild Things

I was cruising, one early spring morning, the Sunday-morning talk shows: *Meet the Press, This Week with David Brinkley, Face the Nation.* But along the way I ran across a couple of video events that I have not yet recovered from seeing. The first was a Jerry Falwell commercial, played during the *Old Time Gospel Hour.* In this minute-long segment he offers us the opportunity to spend four dollars engaging in citizenship acts. We might call 1-900-288-3402 in support of "the new homosexual rights agenda" soon, he says, to be signed into law by President Clinton. Or we might call 1-900-288-3401 to say that although we pray for the president, we do not support "the new homosexual rights agenda," we do not want our "children to grow up in an America where a new homosexual rights agenda" is law. He keeps repeating the phrase "new homosexual rights agenda" and posts the phone numbers on the TV screen, the background for which is a purple, and not a lavender-tinted, American flag. Next I flipped to C-SPAN, which happened—I say "happened" as though it were random—to be showing a tape of a speech given by Major Melissa Wells-Petry, sponsored by the Christian Action Network, a speech shown at least once later the same day, which I taped and watched compulsively. Major Wells-Petry, a U.S. military attorney, is giving a speech about why gays ought to be barred from the military. She describes the vast incompatibility of the nation and the gay man; she knows the law, well, colloquially. Her reason for rejecting a gay presence in the military is that when someone says, "I am a homosexual," there are "data" to support that he is "likely to engage in homosexual acts." There is no possibility that a homosexual has an identity that is not evidenced in acts. She says the courts have proven that to be homosexual is to behave as a homosexual, just as a pilot can be said to be a pilot because he flies airplanes. I have no idea if she is secretly thinking about the "cruising" altitude of planes, or about the cliché that queers are light in the loafers. In any case, she also argues that gayness is only one of many behavioral identities the army bars from service, and she names two others: in an aside, she notes that fatness makes you unfit for service; more elaborately, she recounts a case where a Nazi walked into a recruiting station and asked to enlist, but was barred from enlisting because being a Nazi makes you unfit to serve in the U.S. military. I fell into a dream that day, about *Griswold v. Connecticut* and *Roe v. Wade,* two cases I was teaching the following week. These two cases are generally thought to be crucial to the struggle to gain sex equality in the United States. *Griswold v. Connecticut* made it possible for married couples to buy birth control; *Roe v. Wade* made it possible to abort some fetuses birth control didn't prevent from being conceived. But the language about heterosexuality and pregnancy these cases promoted did nothing to shake up the normative relations of sex and nationality in modern America. In my dream, I tried to explain to someone in a supermarket how the zone of privacy established for married sex acts in *Griswold* even further enshrined heterosexual reproductive activity as the fundamental patriotic American fetish, so powerful it was entirely private, it was the only fixed sign in the national language. Indeed, I insisted on telling her, and with great painful prolixity, of Justice Harlan's cited opinion: "The right of privacy is not an absolute. Thus, I would not suggest that adultery, homosexuality, forni-cation and incest are immune from criminal enquiry, however privately practiced. . . . [But] the intimacy of husband and wife is necessarily an es-sential and accepted feature of the institution of marriage, an institution which the State not only must allow, but which always and in every age it has fostered and protected."[40] Then, somehow bored in my own dream, I turned my back and looked out the window, where I saw a pregnant woman wandering naked in traffic. I watched her, transfixed, for the longest time. When I awoke, I asked myself, what is the wish of the dream? I didn't know, but what flashed up instead was a line from *Roe v. Wade* that goes, "The pregnant woman cannot be isolated in her privacy."[41]

Let me review the argument: insofar as an American thinks that the sex he or she is having is an intimate, private thing constructed within the lines of personal consent, intention, and will, he or she is having straight sex, straight sex authorized by national culture; he or she is practicing national heterosexuality, which makes the sex act dead, in the sense I have described, using a kind of metaphor that foregrounds heterosexuality's function as a sacred national fetish beyond the disturbances of history or representation, protected by a zone of privacy.

The privacy zone that projects national culture as a shadow effect of scandalous or potentially destabilizing acts of sexual alterity has a history, and I have tried to telegraph it here as a history of some live acts that counter an ideology of dead citizenship. Most important, until recently there has never been, in the United States, a public sphere organized around sex and sexuality—that is to say, a public sphere demarcated by what Geoff Eley has described as a political culture.[42] The prehistory of this moment must transform our accounts of the contemporary public sphere as well as of citizenship, nationality, acts, identities, sex, and so on. It might start with racial and gendered corporeal counterpolitics of the period after the Civil War, part of a general citizen reform movement, but also specifically around issues of property and reproduction, the two most sacrosanct areas the Constitution designates. Suffrage meant to bring these nineteenth-century primitivist categories into national modernity, and the history of national sentimentality this essay partly tells has to do with the public failure of suffrage to solve the relation between the body and the state in the United States, such that a tactical shuttling between assimilation and banishment remains central to the complicated histories of those sexed, racialized, female, underclassed subjects who can be seen animating the live margins of the U.S. scene. In any case, as the Queer Nation motto "We Are Everywhere, We Want Everything" suggests, the scandal of sexual subculture in the contemporary American context derives in part from its insistence on a noninfantilized political counterpublic that refuses to tie itself to a dead identity; that sees sexuality as a set of acts and world-building activities whose implications are always radically TBA; that seeks to undermine the patriotic ethics in which it is deemed virtuous to aspire to live in abstract America, a place where bodies do not live historically, complexly, or incoherently, guided by a putatively rational, civilized standard. The basic sex-radical tactic has been to countercorporealize at every moment, and so to de-elect the state and other social formations that have patriarchalized and parentalized national culture. This is not enough, as Michael Warner has argued.[43] But it is the beginning of a *movement*, and it's a live one.

This is to say that a radical social theory of sexual citizenship in the United States must not aspire to reoccupy the dead identities of privacy, or name the innocence of youth as the index of adult practice and knowledge, or nationalize sexuality or sex as the central mode of self-legitimation or public identity making. In this way it can avoid repeating the utopian identification that infantile citizenship promises, which distracts everyone from turning to the nation form and thinking about its inexhaustible energy for harnessing capitalism to death through promises of eternal identity and images of life activity. It can then avoid repeating the struggle between crassness and sentimental sublimity that defines all of our bodies in the United States; all of our live sex if we're lucky enough to have it; our dead citizenship; and our potentially undead desires to form a live relation to power, nature, sensation, and history within or outside the nation form as we know it. The risk is that peeling away the fantasies that both sustain and cover over the sexual bodies living the good life in the zone of privacy will also tear away some important protective coverings, like the fantasy of privacy itself, the way a Band-Aid covering an unhealed wound will take away part of the wound and its bit of healing with it. But such violence and failure, such an opening of the wound to air, is a foundational condition for the next steps, which, after all, remain to be taken, seen, and critiqued, though not rated with an X, a PG, or a thumbs-up—unless the thumb is related to something else, like a fist.

Notes

My thanks to Roger Rouse, Kim Scheppele, Michael Warner, Jody Greene, and the great audiences at the University of Michigan, Rutgers, Harvard, and Brown for much-needed conversation and challenge.

1. Andrea Dworkin quoted in Edward de Grazia, *Girls Lean Back Everywhere: The Law of Obscenity and the Assault on Genius* (New York: Random House, 1992), 581.

2. Michael Kammen describes the particularly intensified manipulations of national nostalgia and amnesia during the gestation and rise of the Reaganite right in *Mystic Chords of Memory: The Transformation of Tradition in American Culture* (New York: Vintage, 1993), 618–88.

3. Taussig names this saturation of politics by the nation "state fetishism." This is a condition in which the state uses a sublime and magical official story of national identity to mask the nation's heterogeneity. See Michael Taussig, "*Maleficium*: State Fetishism," in *The Nervous System* (New York: Routledge, 1993), 111–40, 223.

4. The original texts meant to be reviewed were Alison Assiter, *Pornography, Feminism, and the Individual* (London: Pluto, 1989); Gail Chester and Julienne Dickey, eds., *Feminism and Censorship: The Current Debate* (Bridgeport, Dorset, Eng.: Prism, 1988); Andrea Dworkin, *Pornography: Men Possessing Women* (New York: Penguin, 1989); Susan Gubar and Joan Hoff-Wilson, eds., *For Adult Users Only: The Dilemma of Violent Pornography* (Bloomington: Indiana University Press, 1989); Gordon Hawkins, and Franklin E. Zimring, *Pornography in a Free Society* (New York: Cambridge University Press, 1991); Catherine Itzin, ed., *Pornography: Women, Violence, and Civil Liberties* (Oxford: Oxford University Press, 1993). I have also read more widely in the literature pro and con, and assume the entire oeuvre of Catharine MacKinnon in this essay as well. Of those listed above, the British feminist texts (Assiter, Itzin, Chester and Dickey) share with the work of MacKinnon and Dworkin a sense that issues of sexual difference cannot be solved by U.S.-style liberal thinking about ontological selfhood, but must address the ways the state and the nation frame the conditions of sex, sexual identity, and gender value. Of the U.S. texts that do not take a clear pornography-is-patriarchy position, the most useful is *For Adult Users Only*, which rehearses and I think extends the feminist debate over the causes, effects, and possibilities pornography poses for American women. But the discussion of sexuality and public life is stunted by the referential dullness or

hyperelasticity of the category of "pornography," along with the unstated hetero-normative assumption (about what "good" sexuality is, about the relation of the natural and the normal, about what "bad" representations do) that almost always accompanies these discussions. A scrupulous specificity is necessary for any discussion of politically rezoning the place where national culture meets intimacy forms of sex. That is why in this chapter I seek to place this discussion of national sexuality in a context of thinking the sexual politics of citizenship in the United States.

5. Quoted in *New York Times,* May 25, 1993, A8.

6. I take this way of thinking about the processes of making an institution appear hegemonic from Chandra Mohanty, who takes it from Dorothy Smith. See Chandra Mohanty, "Cartographies of Struggle: Third World Women and the Politics of Feminism," in *Third World Women and the Politics of Feminism,* ed. Chandra Mohanty, Ann Russo, and Lourdes Torres (Bloomington: Indiana University Press, 1991), 15–16; Dorothy E. Smith, *The Everyday World as Problematic: A Feminist Sociology* (Toronto: University of Toronto Press, 1998), 108.

7. John Frohnmayer, *Leaving Town Alive: Confessions of an Arts Warrior* (Boston: Houghton Mifflin, 1993), 3, 337, and passim.

8. Ibid., 314, 202.

9. Quoted in ibid., 324.

10. Ibid., 326.

11. Wodiczko's "Homeless Vehicle" has generated a number of consequential essays, the most important of which, for thinking subjectivity, capitalism, and citizenship, is Neil Smith's, "Contours of a Spatialized Politics: Homeless Vehicles and the Production of Geographical Space," *Social Text* 33 (1992): 54–81.

12. Frohnmayer, *Leaving Town Alive,* 291, 324–25.

13. Ibid., 69. The "Helms amendment" was offered to the U.S. Senate on October 7, 1989. It reads: "None of the funds authorized to be appropriated pursuant to this Act may be used to promote, discriminate, or produce materials that are obscene or that depict or describe, in a patently offensive way, sexual or excretory activities or organs, including but not limited to obscene depictions of sadomasochism, homo-eroticism, the sexual exploitation of children, or individuals engaged in sexual intercourse." See *Congressional Record,* 135, no. 134 (1989): S 12967.

14. De Grazia, *Girls Lean Back Everywhere,* 637.

15. Frohnmayer, *Leaving Town Alive,* 326, 328–29.

16. De Grazia, *Girls Lean Back Everywhere,* 4–5.

17. Ibid., 436–37. See also Edward de Grazia, *Censorship Landmarks* (New York: Bowker, 1969).

18. Andrea Dworkin and Catharine A. MacKinnon, *Pornography and Civil Rights: A New Day for Women's Equality* (Minneapolis: Organizing against Pornography, 1988), 48.

19. *Jacobellis v. Ohio,* 378 U.S. 184 (1964); see also de Grazia, *Girls Lean Back Everywhere,* 423–33.

20. Carole S. Vance, "The Pleasures of Looking: The Attorney General's Commission on Pornography versus Visual Images," in *The Critical Image: Essays on Contemporary Photography,* ed. Carol Squiers (Seattle: Bay, 1990).

21. See Robin West, "Pornography as a Legal Text," in Gubar and Hoff-Wilson, *For Adult Users Only,* 108–30.

22. Quoted in Attorney General's Commission on Pornography, *Final Report,* vol. 1, July 1986, 839.

23. Ibid.

24. Ibid., 839–40.

25. Dworkin and MacKinnon, *Pornography and Civil Rights,* 43, 45–46.

26. Leo Bersani, "Is the Rectum a Grave?" in *AIDS: Cultural Analysis/Cultural Activism,* ed. Douglas Crimp (Cambridge: MIT Press, 1988).

27. Dworkin and MacKinnon, *Pornography and Civil Rights,* 46.

28. Attorney General's Commission on Pornography, *Final Report,* vol. 1, 849.

29. Tipper Gore, *Raising PG Kids in an X-Rated Society* (Nashville: Abingdon, 1987).

30. Ibid., 17.

31. Ibid., 18.

32. Ibid., 41.

33. Ibid., 28.

34. Ibid., 39.

35. Ibid., 42.

36. Ibid., 43–48.

37. Ibid., 11.

38. For all its greater liberalism and greater belief in the wisdom of a welfare state, Hillary Rodham Clinton's *It Takes a Village and Other Lessons Children Teach Us* (New York: Simon & Schuster, 1996) fully joins Gore's *Raising PG Kids* in characterizing the ideal United States as a parental public sphere.

39. Gore, *Raising PG Kids,* 167.

40. *Griswold v. Connecticut,* 381 U.S. 479 (1965).

41. *Roe v. Wade,* 410 U.S. 113, 159 (1973).

42. Geoff Eley, "Nations, Publics, and Political Cultures: Placing Habermas in the Nineteenth Century," in *Habermas and the Public Sphere,* ed. Craig Calhoun (Cambridge: MIT Press, 1996), 289–339.

43. Michael Warner, "The Mass Public and the Mass Subject," in *Habermas and the Public Sphere,* ed. Craig Calhoun (Cambridge: MIT Press, 1996), 399–400.

Narrating the Child's Queerness in *What Maisie Knew*

Kevin Ohi

Innocence is a lot like the air in your tires: there's not a lot you can do with it but lose it.

—*James R. Kincaid,* Erotic Innocence, *1998*

Eve Kosofsky Sedgwick has written about the punitive effects on children of the homophobic regulation of gender identity in psychiatric practice, the murderous cultural and institutional reaction to perceived signs of gay incipience guided, she suggests, by the overarching fantasy of the eradication of the homosexual.[1] Her reading also implies the possibility of a more thoroughgoing fantasy of queer extinction—*queer* in the sense not just of other dissident sexualities (sadomasochism or intergenerational desire, for instance) that might thereby be named, but of a resistance to containment in such legible identity categories. This fantasy might be emblematized by our culture's frantic regulation of childhood sexuality. Sedgwick's argument makes manifest, among other things, the homophobic violence implicit in understandings of childhood sexuality even when homosexuality—or its expunging—is not explicitly or thematically at stake, a violence that extends to all desires outside of heteronormativity.

The fantasy of queer extinction is made manifest in the impossibility, within the dominant language of our culture, of conceiving of an identification with queerness, which means that even those (allegedly laudable) representations—more or less "positive" though they might be—of various dissident sexualities are nearly always given (however tendentiously) from a perspective other than their own, or (in what amounts to the same thing) from a perspective reductively ascribed or attributed to them, as an object of a gaze that is, for instance, condemning, chastening, horrified, fascinated, anthropological, or sympathetic. Framing a resistance to this structure of sexual normativity in terms of recognition—as important as it may be to resist our culture's murderous disregard for proto-gay, proto-pedophilic, proto-masochistic, proto-voyeuristic lives by, among other things, insisting that such desires be recognized and validated in their existence and in their incipience—may, however, persist in maintaining one of the central tenets of the sexual ideology a project of queer liberation would resist. Panics about childhood sexuality concern above all the adult's fears about his or her own desire, the threat posed by the sexual child to the serenity of adult self-understandings. At stake, in other words, is the possibility of recognition itself; children are queer because they thwart such comforting self-recognitions. To say that children aren't queer is a way of asserting that we know what children are and that we therefore know what adults are. To argue that all children are queer, then, is not to argue that all children feel same-sex desire (which, for all I know, they do). Rather, it is to suggest that childhood marks a similar locus of impossibility, of murderous disidentification; the disidentification with childhood queerness presumes, in other words, to recognize it, and to recognize it by emptying it of reference to anything but an incipient normativity. *Innocence* is the term through which this disidentification is achieved, the term that is deployed to contain the queerness of the child.

James Kincaid has explored the disidentification with children through what he calls "erotic innocence": the thoroughgoing eroticization of children in our culture proceeds, he suggests, by way of their emphatic de-eroticization, a cultural doublespeak that allows us the pleasures of imagining and perpetuating the victimization of children while praising ourselves for protecting them. Innocence, he suggests, is a rhetorical category; its particular disavowals, self-justifications, and recriminations mark the traces of a violent disidentification with children that constructs childhood by voiding it of content:

> This new thing, the modern child, was deployed as a political and philo-
> sophical agent, a weapon to assault what had been taken as virtues: adult-
> hood, sophistication, rational moderation, judicious adjustment to the ways

of the world. The child was used to deny these virtues, to eliminate them and substitute in their place a set of inversions: innocence, purity, emptiness. Childhood, to a large extent, came to be in our culture a coordinate set of *have nots,* of negations: the child was the one who *did not have.*[2]

The construction of erotic innocence, Kincaid notes, is hardly innocent: "The constructions of modern 'woman' and modern 'child' are very largely evacuations, the ruthless distribution of eviction notices."[3] Erotic innocence must be continually reasserted; absence and emptiness have to be actively created, entailing a bulldozing of whatever happens to stand in the way. Articulations of erotic innocence thus tend to undermine themselves through the titillating eroticism of innocence. It is not merely that imagining innocence violated is a salaciously enjoyable undertaking in itself; more important, the obliterative operation of naming innocence performs a violation analogous to the imagined illegality. The disavowed erotic thrills of an innocence attribution that is always also innocence's demise account for our fascination with children who are uncannily the opposite of innocent. Children, in other words, are scary because they are purported to be innocent: the unfeeling, undead, uncannily knowing child of horror films is an incestuous sibling of the innocent, transcendently vacant child of our favorite spine tinglers about molested youth. The primary difference is the mode through which desire is disavowed: in the former case, desire is transmuted into salacious ecstasies of self-righteous (and narrative-righting) violence directed toward the child who has uncannily taken the place of our illicit desire for it; in the latter, the violence of our disavowal is played out through salacious ecstasies of self-righteous violence directed toward the demonized molester who desires on our behalf. The disavowal of desire for the child (in each case, through an unacknowledged identification) by way of fantasies of childhood innocence carries, in its various forms, a heavy tax of violence. These dramas of identification and disidentification point to how queer the child is in our culture—and not just the child who dares to utter its queer desires and thus to make itself the unwanted child everyone is afraid to love, but any child insofar as it is purported to be innocent.

Innocence, although valorized in different, if in sometimes overlapping, ways than is heterosexuality, is thus established through a rhetorical violence not dissimilar to the negation of homosexual possibility that Sedgwick has ranged under the rhetorical term *preterition,* the "centuries-long historical chain of substantive uses of space-clearing negatives to void and at the same time to underline the possibility of male same-sex genitality."[4] As Sedgwick suggests of this "quasi-nominative, quasi-obliterative" structure in relation to the denomination of homosexuality, the reifying effect of erotic innocence "is, if anything, more damaging than (though not separable from) its obliterative effect."[5] It is therefore crucial to note that to argue that childhood marks a locus of impossibility, of murderous disidentification, and even to propose the necessity of a corrective identification with childhood is not necessarily to insist on a reified or knowable entity with which to identify. The murderous disidentification with children attempts to ensure not only that all desires be heterosexual but that all desires be recognizable as desires, and the queerness of childhood sexuality might therefore pose a threat not only to heteronormative conceptions of identity but to "positive" or "affirmative" ones (of whatever particular proscribed desire or identity category) as well. An identification with childhood queerness makes manifest that childhood "desire" might not be recognizable as desire, might not be analogous to or recognizable by any adult desire, might not be possible to inscribe in any representational project. At the same time, it is also important to stress that the murderous disidentification with children under the aegis of erotic innocence imposes its rendering intelligible of childhood in specific terms and works in concert with homophobia. Its insistence on the blank innocence of childhood is also an insistence on a (future and legibly incipient) heterosexuality; that which remains unrecognizable to adult heterosexuality is thus voided—either assimilated to heterosexuality or pathologized as a perverse symptom whose source of contamination needs to be (and can be) isolated, reified, and expunged.

Erotic innocence proceeds most importantly through its assumptions of knowingness: it *knows* what a child is, and the certainty of that knowledge—and the knowledge of what adults are that it shores up—is what it seeks, above all, to maintain. To oppose erotic innocence with a certainty of one's own about what children are—for instance, simply to invert its certainties—is to stay within the terms it dictates. The crucial task, therefore, is to make childhood desires legible without reifying them, to recognize them without such presumption of knowledge. Seen from this perspective, Henry James's *What Maisie Knew* (1897) is startlingly prescient and innovative.[6] It tells its story from the perspective of a child while marking the impossibility of that perspective, theorizing both this impossibility and its exploitation of it. It frankly exploits a child without blindly succumbing to the presumptuous knowingness of erotic innocence. It imagines the possibility of identifying with a child by exploring the impossibility of the child's position, and it connects such a desiring identification with a child (and its impossibility) to its own project of novelistic representation, a project that the novel figures, I will suggest, in terms of exchange.

What Maisie Knew is about a desirable child, and it uses this child to articulate larger aesthetic structures and to suggest that these aesthetic structures are also erotic ones; its construction of a narrative voice, its reflection on its own taking shape, its exploration of stylistic and figural effects of irony are all inseparable from the eroticization of a child. Although its premise would have lent itself to a sentimental or gothic narrative about a child's victimization, the novel is less about innocence corrupted by experience than about the pleasures of seducing a child. Part of this pleasure is generated by the way the novel disarticulates assumptions that an identification with a child (victimized or not) prohibits or precludes (or ought to prohibit or preclude) desiring that child, just as it disarticulates an ideology that equates both desiring a child and recognizing a child's desires with, simply, child abuse. The novel urges us to desire and identify with Maisie, to take pleasure in her discoveries. When I read *What Maisie Knew,* I do not "wince," as Dan McCall would have me do, as Maisie loses her innocence and becomes "good at a game she should never have to play."[7] I am less appalled by "the death of her childhood" than I am thrilled by her adventure.[8] I want Maisie to learn, and I want her to know—about her parents and stepparents, about her world, about sex. It is part of the novel's power that it makes such a desiring identification seem inevitable; the pleasure of the novel challenges many of the certainties of the ideology of erotic innocence. Among other things, to read the novel as an unequivocal denunciation of exploitation or corruption is to simplify its narration, which manages complex effects of sympathy and distance through its free-indirect discourse. The various effects—allowing the narrative, for instance, to ironize positions it simultaneously takes—center, as I will discuss, on its focalization through Maisie. The novel's free-indirect narration—which makes the narrator at once a palpable presence in the experience of the text and strangely unlocatable—is largely what allows it to present a desiring identification with Maisie that does not reproduce the knowingness of erotic innocence.

To say that the novel frankly presents Maisie as a figure to be loved, desired, and identified with is not to deny that she is often given rather shoddy treatment. Mark Seltzer suggests that the cult of ambiguity in James studies serves to perpetuate operations of power in the texts themselves, writing that "James advertises . . . the bewilderment and 'muddle' of *What Maisie Knew,* a text that enacts the transformation of sex into discourse in the form of a prurient innocence."[9] To be attentive to this narrative of power suggests that the novel links questions of point of view and form less to a generalizable "ambiguity" than to the particular relations of power that inform Maisie's position. I will return to the overlapping of Maisie's role at the crux of various systems of exchange, establishing, on the one hand, relations among the characters and, on the other, the narration itself as an analogous system of exchange; the potential discomfort of her role in both respects and her relative disempowerment are made manifest in the way she is treated, which the text registers with an unnerving sangfroid. People say astonishingly awful things to her. "Your horrid little mind has been poisoned, . . . [and] you've no more feeling for me than a clammy little fish," says her mother (72), who also calls her a "little nuisance" (164), a "little horror" (169), and a "dreadful dismal deplorable little thing" (170). "It doesn't in the least matter, you know, what you think," she tells her daughter, "and you had better indeed for the future, miss, learn to keep your thoughts to yourself" (22). "Your father," she later informs Maisie, "wishes you were dead" (166). ("You're old enough at any rate to know," she continues, "there are a lot of things I don't say that I easily might; though it would do me good, I assure you, to have spoken my mind for once in my life" [166], but one is hard-pressed to imagine just what she might hold back.) Her father calls her "an obstinate little pig" (147) and a "dirty little donkey" (120), and remarks, "You know your mother loathes you, loathes you simply" (142). Mrs. Beale calls her an "abominable little horror," and even Sir Claude calls her a "dunce" (121).

Beyond being told how horrible she is ("clammy little fish" is my favorite), Maisie is prodded, poked, pushed, pulled, and smothered in hugs to which she is curiously irrelevant, offered as they are not to her but to the gaze of some spectator. If, at the end of the text, Mrs. Beale is said to have "made, with a great fierce jump, a wild snatch at her stepdaughter" (264), Maisie has from the beginning of the novel been made used to such wild snatchings, to more or less violent encounters with adults. "The greatest effect of the great cause," her parents' divorce and feud, the performance they seem to put on for this "mite of a half-scared infant in a great dim theatre," was

> her own greater importance, chiefly revealed to her in the larger freedom
> with which she was handled, pulled hither and thither and kissed, and
> the proportionately greater niceness she was obliged to show. Her features
> had somehow become prominent; they were so perpetually nipped by the
> gentlemen who came to see her father and the smoke of whose cigarettes
> went into her face. Some of these gentlemen made her strike matches and
> light their cigarettes; others, holding her on knees violently jolted, pinched
> the calves of her legs till she shrieked—her shriek was much admired—and
> reproached them with being toothpicks. The word stuck in her mind and
> contributed to her feeling from this time that she was deficient in some-
> thing that would meet the general desire. (15–16)

Her predicament is not only that of being so treated, but also of having to show a greater "niceness" proportionate to the "larger freedom with which she was handled." The "niceness" she is "obliged to show" makes the encountered violence an allegory for (and enactment of) socialization insofar as she must learn to dissimulate her feelings about it. Dissimulated or not, however, no protest would be legible in Maisie's milieu. Her lack of recourse is indicated by the text's neutral tone, which fails to note any registering on Maisie's part of the hostility directed toward her—"her shriek was much admired"—and the narration of such scenes makes it difficult to determine whether the sangfroid is the text's or Maisie's. Such an effect is captured by the description of her sense that "she was deficient in something that would meet the general desire." More than the fact that the language is oddly stilted and almost ostentatiously not hers, and more than the suggestion that Maisie is taking these complaints about her body literally (a literalism that seems nonetheless to understand the motivations, if not the intent, of the teasing), the text joins in with the gentlemen by making a spectacle of Maisie's failure to understand in ways curiously congruent with the gentlemanly nipping and pinching it describes. The passage, that is, seems to correlate the gentlemen's "freedom" with its own studied neutrality of tone, a tone enabled by its free-indirect narration, which hovers at an identificatory middle distance. The moment thus figures the coming together of the treatment of Maisie within the text and the text's treatment of her—that is, its narration. That, finally, the word "toothpick"—which seems to point to an oral rapacity on the part of these "gentlemen," a scarcely disguised, sadistic desire to devour Maisie—is said to have "stuck in her mind" suggests a performative aspect to the passage's language. A word sticking one like a toothpick might represent the congruity between a narrative "word" and a narrated "freedom."

The men around her "pulled and pinched, they teased and tickled her; some of them even, as they termed it, shied things at her, and all of them thought it funny to call her by names having no resemblance to her own" (35). Again, the text connects physical encounters—having things thrown at one, for instance—with linguistic effects, here, of appropriation or disenfranchisement through renaming, through being called names that have no resemblance to one's own. (And, again, the effect is redoubled by the sense that the text registers Maisie's misunderstanding of what seem to be nicknames, even if she does sense the potential hostility of such endearments.) Violence is further tied to language in that it becomes increasingly invisible in the novel, forming a background to Maisie's story, an atmosphere so taken for granted that it becomes not an event to be described but the ground of comparisons describing other events or conditions. Violence becomes part of the novel's own vocabulary, leading to performative effects similar to the "toothpick" that "stuck" in Maisie's mind. We are thus left uncertain, as Dan McCall notes, about the figural status of Sir Claude's description of Ida's desertion of Maisie as a "hideous crime": "She has chucked our friend here overboard not a bit less than if she had shoved her, shrieking and pleading, out of that window and down two floors to the paving-stones." When Maisie is then said to have "surveyed serenely the parties to the discussion," it seems possible that she is less unaware of the figure's violence than inured to it. Mrs. Wix's response further literalizes the violence: "Oh your friend here, dear Sir Claude, doesn't plead and shriek!" (183).

Maisie doesn't plead and shriek in part because she is caught in a peculiar predicament that enforces her passivity: "The child's discipline had been bewildering—it had ranged freely between the prescription that she was to answer when spoken to and the experience of lively penalties on obeying that prescription" (45). "Freely" seems to indicate something more like "arbitrarily" and seems an ironic index of the freedom Maisie does not have. She is not free partly because, as a child, she is dependent on adults; she can establish neither her independence nor the terms of her interaction with the people around her. From this position of exclusion, Maisie registers, much more than any instance of physical violence, the humiliating childhood misery of not knowing. She hates being laughed at and mocked for her childish ignorance, and when, for instance, Mrs. Wix excoriates her for lacking a "moral sense," she seems less ashamed of her lack of morals than of her lack of knowledge (207). In the novel's climactic scene in the hotel room with Mrs. Wix and her stepparents, as Mrs. Wix again accuses her of losing her "moral sense," Maisie's predicament—one, at this moment, of having to choose, impossibly, between people she loves—is phrased in terms of the shame of not knowing:

> It brought back to the child's recollection how she sometimes couldn't repeat on Friday the sentence that had been glib on Wednesday, and she dealt all feebly and ruefully with the present tough passage. Sir Claude and Mrs. Beale stood there like visitors at an "exam." She had indeed an instant a whiff of the faint flower that Mrs. Wix pretended to have plucked and now with such a peremptory hand thrust at her nose. Then it left her, and, as if she were sinking with a slip from a foothold, her arms made a short jerk. What this jerk represented was the spasm within her of something still deeper than a moral sense. She looked at her examiner; she looked at the visitors; she felt the rising of the tears she had kept down at the station. They had nothing—no, distinctly nothing—to do with her moral sense. The only thing was the old flat shameful schoolroom plea. "I don't know—I don't know." (261)

The "present tough passage" marks both her present experience and the present instance of a text that is difficult to memorize, a sentence that, once familiar to the point of being "glib," can no longer be repeated or reproduced. Such a blurring between experience and text—where failure to memorize a passage figures a social uncertainty about what to say in the "present tough passage"—mirrors other blurrings of register in the description. When Maisie's arms make "a short jerk," for instance, they seem to mark a crossing between different registers enacted somatically by Maisie's body. Her arms jerk "*as if* she were sinking with a slip from a foothold," and the disappearance of the "as if" by way of that somatic response—which also parallels her loss of the scent of the pretend flower—parallels the movement from simile to a more identificatory metaphor when, as the figure becomes literalized, Sir Claude and Mrs. Beale cease to be "like visitors at an 'exam'" and become simply "the visitors." Similarly, with this jerk her body also seems to act out a realization or inner revolution in a blending or forcible adequation of registers that the passage correlates to representation: "What this jerk *represented* was the spasm within her." The signifying adequation of outer "jerk" to inner "spasm" both establishes the representative status of her movement and breaches boundaries crucial to such adequation between literal and figural, inside and out, breaches that are enacted by Maisie's seemingly involuntary movement. The figurative patterns in the passage suggest that Maisie's lack of knowledge is less a matter of specific content than it is a generalizable linguistic predicament that Maisie is made, at this moment, to embody.

Maisie's predicament might be familiar to anyone who has been a child with a dawning sense of gay incipience because of the forcible translation of, on the one hand, generalizable linguistic or representational vicissitudes—adequations of inside and out, inner "spasm" and outer "jerk," or inner desire and its outer manifestation—and, on the other, the experience of desire into particularized culpabilities framed by questions of epistemology: Are you or are you not (gay)? Who knows whether (or that) you are (gay)? How do they know—and how do you know—that you are (gay)? It might be familiar, in part, because the translation of desire into a question of what is betrayed or given away (a translation dictated by the phobic context in which gay people come into being, which makes it often dangerous to betray desire) means that desire takes shape as a loss of voluntarity perhaps similar to Maisie's little representative jerk. That said, Maisie's experience here is not specified as a gay experience, and this lack of specification should not be read, I think, as a code (for gayness) or as an evasion (of gayness). It is perhaps not sufficient to expand the definitional reach of queerness beyond homosexuality to assert that the familiarity of Maisie's experience alleged here would extend to the incipience of any nonnormative desires, including those—such as intergenerational desire, voyeurism, and sadomasochism—more obviously relevant thematically to *What Maisie Knew*. Rather, it is important to hold on to the ways Maisie's experience exceeds such analogies—to futures gay, straight, or, for that matter, pedophilic, sadomasochistic, voyeuristic, and so on—and to hold on, more generally, to the child's exorbitance in relation to representational projects that would assimilate it to futures imagined in reference to desires of a specific stamp. Maisie's misery here seems rooted in that exorbitance. It—specifically, disappointment with Sir Claude, the grief she finally expresses at his failure to be worthy of her love—involves having to face the internalization of a structure that has nothing to do with her as the shame of a knowledge that she does not have.

Another way to conceptualize these predicaments, to bring the formal and figurative explorations of linguistic structures together with the explicit concerns of Maisie's situation, would be to suggest that she here registers the predicament of being a child in the context of erotic innocence and its forcible reduction of childhood's exorbitance through a rhetorical operation of voiding or erasure. As the epigraph above might suggest, losing innocence may be the only way to establish that it was ever there. However titillating that may be for the spectator (and protector) of innocence whose moral rectitude is proven all the firmer by every reluctantly indulged moment of absorption in the spectacle of purity's demise, for the innocent child such a structure might prove unlivable. The repository of others' logical and linguistic difficulties, the child of erotic innocence, as the sacrificial lamb who serves to disavow complexities of subjectivity and desire, finds itself—were it allowed to find itself at all—in an untenable position. Thus, if Maisie is continually given contradictory directives, punished for following orders she would have been punished for ignoring, she experiences such double binds as the refracted image of the impression she creates; she reflects during her visit to France on "her tendency to produce socially that impression of an excess of the queer something which had seemed to waver so widely between innocence and guilt" (174). Innocence as an erotic category is compelling because it allows adults to stabilize—but also to perpetuate—that wavering as a way of managing or warning off their own queerness. When Sir Claude pats Maisie's hand, we learn, "such pats and pulls had struck her as the steps and signs of other people's business and even a little as the wriggle or the overflow of their difficulties" (152), and the same could be said of all the pinching, pulling, snatching, and violent hugging in the text, could be said even of grown men's tendency to "shy" things at her.

The effects of the impression Maisie gives of that "excess of queer something which had seemed to waver so widely between innocence and guilt" are registered not only in the violent treatment she receives but also in Sir Claude's emphatically de-eroticized mode of address. "He told her she was an awfully good 'chap'" (63). He calls her "old boy" (64, 191), "old fellow" (85), "my dear old woman" (95), "my dear boy" (102, 243), "my dear old man" (105, 237–38), "my dear man" (176), "dear boy" (177), "Maisie boy!" (195), and "old man" (244). The *OED* defines most of these words—*boy*, *fellow, chap*, and especially *old boy, old fellow, old chap*—in gender-neutral and de-eroticized terms of collegiality that betray, perhaps above all, how the absolute gendering of the paths of entitlement can render invisible that very gendering. One need hardly vociferate an explicit policy of discrimination in a club that admits no women to experience the discrimination. It is certainly true that Sir Claude's style of address registers the effect Maisie has on the adults around her, who are led to treat her as another small adult. Reminding one of the Moreens in "The Pupil," for instance, it is said of Sir Claude that "he was liable in talking with her to take the tone of her being also a man of the world" (65). Like Flora at the end of *The Turn of the Screw* (although without the same sexualized revulsion), Maisie over and over again leaves the impression of being "old," an impression that, for Mrs. Wix, takes the form of a repeated astonishment at how little she is to be corrupted. In stressing that Maisie is treated as if she were an adult, however, it is possible to lose sight of the erotics Sir Claude expresses through negation. It is not merely that Maisie (in most of these cases) has been given a gender reassignment that removes her from Sir Claude's gender of object choice (even if he never gives a reason for desiring women more compelling than that he is very afraid of them), or that she is aged as if to deny the possibility of eroticizing her as a child (or perhaps at all). Sir Claude's "man-of-the-world" collegiality itself marks a realm of de-eroticization that defines a homosociality policed, in Sedgwick's account, by homosexual panic.[10] Such styles of masculine endearment mark an (aggressive) de-eroticization—an endearment dressed up in butch, even hostile, drag—that is one cost of the entitlement secured by the constant paranoia-inducing slippage between prescription and proscription in our culture's choreography of male same-sex erotic intensities. By interpellating Maisie into this world, Sir Claude does not mistreat her by making her an adult that she is not (sexualizing an "innocent" child) so much as he mistreats her by disavowing the erotic charge between them.

Sir Claude's fond mode of address is thus a cognate of the violent pinching and pulling and the calling of her by names bearing no resemblance to her own; they all seem to react to the excess of queer something that had seemed to waver so widely between innocence and guilt. The violence done to Maisie seems to stem in part from her taking cognizance of the split this eroticization as de-eroticization enacts on her person, as if she were split by the contradictory rhetoric of the erotic child. Splitting in fact dominates the language around Beale and Ida's divorce settlement: "The little girl [was] disposed of in a manner worthy of the judgement-seat of Solomon. She was divided in two and the portions tossed impartially to the disputants" (11). "Impartially," describing how "portions" are "tossed," hovers somewhere between "disinterestedly" and "indiscriminately." James also seems to play on the tension between *impartial* as "unbiased" or "just" and the rooting of justice in a wholeness not divided against itself (for instance by desire)— *impartial* as "not in parts." Thus, like the potential synonymity of *heim-lich* and *unheimlich*, *impartial* can mean, at least in one obsolete meaning whose incorrectness is highlighted by the *OED*, simply "partial." However that may be, the proximity in the phrase of "impartially" to "portions" brings out the partialness and division that looms in the word by dint of its negation, the carving up of a child to constitute a justice not riven against itself.[11] "Disputants" then also intensifies the split by combining etymologically a verb meaning to reckon, consider, or calculate, with a prefix highlighting division, pointing to a splitting or separation, to things in twain, asunder, or moving in different directions or apart. Impartiality seems less to resolve the disputants' division than to redouble it, and the language of wholeness and justice replays the divisions and contradictions that mark Maisie's predicament.

It may be possible to assimilate the novel's language of division to a narrative of enlightenment, which would be one way to phrase the traditional reading of the novel. Such a reading charts Maisie's progressive movement toward knowledge; in this view, the splitting at the beginning indexes Maisie's relative powerlessness and lack of knowledge, the gap between, for instance, her surroundings and her awareness of them. Each movement toward knowledge, however, redoubles this splitting; the novel moves not toward the healing of division but toward its culmination or, rather, its repetition. Thus the novel's closing scene reverts to this language of splitting: released by Mrs. Beale and noting "something" in Sir Claude's voice, "the child stood there again dropped and divided" (262). Her experience of being divided by others' conflicts thus traverses the novel as the essence of Maisie's lesson, from the judgment of Solomon at the beginning to her feeling of being "*again* dropped and divided" at the end. Splitting thus describes her experience of establishing relations between others in the text. Throughout, Maisie is used as a weapon or stage prop in others' battles or seductions; perhaps more violent than the pinching and the smoke blown in her face is the tendency for "affection" to "pounce" on her ("a rich strong expressive affection in short pounced upon her in the shape of a handsomer, ampler, older Mrs. Beale; 95). The scenes of hugs and curiously dispassionate "caresses" usually read as choreographed battles for possession that make Maisie the rope in a tug-of-war. When adults are affectionate toward her to express something other than aggression, she is usually used as foreplay—thus, in the first meeting Maisie witnesses between Mrs. Beale and Sir Claude, Mrs. Beale's affection becomes a showy mode of flirtation (103). Beale and Ida's feud, of course, establishes Maisie as a go-between: "What was clear to any spectator was that the only link binding her to either parent was this lamentable fact of her being a ready vessel for bitter-ness, a deep little porcelain cup in which biting acids could be mixed" (13). The comprising of this scene by the knowing gaze of an unspecified "any spectator" links Maisie's role as go-between to her representative status for spectators within and outside of the novel: Maisie is the receptacle of bitter-ness not only for her parents but for those viewing their feud. That feud's ferocity is underlined by the unnerving orality of "biting acids," metaphori-cally placing competing mouths, if not entire persons, within the vessel Maisie represents: the split enacted on Maisie's person results from her being made into a vessel for other people's battles, other people's bitterness. "Any spectator," finally, views a rather detailed figure, linking the splitting to narration and implied differences of readerly acuity (and hence, for the acute, to dramas of affiliation and sympathy in reading); the splitting ex-perienced by Maisie is redoubled by the gap between James's language—"a deep little porcelain cup in which biting acids could be mixed"—and the register of perception in which its insight is placed ("What was clear to any spectator").

Maisie "was the little feathered shuttle-cock they could fiercely keep flying between them. The evil they had the gift of thinking or pretending to think of each other they poured into her little gravely-gazing soul as into a boundless receptacle" (19). Repeating the language of a receptacle into which evil thoughts might be poured, the description also suggests a split within the combatants themselves, who have the gift either of thinking or of pretending to think evil of each other. Maisie tries to interrupt the circuit they establish (18–19), to resist being the bond that keeps them, in their hatred, more married in divorce than they were in marriage, to assert her utter vacancy by refusing to repeat to one parent what the other has said. Achieving a "hollowness beyond her years" (58), an effect of "harmless vacancy" (59), she interrupts the circuit by asserting emptiness. *Hollow* or *vacant*, however, she is still but a receptacle, and the alternative to being filled with bitterness is a melancholy emptiness, a hollowness that the free-indirect narration often registers in its tendency toward dispassionate dead-pan (a deadpan that thereby marks its identification with Maisie's point of view and its distance from it).

Later Maisie becomes the only legitimating link between Sir Claude and Mrs. Beale: she is told, and proudly asserts several times, that she brought them together. In the case of her stepparents, she attempts to claim as her own the status that, in the case of her parents, she had attempted to renounce. Her position enabling exchange, however, remains the same, and the melancholia of Maisie's position is less a matter of the sadness of a child relevant to its parents only as a pawn in their own battles than it is structural to the position of grounding exchange in general. Whatever particular interruptions she creates, then, Maisie's "hollowness" marks the culmination of a logic that makes her the ground of exchange in the novel. Thus one sign of the melancholic structuring of Maisie's position is the difficulty for a person establishing relations between others to speak, as it were, from her own point of view. If, moreover, she is for Beale and Ida, as for Sir Claude and Mrs. Beale, merely a stage prop or a principle of relation, the narrative itself uses her in a similar way. As James notes in his preface, it is Maisie's presence that gives interest to relations between characters whose depiction without her would be merely sordid. In the preface's economic language, Maisie's presence and bewilderment make a scene "appreciable" (8, 9)—that is, set its value, make that value perceptible (or the scene itself perceptible in its value as scene), or increase its value (it appreciates as op-posed to depreciates). The "child's own importance," James writes of the scene with the "Captain," "spreading and contagiously acting, has deter-mined the *total* value otherwise" (9). James is scrupulous to distance this "value" from any simple ratification of Maisie's personhood. The preface's opening sentences feature the impersonal pronoun *it* ten times, with nine of them collocated with the antecedent *infant*. James could, of course, have written *girl* instead of *infant;* the striking recurrence of *it* suggests self-consciousness about Maisie's status as an object of the narrative, an analogy between the novel and her parents in the respective uses they make of her. The depersonalizing pronoun also points to the importance of the preface's first *it,* which refers to the novel itself. Maisie, as an *it,* is implicitly tied to the novel as an imaginative production—in James's figure, to the "tree" his "germ" becomes (1). For the narrative in general, Maisie, by being the locus of focalization, allows experiments not only with characterization but also with point of view, narrative reliability, and ambiguity. (Thus, in the scene where Mrs. Beale's affection for Maisie becomes a mode of flirtation with Sir Claude, the point often seems to be less this particular advance in the plot than the narrative challenge of presenting Mrs. Beale's duplicity across, as it were, Maisie's bewilderment.) The bewilderment and ambiguity that the novel, according to Seltzer, "advertises" is made possible by Maisie's particular relations to knowledge, power, and perception. Her limited consciousness—to a certain extent what Maisie does not know, the very thing that, we remember, makes her most miserable—makes narrat-ing the novel possible.

The novel's free-indirect narration, then, is both from Maisie's point of view and at Maisie's expense. Her position in the novel—making possible various forms of exchange from which she is, simultaneously, excluded—is analogous to the position of the child in erotic innocence insofar as inno-cence constructs the child as a point of blankness outside and constitutive of (setting a temporal and logical beginning to shore up suppositions of autonomy) exchanges underlying language, desire, and subjectivity. It is not merely, therefore, that Maisie is in a position of not knowing—or of not knowing some "thing" in particular. The eponymous designation of what Maisie knew encircles an aporia whose structural importance lies less in specified contents—the fact of sexual intercourse, for instance—that might be known or not known than in the interchange it sets up between the dynamics of power around what Maisie does or does not know and the narration of the novel. Thus Maisie's position of relative disempowerment in relation to adults around her is replayed by the narration itself, to which her powerlessness often seems even structural. That the novel is narrated at her expense is suggested by tonal elements that seem to poke fun at her, not only for what she does not know, but also for being simply so endearingly small. The undercutting and gentle mocking of her point of view appears in the semiautomatic (and often seemingly snide) peppering of adjectives such as *little* and *small* that swathe Maisie in invocations of the diminutive. Thus, intercepting a glance between Mrs. Wix and Sir Claude, she is confronted with a "critical little view" of her mother's behavior (72), and, in the same scene, it is said that she "had even had in the past a small smug conviction that in the domestic labyrinth she always kept the clue" (73). These diminutive adjectives follow Maisie around the text, making her every thought, word, and action stand in metonymically for her endearing little self. The repeated adjectival tributes to her littleness self-consciously remind us of the gap between the narrative voice and Maisie, as if to jar us out of any illusion of a seamless fit between the narrative and the perspective of its focalization, while also reminding us of the narrative's power over her.[12]

The little reiterations of the gap between Maisie and narrator also enable various other textual effects. Thus she reflects:

> It was in the nature of things to be none of a child's business, even when a small child had from the first been deluded into a fear that she might be only too much initiated. Things then were in Maisie's experience so true to their nature that questions were almost always improper; but she learned on the other hand soon to recognize how at last, sometimes, patient little silences and intelligent little looks could be rewarded by delightful little glimpses. (124)

The tautology of things being "true to their nature"—where their nature is to be none of a child's business, thus rendering a child's questions improper—is replayed in Maisie's reward, which compensates "little looks" with "little glimpses." The implied distance between "looks" and "glimpses" suggests the possibility of things becoming less true to their natures, thus opening the way, perhaps, for childish questioning. However that may be, this favored stylistic tic—adjectival references to littleness—is brought together with one of the more straightforward forms of irony enabled by the novel's focalization. Maisie's point of view, that is, allows a defamiliarization that makes understated, satirical jibes at the adults around her. "It was somehow in the nature of plans," the narrator has her observe, "to be expensive and in the nature of the expensive to be impossible. To be 'involved' was of the essence of everybody's affairs, and also at every particular moment to be more involved than usual" (102).[13] The novel makes explicit, however, that the child who points out that the emperor has no clothes is not simply above, beyond, or below experiencing the effects of ignorance or knowledge unveiled. In particular, it makes manifest that the positing of a naïveté through which truth might be revealed often relies on the assertion that the naive child does not understand the revelation it makes. The child able to speak the truth because it does not know what it is saying (who paradoxically reassures us by locating a place—outside of "us"—where knowledge and its utterance are structurally doomed never to coincide) makes necessary the positing of an interpretive faculty (admiring, punitive, indulgent, or whatever) above the child to make the child's speech comprehensible, to bring knowledge and speech back into alignment. This structure characterizes not just romantic cults of childhood but also contemporary child-abuse trials, where a child's silence, speech, accusations, recantations, even indifference, all provide definitive proof that molestation has occurred.[14] From the child's perspective, being placed in the position of innocence—whether by those who praise the child's unprecedented wisdom or by those who deplore its unprecedented victimization—might be experienced as an invasive, even violent, appropriation, a voiding of the child's knowledges and perceptions. Maisie's reductio ad absurdum of the pretensions and foibles of those around her thus comes at her expense as well.

Striking in this regard is a figure that likens a maternal embrace to being tossed through a shopwindow: "The next moment she was on her mother's breast, where, amid a wilderness of trinkets, she felt as if she had suddenly been thrust, with a smash of glass, into a jeweller's shop-front, but only to be as suddenly ejected with a push and the brisk injunction: 'Now go to the Captain!'" (112). The effect is partly comic, offsetting Ida's tastelessness both by tying her bodily display to the advertising solicitation of a jeweler's crowded shopwindow (a "wilderness of trinkets" that emphasizes not only Ida's crowded profusion but her artificiality as well) and by making her visual presentation and physical presence astonishingly violent. The violence seems potentially real; the smashing of the window marks not only her comically loud personal appearance but the violence with which she uses Maisie. If Maisie feels misery at not knowing, enlightenment is perhaps no less violent; patterns of figuration in the text suggest that the shattering of glass also figures the rupturing of Maisie's position as an excluded child. The text often represents her exclusion—from understanding and participation in the plots around her by virtue of her age—as a pane of glass separating her from what she sees. Thus, when she senses that pecuniary pressures will prevent her from attending courses, she "was to feel henceforth as if she were flattening her nose upon the hard window-pane of the sweet-shop of knowledge" (106), an evocative image for the exclusion of a child missing elements of sense or meaning necessary to understand what it sees. True to the paradoxical position of childhood innocence, however, the comprehension that shatters this glass does not ensure a healing reconciliation or inclusion for Maisie, does not come through with the unmediated contact through more informed cognition that the figure of the glass separating her from her experience might seem to promise. Her experience, rather, is to be one of redoubled exclusion, and she achieves clarification only at the cost of irremediable rifts between her and those nearest to her. In this instance, the shattering of glass is figuratively tied to the severing of emotional bonds with her mother: "[Ida] draped herself in the tatters of her impudence, postured to her utmost before the last little triangle of cracked glass to which so many fractures had reduced the polished plate of filial superstition" (164). Offering figures that operate in many (potentially discordant) registers, the passage, with its "tatters of her impudence" and shattered mirror, recalls the splitting that Maisie experiences from the judgment of Solomon until she is left "dropped and divided" at the end of the text and links it to the shattering window of the jeweler. Released from filial superstition by this fracturing of perception, she is also alienated from her mother.

The novel does not sentimentalize such alienation; neither, however, does it simply celebrate it as a freedom purchased through growing knowledge or even disillusionment. Just as the child cast in the isolating and alienating role of erotic innocence cannot simply renounce innocence in favor of knowledge, not least because such a transition is scripted by innocence itself, Maisie's passage to knowledge is inscribed within the economy of a text that uses her as its principle of exchange. It uses her, in other words, to set up a system of tropes, where terms can become exchangeable for one another. The preface's pronominal acrobatics collocating the *it* that names "the infant" with the *it* that names the organic growth of the novel (the novel as tree) remind us of perhaps the most important of these exchanges: the system of exchange linking novelistic representation as a system of tropes to the exchange of persons—Maisie, but also her various sets of parents—within the novel. This is the system of tropes, in other words, that makes Maisie's predicament after the divorce a figure for the novel itself. Maisie's experience of such exchange is an experience of loss, the loss, specifically, of Sir Claude. She learns, perhaps, what she had not been able to read in the absence of his things when Mrs. Beale arrives at the hotel: "She was yet to learn what it could be to recognise in some lapse of a sequence the proof of an extinction, and therefore remained unaware that this momentary pang was a foretaste of the experience of death" (216).

It would be easy to imagine such a melancholy story of loss assimilated to a sentimental narrative of innocence's demise: to lose one's innocence in such stories is often synonymous with losing "everything." One way that the novel avoids such sentimentalizing is by collating this foretaste of death with the experience of the representational—with language as a system of exchange or of tropes that, for Maisie, is linked to the exchange of persons. Her mastery of the representational—her mastery of systems of exchange, which marks her entering into a linguistic competence that would ostensibly promise to close off the mismatch between her and her world—marks not an escape but a final instance of her predicament. Her mastery at the end of the novel—"the death of her childhood"—continues the logic that dictates that when the text represents Maisie's experience of socialization through a dawning sense of the "new freedom" with which she was treated and the "proportionately greater niceness she was obliged to show" (16), the stress is perhaps as much on the "proportionately" as it is on the freedom or the duplicity. The proportionate seems to indicate an experience of representational adequation analogous less to any compensation for loss than to the framework of Maisie's predicament, both to her position enabling exchange between opposed persons and to her position in the ironic symmetry of a novel narrated from her perspective and at her expense.

The most reiterated position of the representative in the novel is that of the stepparents, who are, the text often reminds us, representative, or left standing in the "place" or "shoes," of Maisie's parents:

> She was still, as a result of so many parents, a daughter to somebody even after papa and mamma were to all intents dead. If her father's wife and her mother's husband, by the operation of a natural, or for all she knew, a legal rule, were in the shoes of their defunct partners, then Mrs. Beale's partner was exactly as defunct as Sir Claude's and her shoes the very pair to which, in "Farange *v.* Farange and Others," the divorce court had given priority. (224)

Again, a figure is almost literalized, and the shoes seem to take on an existence independent of the figure. This disruptive literalization results from two kinds of correlations that underlie the possibility of exchange (and representation) here: it relies, first, on the discovery that two partners are "exactly as defunct" as each other—evoking the negated possibility of being more or less defunct—and, second, on a figurative correlation that makes standing in another's shoes a figure for representational adequation. To stand in another's shoes is to be representative of that person almost to the point of becoming him or her; this blending, in turn, stands in for other mergings—for example, between the "legal" and the "natural." As Sir Claude reminds her, these transitions take place through the exchange of Maisie: "There's one thing to remember—I've a right to impress it on you: we stand absolutely in the place of your parents. It's their defection, their extraordinary baseness, that has made our responsibility. Never was a young person more directly committed and confided" (251). Sir Claude asserts a relation between their standing "absolutely" in the place of Maisie's parents and the directness with which she has been "committed and confided." The figure thus suggests an exchange across space (with Maisie committed from one pair to the other) that is so direct and efficient that it makes the places between which she is passed interchangeable to the point of merger ("*in loco parentis*," as the text says of the position a near relative ought to have arrived to fill, before concluding that her family had no such "ornament"; 12). This sort of merger appears in one of the funniest instances of such assertions of the representative, when Mrs. Beale angrily dismisses Mrs. Wix in the climactic scene just before Maisie and her governess leave her and Sir Claude: "Mrs. Beale continued to address her young friend, and her effort to be reasonable and tender was in its way remarkable. 'We're representative, you know, of Mr. Farange and his former wife. This person represents mere illiterate presumption. We take our stand on the law'" (266). Arguably, Mrs. Beale is right to take a stand on this play on *representative*, between "representing" Maisie's parents and "representing mere illiterate presumption" insofar as the novel—by a natural or, for all Maisie knew, a legal rule—casts the law as just such a pun on representation, a sleight of hand (exposed by the novel) that serves to naturalize representation.

This play on the representative also offers a way to describe the Farange marriage-through-divorce, which, leaving them feeling "more married than ever," might be described as agreement through contradiction. This structure is enacted in the syntax early in the novel, which mimes the adversarial divorce court proceedings through parallel structures dominated by conjunctions. Thus "the many friends of the Faranges drew together to differ about them; contradiction grew young again over teacups and cigars. Everybody was always assuring everybody of something very shocking, and nobody would have been jolly if nobody had been outrageous" (14). Drawing together to differ characterizes the syntax as well as the actions described. The oppositions hinging on the coordinating conjunction *and* are mimed by repeated elements that oppose themselves just as the two independent clauses are set in opposition by the parallel structure. "Everybody" and "nobody" each becomes divided from itself, each becoming both sender and receiver of the scandalous address. This division is further en-acted by the peculiar status of *everybody* and *nobody:* as pronouns referring to aggregate bodies or collective groups, they nonetheless function gram-matically as singular (and hence can personify those groups as singular entities divided from themselves). The paradoxical inversion grounding the expression "contradiction grew young again" once again links this splitting effect to an overturning of age difference as a diacritical category. Maisie, then, as the bowl in which poisons are mixed, or as the shuttlecock kept fiercely flying between them, takes the place both of the *and* and of the *everybody/nobody,* the crux of representational exchange left to experience others' adversarial relations as her own division from herself. Her cultivat-ed hollowness, then, both interrupts this grammatical and social structure and marks its culmination, the emptying out of content in its mirroring structure of parallelism.

The ostensible moral conundrum at the end of the text might then be cast in terms of this logic of representation. Mrs. Beale asks Maisie to ac-cept a similar kind of adequation, to make herself a principle of exchange, to legitimate the relation between Mrs. Beale and Sir Claude by making them representative of her parents. Mrs. Wix's contention of an absolute moral value, on the other hand, asks Maisie to be the empty center of an-other system, one in which the possibility of her corruption legitimates Mrs. Wix's disapprobation, legitimates making marriage the standard of moral exchange. These representational adequations might in turn be correlated to the structuring binaries of erotic innocence: Maisie is given the choice of maintaining absolute innocence (siding with Mrs. Wix, or "mere illiterate presumption") or embodying sexualized, urbane (even "man-of-the-world") knowledge (siding with Mrs. Beale). As in her ef-fort to interrupt the circuit of exchange between her parents by cultivating a "hollowness beyond her years," Maisie's attempt to eschew the choice between her stepparents and Mrs. Wix ends up repeating the dilemma she hoped to avoid. The end of the novel might thus be said to present a parallel version of the culmination of her hollowness as Maisie masters structures of representational exchange. Her moral solution—which Sir Claude finds so beautiful—relies on a logic of substitution that attempts to make people equivalent to one another. Her proposal to Sir Claude—she will give up Mrs. Wix if he will give up Mrs. Beale (255)—which Sir Claude calls "the only right one" (263), allows him to express his further admi-ration of Maisie; he has not killed her moral sense, he says to Mrs. Wix, "on the contrary I think I have produced life. I don't know what to call it—I haven't even known how decently to deal with it, to approach it; but whatever it is, it's the most beautiful thing I've ever met—it's exquisite, it's sacred" (261). Maisie's sense of straining for a "describable loss," of having "lost everything," links her sense of Sir Claude's desertion to an intuition of an incommensurability (perhaps "exquisite" or "sacred") grounding representational commensurabilities, a radical loss grounding the possibility of equivalence and exchange. This loss might be described as the realization that losses are not exchangeable or comparable: by formulating to Sir Claude the proposition that each give up a loved person, Maisie formulates a commensurability that, in opening up the possibility (or fantasy) of exchanging one person—without loss—for another, leads to an intuition of incommensurability, of what will be lost—absolutely—for her in her and Sir Claude's unmourned losses of each other.

To say, then, that the narration of the novel is simultaneously from Maisie's perspective and at her expense is also to suggest that Maisie has throughout been made to play the part of this founding disjunction. She is the *it* that names the infant and the novel; she is the *scale* through which the preface names the possibility of the novel itself (7). She is the cup in which biting acids are mixed (13) or the vanishing point that, by establishing perspective, creates what James in the preface calls a "scene": "Yet the thing has but to become a part of the child's bewilderment for these small sterilities to drop from it and for the *scene* to emerge and prevail" (8). The "special scale she creates for them" gives, James writes, the novel's "poorer persons and things . . . a precious element of dignity" (7). Giving moral and aesthetic interest to the merely sordid, Maisie seems to realize the untenable vacancy of this position, a position simultaneously of making possible the narration and of inhabiting erotic innocence. This double articulation prevents the novel from merely reproducing erotic innocence, where the innocent child is called upon to play the part of a founding disjunction. The novel, in other words, foregrounds disjunctions that sentimental or gothic stories of victimization or nostalgia strive to obscure: it makes explicit the ways in which the child, as pure, impermeable blankness or as nothing but the facticity of its violation, allows us to imagine a self-sufficient subjectivity (specifically, our own) not rent by the vicissitudes of language, representation, or desire.

What Maisie Knew is remarkable simply because Maisie is allowed to take cognizance of her situation and because it tries to imagine what innocence might look like from her point of view. After Mrs. Beale appears in France instead of Sir Claude, Maisie "put it together with a suspicion that, had she ever in her life had a sovereign changed, would have resembled an impression, baffled by the want of arithmetic, that her change was wrong: she groped about in it that she was perhaps playing the passive part in a case of violent substitution" (222–23). Her bafflement is redoubled: sensing that she has been given the wrong change (if ever she were to experience getting change), she lacks the arithmetic to verify her intuition. Mrs. Beale's appearance in France and Maisie's realization that it does make a difference to her which of her stepparents takes her parents' place, her realization that Sir Claude cannot, as Mrs. Beale would have it, simply be exchanged ("if she can live with but one of us alone, with which in the world should it be but me"; 223) sets the stage for her understanding of loss as a "violent substitution" or as the forcible assertion of equivalence: you give up Mrs. Beale, and I'll give up Mrs. Wix. Her formulation of an incommensurability of loss rooted in an assertion of a commensurable exchange seems to be her answer to the impossible choice that Sir Claude gives her. Made to choose between him and Mrs. Wix, Maisie is left with the impression of "her choice . . . there before her like an impossible sum on a slate" (252). Her intuition of an impossible choice or a violent substitution might then figure both the child's relation to erotic innocence and Maisie's relation to the narration of the novel, and "queer" is one way to phrase the paradoxical untenability of her position. Experienced as a sense of loss, perhaps, an unveiling of an exorbitance to systems of representational or tropological exchange, an incommensurability within structures of commensurability, *queerness* names the untenability of Maisie's position and, too, its possibility of radically unsettling the structures underlying the ideology of erotic innocence.

The novel theorizes Maisie's queer position, the founding disjunction she experiences as the grounding of equivalence, through a constitutive mismatch between "names" and "conceptions." "She had ever of course in her mind fewer names than conceptions," the novel says of her early on, and the preface discusses the gap between "seeing" and "experience" on the one hand and "understanding" and "vocabulary" on the other (154, 155–57). Initially, it seems possible to imagine that this mismatch is merely a pragmatic concern, a novelistic challenge to represent experience in spite of a child's insufficient vocabulary and understanding. One might expect, then, a growth toward representational sufficiency as the child finally grasps the words it lacks. As the novel moves on, however, it is increasingly the narration itself that is said to lack names for Maisie's conceptions. More and more appear such protestations as "Oh decidedly I shall never get you to believe the number of things she saw and the number of secrets she discovered!" (155) and "I so despair of courting her noiseless footsteps here that I must crudely give you my word for its being from this time forward a picture literally present to her" (208). Although a strange admission for a Jamesian narrator—who seems to lack words for almost nothing and whose super-refined, discriminating specification need never, perhaps, despairingly concede to crudity—the reversal, beyond asserting Maisie's growing knowledge, also asserts the necessity of an imbalance, of a failure of equivalence between "names" and "conceptions" to maintain the system of naming. The more names Maisie can give to her conceptions, the more the narration must protest the inadequacy of its own nomenclature. Thus Maisie thinks of herself and Sir Claude "in a little place in the south," while Mrs. Wix and Mrs. Beale, "in a little place in the North, remained linked by a community of blankness and by the endless series of remarks it would give birth to" (253).

In a paragraph in the preface detailing the relations between her parents that Maisie sets up and the reduplication of this "system of misbehaviour" with the stepparents, James writes of the "human" themes of the novel in terms of a reflexively phrased "mixing" of life's elements: "No themes are so human as those that reflect for us, out of the confusion of life, the close connection of bliss and bale, of the things that help with the things that hurt, so dangling before us for ever that bright hard metal, of so strange an alloy, one face of which is somebody's right and ease and the other somebody's pain and wrong" (4). An image of exorbitant pathos, it is also one of inseparable fusion (like standing in another's shoes until you become him or her) that maintains "faces" that can never see one another. The repetition of "somebody," like the passage about the gossiping everybody and nobody, divides *somebody* from itself through the movement of merger that transforms "the confusion of life" into a representative emblem. The symmetrical pairings set up by "themes" that "reflect"—of "bliss and bale," "help" and "hurt," and the opposed faces of that "strange . . . alloy"—condense in this description of the "human" the structure of commensurability and incommensurability in representation and desire that Maisie discovers in the novel. Her realization of imbalance or disjunction is correlated both with her experience of desire and with her place within the economy of the novel, the untenable position of grounding both exchange among the characters and representation in the novel itself.

"To live with all intensity and perplexity and felicity in its terribly mixed little world," James continues, "would thus be the part of my interesting small mortal." Maisie is cast as the connection between bliss and bale, help and hurt, and the opposed faces of the alloy of right and ease, pain and wrong, "bringing people together who would be at least more correctly separate; keeping people separate who would be at least more correctly together." As in the divorce settlement, Maisie is representationally at the crux of such recursive structurings. This position, much more than the simple, gothic, or sentimental victimization of innocence and the concomitant moralized reaction it arouses against the predations of maturity, makes her able to "keep the torch of virtue alive in an air tending infinitely to smother it . . . sowing on barren strands . . . the seed of the moral life." As James notes, this "fragrance of an ideal," the moral life Maisie fosters, "makes confusion worse confounded," tying the "moral" and the "ideal" to the interruption or confusion of such reflexive structures and representational symmetries

(4).[15] What James casts as the "moral life" seems tied to Maisie's taking cognizance of her position grounding exchange and representation in and for the novel. Her discovery of loss through these structures of symmetry and adequation also takes a specific shape, namely, the loss of Sir Claude, the final instance in the novel of an adult who proves inadequate to Maisie's love. Her position is thus that of the queer child as the victim of childhood's construal exclusively in the terms of erotic innocence. If, however, the text allegorizes a position of innocence and its various excruciations, it avoids the usual ruses by which an identification with the child—as with the queer—is warded off. By tying Maisie's predicament to that of the reader, the novel makes an identification with her both inevitable and impossible. Telling the story of a child victimized by circumstance and by the adults around her, it thwarts a sense of an easy identification that, by casting the child as a blank victim inspiring gratifying reactions of pity and outrage, apotropaically wards off the possibility of identification.

Thus turning too credulously to identification as a valorized term ignores the ways in which identification understood as empathy or as the seamless inhabiting of another's identity merely repeats the structures of representational adequation that Maisie discovers. To insist, then, on the impossibility of identification—to point to the ways that the novel makes Maisie's position one of the impossible or the untenable—is also to suggest that there is no easy alternative to the rhetoric of erotic innocence. Thus Maisie experiences at the end of the novel the kind of impossible identification I believe the text asks of its reader. Her sense of loss grows in part out of an incommensurability of desire, out of Sir Claude's failure to live up to his desire for her. In the climactic scene in the train station, Maisie shows Sir Claude her two armfuls of books, "smiling at him as he smiled at her, but so conscious of being more frightened than she had ever been in her life that she seemed to see her whiteness in a glass. Then she knew that what she saw was Sir Claude's whiteness" (254). The remarkable phrasing figures an incommensurability through perfect mirroring, evoking both the psychological experience of terror in discovering the fear of a loved one on whom one relies and the disconcerting experience of a recognition from another in a mirroring structure that confounds that person with oneself. Seeing her whiteness in a glass and realizing that her terror is his terror offers an image for an unnerving identification, one that might result in a "community of blankness" (253) or an exchange of silences (255). The pathos of the emptiness Maisie discovers, however, is perhaps difficult to distinguish from sentimentality, from the reification of innocence as the perfect victim or as the repository of all that should have been. The extent to which a desiring identification is possible that would not cast Maisie as the child in "The Emperor's New Clothes"—whether unveiling linguistic structures of impossibility or the rhetoric of childhood innocence—remains open to question. In other terms, *What Maisie Knew* is not simply about "ambiguity," and yet it also resists a reification of the specific story of power it tells within terms of innocence and victimization. The question might then be to what extent it is possible to read outside of these terms, to what extent it is possible to make the queer child legible—that is, to attend to the child's illegibility or its exorbitance—without duplicating a reification that enacts the ideological voiding/comprehension of the child in erotic innocence.

Notes

Special thanks to Henry Russell Bergstein, T. Bodenheimer, Cynthia Chase, Bob Chibka, Ellis Hanson, James Kincaid, and Daniel Heller-Roazen.

1. See Eve Kosofsky Sedgwick, "How to Bring Your Kids Up Gay: The War on Effeminate Boys," in this volume.

2. James R. Kincaid, *Erotic Innocence: The Culture of Child Molesting* (Durham, NC: Duke University Press, 1998), 15. See also Kincaid's essay "Producing Erotic Children" in this volume.

3. Kincaid, *Erotic Innocence*, 16.

4. Eve Kosofsky Sedgwick, "The Beast in the Closet: James and the Writing of Homosexual Panic," in *Epistemology of the Closet* (Berkeley: University of California Press, 1990), 202.

5. Ibid., 203–4.

6. Henry James, *What Maisie Knew* (Oxford: Oxford University Press, 1980). Page numbers from this edition are hereafter cited in text.

7. Dan McCall, "What Maisie Saw," *Henry James Review* 16, no. 1 (1995): 52.

8. "The death of her childhood" is a quotation from James's preface to the novel (7).

9. Mark Seltzer, *Henry James and the Art of Power* (Ithaca, NY: Cornell University Press, 1984), 157.

10. See Sedgwick, "The Beast in the Closet."

11. My comments on the relation of "impartiality" to parts and wholes rely on my (partial) memory of remarks made to me by Eva Badowska.

12. That these adjectives are markers, potentially, of an authorial identification is suggested by a similar constellation of diminutive adjectives in James's descriptions of himself in *A Small Boy and Others*. At the same time, these adjectives in that text also seem—as they do in *What Maisie Knew*—to drive a wedge between James as narrator and James as a remembered small boy.

13. Affairs, according to the *OED*, were primarily business affairs and not erotic or romantic ones. An erotic affair took the French spelling—*affaire*—at least until 1958. The insistent repetition of complicated "affairs" in this text, as in *The Golden Bowl*, however, suggests that James was playing on the phonetic resonance for ironic effect, here to allow Maisie to utter, seemingly unknowingly, what is going on around her.

14. James Kincaid is incisive and funny about such dynamics of belief around child-abuse accusations. See, for example, "The Trials: Believing the Children," in *Erotic Innocence*, 192–212.

15. It is also unclear to me whether to "make confusion worse confounded" is to exacerbate confusion or to thwart it.

Knowing Children: Desire and Interpretation in *The Exorcist*

Ellis Hanson

> But while reviewers argue and the more salacious sections of the press drum up increasingly sensational stories, let's look at some of the facts: The book was based on the last recorded incident of exorcism in America which took place in 1949. A fourteen-year old boy was possessed by a demon. He met all the Church requirements for an exorcism. He was speaking in a voice not his own, in a language not his own. He was possessed of superhuman powers. He broke the arm of the priest performing the exorcism. His bed shook up and down. Furniture moved to block his way. He was burning up with pain and in tears and then there was the sound of a slap and suddenly there was the imprint of a hand across his face. . . . Today that boy is a thirty-eight year-old married man with three children and he remembers nothing of what happened. All this is authenticated in Church records.
>
> —*from a review of* The Exorcist[1]

N ow that you have been rescued from salacious and sensational stories, I thought I should put you in possession of the facts. In case you did not know, the opposite of demonic possession is marriage. The opposite of the child who acts out is the adult who forgets. Finally, if you have three children of your own, you will speak in your own voice and your furniture will lead a perfectly sedentary existence. All this is authenticated in Church records, so relax. The occasion for this journalistic melodrama of normalization was the brouhaha over William Friedkin's film *The Exorcist,* which first leaped onto the screen and barked and spat vomit on the day after Christmas in 1973. Despite a barrage of nasty reviews that deemed it exploitative and just plain lousy, it quickly became the most popular horror film ever made. Satan got considerable press for months afterward, as any little treatise on demonic possession, especially where children and sex were involved, magically became a newsworthy item of scholarly interest to the readers of magazines. Even psychologists and theologians got in on the act. The finer distinctions between psychosis and satanism inevitably became more pressing when the audience was lining up to see a girl violently stab herself in the crotch with a crucifix (I believe "masturbate" was deemed the mot juste in the reviews).

The Exorcist proved critic-proof evidently because it had not just a demon-possessed girl, but also impressive special effects, well-orchestrated melodrama, excellent performances by respected actors, realistic violence, unnerving obscenity and blasphemy, and a degree of profanity unprecedented on a mainstream screen—what was not to like? It also had Linda Blair. I learned from various magazines that she was a sweet-voiced girl-woman from a suburb of Connecticut, and I kept reading. Her own sexual corruption, or lack thereof, became the stuff of popular speculation, as if the conventional bourgeois background rather too exhaustively attributed to her was at once a reassurance and an instigation to suspicion. As in the review quoted above, reassurances on the subject of demonic behavior in children are often curiously framed as incitements to further panic. In the personal interviews she gave at the time, Linda Blair was quizzed about her understanding of her role as if at any moment she might convulse into an obscene tirade. The naïveté attributed to children is always serviceable as a stimulant to biographical fantasy. In such discussions, the distinction between art and life in a child's work before the camera remains reliably and deliciously unclear. The director's pursuit of good child acting slides effortlessly and predictably into child molesting as we speculate about whether the girl was traumatized by the sexual content of her own performance. The interview in *Newsweek* provides a typical example:

> Most horrifying to moviegoers are the violent sexual actions of the possessed child, who makes lewd overtures to the adults (including her mother, played by Ellen Burstyn) in the most fearsome language. Although the masculine-sounding voice of actress Mercedes McCambridge was eventually dubbed in as the voice of the demon, Linda had to say all her lines. But she treated the obscenities as mere jargon just like the Latin and the backwards sentences she also had to speak. "Billy Friedkin told me what to do and I just figured I'd get down there and do it," says Linda. "It could have been about a girl eating a lollipop."[2]

The lollipop clinches it: Shirley Temple meets Lolita, and "Billy" ends up looking like a stereotypical molester, insinuating himself into the easy trust of a girl and then instructing her how to get down there and do it. Even the quaint circumlocutions, the "lewd overtures" and "the most fearsome language," seem calculated to prick our imaginations to life with a prurient vagueness, though they read like a parody of Victorian erotica.

▼ Ellis Hanson

Luckily for Linda, there were several Roman Catholic priests on hand to exorcise the demon of child sexuality and trauma, though she herself, as the *Newsweek* interviewer is quick to note, was raised Congregationalist. After the myriad pedophile priest scandals of the past decade, the idea of Catholic clergy as defenders of youthful sexual innocence may now be even more dubious than it was in 1973, but the sheer earnestness of the concern lavished on Linda's besieged virginity is worthy of a conduct book for ladies in the age of Jane Austen: "Some of the tension was eased by cast and crew members, including the priests who acted as advisers on the film. Their concern for Linda, together with her soundness and common sense, have left her unmarked by the experience. 'I don't feel any different,' Linda says, and her mother confirms that 'she hasn't changed. That's one of the healthy things about her.'" This sweet mother-daughter relationship, buttressed on all sides with clerical concern, is a virtual reenactment of the Oedipal dynamics of the film, and therefore not likely to set us at ease—but we do not want to be set at ease.[3] We are aching for Ellen Burstyn to show up uninvited so that we can see Linda go beserk again. The suspense intensifies with the hand-wringing invocation of a trauma that, much to our disappointment, has failed to materialize, that has indeed been displaced onto the exceedingly adult actor/actress Mercedes McCambridge, who is assumed to be immune to any sort of corruption we might care about. The title of this article, "The Ghoul Next Door," plays on one of the most unnerving aspects of the film: its realism, the sheer banality of the characters and their lives, the domesticated banality even of the supernatural evil the film invokes. The article includes a photograph of Linda Blair with her mother, who is eying her smilingly as if to assure us that she has not blinked and missed any signs of possession. We are told that this girl has a father at home, not to mention siblings, but *Newsweek* would prefer that we not see them or hear from them. Regan too is an only child with an estranged father, and her mother is seen to loom suspiciously large in her daughter's life. Flanking this illustration on either side are pictures not of those helpful priests and crew members but of the demon-possessed Regan looking especially gruesome, as if to provide the family photo with a suitably Oedipal and cinematic unconscious at its margins. The indexical vagueness of the caption reinforces the ambiguity: "Linda at home with her mother, and as the possessed child." Which is which?[4]

As Henry James made abundantly clear in his 1898 gothic novella *The Turn of the Screw,* the occult possibility of demonic possession, a paradox of innocence and licentiousness in the same character, serves as a fine allegory for the erotic enigma that is the modern child.[5] James was the first writer to put the eroticized child at the center of the gothic novel, a convention that had previously relied on, to put it simply, perverse men who make pacts with the devil and nubile women with only the vaguest conception of the floor plans of large, dark, and creaky houses. Miles and Flora, his enigmatic child protagonists ever on the verge of being antagonists, drive the new governess to distraction with teasing suggestions that they may be communing with ghosts with whose supposedly appalling sexual secrets they appear to be familiar. James will not tell us whether Miles and Flora are possessed, whether indeed they are traumatized by ghosts, by sexual knowledge, or merely by the cruel intrusions of a prudish governess. The children become ciphers for a maddeningly, invitingly, titillatingly irresolvable regime of questions that we as readers ask, not without a sexual and political investment of our own, a very modern need to place child sexuality, our own sexuality, our own childhood experience, within a language of trauma whose significance we could never underestimate. At roughly the same time, Sigmund Freud invented the gothic child for the burgeoning field of psychology by making repressed childhood sexual trauma the basis for his theory of adult subjectivity. The inherently polymorphously perverse child upstaged the corrupted adult as the uncanny progenitor of trauma, horror, pathology, and sexual secrets, such that what is most modern about psychoanalysis seems also most gothic. For what contemporary political issue, what recent theory of child psychology, what modern conception of the origins of subjectivity does not involve a pressing concern with trauma and the sexual secrets that supposedly lurk within the mysterious psyches of children? As James Kincaid has made amply evident, the sexuality of children is now almost always evoked as a gothic melodrama, "a ritual that seems to be directed by and enacted through panic," and its shrillness and redundancy have inflected a vast array of public debates and scandals—over Internet access, the Roman Catholic priesthood, sexual harassment codes, pornography and censorship, gay rights, day care, public education, welfare policy, and of course the validity of psychoanalysis, to name just a few arenas of contestation.[6] Children are queer. Their sexual behavior and their sexual knowledge are subjected to an unusually intense normalizing surveillance, discipline, and repression of the sort familiar to any oppressed sexual minority. My intention here is to use queer theory, by which I mean the deconstruction of sexual rhetoric, to analyze the erotic motives, the ambiguities, the disavowals, the paradoxes, and the violence in our relationship to this gothic figure, this illicitly sexual child we have invented, as it appears in one of its most famous and complicated cinematic instances.[7]

The gothic child may have appeared in literature and in psychological theory around the turn of the century, but it did not gather momentum in cinema for at least another fifty years. I can only speculate on the cultural forces that kept this gothic sensibility in check for so long: the relatively late popularization of the "battered child" in sociology around 1960; Hollywood censorship codes, which were drastically liberalized at about the same time; an increasingly rebellious postwar youth culture; the increased marketing of cinema to younger audiences with more sensationalist tastes; and Shirley Temple and the cult of cuteness in Hollywood (though I would argue that cuteness as a sentimental sensibility is merely the flip side of gothic, which is cuteness run amok). In *The Village of the Damned* (1960), where the women of a small English town mysteriously give birth to an intergalactic race of weirdly Aryan children with a taste for regimentation and world domination, we even see that classic Cold War cliché, the space alien who represents a displaced fear of communism and fascism. Whatever the reason, the late fifties and early sixties heralded the spectacular appearance of the gothic child in cinema with such popular, sometimes controversial fare as *The Bad Seed* and *Baby Doll* (1956), *Suddenly, Last Summer* (1959), *The Innocents* (1961, the first and most impressive of the film adaptations of *The Turn of the Screw*), *The Children's Hour* (1961, a remake of the much tamer *These Three,* a 1936 film by the same director), *The Village of the Damned, Lolita* (1962), and *The Haunting* (1963), all of which turned on secrets, in particular the scandalous secret of the violent, violated, or sexual child. After 1968, anxieties about the rebelliousness of youth culture seemed to come to the fore in this genre (*The Exorcist* was discussed at the time with respect to such supposed threats to youthful innocence and family life as the Vietnam War, feminism, and atheism), and in the course of the 1970s the gothic child acquired a degree of popularity that has not yet abated and is often associated with a wider cinematic appetite for violence, sexual explicitness, and the occult. Children and adolescents with demonic powers became a staple of the horror genre, and their popularity was secured by the financial success of Roman Polanski's film *Rosemary's Baby* (1968) and *The Exorcist*. It was further assured by the rising star of Stephen King, whose gothic novels about children and adolescents helped to establish him as the best-selling author of all time and have frequently been made into films, among them *Carrie* (1976), *The Shining* (1980), *Firestarter* (1984), *It* (1990), and the several incarnations of *Children of the Corn* (1984). *The Exorcist* was followed by a number of other films that kept the genre in play: *Audrey Rose* (1977), *The Fury* (1978), *The Changeling* (1979), the two *Exorcist* sequels, *The Omen* (1976) and its sequels, *Poltergeist* (1982) and its sequels, *Child's Play* (1988) and its sequels—any sign of audience interest in the gothic child usually resulted in triplets at least.

Although moviegoers flocked to *The Exorcist*, critics claimed that it was pornographic and made no sense. Without seeming to realize it, they summed up two of the key aspects of the gothic genre—two ways, I believe, that the film is ingenious: it plays with our desire and our knowingness. The critics complained that they felt manipulated and nauseated by what they saw, but as the numerous accounts of fainting and vomiting and religious conversions at screenings of the film might attest, the visceral and psychological impact is not easily dismissed. The critics also complained that there were too many loose ends in William Peter Blatty's screenplay, too many things that did not make sense even if one read his novel, itself a best seller written and packaged with the film in mind. The story seemed simple enough. A twelve-year-old girl, Regan MacNeil (Linda Blair), is possessed by the devil, causing her to puke, blaspheme, talk dirty to a priest, bounce on her bed, move furniture about the room, toss a sizable film director out her bedroom window, and (did I mention this?) violently stab herself in the crotch with a crucifix. In the recent director's cut she even trots down the stairs like a spider. When medical authorities fail to explain the phenomenon, Chris MacNeil (Ellen Burstyn), her movie-star mother, requests an exorcism from a priest, Damian Karras (Jason Miller), who is also a psychiatrist and who is struggling with his religious doubts. Karras's doubts, never wholly unassailable, are challenged by the spectacle of Regan's possession, and with the help of an experienced and elderly exorcist, Lankester Merrin (Max von Sydow), who knows not the meaning of the word *doubt,* he tries to cast out the demon. When, in the course of this grueling contest between good and evil, Father Merrin dies in mid-exhortation, Karras saves Regan by inviting the girl's demon into himself and then throwing himself out the window.

The question remains, however, why is Regan possessed? Is it because the devil works in mysterious ways, because Regan has been playing with a Ouija board, because she is somehow guilty, because her parents are divorced, because her mother is independent and her father absent, because a priest has doubts, or just because she happens to be a girl of twelve? Why this particular girl of twelve? Why a girl at all, when Blatty based his novel on a historical account of an exorcism performed on a boy? Further mysteries abound. The film begins with a lengthy account of Father Merrin digging up a sculpture of a demon in northern Iraq, where he is working on an archaeological excavation of the site of ancient Nineveh. I can understand why an American film would be eager to locate the ultimate evil in the Middle East, particularly Iraq, but what does the demon have to do with Nineveh? Why would it move to Georgetown? (Given the date of the film, it is often supposed that Richard Nixon had something to do with it.) There are still other mysteries and red herrings, such that one begins to suspect the film is about suspicion itself, not to mention its more religious sidekick, doubt. Chris's German servant Karl is accused of being a Nazi and leaves the house for mysterious reasons, but we never learn why. Regan tells an astronaut he is going to die in space, but we never find out if he does. Detective Kinderman (Lee J. Cobb) has three corpses to ponder in the

MacNeil case, but we never learn what becomes of his criminal investigation. Some people who saw the film were understandably unsure whether Regan was possessed rather than just bonkers, whether Merrin released the demon by digging it up, whether the demon lives on in Karras, or how he got thrown from the window. Many of the first people who saw the film thought that the devil pushed Karras out the window and was triumphant, and Blatty was so distressed by this misreading that he proposed reshooting the ending to allay confusion. One wonders if he was not himself missing the point.

The press accounts of traumatized audiences led some reviewers to observe wryly that it was not the devil but the film itself that was in need of exorcism. It is an assault on the senses and on vulnerable emotional sensibilities, they said, and children were especially at risk. I would add that, with its myriad mysteries, the very narrative structure is out to get us, to make us feel confused and paranoid. It keeps us guessing long after Satan has revealed himself and left the premises. The question is not, as in *The Turn of the Screw*, whether we are dealing with insanity or the supernatural, since Blatty goes to great pains to replace every scientific explanation with a religious one. The film does resemble James's narrative, however, in that we are left to wonder why the devil is there at all, through what psychological, sexual, or moral flaw he is admitted to the film, and why there are so many unexplained mysteries. As in all gothic narratives, we are infantilized by secrets that leave us feeling vulnerable and ignorant: we feel we have traded places with the child in that Regan knows too much and we know too little. Merrin too seems to know more than we do and know more than anyone ought. We are also confronted with characters, the devil only the most egregious among them, who lie, mislead, or conceal things. The film itself, like the body of the child, seems to be possessed, to play games with us, to put things where they do not belong.

Like *The Turn of the Screw* and its film adaptation *The Innocents, The Exorcist* generates an epistemological crisis, a panic about the validity of interpretation, that hinges on our perception of a queer sexuality, in particular the illicit sexual desires and sexual knowledge of a child. Both films also perform the classic gothic ruse of sexual ambiguity by embodying perfect innocence and outrageous licentiousness in the same character, in this case a child, without offering any convincing resolution to the contradiction. We may be able to persuade ourselves that it is really the devil talking through Regan, but it is still the girl's body that makes the obscenity truly shocking. We are assured of her innocence, her sexual naïveté, her failure to remember anything, but the violently erotic spectacle of her possession also invites us to ponder the sexuality of the girl even when she is not possessed, to find some psychological parallels between her normal and her demonic personalities, to examine closely her Oedipal longings, her unconscious fixations, her frustrated pleasures. As in all child-gothic narratives, we are invited to take a closer look, a sexy peek, though always under the aegis of innocence, the highly dubious, albeit ubiquitous presumption that there could not possibly be anything to find out, either in the kid or in our own insistent curiosity.

The Exorcist also resembles its Jamesian predecessor by dropping entirely too many psychosexual hints for us to be content with the explanation that we are looking at a simple ghost story, a tale about demons who are motivated by nothing more profound than their inherent cussedness. The film aspires to be a conservative psychosexual morality tale whose only resolution is to be found in the Church, not the clinic. I gather from published interviews that Blatty is fanatical about the existence of devils, and he is certainly offering us a story of the occult; nevertheless, he invites psychological readings of the sort he is eager to disqualify in his characterization of psychiatrists and doctors as materialist buffoons. His faith is relentlessly Freudian. My approach here is not psychoanalytic, but it is important to recognize the implicit influence of psychoanalysis in the film's conception of character and spectator motivation. Regan, Chris, and Damian Karras are all sexually unconventional, little neurotic hotbeds of unacceptable inclinations unconvincingly repressed, and the narrative of possession allows for much indirect moral commentary from the author. As in vampire tales, the demon enters the house only because in some unspoken way he has been invited, because the unconscious desires of the inhabitants have beckoned him as if through some erotic equivalent of Regan's Ouija board. After all, the Ouija board is etymologically linked to a double affirmative in two languages: it is both a *oui* and a *ja*—and as we know from Freud, there is no such thing as a *no*, or even a *non* or a *nein*, in the unconscious.[8] The devil arrives at the MacNeils' house in Georgetown because, sexually speaking, he feels quite at home there, mischievous creature of persuasion and seduction that he is.

I do not mean to say that the doctors in the film are correct to diagnose Regan as hysterical or brain damaged rather than possessed; on the contrary, the doctors have missed the point, and despite their conscious good intentions, they are unconscious coconspirators in the invasive gaze at the sexual child whose suffering they claim to want to alleviate. In other words, they have not diagnosed a pathology, but colluded in a seduction. The invitation to the demon is a *oui* and *ja* that we all enact simply by the voyeuristic pleasure we take in interpretation, in speculating, however violently and erotically, on the body and the psyche of the girl. That phallic invasiveness is never more excruciating than when we have to sit through Regan's spinal exam, with its hovering, humming, menacing X-ray machines like so many technological witches swooping about the girl's body. The film seems to evoke Freud most strikingly in the scene where Father Karras examines Regan's artwork in the basement. By this time, the doctors have been disproved, and even Karras is beginning to lay aside his medical and psychiatric training in favor of a religious explanation. Regan has just vomited on his sporty Georgetown University jacket, and Chris, in an uncharacteristic but endearing bit of housewifery, has laundered it and is now ironing it while he waits. Suddenly, the celibate priest and the divorced movie star have settled down for a quiet moment of domestic bliss in which it is implicitly marked, in the most traditional terms, who is playing father and who mother, who is playing husband and who wife.

No doubt aware that fairy tales and scribblings in crayon are the happy hunting ground of child psychology, Karras and the camera glance over Regan's artwork and the pictures on her wall. He is now at play in the playroom; he thinks he is a sage adult, when in fact he is appealing to the child to explain what he does not understand. We see a version of Little Red Riding Hood, whom Freud discusses along with the Seven Little Goats in his case study of the Wolf-Man and who has been the subject of much psychoanalytic speculation ever since. Red Riding Hood rivals Sleeping Beauty as the fairy-tale ur-text of the sexuality of girls. It speaks with mythic simplicity of an abandoned mother and a devoured grandmother helpless in the battle between the seductive Wolf-father and heroic Hunter-father for the Oedipal allegiance of the little girl who strays from the straight and narrow path to indulge the pleasure of picking flowers and flirting with rapacious beasts. On the wall in this scene we see a cartoonish figure of Red Riding Hood offering a flower to the Big Bad Wolf, who is disguised as a gentleman wearing spectacles and bearing a cane. On a branch nearby is a bird like a toucan with a long and colorful beak. The bird is abundantly phallic, and we have already seen it in a number of guises in the film, including a stone bird-demon, the bird-spout of a water pitcher in Iraq, and, most important, a bird sculpture that Regan was painting earlier and presented to her mother. The bird also recalls the beaky and garishly painted breasts and penis that desecrate a statue of the Blessed Virgin in a nearby church in an earlier scene, and it is significant that this statue is discovered by a priest, an innocent, whose hands are full of the flowers he has been arranging. In Regan's picture of Red Riding Hood, the possession of this phallic bird remains in question. Is it the girl's to bestow where she pleases, as she extends with arm erect the gift of the flower to the Wolf or the gift of the bird sculpture to the divorced mother or the gift of the phallus to the virgin mother? In a visual pun, the phallic bird at one point looks as if it were strapped to Chris's groin.

The Wolf in the picture is of course easily identified with the demon, who is sometimes birdlike but who most often appears here in traditional guise as a creature, half man and half animal, with a growling countenance like that of a wolf or dog. Oddly, the Wolf also resembles Father Merrin, a gentleman who gets his spectacles vomited on and who, in Iraq, watches a man lead a blind person who carries a cane. There is also a doctor who wears spectacles in which Regan's X-rays are reflected. The better to *see* you with, my dear, says the Wolf who would like to devour Red Riding Hood. There seems to be no safe position from which to gaze at the little girl in this film, no look that is free from the carnivorous paternal desire it seeks to exorcise. Karras gazes at the Wolf gazing at the girl, even as he aspires unconsciously to betray his vow of celibacy and take the place of the absent Hunter-father, the absent Mr. MacNeil. In his final gesture of self-sacrifice, when Karras invites possession and his eyes take on the bestial, glowing greenness of the devil, we are left to wonder whether there is a difference between the Hunter and the Wolf. As in the fairy tale, the distinction between the dual roles of the sadistic father, whether evil-Wolf or good-Hunter, is always in danger of collapse. In both the fairy tale and the film, the arduous narrative effort at idealizing the desires of father and daughter is always in question. Are there any innocents here? Does Regan not secretly long for her demon, is not Merrin a little too creepy to be a redeemer, is Karras not at heart a lover and a murderer? Are they not all involved in the same Oedipal game? Are not we as spectators appreciating the figure of Regan's Red Riding Hood with the interpretive gaze of a Hunter and a Wolf?

In one of Regan's drawings we see a bare tree with a number of vague figures perched in the branches. The image plays on the figure of the bird on the desk and in the Red Riding Hood drawing, but it is also very nearly a replica of the drawing of the dream of the wolves in Freud's case of the Wolf-Man. Freud's analysand has a homosexual fixation on his father, and he fears that the phallic wolves outside his bedroom window are going to devour him. Regan appears to have a homosexual fixation on her mother rendered all the more rapacious by the absence of her father, whose place she is in hot competition with Sharon (Chris's secretary) to usurp. Like Red Riding Hood, her naive desire for the father has allowed him to seduce and devour her in the person of the demon. Like the Wolf, the demon tells Father Karras that he is not Regan, that Regan is inside him. Nevertheless, it is Regan's body that we see, not a Wolf's, not even Grandma's nightgown and spectacles, though at one point Father Karras imagines the girl's transformation into his ailing and elderly mother (the better to eat her, I suppose). We are led to suspect an ironic reversal: the girl has swallowed the Wolf. She has incorporated the phallus and taken the place of her father. In this sense, Regan becomes a touchstone for the representation of the gothic child, possessed of a maturity, a masculinity, and a paternal power that renders her grotesque. The girl is the Wolf. Her proffered flower has blossomed, and that is, after all, a message of the gothic ur-child Little Red Riding Hood, whose innocence is preserved, however improbably, through the displacement of her desire onto a seducer, as if she could simply hand it over with her basket from her mother.

I come to this interpretation not merely through the girl's artwork, but also through the deceptively banal dialogue between Regan and her mother before the possession. The mother's basket is unusually bountiful. Much to the irritation of the numerous film reviewers who thought the characterization vacuous, Blatty won an Oscar for his screenplay. I think he deserved it, since the film's dialogue is symbolically dense and much tighter and more ironic than the kitschy chatter of his novel. There is a subtle tension and eroticism between mother and daughter, an unconscious, understated, but relentless aggression that builds almost imperceptibly during the first half hour until it finally bursts out on the screen in Regan's mother-hating, mother-loving possession. As we watch, we are ourselves possessed of a suspicion—we are scarcely able to account for it at first—that the mother is to blame. The summer after *The Exorcist* was released, the sociologist Herbert J. Gans published an essay in *Social Policy* that was a blistering attack on Blatty's sexism. He noted that all the sick people in the film are female and that the "social cause of Regan's illness is her mother's life-style."[9] Other people blamed Vietnam and Watergate for the success of the film, claiming with good reason that Blatty's demon gave us a simple personification of evil for a scapegoat in a time of political chaos (the gothic child as ideological weapon is nothing if not protean), but Gans saw the film as a backlash against the women's movement in particular. In other words, the mother is the real demon. Gans explained, "the social underpinnings of *The Exorcist* suggest, therefore, that it is about manly—and Christ-like—priests of lowly origin in the service of a rational and modern Catholic church, who save the daughter of a rich and famous woman from a destructive sexual psychosis caused by her mother's putting her career before her family."[10] The problem, therefore, is not the devil but the liberated woman who unwittingly invites the devil into her home. To support his thesis, Gans quotes a passage from the novel that does not occur in the film: the devil, speaking through Regan, berates Chris (the "sow-mother") for having a career: "Are you pleased? It is *you* who have done it! Yes, *you* with your career before *anything,* your career before your *husband,* before *her,* before . . ."—before, well, just about everything that Blatty cares about.[11]

I agree with Gans's general argument, though he is taking this passage out of context, making Blatty sound as if he concurred with the opinion of his own villain. It is clearer in the novel than in the film that the devil can read the minds of the people in Regan's bedroom and that he plays on their guiltiest fears (Karras's feeling that he is a failure as a priest and as a son, for example)—and of course, the devil lies. We are left in a difficult interpretive position, a dilemma in which the gothic child always leaves us. Do we believe those disturbing assertions that slip from the mouths of babes, especially those babes who are possessed? Are we to take this passage literally or as a taunting and unfair exploitation of Chris's unjustified guilt? Do we dare take the devil—and the child, and the sociologist—at his word? Gans is right to point out the antifeminist politics of the script, since the film spews it like vomit all over our spectacles. Nevertheless, the sexual psychology of that narrative is more elaborate and subtle than he suggests. The thread of doubt that the film instills—is Regan innocent, is the mother innocent, dare we listen to the devil—makes us all the more suspicious and watchful. We are summoned to the voyeuristic pleasure of analyzing the sexual motives of those alleged innocents, the mother and daughter. The lasciviousness of Regan's demon calls into question the seemingly mundane and innocent banter that precedes his invasion of the girl's body, but as in *The Turn of the Screw,* the text tends to disavow the sexual speculations and investments that it is eager to excite. Every exchange between mother and daughter has, therefore, a double face, like the bestial face superimposed briefly over Regan's when the demon is urged to depart. Sexual suspicions possess us.

These suspicions are impressive in their complexity. Indeed, our suspicion is so neatly bound up with Chris's career as a movie star, that the erotics of interpretation and suspicion are thematized as a peculiar function of the cinematic apparatus itself. We suspect the film is out to get us; as a genre, it is up to no good. Chris is a skillful actor, especially when it comes to dissembling her own desire and guilt, and the film tempts us to see through her fakery, to expose her lies as if she too were the devil and disguised as an innocent mother. Both Regan and Chris are rather stagy in their demonstrations of mutual affection. We are impressed with what appears to be their genuine love for each other, but at the same time we have a nagging feeling that we are impressed with it too often, that we are constantly reminded of it because we need reminding, we need some conspicuous sign of a connection that we would otherwise question. With her role in *Alice Doesn't Live Here Anymore* (1974), Ellen Burstyn became a potent symbol of feminism in Hollywood by playing a woman who bravely set out to make a better life for herself after divorcing her abusive husband. *The Exorcist* takes a decidedly different tack, telling us that no matter how successful and independent a divorced woman might be, if her ex-husband does not exact his revenge, the devil will.

Chris MacNeil is what was once referred to quaintly and with some trepidation as a "career woman." The film suggests not only that she puts her career before her family, as it were, but that her career is a sign of her pathological sexuality, about which she feels guilty. In the novel she is divorced from her husband because she found her career more exciting and he just found someone else. The film leaves the reasons for the divorce vague, and so a heavy cloud of blame is permitted to hover over both Regan and Chris for no clear reason. In the film the father enjoys a curiously undeserved odor of sanctity. Apart from his failure to phone, his faults go unenumerated. Like the Christian god, he hides himself from human eyes. Like the pope, he resides in Rome, and his hotel, the Excelsior, suggests through its latinate loftiness that Chris might as well be trying to phone the Vatican on a Sunday. She is out of touch with the holy father in Rome, improbably symbolized by the guy from whom she is sinfully divorced. He may be a cad for not calling his daughter on her birthday, but when Chris screams at the telephone operator, we are given our most obvious clue as to why the marriage did not go well: she loses her temper and fires off a round of obscenities, a barrage of bullshits and Jesus Christs and fucking this and fucking that, that was unprecedented for a woman, especially the mother of a small child, in a mainstream film. She is, of course, well justified in her frustration and anger, not only with the operator but also with the various father figures in her life, but the film nudges us along in the suspicion that she is not necessarily what Kinderman says she is, "a very nice lady."

Her very name makes clear that she has usurped a paternal role at home and more generally; Chris is often a man's name, and it refers etymologically to Christ himself, such that her full name, when her husband's surname is added, sounds like a prayer or a commandment: "Christ, make kneel!" or the anagrammatical "Christ, I'm clean!" Despite her strange retention of the father's name, not to mention the husband's, she insists upon her atheism. Even when the priests rescue her daughter, she shows no sign of joining the fold, no desperate prayers, no retreats to a convent. In the final scene, she is relieved that her daughter remembers nothing, and she appears to wish she could do the same. She even returns to another priest, Father Dyer, the Saint Joseph medal that the demon ripped from Father Karras's neck, as if only he and not she could desire such a souvenir.[12] In the final scene she wears her usual sunglasses to cloak her identity, and she drives off with her daughter in a big black Mercedes, Hitler's favorite car, packed by her own servant, who is accused of being a Nazi—her shadow of evil intact. Her shadow of gender indeterminacy is also intact; the very name Mercedes is a playful pun on the gender-bending Mercedes McCambridge, the female actor whose gravelly baritone provides the voice of the demon, who is supposed to be male. Chris is named for the son of a god whose power she is reluctant to accept and whose name she is quick to use in vain in a tantrum, as if blaspheming in some Black Mass of her own. In her violent outbursts and cursing, she becomes ironically the double of her possessed daughter, calling on the father all the better to incorporate and displace him.

Before the women's movement set us all straight, Chris's career no doubt looked like the quintessential threat of feminism, a radical politics widely presumed to turn very nice ladies into aggressive careerists who neglect their proper domestic duties. We are told that she has sold her house in Los Angeles, she has just started renting this one in Georgetown (where she is currently filming), and she has plans to take Regan to Europe with her. Her relationship to a "home" is rendered all the more uncertain by the scenes in which she gives orders to her two servants and her secretary, who seem responsible for even the most minute domestic arrangements, from making tea to throwing parties. Having circumnavigated the traditional place of middle-class women in a home lorded over by a husband, she suffers the revenge of her own house in true gothic style: strange noises (rats, she thinks), migrating furniture, and blinking lights. We are also invited to suspect she is not necessarily a very attentive mother. Fathers in Hollywood are rarely plagued by this suspicion, but mothers who check their calendars to pencil in quality time with their young children have always been dubious candidates for sympathy.

Regan's relationship with her mother is characterized as a frustrated erotic longing frequently pursued in a bed (or, in one case, a bathtub, though usually by the age of twelve girls no longer need their mothers to bathe them). In one scene, Chris removes a fan magazine from Regan's bed while tucking her in. Mother and daughter appear on the cover, but Chris tells Regan she is silly to keep it in bed with her, apparently oblivious to the intensity of feeling in a girl who would do such a thing. She also says it is a bad picture that makes her look old, and so she gets further demerits for narcissism. Their conversation continually evokes Regan's capacity for vision as a potently cinematic gift from her mother, a way of looking with her and at her. Chris removes an eyelash from Regan's eye and observes, "We never finished seeing all the sights in Washington." She draws Regan into the specular world of her own film career, not only by posing with her for the fanzine but by promising to take her to a movie on her birthday (on Sunday, of course). In their relationship, the movies represent the gaze as an illicit mode of desire. Chris's banter is never less than indulgent and sweet, but there is always a hollow echo in her words that is easily given voice, in the typical manner of gothic projection, by the growling rumble in the attic. She nuzzles her daughter and promises to take her horseback riding on the weekend, as if merely spending time with her were a special gift. Then Regan pops the question: is Chris going to marry Burke Dennings, her director, the sexually dubious cinematic father, and does Chris feel the same way toward him as toward the father in Rome? Sensing her daughter's anxiety, Chris denies a relationship with Burke, comparing her fondness for him to her fondness for pizza, a rather troubling oral-sadistic allusion, given the Red Riding Hood theme. We are never any more certain than Regan about her mother's feelings for Burke, whether he is even heterosexual, or whether the pressing thing he fails to tell her at the front door is a proposition of marriage of the sort Regan has heard of, though from whom she does not say. Chris's reassurances to her daughter are improbable, especially when she says, "I'll always love your daddy, honey," shortly before Regan overhears her screaming about what a bastard he is. We suspect double-talk, and the girl's sexual curiosity hangs in the air along with ours, ungratified by what it cannot visualize.

Every interaction between mother and daughter entails a show of lavish affection that is nevertheless fraught with incestuous undertones in the usual manner of gothic-child narratives to undermine the tenuous distinction between parental love and parental seduction. The reference to horseback riding, for example, is less than innocent, given an earlier conversation about Regan's passion for horses. For reasons that are perhaps obvious, when American girls arrive at the age of twelve, their sexual preference seems often to take a turn that can only be described as equine. Regan is no exception, and she had been admiring a horse that is vaguely associated with the secretary Sharon's boyfriend, another father figure who is conspicuously absent from the film. If the expendable fathers were not a sufficient symbol of castrating female desire, Blatty offers us a more literal rendering. Chris asks her daughter if the horse was a gelding or a mare, and Regan says she thinks it was a gelding. I begin to suspect a conspiracy in this presentation of a choice between the castrated male and the female. Why is the gender of the horse, conceived in such a strikingly gonadal term, thought to be of pressing interest? Why would Regan have noticed? Regan's appeal to her mother—"Oh mom, can't we get a horse?"—would appear to have a very specific sexual impetus, her unconscious recognition that her mother has castrated the father and now has the phallus at her disposal, along with horses, movies, and other substitutes for the dad's body.[13] Like all Freudian girls, good and evil, Regan would like that phallus for herself, or anyway just a taste of it, something she can take to bed with her at night, and she reenacts her wish in the style of Red Riding Hood by tricking her mother and stealing a snack from a jar on her mother's desk. When she tries to escape with the loot, she is tackled by her mother in the hallway. Chris pins her to the floor in a bit of horseplay, so to speak, and teasingly demands that Regan "give it up." "You'll be sorry," she warns the girl, her playfulness seemingly ripe with unacknowledged aggression. The phallus, once detached from the father, is up for grabs, but despite her jocular demeanor, mom is none too eager to "give it up" herself.

This wrestling scene is repeated later on as a motif of visual puns—when, for example, Regan's bed begins to shake. First, we are as surprised as Chris to see that Regan has sneaked into bed with her, though the girl's need to escape a shaking bed seems not nearly as strong as her need to ride one. When Chris, summoned by Regan's cries for mother, finally witnesses the shaking bed for herself, she leaps on top of it and her daughter, screaming all the while, in an incestuous embrace suitably disguised as a terrified response to supernatural violence. This wrestling motif is further elaborated when the boxer Karras jumps on Merrin (who has just died of a heart attack) and pounds his chest, and when Karras jumps on Regan in a rage to do battle with her demon. In each case, a ghost of erotic aggression inhabits an otherwise innocent scene in which someone is ostensibly acting in the best interest of another. Only through Regan's possession does the erotic dimension become legible, most notably when Regan jumps on her quack hypnotist and wrenches his scrotum in her hands (recalling the gelding she covets). The delectably polymorphous perversity of Regan's obscenities calls everyone's sublimations and displacements into question. When she masturbates for Chris, when she (let me say it again) stabs at her bleeding vagina with the crucifix, when she slams Chris's head between her legs and cries in a gruff masculine voice, "Lick me! Lick me!"—she makes grotesquely literal the symbolic seduction that has already taken place between herself and her mother. When the demonic Regan screams at Merrin and Karras, "Stick your cock up her ass, you mother-fucking, worthless cocksucker!" or when she says to Damian, "Fuck him! Fuck him, Karras!" she is rendering explicit those illicit sexual possibilities that are already latent in the text in a more figurative and therefore more elusive and "innocent" form.

The scene with the crucifix is especially dense with sexual symbolism beyond what is literally and graphically taking place before our eyes. Chris bolts up the stairs to Regan's bedroom in response to that gruff masculine voice and the high-pitched screams of her daughter. By the sound of it, Regan is being raped by a man, but when Chris enters the room, she sees that her daughter is alone. Regan has incorporated her own paternal rapist. The crucifix as dildo renders literal the phallus as detachable paternal penis, especially given that Chris is shocked by its very presence in Regan's bedroom. In another scene, she confronts the servants and asks who put the crucifix under Regan's pillow, but no one will claim it, not Sharon, not Karl. In a symbolic sense, Chris herself put it there. In a fatherless drama between mother and daughter, she has made a spectacle of the paternal penis. It has become a free-floating signifier, possessed by no one, possessing everyone, easily appropriated for the most profane of purposes even by the girl herself. We might be tempted to read this scene as a sign of Regan's frustrated love for her father. This reading would make no sense, however, given her contempt for fathers when they finally appear on the scene in the form of priests. We might also be stirred to fashionable accusations of sexual abuse by the father. The text is game for just about anything salacious.

The failed telephone call to the father in Rome allows Chris to justify her rage, to stage it dramatically not only for Sharon but also for Regan, since she must know as well as we do that her daughter is well within earshot in the next room. The message of that failure, the return call of the operator in the middle of the night, is what wakes Chris to the presence of Regan in her bed. When she forces her mother to lick her, however, we witness the rebellion within the rebellion, the moment when the daughter becomes the father, the abusive husband and father, and assaults the mother. The shift in gendered address is jarring, an invitation to both fellatio and cunnilingus, which reads as a girl's masculine and sadistic appeal for submission from her mother. Regan's sexuality is defined by rage. In fact, her very name is an anagram for "anger." Her anger, like her desire, is directed at both her father and her mother. Anyone who thinks that Regan is a classic Oedipal girl, motivated by a frustrated love for her father, would do well to remember that she is the namesake of the Shakespearian princess who betrayed her father, King Lear. Blatty makes this name game explicit in the novel: in true Red Riding Hood fashion, Regan woos her mother in the morning with a flower, a blush-red rose, as might a lover: *"That angel,"* Chris thinks—but then we read, "Chris shook her head; rueful; recalling: she had almost named her Goneril. *Sure. Right on. Get ready for the worst."*[14] Do you sense a certain heavy-handed ambivalence here? What mother in her right mind would name her daughter after Regan or Goneril? Not only do Shakespeare's ambitious, scheming characters betray their father, tricking him out of a kingdom by faking filial love, they also have no mother. Chris plays on her own career as an actor, a woman who, like Shakespeare's Regan, makes an occupation of dissemblance, and yet she has written the maternal role out of existence and, even more curious, cast the father, whose role she has (like Regan and Goneril) usurped, as a tragic dupe. This passage in the novel is rendered all the weirder when Regan's flower reminds Chris of her dead son Jamie, as if through some unspecified incestuous union, Regan could present her mother with a child, a son no less, from the grave.

The scene with the crucifix is further complicated by the blood flowing from Regan's vagina, which has been lacerated by the crucifix. The blood suggests a forcible breaking of the hymen by the father, but also menarche, here construed as a symbol of feminine abjection. Like many a Lolita in contemporary film and literature, Regan is twelve, an age of sexual transition that has proven irresistible, if not wholly magical, to the popular erotic imagination. By forcing her mother to lick the blood in this approximation of her first period or her "deflowering," Regan enacts a complex gesture of resentment and desire toward her mother because—to offer the most prob-able psychoanalytic explanation—she holds her mother responsible for the castration they are both struggling to disavow. There is also a hint of vam-pirism here, a retaliation against her mother's parasitic desire, now rendered literal in a grotesque parody of their relationship (followed by a brutal slap of rejection). By incorporating the father and forcing herself on her mother, Regan realizes most dramatically a fantasy of seduction previously frus-trated and reconceptualized by her mother, who sought to appropriate the unconscious paternal role from the husband she divorced and take the girl as phallus and lover.

Regan and Chris trade places in this scene. Regan now stands erect on the bed, towering over her mother and far superior to her in strength. Chris is made to kneel or scramble on the floor at Regan's feet, as though tossed from the bed of father and daughter and made to peer over the footboard, the locus classicus for the child detective in the primal scene who cannot yet grasp the significance of the erotic spectacle that excludes her. Chris has passed from an urbane and even cynical knowingness to an infantilized bafflement. As the girl turned woman turned father, Regan has beat Chris at her own game. She has mimicked her mother's earlier position of autonomy and dominance, and then turned it against her. With a few exceptions, the camera in this scene is positioned so that it invites us to identify with the mother's perspective as she gawks in horror and confusion at the spectacle on the bed. We too are the child-mother positioned at the foot of the bed, jolted with sensational scenes of blasphemy, genital mutilation, and assault by furniture. The gothic child is threatening, not only in its omniscience and omnipotence, but also in its power to infantilize the adult viewer into a child-man, a kinder-man, to play upon the German name of the child-like detective who poses as his own little daughter to get an autograph from Chris. Kinderman is a kinder man than any other in the film, but he never does get a clue, no matter how often he lingers at the margin of events and peers in at them. Like him, like Chris at the foot of the bed, we are presented once again with a primal scene of desire and murder, a violent sexuality we would rather not remember, one that makes us feel fascinated, powerless, confused, frightened, and, once again, very, very small.

In the final shots of this notorious scene, Regan's head turns all the way around with bone-cracking verisimilitude and faces backward, one of many inversions ascribed to the demon. She then poses a rhetorical question that reverberates through the film, not the least because it is answered only by her mother's scream, which echoes into the empty sky of the following scene. She asks in Burke Denning's voice, "Do you know what she did, your cunting daughter?" The answer ought to be yes, we do know, or at any rate we have guessed, that Regan has murdered Denning in a jealous rage by wrenching his head around backward and flinging him out the window. Her turning head is then not only a sign of her "perversion" but a parody of yet another ineffectual father figure (a "père-version," to lift a French pun from Lacan) whom she has murdered and incorporated, speaking as she sometimes does with his voice. Beyond this immediate confession, posed oddly as a question rather than an answer, we might ask what *did* she do, after all, that made her the ideal candidate for possession by the devil? And what does that obscure British practice "cunting" have to do with it? Why is her possession defined relentlessly in sexual terms? Once again, the demon's question seems to provide its own set of answers, though we accept them at our peril. As usual, Regan's demon may be looking to confirm our worst suspicions, even when the truth may well be otherwise. Does Karras's mother really suck cocks in hell, as the demon says? One could do worse, I suppose, but it seems a bit out of character for Grandmother to act on her desire for the Wolf so boldly. But how does one know for sure? We are always afraid—indeed, we are warned repeatedly—that we might be the victim of an occult tattletale, a gossip who goes about dispensing salacious disinformation prefaced by the obsessive and irresistible come-on, "Do you know? Do you know what she did?" In its teasing, quizzing incitement to speculate about evil—*honi soit qui mal y pense*—the question raises the question of interrogation itself and the status of the sexual child as an epistemological paradox, a play of questions that are pleasurable, even sinful, precisely because they are their own answer.

In her erotic innocence, Regan is the very emblem of the symbolic as game or child's play. Even before she is possessed, she plays one Oedipal language game after another with Chris. For example, in their exchange over the Ouija board—which is a language game, and a rather childish one at that—Regan and Chris reenact their ambivalence toward each other. After the fashion of a seance, the players place their hands lightly on an indicator that, supposedly inspired by occult forces, glides over letters and words on a board, spelling out messages from the Beyond. As usual, the Beyond seems to be a metaphor for the unconscious. Chris wonders where the Ouija board came from. She is always wondering where something came from, usually because, unconsciously, she has already guessed, she has already identified herself as the culprit. Regan says she has found the Ouija board in a closet in the basement, which is generally not a good place to hide things from Dr. Freud. Like every scene between Chris and Regan, this one is ripe with erotic symbolism. Consider this little snatch of dialogue, which positively drips with sexual innuendo:

CHRIS: Been playing with it?
REGAN: Yup.

CHRIS: You know how?
REGAN: I'll show you.
CHRIS: Wait a minute, you need two.
REGAN: No I don't. I do it all the time.
CHRIS: Oh yeah? Well, let's both play.

What could the Ouija board come up with that could possibly be more revealing or more enigmatic than this? In fact, the figurative sexual game is eventually literalized when Chris first brings doctors home to "see" Regan again: the girl stands up on the bed and starts wanking for her mother. Yes she has been playing with it, yes she certainly knows how, no it does not take two, but she would like to get her mother to watch. The Ouija board tugs the indicator away from Chris's hands—another snatching game, but this time the girl gets away with it. Regan then demonstrates for her mother how to communicate with the Beyond, as represented by a mysterious man named Captain Howdy (the phallus as cartoon character in the capable hands of a child). The reference to Howdy Doody escapes Chris, I guess, though in the novel, she is sharp enough to notice that "Howdy" sounds like "Howard," her ex-husband's name. Regan asks the Captain if her mother is pretty, but there is silence on the line. Chris makes a joke of Regan's apparent aggression, but really neither one of them has been able to get an answer out of the father, perhaps because they have both already eaten him. Through the Ouija board, Regan unwittingly summons the demon who possesses her; however, through her other language games, we find hints that he has been in residence for quite some time.

In the scenes where Regan is possessed, her language games become all the more elaborate; in fact, she embodies a perverse textuality that is insidiously foreign and technological in character, one that implicates the very practice of filmmaking. We prefer to think she cannot possess such a text, but can only be possessed by it. The sexual child is always nothing but uncanny recordings, a tabula rasa turned symptom or cipher of the spectator's desire. When Chris discovers Regan doing the nasty with the crucifix, she also sees a whirlwind of smashed phonograph records spinning out the window. They are recordings gone haywire, spun not on their proper mechanism but thrown perversely about the room in a demonic tantrum. They serve as metaphors for the multiple and fragmentary voices of Regan's demon, a dubbed voice that makes Regan sound as though she were possessed not by the devil but by a recording of the devil, by the very technology of recording and inscription in general. Hers is a mystical-hysterical textuality, as when, at the instigation of Sharon's flashlight, the words "HELP ME" appear on the girl's denuded belly as if symptomatically in childish scrawl in the form of hives. Is Regan sending a desperate message for help, or is the demon teasing us again even as he seems to sleep, trying to seduce Karras into an exorcism so that the girl's appropriation of the father will be complete? We are warned repeatedly (by Merrin, by Freud) that the child is not to be trusted to speak for herself. Her demon lies, it plays games, it perverts the language, it speaks in enigmatic signs.

Nowhere is this perversity more evident than in Karras's efforts to tape-record Regan's voices. He is trying to analyze her speech and to gather proof for either possession or psychosis, but he cannot interpret the information he gathers. Regan's demon plays language games with him. He would like to get her to speak in a foreign language that Regan does not know, as such knowledge would be a telltale sign of possession. She starts to speak in simple Latin phrases of the Jesuit variety, either because the demon is an accomplished linguist or because he can read the phrases in Karras's mind. Karras tries to engage her in a Latin conversation, and she quickly shifts to speaking nonsense in French. "La plume de ma tante!" she exclaims, "my aunt's pen," the sort of phrase one finds in a grammar textbook for schoolchildren, and she gives a guttural chortle. The very phrase, pointedly random though it appears, evokes an evil specter of female writing, like the mystical-hysterical message scrawled across Regan's belly, seemingly pregnant with her former self. She wields the pen, with all its phallic plumage, and she uses it to play a game. Karras then tells her he has some holy water, and he splashes her with it. He is lying—it is only tap water—but the demon cries out, "It burns!" We know that Karras is lying, though we never suppose he would lie to us, and so it makes no sense that the holy water should burn. Presumably, then, Regan is also lying, playing a game that is intended to confuse. In other words, she has read Karras's mind or simply recognized his ruse, and she is toying with his powers of interpretation, beating him at his own game of lies. In so doing, she blurs the distinction between the priest and Satan, who is after all the "man of lies."

When Karras interrogates Regan about her identity, she speaks in a language he does not recognize. She writhes and groans, apparently speaking in tongues and abandoning reference altogether. Karras takes the tape recording to a language lab at the university because he is incapable of analyzing it himself. He is then informed that Regan was indeed speaking English, but backward. When the tape is reversed, we hear her say, "I am no one," and cry out the name of Merrin, whom she has not yet met. Here, Regan's queer status as recording, as a perverted or inverted technology of the textual, is most evident, as is her eerie playfulness with language. Through her language games she announces her negation of identity, or rather her identity as negation, her refusal to be read, which is also a cry to be read more closely, to seduce through her child's play the father, the interpreter of the paternal word, embodied even more effectually in Merrin than in Karras. The exorcism, then, will be successful only if it rejects the contaminated modern technologies of recording to embrace the revealed word, albeit the word revealed within the modern recording technology of film. Thus Merrin calls for consecrated texts, cracking open his prayer book in true apocalyptic style, though how one can tell which texts bear the truth strikes me as a bit elusive. It is simply a matter of the Church's blessing, that sweet odor of sanctity that patriarchy exudes throughout the film. Some texts have it, some texts do not. But the high-tech ones are always suspect, a rather troubling distinction to be made in so high-tech a genre as film. What we are left with, then, is an archaic defense, a superstitious technophobia, that fails to resolve the question of who has the truth, whose language is not merely a seductive game. In the final scenes, once Regan is happily exorcised and Chris is packing her bags to leave the house, Sharon asks what they should do with the phonograph. "Storage," Chris responds simply—a wonderful ironic touch, but what of the film, which has a sound track of its own? Back in the closet, back in the basement where the Ouija board was tucked away. Repression is restored, even the repression of our own mode of perception, but we know what happens then. Some kid will always stumble on the evil technology while playing. Chris has changed nothing, but she has learned how to play a certain game with language, a certain game with priests and the paternal word, so that she does not get burned.

The elusiveness or duplicity of the sexual child is reinforced by the instability of the symbolic itself, as it is thematized in numerous references to various modes of communication, including writing, photographing, filming, phoning, painting, sculpting, and even just conversing, that all go mysteriously awry. All the characters in this film have considerable difficulty making themselves understood, and they have even less success interpreting other people. Just about everyone is interrupted in midsentence. Merrin leaves off writing in his notebook to ponder the broken sculpture of the demon he has unearthed. Chris is also writing in a diary or notebook (in the novel, she is reading her script) when we first see her, but she is interrupted by inarticulate growls from the attic. The ever-brooding Karras can scarcely put two words together, not even when he is with his crypto-queer friend, Father Dyer, the man most likely to understand him. The party around the piano is interrupted by Regan, who pees on the floor and says something utterly mysterious about the death of the astronaut. Then there is the telephone: the very technology that should bring people together and allow them to communicate more easily has only driven people apart. As Freud remarks in *Civilization and Its Discontents*, telephones and trains may make connection easier, but they also make distance easier. That astronaut is doomed in his spaceship. Chris curses the telephone operator who fails to connect her. When she first hears Karras's voice, he is offering consolation, but he is drowned out by the noise of a jet. With the aid of a television monitor, the doctors watch a recording of Regan howling, but they are still theorizing in the dark. The scanning machines make an enormous amount of mechanical racket, while filming and while displaying the slides in front of the light, but they tell the doctors nothing about Regan's condition. With its terrifying noise and impersonality, its ganglia of electrodes, its vampiric needle puncturing her neck, this technology of recording is anything but the redemptive gaze that the doctors promise it will be. This machinery of intensified gazing allows us to look all the more closely, down through the skin in a procedure that is painfully invasive. All we discover are repeated X-rays of Regan's exposed skull, a somewhat ghoulish death's-head, with wiry tissue that makes the image look as though it had been scribbled over by a child.

The X-ray machines are one of many paradoxical commentaries on the cinematic apparatus, all of which focus on the eroticized body of the child as an enigma, the vanishing point of vision. *The Exorcist* is a film about the failure of filming. As the X-rays shift slowly in and out of our line of vision, leaving a perfectly blank white screen ("I am no one") in their wake, they play on the blank screen of the cinema and suggest the futility of trying to capture a spiritual truth, to capture the invisible and ineffable, in a materialist technology of the visual such as film. Through the X-rays, we see that we cannot see, no matter how closely we look. There are a number of references to projected lamplight in the film, artificial rays that, like the faulty cinematic beam of light, reveal nothing but signs the characters cannot yet understand. I have already mentioned Sharon's flashlight on Regan's belly, and there are many other similar metaphors for cinematic illumination. There are also the movie lights that snap on loudly as Burke begins shooting his vapid film. Chris's headlights grope the pavement as she makes her way home in the dark. A ghoulish lamplight projects from Regan's bedroom window onto the street where Merrin emerges from a cab. Even Damian Karras's nickname, "Dimmy," characterizes him as a dim bulb who cannot see because his faith has all but flickered out. Despite all this artificial illumination, the film retreats into an ever more pervasive gloom and darkness until the exorcism has been accomplished and daylight returns.

Can the film survive its own assault on film as a medium? Blatty longs for revelations of prophetic clarity, nothing but the sublime illumination of pure truth, and like most such writers he has a weakness for biblical references. In an epigraph in the novel he cites the gospel according to Saint John: "They said, 'What sign can you give us to see, so that we may believe you.'"[15] His other epigraphs speak of the horrors of the Holocaust or the war in Vietnam, as if they were all chapter and verse of the same eminently readable sacred text, the same Christian apocalyptic narrative. In the context of his religious perspective, the various beams of light, the X-rays and the cinema, like the doctors and the filmmakers who orchestrate their images, are inadequate to the task of revelation. They attribute occult experiences to physiological and psychological origins, as if one could understand the spiritual as a mere symptom through a minute examination of the body. As a social construction, as well as an aesthetic one, the cinematic gaze is seen as limited by its own frame of reference, by the set of allowable questions motivating the inquisitive eye that searches for meaning. Film in this context is too modern for its own good.

Blatty was a screenwriter long before he published his novel; indeed, the film rights were sold before he finished writing it. The novel seems to have been designed with its cinematic adaptation in mind. It is strange, then, that a writer who has invested so much faith in cinema as a form should express so many doubts as to its efficacy. Within the film, movies are presented as a paradigm for the failure of symbolic expression in modernity. Film here does not stabilize identity, facilitate perception, or secure authority. For example, when Kinderman interviews Chris, he presents himself as a critical authority on her films, especially a film titled *Angel,* which in this context we can see only as a joke. Despite his insights into her acting career, he learns nothing useful about Regan or the murder he is supposed to be investigating. When he interviews Karras, he likens him to John Garfield and then, in a subtle bit of gay-baiting, to Sal Mineo, but Karras points up the absurdity of the game by likening Kinderman to Paul Newman. He tries to get Karras to come to the movies with him to see a production of *Othello,* about which he jokes, but the priest is not game. Film is seen as a trivial medium that can tell us nothing true, nothing we really need to know.

Aesthetically and politically, the film that Chris and Burke are shooting is clearly twaddle. Even Blatty, not above creating twaddle of his own, thinks so. In the novel it is described as "a musical comedy remake of *Mr. Smith Goes to Washington.* A subplot had been added dealing with campus insurrections." Blatty, ever the conservative, obviously did not think highly of campus insurrections, and Chris feels she has outgrown the radical politics that she refers to as "dumb."[16] In Blatty's screenplay, she shouts at the students that they have to bring about change "within the system," and then later, at home, she describes the project dismissively as a "Walt Disney version of a Ho Chi Minh story." By her own admission, she does not understand her role. She can read, she tells Burke, but the screenplay is ludicrous—and many said the same thing about the screenplay for *The Exorcist.* She is caught in two reactionary films that are perfectly happy to make no sense. Burke then jokingly asks if they should call up the writer, but unfortunately the writer is in Europe. "Writing?" she asks. "Fucking!" he answers. Everyone laughs. Even Karras the brooding priest laughs for the first and only time as he watches from a crowd of onlookers, the first audience for the film. Like Howard MacNeil, the screenwriter should stand in for the holy father in Europe, but in fact he has just abandoned us. The guy is off fucking when he should be writing. Fucking and writing seem to amount to the same thing in this film, where desire is always eager to interrupt one's composition and even determine the significance of one's every utterance. Fucking is all the devil can talk about, now that the paternal word is free to play as it pleases. Here we have writer, director, actor, and audience all in one scene, and they are all blind, all moral failures. The director is especially egregious, impotent kitschmeister that he is, though it seems to me that both Blatty and Friedkin are sawing at their own limb here. Burke Denning is a vulgar and pretentious ass, as well as a mean drunk, a party bore, and a less-than-virile wooer of women. He is not a man who can step easily into the role of father to Regan, certainly not with the lofty conception of paternity this film puts forward. We do not much miss him when he is murdered and flung from her bedroom window. It is as if the shutters and drapes on Regan's window were a metaphor for the shutters and drapes of a camera and he were expelled quite literally not only from the film but from the cinematic apparatus he has failed to master. What we need is a good writer like Blatty, a good director like Friedkin, a good actor like Burstyn, and a good audience like you and me to restore the word and the image to its paternal symbolic role, to rescue the child from her queerness, and to make the cinema see again.

Presumably, Blatty believes that the cinema might transcend the limitations of so materialist a mode of filmmaking as the X-ray, which is after all the ultimate documentary, the ultimate metaphor for documentary as a form, a way of using film to expose those elusive "inner workings" of the real. Here, the film is looking to the occult and to the wizardry of special effects to subvert its own efforts at realism. Like Regan and her demon, the film perverts its own genre, getting it all backward so that we can hear the devil speaking. Along with *Rosemary's Baby,* Roman Polanski's ironic foray into satanism, the film initiates a popular horror tradition in which the supernatural seems perfectly natural, as though the devil were appearing, tail and all, in a documentary. Friedkin offers gothic with a minimum of shadows and cobwebs, presenting the possessed child in a realist style, imposing the occult on the everyday, in order to exploit the audience's formal expectations and introduce demonic chaos into a world that would otherwise be reassuringly familiar. Paradoxically, the film renders the devil all the more strange by banishing strangeness, by plunking him down amid bourgeois atheists in a well-lit modern townhouse where there are cocktail parties, kitchens, ironing boards, wall-to-wall carpeting, and a surprisingly ordinary twelve-year-old girl. The visual style generates an aesthetic dissonance, the clash of gothic realism.

As the novelist Jeanette Winterson once pointed out, great art introduces us to the unexpected: your favorite aunt in your favorite poker parlor or your favorite poker in your favorite aunt. In *The Exorcist* a gothic spectacle seems out of place in a realist film, just as the devil seems out of place in such an ordinary twelve-year-old girl. The juxtaposition invites us to unearth, or perhaps merely to generate, a psychological or moral narrative of trauma that rises to the occasion of explaining the mayhem on the screen. In the expectation that we might make the wild leap into the mysterious and the unknowable, the screenplay continually presents us with the enigma of things that are out of place. Obviously, the devil can be blamed for some of this mischief, but there are a few enigmas that the film is eager to leave unresolved. Where did the Ouija board come from? Who desecrated the statue of the virgin? Who put the crucifix under Regan's pillow? How does a medal of Saint Joseph find its way into an archaeological excavation of ancient Nineveh? How did the broken image of Pazuzu like the one dug up by Merrin in Iraq find its way to the bottom of the steps outside the MacNeils' apartment in Georgetown even before Merrin has appeared on the scene? What does Kinderman do with it after picking it up? More than the furniture is migrating. There is a tendency for things to show up in the narrative where they do not—or could not—belong, and we are left to our own devices to provide plausible explanations. Like Karras and Kinderman, we are always a little bit in the dark, never quite certain. Karras has a wavering faith in God, and we have a wavering faith in the film. These mysterious religious objects—the Ouija board, the statue of the virgin, the crucifix, the medal, the demon head—are the pawns in a playful narrative game, an affront to realism that obliges us to relinquish our engagement in the seemingly realistic, rational, familiar world of the film. The devil really is out of place in modernity, just as Christianity is out of place in ancient Nineveh. Nevertheless, there it is. We are called upon to revise our modes of perception and understanding, and certainly our horizon of expectations. At the same time, this film is caught in a paradox: it seems to be as elusive, as difficult to interpret, as the body of the sexual child it seeks to redeem. The film is itself a possessed child who plays seductive games with us—and is therefore an improbable source of theological enlightenment.

How are we then to interpret its archaic appeal to Christian orthodoxy? How are we to know that its flight from reason, from science, even from interpretation is not itself on the side of the devil, part of the seductive game by which, like Karras, we are included in the child's narrative of illicit desire? We are presented with what looks like a redemptive narrative, but a closer inspection leaves us with doubts. We are offered the example of Father Merrin, who seems to have an unshakable faith in Christ. Like the devil he exorcises, he seems to know everything without needing to be told.

Ellis Hanson

When confronted with the unknown, he eschews his own scientific training in favor of mystical thinking. As he stands over the ruins of Nineveh, face-to-face with the statue of Pazuzu, with only the blood-red sun between them, we might suspect that the two figures represent a dichotomy of good and evil, but the opposition is always in danger of collapse, because good and evil are in such intimate communication with each other. They seem to be two sides of the same medal, like the two-sided medal of Saint Joseph that Merrin flips over in his hand. "Evil against evil," he says of the Pazuzu fragment, which was supposedly used superstitiously to ward off the demon. Are he and his Christian medal any different? One side has a picture of Joseph with the infant Christ in his lap, an image that enacts yet another act of paternal vengeance on the mother it envies but has displaced. Here we see only the father can redeem the child: it reads, "Sancte Joseph, ora pro nobis." The other side, however, is blank, like the blank white screen where the X-rays appear. "I am no one," it seems to tell us, but only backward of course, its head turned all the way around. Then again, perhaps the Father is also legion: when Karras says there are at least three demons in Regan, Merrin insists there is only one, an image that ironically mirrors the mystery of the holy trinity, the three in one. Like Regan, Merrin speaks in many voices in that he claims to command her in the name of Christ, the martyrs, God himself, and so on. Merrin even appears as a blank when he first turns up on the MacNeils' doorstep. For a moment, he is ghoulish as he looms in from the darkness, visible to us only as an empty black silhouette. His colleagues in the Church describe him as still "digging up tombs," a curiously vampiric turn of phrase. Max von Sydow is earnest to the point of creepiness, arriving less than fresh from his famous chess game with death in *The Seventh Seal*. If Merrin is the vessel of redemption, why is he so spooky? Why is he weaker than the demon?

Father Karras poses still another problem. He slowly recovers his faith over the course of the film, judging from his increasing earnestness at Mass and his final conviction that Regan is possessed and the power of Christ compels her. In the novel he explains that he was named after a priest who devoted his life to caring for lepers and who finally caught the disease himself; thus he is characterized as a paragon of self-sacrifice, taking the evil of others onto himself just as he invites Regan's demon to possess him instead. His final act of rescue may be seen as a good Christian's act of self-sacrifice, but it might also be seen in more orthodox terms as a sin, a suicide. In the novel, Blatty cites the passage in the Bible in which Christ exorcises demons, casting them into the bodies of pigs who then drown themselves. Karras is evidently a pig in this film, a father who turns his own failure into the redemption of another. "The sow is mine!" as Regan announces.

Once Regan has been exorcised, once the paternal presence has been restored in her psyche, she is her chirpy old self again, chatting to the priest, Father Dyer, like the good little girl she is not. In fact, nothing has changed. She is a model of repression and Oedipal trauma in that, so her mother assures us, she remembers nothing. The priest ponders her window, which has been temporarily boarded up, but as the spine-tingling musical score reasserts itself, we wonder, as perhaps this priest wonders, what manner of closure is this? How long will the film maintain a blind eye? In one of the more ambiguous scenes in the film, Regan gazes at the priest's collar and then suddenly kisses him for no apparent reason. For a moment, she seems to have forgotten that she forgot. She offers a grateful kiss to the father, which has already been rendered suspect, even volatile, by the salacious invitations that Regan offered the priests while she was possessed. In fact, she still has no father, and she is off again with her mother in the car. If she has faith in the father, it shows itself only latently and unreliably in her Oedipal kiss. As always, Regan's innocence, which is to say her desire, is seductively paradoxical. Her exorcism is profoundly queer, a ritual that produces the sexual child it seeks to redeem. Regan offers the viewer a kiss readable as both innocence and its antithesis.

James Kincaid argues that the modern child is an erotically appealing blank. Filmmakers, talk-show hosts, journalists, police, psychologists, concerned parents—in short, all of us—have a stake in propagating the image of the sexual child through the same endlessly repeated and repeatable gothic narrative of protection and redemption that allows us to disavow our own sexual investment. It is a tale of monstrous adults preying on angelic children, and it produces the child as a blank screen ideal for projections of innocence and fantasies of corruption: "Such frenzied denunciations of the villains, such easy expressions of outrage, such simple-minded analyses of the problem of child-molesting as we love to repeat serve not simply to flatter us but to bring before us once again the same story of desire that is itself desirable, allowing us to construct, watch, enjoy the erotic child without taking any responsibility for our actions."[17] Our narratives of protection and redemption are endlessly serviceable as pornography for puritans. *The Exorcist* does indeed exploit this gothic tradition, but it might also serve as an allegory, a way for us as critics to tell the story of the story. Despite its conservative effort to reaffirm our faith in the power of paternal authority to bring closure to the story, to save the child and indeed to save ourselves from an illicit desire, the film seduces us finally by baffling us, by invoking an unabashedly gothic spectacle of the sexual child and then rendering it hopelessly ambiguous. It questions the validity of its own powers of interpretation—whether scientific, religious, or cinematic—defying our certainty that we know what we are wrestling with. The sexual child is a figure rich in paradox, at once familiar and strange, naive and knowing, transparent and inscrutable, docile and dangerous, innocent and guilty. In Kincaid's analysis, it has acquired all the makings of a modern myth, and we find ourselves called upon to participate in the voyeuristic popular obsession with decrying an evil and enjoying it at the same time. *The Exorcist* may be seen to allegorize this paradox, gratifying us not with moral certainty, but with a spectacle of child sexuality that flirts with us by remaining always erotically overdetermined, always seductively ambiguous, always at play for our inquisitive gaze.

Notes

1. Review of *The Exorcist, Films Illustrated* 32 (1974): 303–4.

2. "The Ghoul Next Door," *Newsweek,* January 21, 1974, 97.

3. By "we," I mean you and me. You have my permission to opt out of this category if you are so inclined, though I formulated it to invite you to question the instinct, indeed the eagerness, for just such a disavowal.

4. Ibid., 4. Since it is one of the pleasures of this film that we should never be able to distinguish clearly between Regan and her demon, it is especially difficult to determine to whom we should attribute her more diabolical behavior. By assigning that agency to "Regan" and attributing to her all of Mercedes McCambridge's best lines, I intend not to cloak this important ambiguity but to highlight it. I cannot speak, however, for the intentions of any party by whom I myself might be possessed.

5. See Ellis Hanson, "Screwing with Children in Henry James," *GLO* 9, no. 3 (2003), 367–91.

6. James R. Kincaid, *Child-Loving: The Erotic Child and Victorian Culture* (New York: Routledge, 1992); and James R. Kincaid, *Erotic Innocence: The Culture of Child Molesting* (Durham, NC: Duke University Press, 1998).

7. For a more thorough discussion of the term *queer* and the uses of queer theory in cinema studies, see my introduction to my edited collection *Out Takes: Essays on Queer Theory and Film* (Durham, NC: Duke University Press, 1999), 1–19.

8. See, for example, Freud's case study of Dora: "No other kind of 'Yes' can be extracted from the unconscious; there is no such thing at all as an unconscious 'No.'" Sigmund Freud, "Fragment of an Analysis of a Case of Hysteria" (1905), in *The Standard Edition of the Complete Psychological Works of Sigmund Freud,* ed. and trans. James Strachey (London: Hogarth, 1955–74), 7:57.

9. Herbert J. Gans, "*The Exorcist*: A Devilish Attack on Women," *Social Policy* 5 (1974): 73.

10. Ibid.

11. Ibid., quoting William Peter Blatty, *The Exorcist* (New York: Harper & Row, 1971), 309.

12. Significantly, in the recently released "director's cut" of the film, Father Dyer gives the medal back to Chris, thus insisting on her acceptance of the Church's role in her future life.

13. In the *Newsweek* article, Linda Blair is referred to as a "live-wire adult-child" who is a "prize-winning equestrienne." When asked whether she wants to do any

more acting, she replies in the affirmative but adds, "The horses come first." "The Ghoul Next Door," 97.

14. Blatty, *The Exorcist,* 15.

15. Ibid., 197.

16. Ibid., 13.

17. Kincaid, *Child-Loving,* 375.

Part II
The Queers We Might Have Been

How to Bring Your Kids Up Gay: The War on Effeminate Boys

Eve Kosofsky Sedgwick

In the summer of 1989 the U.S. Department of Health and Human Services released a study titled *Report of the Secretary's Task Force on Youth Suicide*. Written in response to the apparently burgeoning epidemic of suicides and suicide attempts by children and adolescents in the United States, the 110-page report contained a section analyzing the situation of gay and lesbian youth. It concluded that, because "gay youth face a hostile and condemning environment, verbal and physical abuse, and rejection and isolation from families and peers," young gays and lesbians are two to three times more likely than other young people to attempt and to commit suicide. The report recommended, modestly enough, an "end [to] discrimination against youths on the basis of such characteristics as . . . sexual orientation."

On October 13, 1989, Dr. Louis W. Sullivan, secretary of the Department of Health and Human Services, repudiated this section of the report—impugning not its accuracy but, it seems, its very existence. In a written statement Sullivan said, "The views expressed in the paper entitled 'Gay Male and Lesbian Youth Suicide' do not in any way represent my personal beliefs or the policy of this Department. I am strongly committed to advancing traditional family values. . . . In my opinion, the views expressed in the paper run contrary to that aim."[1]

It's always open season on gay kids. But where, in all this, are psychoanalysis and psychiatry? Where are the "helping professions"? In this discussion of institutions, I mean to ask not about Freud and the possibly spacious affordances of the mother-texts, but about psychoanalysis and psychiatry as they are functioning in the United States today.[2] I am especially interested in revisionist psychoanalysis, including ego psychology, and in developments following on the American Psychiatric Association's much-publicized 1973 decision to drop the pathologizing diagnosis of homosexuality from its next *Diagnostic and Statistical Manual (DSM-III)*. What is likely to be the fate of children brought under the influence of psychoanalysis and psychiatry today, post-*DSM-III,* on account of parents' or teachers' anxieties about their sexuality?

The monographic literature on the subject is, to begin with, as far as I can tell, exclusively about boys. A representative example of this revisionist, ego-based psychoanalytic theory is Richard C. Friedman's *Male Homosexuality: A Contemporary Psychoanalytic Perspective,* published by Yale University Press in 1988.[3] (A sort of companion volume, though by a non-psychoanalyst psychiatrist, is Richard Green's *The "Sissy Boy Syndrome" and the Development of Homosexuality,* 1987, also from Yale.)[4] Friedman's book, which lavishly acknowledges his wife and children, is strongly marked by his sympathetic involvement with the 1973 depathologizing movement. It contains several visibly admiring histories of gay men, many of them encountered in nontherapeutic contexts. These include "Luke, a forty-five-year-old career army officer and a life-long exclusively homosexual man" (152), and Tim, who was "burly, strong, and could work side by side with anyone at the most strenuous jobs": "gregarious and likeable," "an excellent athlete," Tim was "captain of [his high school] wrestling team and editor of the school newspaper" (206–7). Bob, another "well-integrated individual," "had regular sexual activity with a few different partners but never cruised or visited gay bars or baths. He did not belong to a gay organization. As an adult, Bob had had a stable, productive work history. He had loyal, caring, durable friendships with both men and women" (92–93). Friedman also, by way of comparison, gives an example of a *hetero*sexual man with what he considers a highly integrated personality, who happens to be a combat jet pilot: "Fit and trim, in his late twenties, he had the quietly commanding style of an effective decision maker" (86).[5]

Is a pattern emerging? Revisionist analysts seem prepared to like some gay men, but the healthy homosexual is one who (a) is already grown up and (b) acts masculine. In fact, Friedman correlates, in so many words, adult gay male effeminacy with "global character pathology" and what he calls "the lower part of the psychostructural spectrum" (93). In the obligatory paragraphs of his book concerning "the question of when behavioral deviation from a defined norm should be considered psychopathology," Friedman makes explicit that, while "clinical concepts are often somewhat imprecise and admittedly fail to do justice to the rich variability of human behavior," a certain baseline concept of pathology will be maintained in his study, and that that baseline will be drawn in a very particular place: "The distinction between nonconformists and people with psychopathology is usually clear enough during childhood. Extremely and chronically effeminate boys, for example, should be understood as falling into the latter category" (32–33).

"For example," "extremely and chronically effeminate boys"—this is the abject that haunts revisionist psychoanalysis. The same *DSM-III* that, published in 1980, was the first that did not contain an entry for "homosexuality" was also the first that *did* contain a new diagnosis, numbered (for insurance purposes) 302.60: "gender identity disorder of childhood." Nominally gender neutral, this diagnosis is actually highly differential between boys and girls: a girl gets this pathologizing label only in the rare case in which she asserts that she actually is anatomically male (e.g., "that she has, or will grow, a penis"), whereas a boy can be treated for gender identity disorder of childhood if he merely asserts "that it would be better not to have a penis"—or, alternatively, if he displays a "preoccupation with female stereotypical activities as manifested by a preference for either cross-dressing or simulating female attire, or by a compelling desire to participate in the games and pastimes of girls."[6] While the decision to remove "homosexuality" from *DSM-III* was a highly polemicized and public one, accomplished only under intense pressure from gay activists outside the profession, the addition to *DSM-III* of "gender identity disorder of childhood" appears to have attracted no outside attention at all—or even to have been perceived as part of the same conceptual shift.[7]

Indeed, the gay movement has never been quick to attend to issues concerning effeminate boys. There is a discreditable reason for this in the marginal or stigmatized position to which even adult men who are effeminate have often been relegated in the movement.[8] A more understandable reason than effeminophobia, however, is the conceptual need of the gay movement to interrupt a long tradition of viewing gender and sexuality as continuous and collapsible categories—a tradition of assuming that anyone, male or female, who desires a man must by definition be feminine and that anyone, male or female, who desires a woman must by the same token be masculine.

That one woman, *as a woman,* might desire another; that one man, *as a man,* might desire another—the indispensable need to make these powerful, subversive assertions has seemed, perhaps, to require a relative deemphasis of the links between gay adults and gender-nonconforming children. The move toward theorizing gender and sexuality as distinct though intimately entangled axes of analysis has been, indeed, a great advance in recent lesbian and gay thought.

There is a danger, however, that this advance may leave the effeminate boy once more in the position of the haunting abject—this time the haunting abject of gay thought itself. This is an especially horrifying possibility if—as many studies launched from many different theoretical and political positions have suggested—for any given adult gay man, wherever he may be at present on a scale of self-perceived or socially ascribed masculinity (ranging from extremely masculine to extremely feminine), the likelihood is disproportionately high that he will have a childhood history of self-perceived effeminacy, femininity, or nonmasculinity.[9] In this case the eclipse of the effeminate boy from adult gay discourse would represent more than a damaging theoretical gap; it would represent a node of annihilating homophobic, gynephobic, and pedophobic hatred internalized and made central to gay-affirmative analysis. The effeminate boy would come to function as the discrediting open secret of many politicized adult gay men.

One of the most interesting aspects—and by "interesting" I mean cautionary—of the new psychoanalytic developments is that they are based on *precisely* the theoretical move of distinguishing gender from sexuality. This is how it happens that the depathologization of an atypical sexual object choice can be yoked to the *new* pathologization of an atypical gender identification. Integrating the gender-constructivist research of, for example, John Money and Robert Stoller, research that many have taken (though perhaps wrongly) as having potential for feminist uses, this work posits the very early consolidation of something called *core gender identity*—one's basal sense of being male or female—as a separate stage prior to, even conceivably independent of, any crystallization of sexual fantasy or sexual object choice. Gender identity disorder of childhood is seen as a pathology involving the core gender identity (failure to develop a CGI consistent with one's biological sex); sexual object choice, on the other hand, is unbundled from this core gender identity through a reasonably space-making series of two-phase narrative moves. Under the pressure, ironically, of having to show how gay adults whom he considers well-integrated personalities do sometimes evolve from children seen as the very definition of psychopathology, Friedman unpacks several developmental steps that have often otherwise been seen as rigidly unitary.[10]

One serious problem with this way of distinguishing between gender and sexuality is that, while denaturalizing sexual object choice, it radically renaturalizes gender. All ego psychology is prone, in the first place, to structuring developmental narrative around a none-too-dialectical trope of progressive *consolidation* of self. The placement of a very early core-gender determinant (however little biologized it may be) at the center of that process of consolidation seems to mean, essentially, that for a nontranssexual person with a penis, nothing can ever be assimilated to the self through this process of consolidation unless it can be assimilated *as masculinity.* For even the most feminine-self-identified boys, Friedman uses the phrases "sense of masculine self-regard," (245), "masculine competency" (20), and "self-evaluation as appropriately masculine" (244) as synonyms for any self-esteem and, ultimately, for any *self.* As he describes the interactive process that leads to any ego consolidation in a boy:

> Boys measure themselves in relation to others whom they estimate to be
> similar. [For Friedman, this means only men and other boys.] Similarity of
> self-assessment depends on consensual validation. The others must agree
> that the boy is and will remain similar to them. The boy must also view
> both groups of males (peers and older men) as appropriate for idealization.
> Not only must he be like them in some ways, he must want to be like them
> in others. They in turn must want him to be like them. Unconsciously, they
> must have the capacity to identify with him. This naturally occurring [!]
> fit between the male social world and the boy's inner object world is the
> juvenile phase-specific counterpoint to the preoedipal child's relationship
> with the mother. (237)

The reason effeminate boys turn out gay, according to this account, is that other men don't validate them as masculine. There is a persistent, wistful fantasy in this book: "One cannot help but wonder how these [prehomosexual boys] would have developed if the males they idealized had had a more flexible and abstract sense of masculine competency" (20). For Friedman, the increasing flexibility in what kinds of attributes or activities *can* be processed as masculine, with increasing maturity, seems fully to account for the fact that so many "gender-disturbed" (effeminate) little boys manage to grow up into "healthy" (masculine) men, albeit after the phase where their sexuality has differentiated as gay.

Or rather, it *almost* fully accounts for it. There is a residue of mystery, resurfacing at several points in the book, about why most gay men turn out so resilient—about how they even survive—given the profound initial deficit of "masculine self-regard" characteristic of many proto-gay childhoods and the late and relatively superficial remediation of it that comes with increasing maturity. Given that "the virulence and chronicity of [social] stress [against it] puts homosexuality in a unique position in the human

▼ How to Bring Your Kids Up Gay

143

behavioral repertoire," how to account for "the fact that severe, persistent morbidity does not occur more frequently" (205) among gay adolescents? Friedman essentially throws up his hands at these moments. "A number of possible explanations arise, but one seems particularly likely to me: namely, that homosexuality is associated with some psychological mechanism, not understood or even studied to date, that protects the individual from diverse psychiatric disorders" (236). It "might include mechanisms influencing ego resiliency, growth potential, and the capacity to form intimate relationships" (205). And "it is possible that, for reasons that have not yet been well described, [gender-disturbed boys'] mechanisms for coping with anguish and adversity are unusually effective" (201).

These are huge blank spaces to be left in what purports to be a developmental account of proto-gay children. But given that ego-syntonic consolidation for a boy can come only in the form of masculinity, given that masculinity can be conferred only by men (20), and given that femininity in a person with a penis can represent nothing but deficit and disorder, the one explanation that could *never* be broached is that these mysterious skills of survival, filiation, and resistance could derive from a secure identification with the resource richness of a mother. Mothers, indeed, have nothing to contribute to this process of masculine validation, and women are reduced in the light of its urgency to a null set: any involvement in it by a woman is overinvolvement, any protectiveness is overprotectiveness, and, for instance, mothers "proud of their sons' nonviolent qualities" are manifesting unmistakable "family pathology" (193).

For both Friedman and Green, then, the first, imperative developmental task of a male child or his parents and caretakers is to get a properly male core gender identity in place as a basis for further and perhaps more flexible explorations of what it may be to *be* masculine—that is, for a male person, to be *human*. Friedman is rather equivocal about whether this masculine CGI necessarily entails any particular content or whether it is an almost purely formal, preconditional differentiation that, once firmly in place, can cover an almost infinite range of behaviors and attitudes. He certainly does not see a necessary connection between masculinity and any scapegoating of male homosexuality; since ego psychology treats the development of male heterosexuality as nonproblematic after adolescence, as not involving the suppression of any homosexual or bisexual possibility (263–67), and therefore as completely unimplicated with homosexual panic (178), it seems merely an unfortunate, perhaps rectifiable, misunderstanding that for a proto-gay child to identify "masculinely" might involve his identification with his own erasure.

The renaturalization and enforcement of gender assignment is not the worst news about the new psychiatry of gay acceptance, however. The worst is that it not only fails to offer but seems conceptually incapable of offering even the slightest resistance to the wish endemic in the culture surrounding and supporting it: the wish that gay people *not exist.* There are many people in the worlds we inhabit, and unmistakably among them are psychiatrists who have a strong interest in the dignified treatment of any gay people who may happen already to exist. But the number of persons or institutions by whom the existence of gay people is treated as a precious desideratum, a needed condition of life, is small. The presiding asymmetry of value assignment between hetero and homo goes unchallenged everywhere: advice on how to help your kids turn out gay, not to mention your students, your parishioners, your therapy clients, or your military subordinates, is less ubiquitous than you might think. On the other hand, the scope of institutions whose programmatic undertaking is to prevent the development of gay people is unimaginably large. There is no major institutionalized discourse that offers a firm resistance to that undertaking: in the United States, at any rate, most sites of the state, the military, education, law, penal institutions, religious institutions, medicine, and mass culture enforce it all but unquestioningly, and with little hesitation at even the recourse to invasive violence.

These books, and the associated therapeutic strategies and institutions, are not about invasive violence. What they are about is a train of squalid lies. The overarching lie is the lie that they are predicated on anything but the therapists' disavowed desire for a nongay outcome. Friedman, for instance, speculates wistfully that—with proper therapeutic intervention—the sexual orientation of one gay man whom he describes as quite healthy might not have *been changed* but might conceivably "have shifted *on its own*," a speculation, he artlessly remarks, "not value laden with regard to sexual orientation" (212). Green's book, composed largely of interview transcripts, is a tissue of Green's lies to children about their parents' motives for bringing them in for therapy. (It was "not to prevent you from becoming homosexual," he tells one young man who had been subjected to behavior modification, "it was because you were unhappy;" but later on the very same page, he unself-consciously confirms to his trusted reader that "parents of sons who entered therapy were . . . worried that the cross-gender behavior portended problems with later sexuality"; 318.) He encourages predominantly gay young men to "reassure" their parents that they are "bisexual" ("Tell him just enough so he feels better; 207) and to consider favorably the option of marrying and keeping their wives in the dark about their sexual activities (205). He lies to himself and to us in encouraging patients to lie to him. In a series of interviews with Kyle, for instance, the boy subjected to behavioral therapy, Green reports him as saying that he is unusually withdrawn—"I suppose I've been overly sensitive when guys look at me or something ever since I can remember, you know, after my mom told me why I have to go to UCLA because they were afraid I'd turn into a homosexual'" (307), as saying that homosexuality "is pretty bad, and I don't think they should be around to influence children. . . . I don't think they should be hurt by society or anything like that—especially in New York. You have them who are into leather and stuff like that. I mean, I think that is really sick, and I think that maybe they should be put away" (307), as saying that he wants to commit violence on men who look at him (307), and as saying that if he had a child like himself, he "would take him where he would be helped" (317). The very image of serene self-acceptance? Green's summary:

> Opponents of therapy have argued that intervention underscores the child's "deviance," renders him ashamed of who he is, and makes him suppress his "true self." Data on psychological tests do not support this contention; nor does the content of clinical interviews. The boys look back favorably on treatment. They would endorse such intervention if they were the father of a "feminine" boy. Their reason is to reduce childhood conflict and social stigma. Therapy with these boys appeared to accomplish this. (319)

Consistent with this, Green is obscenely eager to convince parents that their hatred and rage at their effeminate sons is really only a desire to protect them from peer-group cruelty—even when the parents name *their own* feelings as hatred and rage (391–92). Even when fully one-quarter of parents of gay sons are so interested in protecting them from social cruelty that when the boys fail to change, their parents kick them out onto the street! Green is withering about mothers who display any tolerance of their sons' cross-gender behavior (373–75). In fact, his bottom-line identifications as a clinician actually seem to lie with the enforcing peer group: he refers approvingly at one point to "therapy, be it formal (delivered by paid professionals) or informal (delivered by the peer group and the larger society via teasing and sex-role standards)" (388).

Referring blandly on one page to "psychological intervention directed at increasing [effeminate boys'] comfort with being male" (259), Green says much more candidly on the next: "The rights of parents to oversee the development of children is a long-established principle. Who is to dictate that parents may not try to raise their children in a manner that maximizes the possibility of a heterosexual outcome?" (260). Who indeed—if the members of this profession can't stop seeing the prevention of gay people as an ethical use of their skills?

Even outside the mental health professions and within more authentically gay-affirmative discourses, the theoretical space for supporting gay development is, as I've pointed out in the introduction to *Epistemology of the Closet*, narrow.[11] Constructivist arguments have tended to keep hands off the experience of gay and proto-gay kids. For gay and gay-loving people, even though the space of cultural malleability is the only conceivable theater for our effective politics, every step of this constructivist nature/culture argument holds danger: the danger of the difficulty of intervening in the seemingly natural trajectory from identifying a place of cultural malleability, to inventing an ethical or therapeutic mandate for cultural manipulation, to the overarching, hygienic Western fantasy of a world without any more homosexuals in it.

That's one set of dangers, and it is against them, as I've argued, that essentialist and biologizing understandings of sexual identity accrue a certain gravity. The resistance that seems to be offered by conceptualizing an unalterably *homosexual body* to the social-engineering momentum apparently built into every one of the human sciences of the West can reassure profoundly. At the same time, however, in the postmodern era it is becoming increasingly problematic to assume that grounding an identity in biology or "essential nature" is a stable way of insulating it from societal interference. If anything, the gestalt of assumptions that undergirds nature/nurture debates may be in the process of direct reversal. Increasingly it is the conjecture that a particular trait is genetically or biologically based, *not* that it is "only cultural," that seems to trigger an estrus of manipulative fantasy in the technological institutions of the culture. A relative depressiveness about the efficacy of social-engineering techniques, a high mania about biological control—the Cartesian bipolar psychosis that always underlay the nature/nurture debates has switched its polar assignments without surrendering a bit of its hold over the collective life. And in this unstable context, the dependence on a specified *homosexual body* to offer resistance to any gay-eradicating momentum is tremblingly vulnerable. AIDS, though used to proffer every single day to the news-consuming public the crystallized vision of a world after the homosexual, could never by itself bring about such a world. What whets these fantasies more dangerously, because more blandly, is the presentation, often in ostensibly or authentically gay-affirmative contexts, of biologically based "explanations" for deviant behavior that are absolutely invariably couched in terms of "excess," "deficiency," or "imbalance"—whether in the hormones, in the genetic material, or, as is currently fashionable, in the fetal endocrine environment. If I had ever, in any medium, seen any researcher or popularizer refer even once to any supposed gay-producing circumstance as the *proper* hormone balance or the *conducive* endocrine environment for gay generation, I would be less chilled by the breezes of all this technological confidence. As things are, a medicalized dream of the prevention of gay bodies seems to be the less visible, far more respectable underside of the AIDS-fueled public dream of their extirpation.

In this unstable balance of assumptions between nature and culture, at any rate, under the overarching, relatively unchallenged aegis of a culture's desire that gay people *not be,* there is no unthreatened, unthreatening theoretical home for a concept of gay and lesbian origins. What the books I have been discussing, and the institutions to which they are attached, demonstrate is that the wish for the dignified treatment of already gay people is necessarily destined to turn into either trivializing apologetics or, much worse, a silkily camouflaged complicity in oppression—in the absence of a strong, explicit, *erotically invested* affirmation of some people's felt desire or need that there be gay people in the immediate world.

Notes

I wrote the original version of this essay in 1989 for a Modern Language Association panel. Jack Cameron pointed me in the direction of the texts discussed here, and Cindy Patton fortified my resistance to them.

1. This information comes from reports in the *New York Native,* September 23, 1989, 9–10, and November 13, 1989, 14; *VJ* November 1989, 7.

2. A particularly illuminating overview of psychoanalytic approaches to male homosexuality is available in Kenneth Lewes, *The Psychoanalytic Theory of Male Homosexuality* (New York: Penguin/NAL/Meridian, 1989).

3. Richard C. Friedman, *Male Homosexuality: A Contemporary Psychoanalytic Perspective* (New Haven, CT: Yale University Press, 1988). Page numbers from this edition are hereafter cited in text.

4. Richard Green, The *"Sissy Boy Syndrome" and the Development of Homosexuality* (New Haven, CT: Yale University Press, 1987). Page numbers from this edition are hereafter cited in text.

5. It is worth noting that the gay men Friedman admires always have completely discretionary control over everyone else's knowledge of their sexuality: no sense that others may have their own intuitions that they are gay, no sense of physical effeminacy, no visible participation in gay (physical, cultural, sartorial) semiotics or community. For many contemporary gay people, such an existence would be impossible; for a great many, it would seem starvingly impoverished in terms of culture, community, and meaning.

6. American Psychiatric Association, *Diagnostic and Statistical Manual of Mental Disorders,* 3rd ed. (Washington, DC: American Psychiatric Association, 1980), 265–66.

7. The exception to this generalization is Lawrence Mass, whose *Dialogues of the Sexual Revolution,* vol. 1, *Homosexuality and Sexuality* (New York: Harrington Park, 1990) collects a decade's worth of interviews with psychiatrists and sex researchers, originally conducted for and published in the gay press. In these often illuminating interviews, a number of Mass's questions are asked under the premise that "American psychiatry is simply engaged in a long, subtle process of reconceptualizing homosexuality as a mental illness with another name—the 'gender identity disorder of childhood'" (214).

8. That relegation may be diminishing as, in many places, "queer" politics comes to overlap and/or compete with "gay" politics. Part of what I understand to be the exciting charge of the very word *queer* is that it embraces, instead of repudiating, what have for many of us been formative childhood experiences of difference and stigmatization.

9. For descriptions of this literature, see Friedman, *Male Homosexuality*, pp. 33–48; and Green, *The "Sissy Boy Syndrome,"* 370–90. The most credible of these studies from a gay-affirmative standpoint would be Alan P. Bell, Martin S. Weinberg, and Sue Kiefer Hammersmith, *Sexual Preference: Its Development in Men and Women* (Bloomington: Indiana University Press, 1981), which concludes, "Childhood Gender Nonconformity turned out to be more strongly connected to adult homosexuality than was any other variable in the study" (80).

10. Priding himself on his interdisciplinarity, moreover, Friedman is much taken with recent neuroendocrinological work suggesting that prenatal stress on the mother may affect structuration of the fetal brain in such a way that hormonal cues to the child as late as adolescence may be processed differentially. His treatment of these data as data is neither very responsible (e.g., problematic results that point only to "hypothetical differences" in one chapter [24] are silently upgraded to positive "knowledge" two chapters later [51]) nor very impartial (for instance, Friedman invariably refers to the conditions hypothesized as conducive to gay development as *inadequate* androgenization [14], *deficit* [15], and so on). But his infatuation with this model does have two useful effects. First, it seems to generate by direct analogy this further series of two-phase narratives about psychic development, narratives that discriminate between the circumstances under which a particular psychic structure is *organized* and those under which it is *activated,* that may turn out to enable some new sinuosities for other, more gay-embracing and pluralist projects of developmental narration. (Friedman makes this analogy explicit on pp. 241–45.) And second, it goes a long way toward detotalizing, demystifying, and narrativizing in a recognizable way any reader's sense of the threat (the promise?) presented by a supposed neurobiological vision of the already gay male body.

11. Eve Kosofsky Sedgwick, *Epistemology of the Closet* (Berkeley: University of California Press, 1990).

How to Do Things with Perversion: Psychoanalysis and the "Child in Danger"

Paul Kelleher

This essay seeks to understand the strange insistence that, in order to reflect on our relationships with children, in order to conceive of childhood as such, we must put the child in danger. Why, as a way to think about children, have we become accustomed to beginning with an image of the "child" in "danger," and only then (assuming *then* ever comes) working our way back to the boy or girl in the room? The "child" I speak of here refers not to a group or class of children, or any one identifiable child, but rather the figure of *no child in particular,* a figure whose lack of particularity enables a great deal of thinking and speaking—not to mention legislating and policy making—about matters of so-called general, national, or universal concern. Accordingly, when we encounter concepts such as "the general population," "national security," or the "universal human condition," we find the child buckled into the logic of these abstract bodies, and, more often than not, this child is in danger.

Consider, in this regard, Neil Postman's *The Disappearance of Childhood*, a book that articulates symptomatically the ideological reflexes this essay interrogates at length. Postman, we find, has a number of good things to say on behalf of "shame," particularly regarding its role in the civilizing process of controlling "impulses . . . toward aggression and immediate gratification."[1] He's worried, however: in the mass-mediated culture of the contemporary United States, shame isn't doing the social work it used to, namely, the disciplinary labor of, in his words, "social control and role differentiation."[2] Exhibit A for Postman's argument is as sinister as it is, unfortunately, unsurprising: "It is one thing to say that homosexuality is a sin in God's eyes, which I believe to be a dangerous idea. It is altogether different to say that something is lost when it is placed before children's eyes."[3] The question of what that something *is,* what precisely is lost when the image of "homosexuality" is placed before children's eyes, remains—as usual—unanswered. Or, more to the point, the question is strategically unanswerable. As long as no answers are forthcoming, you can do things with *perversion,* with all the psychological and social phenomena it purports to describe ("homosexuality," for one, but also any nonreproductive forms of sexuality, as well as any nontraditional forms of intimate, social, or political life). This also means, of course, that you can do things *to* "perverts," in the name of, for instance, the "child."

In this essay, I explore how the imperative to protect the "child," to guard against the loss of childhood's *je ne sais quoi,* defines—and, at the same time, is defined by—the psychological and social "danger" imagined to reside in the figure of the "pervert." I begin with a reading of Freud's *Three Essays on the Theory of Sexuality* (1905) in order to retrace how psychoanalysis began its love affair with children and perverts, and in the process set the terms and shaped the assumptions that, nearly a century later, we still are obliged to rely on for approaching the question of sexuality, be it child, "perverse," or "normal" sexuality. In the second half of the essay I investigate the convergence of psychoanalysis and criminology—specifically, the ways in which the psychoanalytic theory of "perversion" informed the late-nineteenth- and early-twentieth-century effort in criminology to profile certain individuals as species and agents of social "danger." Foucault's lecture on "The Dangerous Individual" opens the way to a reading of Melanie Klein's 1927 paper "Criminal Tendencies in Normal Children," in which a phantasmatic lineup of child, pervert, and dangerous criminal brings the social logic under discussion to its lurid climax: the danger embodied in the figures of pervert and criminal is rhetorically internalized and recast as the child's sexual danger to *itself* and *others.* As psychoanalysis increasingly tightens the conceptual relations among perversion, childhood, and criminality, we are given not a more penetrating or more accurate account of psychic and social determination, but rather a more compelling method for overcoming—that is, refusing to recognize—the limits of what theory, or we, can know or explain.

Intimations of Perversity; or, Freud's *Three Essays* on the *Theory of Sexuality*

> When in analysis two things are brought out one immediately after the other, as though in one breath, we have to interpret this proximity as a connection of thought.
>
> —*Sigmund Freud, "A Childhood Recollection from* Dichtung und Wahrheit," *1917*

Whereas nineteenth-century sexology amassed a vast body of empirical documentation and scientific (and, often, pseudoscientific) speculation— in the work, for instance, of Krafft-Ebing, Moll, Ellis, and Hirschfeld— Freud's *Three Essays on the Theory of Sexuality* theoretically streamlined the Victorian sexual body. In addition to organizing its economy (the component drives; object/aim-oriented) and rezoning its pleasures (the oral, anal, and genital erogenous zones), Freud's theory of sexuality articulated a dense profile of sexual subjectivity and practice. Among the many aftereffects of Freud's sexual theory, I will concentrate on two principal figures advertised by Freud's text, two figures that are actively recruited into contemporary dispensations of society and sexuality: the *perverse child* and the *manifest pervert*. Freud's *Three Essays* methodologically mapped, and largely inaugurated, the theoretical interface between the "child" and the "pervert." The proximity of pervert and child, I will argue, organizes the body, and orients the desire, of Freud's sexual theory.

Recall the structure of the *Three Essays:* before reaching "Infantile Sexuality" and "The Transformations of Puberty" (the second and third essays, respectively), we first face and traverse "The Sexual Aberrations" (the first essay). One "scandal" of the *Three Essays* followed their announcement that infant sexuality closely "approximates" its later adult manifestations, and more, that this approximation, this approach toward the end-pleasures of heterosexuality, is thoroughly mediated by the perversions. Freud's *Three Essays,* in other words, remodel perversion as the vehicle of human sexuality. "Thus the extraordinarily wide dissemination of the perversions forces us to suppose that the disposition to perversions is itself of no great rarity but must form a part of what passes as the normal constitution."[4] Having domesticated the perversions as constitutive of "the normal constitution," Freud stops short of articulating what, by the terms of his analysis, seems evident: strictly speaking, the "perversions" dispose us to the experience of sexuality, and may, in fact, be another word for sexuality itself. In Jean Laplanche's words, "Sexuality in its entirety is in the slight deviation, the *clinamen* from the function."[5]

The *Three Essays* instate and cultivate the principle of perversion that, at the same time, they wish to limit conceptually and prevent or cure therapeutically. Theorizing "perversion," we find, simultaneously multiplies the pervert population: "By demonstrating the part played by perverse impulses in the formation of symptoms in the psychoneuroses, we have quite remarkably increased the number of people who might be regarded as perverts."[6] As the following summary of perverse, neurotic, and normal sexuality makes clear, perversion emerges as the fundamental trope and substance of sexual development:

> What is in question are the innate constitutional roots of the sexual instinct. In one class of cases (the perversions) these roots may grow into the actual vehicles of sexual activity; in others they may be submitted to an insufficient suppression (repression) and thus be able in a roundabout way to attract a considerable proportion of sexual energy to themselves as symptoms; while in the most favourable cases, which lie between these two extremes, they may by means of effective restriction and other kinds of modification bring about what is known as normal sexual life.[7]

Teresa de Lauretis detects a "certain discrepancy of tone" between the closing pages of the first essay, in which this passage appears, and the pages that open the second essay. These pages mark for us the fraught space between the adult aberrations and infantile sexuality. Whereas the first essay, "The Sexual Aberrations," indicates that normal adult sexuality "could be said to be *brought about,* to be achieved, even induced 'by means of effective restriction and other kinds of modification,'" in the second and third essays, de Lauretis observes, "'normal' sexual life is taken as the premise, rather than the end result, of sexual development and assumed to be coincident with adult, reproductive, lawful heterosexual intercourse."[8] The "discrepancy of tone" that de Lauretis detects in Freud's writing no doubt speaks to Freud's own shifting relation to the idea of the normal and the measures that should, or can, be taken on its behalf. This discrepancy also draws our attention to a certain *risk* in theorizing perversion, in which thinking or speaking "perversion" becomes more and more indistinguishable from enacting perversion. Freud's rhetoric—its slipperiness, its shifts in emphasis and valuation—formalizes the uncertainty at the heart of psychoanalysis: if psychoanalytic practice works to prevent or remedy deviations from "normal sexual life," does psychoanalytic theory at the same time rationalize and legitimate these very deviations, perhaps even encourage them?

The problem of psychoanalysis—namely, that one is not born, but rather, *becomes* normal—also defines its purpose. The becoming-normal of the sexual body, the straightening of its perverse possibilities, entails the theoretical superimposition of the Freudian developmental narrative, in which the perversions are the unproductive detours passed through, and left behind, en route to the final destination of heterosexual reproductive life. Freud's debt to narrative protocols has received extensive critical scrutiny, not least from Freud himself.[9] In his groundbreaking work *The Freudian Body,* Leo Bersani demonstrates how Freud's writings struggle against the poignant, disorienting theoretical insights they themselves produce: for instance, the *Three Essays* endeavor to maintain the form of narrative development in the face of their own intimation of "the inherently antinarrative psychoanalytic notion of sexuality." The *form* of narrative development and the *norm* of heterosexual maturation, in other words, reflect and reinforce one another's ideological designs.[10] As Bersani observes, "Heterosexual genitality is the hierarchical stabilization of sexuality's component instincts," and "the perversions of adults therefore become intelligible as the sickness of *uncompleted narratives.*"[11] More recently, Paul Morrison has extended Bersani's insights into the narrative anxieties and ambivalences of Freud's sexual theory, bringing them to bear on the question of the AIDS epidemic and its reactionary fabulations in popular culture. The Freudian "narrative of psychosexual development," by Morrison's account, scripts "perversion" as "a narrative in which each and every moment is contaminated by its past, and hence threatening to its future."[12] Media representations of AIDS, he argues, have indulged in a kind of narrative wish-fulfillment: the homophobic social logic that understands the advent of AIDS as a "consequence" of gay sexual and social liberation is underwritten by another fantasy, the fantasy of "the revenge *of* narrative *on* gayness, the assimilation of the 'male homosexual' to the fully satisfying teleology that, in our standard technologies of self-fashioning and self-knowledge, he is said to resist."[13] By the lights of queer theory, Freud's *Three Essays* read as an exemplary instance of heterosexual novelization, a cautionary tale that opens with an obligatory bad example—the essay on "the sexual aberrations"—and proceeds to install a vision of healthful sexual normality as two modes of uninterrupted serial (re)production: heterosexuality and narrativity. In Morrison's words, "Where the well-made narrative is, the pervert is not."[14]

Building on the lessons of Bersani and Morrison, I want to bring out some of the rhetorical tendencies that underwrite Freud's thinking of sexuality, and focus particularly on how the *Three Essays* enact, indeed found, Freud's sexual theory via an entanglement between perverts and children. If the official story told by the *Three Essays* is the developmental narrative of how to enjoy and then leave the perversions behind, I want to consider how, without Freud's putting and always keeping the pervert and the child in play rhetorically, there would be no theory of sexuality to speak of, or speak through. For Freud's first readers (not to mention his first analysands), the "kinship" of child and pervert was, it's fair to say, anything but obvious. How, then, was it accomplished? Freud's *Introductory Lectures on Psycho-Analysis* offer an instructive angle from which to view the theoretical and social challenges posed by the *Three Essays*. Given over the course of two academic years at the University of Vienna from 1915 to 1917, the *Introductory Lectures* were presented to mixed audiences of medical practitioners, academicians, and laypersons. The first two parts of the *Introductory Lectures* treat, respectively, Freud's work on parapraxes and dreams, and the third part covers the "general theory of the neuroses." The *Introductory Lectures* give us a sense of how Freud enacted what we might call the public relations of the *Three Essays:* the various forms of rhetorical persuasion and theoretical reorientation that Freud's sexual theory at once called for and called into being. At the close of the twentieth lecture, Freud briefly takes on the central charge brought against psychoanalysis: namely, that psychoanalytic theory has "unduly extended" "the concept of what is sexual" in order to prove its theses regarding "the sexual causation of the neuroses and the sexual meaning of the symptoms."[15] But Freud invokes this charge only in order to counter it: "We have only extended the concept of sexuality far enough to be able to comprise the sexual life of perverts and of children. We have, that is to say, given it back its true compass."[16] The *Three Essays* revised the popular understanding that "sexuality" comprises the reproductive function only (or *should*, in any case). There Freud argues that "[t]he final outcome of sexual development lies in what is known as the normal sexual life of the adult, in which the pursuit of pleasure comes under the sway of the reproductive function."[17] "Normal adult sexuality," as a synonym exclusively for man and woman engaged in reproductively oriented, genital-to-genital contact, overlooks the role of pleasure in sexual life. Bringing the "child" and the "pervert" back into the fold of sexuality, comprehending the "true compass" of sexuality, reclaims for sexuality what is, in fact, its originary orientation toward *pleasure*. In other words, before it "comes under the sway of the reproductive function," the "pursuit of pleasure" *is* sexuality *as such*. Nevertheless, what Freud gives with one hand (the reassertion of pleasure), he takes away in large part with the other (the imposition of normal sexuality).

The next lecture (the twenty-first) opens with Freud worrying that he "ha[s] not succeeded in bringing home to you quite convincingly the importance of the perversions for our view of sexuality." By Freud's account, "It is not the case that the perversions alone would have obliged us to make the change in the concept of sexuality which has brought such *violent contradictions* down on us. The study of infantile sexuality had even more to do with it and it was *the concurrence of the two* which was decisive for us."[18] With every sense of *concurrence* rhetorically in play—simultaneity of events, unity of action, and availability of consent—the concurrence of pervert and child founds the psychoanalytic theory of sexuality. The strength with which Freud's model of sexuality *takes hold theoretically* follows, thus, from his routing of the perversions through the figure of the "child" and vice versa. It is important to note, as well, that the roots of the *violent* opposition to Freud's theory of sexuality—in his day and in our own—are to be found in this entanglement of pervert and child. On the face of it, the manifest perversions of adults were not front-page news for Freud's readers. This is not to deny that the internal dynamics of the perversions were articulated with a newfound sophistication in the *Three Essays*. But the perversions come to life, come into being, become a constitutive aspect of all sexual and social life, only once they are refracted through the "child."[19]

Freud's counterintuitive revision of the theory of sexuality—that normal sexual development entails a necessary deviance that precedes normality—participates in what Jonathan Dollimore has termed the "paradoxical perverse."[20] Dollimore's reading of psychoanalysis brings out a deconstructive Freud and sets him against those inheritors of his theory for whom the "normal" is shorthand for the metaphysics of "essence, nature, *telos,* and universal."[21] Freud's sexual theory subverts the metaphysics of presence by "retain[ing] and intensif[ying] the major paradox [that] . . . the shattering effect of perversion arises from the fact that it is integral to just those things it threatens."[22] Another paradox is broached in these further observations, and here we begin to detect where Dollimore's rendering of a deconstructive Freud threatens to stall: "If culture's repeated disavowal of the centrality of perversion is expressed in and through the endless demonizing of the manifest pervert, it is also true that the perverse dynamic both reveals and undermines the double process of disavowal and displacement which demonizing entails. Perversion, in the form of the perverse dynamic, destroys the binary structure of which it is initially an effect."[23] While I would agree that Freud's contribution to sexuality embodies, in many respects, a deconstruction *avant la lettre*, we need to account more fully for the social logic that permits the integration of "perversion" into "normal" sexuality, while at the same time authorizing the demonization of "manifest perverts."

Rather than focusing exclusively on the dynamic opposition between the "normal" and the "perverse," we can begin to understand the double movement of domesticating "perversion" and demonizing the "pervert" by widening our angle of analysis. Specifically, we need to attend to the triangulation that Freud implicitly stages within his sexual theory, a tense and indeterminate play among the figures of the pervert, the child, and the "normal" adult. The triangle of pervert–child–normal adult operates as ideological fantasy, a screen for desiring and deferring what might be called the impossible *thing* behind the fantasy of normal life.[24] In this regard, don't Freud's *Three Essays* betray the scandalous truth that normal heterosexual adulthood—that infinitely desirable and desired thing—is not, in fact, an actually existing state (of being)? Consider Morrison's apposite observation: "Readers of *Three Essays* . . . might reasonably expect a fourth: Freud takes us to the threshold of normativity, 'The Transformations of Puberty,' but stops short of a full discussion of a fully realized heterosexuality."[25] The *Three Essays,* in other words, can only formalize, without ever concluding, our asymptotic approach toward the end-pleasure of heterosexuality. Crossing over, shutting down the panicked fantasy of pervert–child–normal adult would risk ending a host of other pleasures—the pleasures, for instance, of epistemological regulation and social discipline.

The figure of the child, at every moment, choreographs the paradoxical interrelation of perversion and normality. This interrelation can be suggestively unfolded in light of the question Derrida cryptically poses in *Of Grammatology:* "How is a child possible in general?"[26] This question appears in a well-known discussion of Rousseau, in which Derrida develops the concept of the "dangerous supplement" in the course of a reading of Rousseau's meditations on education, writing, and perversion. The supplement, as Derrida demonstrates at length, preserves at every moment its double valence: the supplement as addition to a full presence, the supplement as substitution for a replaceable, or already absent, presence. "It is indeed culture or cultivation," Derrida writes, "that must supplement a deficient nature, a deficiency that cannot by definition be anything but an accident and a deviation from Nature."[27] The supplement—or, indeed, whatever goes by the name of "culture"—in adding to or completing Nature, implicitly reveals that Nature is insufficient, imperfect, lacking. Culture, consequently, must be said to precede Nature, despite the fact that its traditional place is to (in every sense) "follow" nature, temporally and conceptually. In these passages, Derrida affords the child a notable priority:

> Childhood is the first manifestation of the deficiency which, in Nature, calls for substitution [*suppléance*]. Pedagogy illuminates perhaps more crudely the paradoxes of the supplement. How is a natural weakness possible? How can Nature ask for forces that it does not furnish? How is a child possible in general? . . . Without childhood, no supplement would ever appear in Nature. The supplement is here both humanity's good fortune and the origin of its perversion.[28]

While the notion of childhood is meant to signal and embody the pure plenitude of Nature, it will in fact name the place from which culture scandalously emerges—or, more accurately, *reemerges.* "Childhood" marks the space in which nature and culture will do battle, without end, for authority. Culture, in short, is the repressed of Nature, and the peculiar fate of the "child" demands that it both symbolize and negotiate this dangerous intersection.

The chain of supplements Derrida envisions—especially the perverse play of too much/too little, too early/too late—speaks to one of the double binds Freud offers in the *Three Essays.* In a brief section of the summary, devoted to the "accidental experiences" of sexual life, Freud notes how "[t]he constitutional factor must await experiences before it can make itself felt; the accidental factor must have a constitutional basis in order to come into operation."[29] Psychoanalysis, in this regard, offers a theoretical account of *erotic accidents,* the series of encounters between chance and disposition that "govern the evolution of infantile sexuality till its outcome in perversion, neurosis or normal sexual life."[30] This risky tacking between the constitutional and the accidental, what Freud calls an "aetiological series," comprises the drama of human sexuality and its potential failures. These developmental failures signal both an arrest and a departure, a regression and an advance: the child's vulnerability, the pervert's fixations, and the neurotic's hesitations, in a sense, are the preconditions for the diagnostic freedom and theoretical mobility of psychoanalytic theory.

As a theory of erotic accidents, psychoanalysis also incites a wish for risk management: not only sexual normality in the here and now, but also an achievable future of reproducible sexual normality.[31] But on this score, Freud offers (at best) cold comfort. When in the *Introductory Lectures* he revisits the topic of the constitutional and the accidental factors of child sexual life, Freud turns the screw of developmental failure yet again:

> Strict protection of the young loses value because it is powerless against the constitutional factor. Besides, it is more difficult to carry out than educationists imagine and it brings with it two fresh dangers which must not be underestimated: the fact that it may achieve too much—that it may encourage an excess of sexual repression, with damaging results, and the fact that it may send the child out into life without any defence against the onrush of sexual demands that is to be looked for at puberty.[32]

Where, then, does this leave "us"? Do "we" imagine that the child needs protection from the idea or the representation of perversion, from individuals who qualify (by whatever criteria, whether they know it or not) as perverts, or from the perversion that is congenital to the child? Perhaps all three, at once. Or rather, is "protection" always a belated gesture, a compensatory strategy that admits, by denying, the impossibility of cure, the permanently unfinished business of normalization?

> But thought is one thing, the deed is another, and the image
> of the deed still another: the wheel of causality does not roll
> between them.
>
> —*Friedrich Nietzsche, "On the Pale Criminal,"*
> Thus Spoke Zarathustra

In a preface to August Aichhorn's volume *Wayward Youth,* Freud memorably comments on the difficulties of psychoanalytic theory and practice: "At an early stage I had accepted the *bon mot* which lays it down that there are three impossible professions—educating, healing and governing."[33] Freud would have done just as well to include criminology in this roster of impossible professions. Indeed, in the wake of Foucault's work, we are able to discern the criminal element, so to speak, already at work in the impossible professions of "educating, healing and governing." Turning to Foucault's lecture "The Dangerous Individual" enables us to specify further the convergence of child and pervert, as well as begin to retrace how the discourses of law and order established a "criminal continuity" between sexual immaturity and sexual dissidence.[34] With Foucault, we are able to disentangle the speculations of psychoanalytic analysis from the protocols of criminological investigation and begin to understand what roles the "child" and the "pervert" played in the historical-discursive formation of what Foucault terms "the psychiatrization of criminal danger."[35]

In the early nineteenth century, coincident with psychiatry's advance into the legal domain, a series of crimes emerged whose pattern was the absence of apparent motive. Foucault notes:

> Another common feature of these great murders is that they take place in
> a domestic setting. They are family crimes, household crimes, and at most
> neighborhood crimes. . . . [T]hese are crimes which bring together partners
> from different generations. The child-adult or adolescent-adult couple is
> almost always present. . . . Rather than crimes against society and its rules,
> they are crimes against nature, against those laws which are perceived
> to be inscribed directly on the human heart and which link families and
> generations.[36]

In order to account for these unnatural crimes committed "without reason . . . without profit, without passion, without motive," another species of human nature was posited: the pathological criminal, understood not as a juridical status through which any social actor might pass, but rather as a fixed category of being. Foucault's analysis in "The Dangerous Individual" relies on the hypotheses offered in the first volume of *The History of Sexu-*

ality, in which he traces the discursive emergence of the "homosexual" in terms that inform his account of the discursive profiling of the modern criminal. At the intersection of legal and psychiatric discourses, the pathologization of crime rendered instances of unmotivated violence intelligible by bringing out the criminal as "a personage, a past, a case history, and a childhood, in addition to being a type of life, a life form, and a morphology, with an indiscreet anatomy and possibly a mysterious physiology."[37]

This was, in short, the birth of the "natural-born killer": a set of discrete criminal acts, arranged within the evidentiary patterns of a case history, is theoretically redescribed as the true confessions of the criminal's (or what will come to the same, the homosexual's) nature. In one respect, the positive identification of the criminal subject (in a sense, its "minoritization") would seem to have promised a stabilization, at the very least, a localization of social menace; the specification of the criminal individual, however, entailed the "universalization" of criminal tendencies.[38] This ironic development introduces, against its official directives, an explosion in the criminal population. Freud, for one, would have been less than surprised by this untoward development, for his own labors on behalf of making a set of positive identifications—perversion, neurosis, normalcy—required "the wide dissemination of tendencies to perversion." Here it is useful to recall once again Freud's observation in the *Three Essays:* "By demonstrating the part played by perverse impulses in the formation of symptoms in the psychoneuroses, we have quite remarkably increased the number of people who might be regarded as perverts."[39] In this respect (but not only this), psychoanalysis and criminology draw from the same repertoire of rhetorical-analytic gestures: whether the objective is to cure or to incarcerate (or, perhaps, some of both), the social imperative to identify more precisely a kind of person (pervert or criminal) entails universally redefining the psychological makeup of every member of society, thereby rendering every individual a possible candidate for psychological investigation, as well as a possible agent of social danger.

Circa 1905, it seems, perverse tendencies and criminal tendencies were understood, more and more, as two profiles of the same subject. In that year, Freud published his *Three Essays on the Theory of Sexuality;* also in that year, as Foucault suggests, the criminal anthropologist Prins likely introduced the category of the "dangerous being" at a meeting of the International Union of Penal Law.[40] With the "dangerous being" foregrounded as a matter of public concern, the social body could be reimagined as a pervertible organism and social life could be rethought as a protracted exercise of risk management. For Foucault, the progressive psychiatrization of crime in the nineteenth century "enlarged, organized, and codified the suspicion and the locating of dangerous individuals, from the rare and monstrous figure of the [homicidal] monomaniac to the common everyday figure of the degenerate, of the pervert, of the constitutionally unbalanced, of the immature, etc."[41] The intensified overlap between social disciplines did not mean that one discipline yielded its authority to another, but rather that "through a perpetual mechanism of summoning and of interacting between medical or psychological knowledge and the judicial institution . . . [a] set of objects and of concepts was born at their boundaries and from their interchanges."[42] We can understand these disciplinary interchanges as the mutual borrowing and sharing of both theoretical methods and rhetorical forms. In this way, the protocols of criminological investigation— "Are there individuals who are intrinsically dangerous? By what signs can they be recognized, and how can one react to their presence?"[43]—became the free-ranging means for psychological description and apprehension. Pervert or criminal—at the end of the day, everyone looks the same.

At this point, we are well positioned to appreciate a handful of paradoxes, as well as the striking resemblances they share: on the one hand, Freud and criminology counsel that the child and society need to be protected and defended against, respectively, deviant sexualities and dangerous individuals; on the other hand, "strict protection of the young" and adequate "social defense" are interminable, if not impossible, projects—which ultimately may injure or compromise, through their overzealous application, the very things they ostensibly wish to protect. In order to measure the extreme reach of this convergence of psychological and social fears, I want to consider how the strange entanglement of child, pervert, and criminal is formulated in Melanie Klein's 1927 paper "Criminal Tendencies in Normal Children."[44] In this extraordinary piece of writing, Klein attempts to demonstrate "how we can see criminal tendencies at work in every child and to make some suggestions as to what it is which determines whether those tendencies will assert themselves in the personality or not."[45] Klein builds on Freud's speculations in his 1916 paper "Some Character-Types Met with in Psycho-Analytic Work," in which he suggests that adult criminal behavior might represent a defensive response intended to "fix" the guilty residues left over from the Oedipus complex, what he calls "the two great criminal intentions of killing the father and having sexual relations with the mother."[46]

Before turning to Klein's paper, it will be useful to rehearse Freud's claims in "Some Character-Types" regarding what he calls "criminals from a sense of guilt." Given the "weakness of moral inhibitions at that period of life," Freud, by his own account, was in the "habit" of "dismissing" as unexceptional behavior his patients' reports of their criminal exploits as children ("thefts, frauds and even arson"); however, Freud "was led to make a more thorough study of such incidents by some glaring and more accessible cases in which the misdeeds were committed while the patients were actually under [his] treatment, and were no longer so youthful."[47] Readers of psychoanalysis will recognize Freud's rhetorical strategy of obligation and persuasion: when faced with unusual, paradoxical, or shocking analytic material, Freud characteristically claims to have been compelled into a certain theoretical formulation by the irresistible force of the facts at hand. "Analytic work then brought the surprising discovery that such deeds were done principally because they were forbidden, and because their execution was accompanied by mental relief for their doer. He was suffering from an oppressive feeling of guilt, of which he did not know the origin, and after he had committed a misdeed this oppression was mitigated. His sense of guilt was at least attached to something."[48] Through a notably counterintuitive diagnosis, in which empirical expectations are submitted to a causal reversal, Freud links the dynamics of the Oedipus complex with adult criminality: "Paradoxical as it may sound, I must maintain that the sense of guilt was present before the misdeed, that it did not arise from it, but conversely—the misdeed arose from the sense of guilt. These people might justly be described as criminals from a sense of guilt."[49]

Two years earlier, in his 1914 essay "On Narcissism: An Introduction," Freud had the following to say regarding the "sense of guilt" and its relation to the "ego ideal": "In addition to its individual side, this ideal has a social side; it is also the common ideal of a family, a class or a nation. It binds not only a person's narcissistic libido, but also a considerable amount of his homosexual libido, which is in this way turned back into the ego. The want of satisfaction which arises from the non-fulfillment of this ideal liberates homosexual libido, and this is transformed into a sense of guilt (social anxiety)."[50] A page earlier, Freud has observed that "[w]here no such ideal has been formed, the sexual trend in question makes its appearance unchanged in the personality in the form of a perversion."[51] Two lessons, then, regarding the ego ideal: where the ego ideal remains unformed, perversion persists unchanged; where the ego ideal's great expectations are disappointed, homosexual libido is liberated and transformed into a sense of guilt,[52] which, as Freud observes in "Some Character-Types," paradoxically compels individuals to embark on a life of crime. According to Freud's logic, the ego ideal works on behalf of reducing the antisocial population, and a disturbance in its formation or efficacy increases the incidence of both perversion and criminality. What Freud leaves unsaid, but what his logic lets settle into place, is the notion that between perversion and criminality there are only differences of degree, not kind.

With much less reservation and in much stronger terms than Freud himself, Klein argues that "normal," or mostly "normal," children should undergo psychoanalytic treatment for "prophylactic reasons."[53] Not unlike Freud's methodological itinerary in the *Three Essays*, Klein approaches the question of a "normal" child's criminal tendencies by way of the perversions and the stages of pregenital development. In the first year, the child passes through the oral fixations of oral-sucking and oral-biting. She notes that in the first year also, "a great part of the anal-sadistic fixations take place. This term, anal-sadistic erotism, is used to denote the pleasure derived from the anal erotogenic zone and the excretory function, together with the pleasure in cruelty, mastery, or possession, etc., which has been found to be closely connected with anal pleasures."[54] From her clinical interaction with children, Klein finds that a severely punishing superego, formed in relation with the Oedipus complex, may be discovered in the child as early as the second year; for Klein, this superego comprises an admixture of the child's own sadistic tendencies with his familial inheritance, such as parental prohibitions and commands. With the ascendancy of the Oedipus complex, the child finds himself unhappily positioned: the child is faced either with acceding to the imperatives of his life to come, his hetero-genital life, or transgressively prolonging his tenure in oral- and anal-sadism.

Importantly, Klein revises Freud's hypothesis that the superego is heir to the Oedipus complex; her analysis suggests that the superego erected in the child's psyche partly comprises the "perverse constituents" of the child's sexuality. "When the Oedipus complex sets in . . . the early stages . . . the oral-sadistic and anal-sadistic—are fully at work. They become connected with the Oedipus tendencies, and are directed towards the objects around which the Oedipus complex develops: the parents."[55] Although Klein perhaps offers a more complex model of the superego, her efforts to backdate its development rely crucially on a selective distillation of its pregenital components; in order to advance the role of the oral and anal stages in child development, Klein's analysis simplifies pregenital erotism into sadism as such (that is, after one early mention, the functions of pregenital pleasure and passivity are for the most part elided). The aggressiveness of the child's "Oedipus tendencies," which are performing the arduous task of hetero-sexualization, then receive particular force from the child's now unalloyed perverse reserves: "The little boy, who hates the father as a rival for the love of the mother, will do this with the hate, the aggression and the phantasies derived from his oral-sadistic and anal-sadistic fixations. Phantasies of penetrating into the bedroom and killing the father are not lacking in any boy's analysis, even in the case of a normal child."[56] Even a seemingly normal child, such as her patient Gerald, will produce phantasies of "cutting his father and mother into pieces, these phantasies being connected with anal actions, [and] with dirtying his father and mother with his faeces."[57] The shock of this scene, however, radiates from a tableau of an unreasonably punished child: "It is difficult to illustrate how such a warm-hearted child, as this one was, in particular suffers through such phantasies, which the cultivated part of his personality strongly condemns."[58]

Whereas Freud's *Three Essays* overturn the notion of childhood asexual innocence, Klein's child analysis disabuses us of a no less tenacious or cherished belief: that childhood, in a word, is happiness itself. In Klein's words:

> Although psychology and pedagogy have always maintained the belief that a child is a happy being without any conflicts, and have assumed that the sufferings of adults are the result of the burdens and hardships of reality, it must be asserted that *just the opposite is true*. What we learn about the child and the adult through psycho-analysis shows that all the sufferings of later life are for the most part repetitions of these early ones, and that every child in the first years of its life goes through an immeasurable degree of suffering.[59]

Klein recasts the Freudian drama of infantile sexual misprision (à la the Wolf Man, who fantasizes the primal scene of parental sex as a violent episode of coitus *a tergo*)[60] and offers in its place the more lurid spectacle of a child's forcible impression into perversion. By Klein's account, the child's psychic history entails another kind of primal scene; the Kleinian superego, constitutively perverse and functionally sadistic, stages a primal scene of child abuse. A child is being beaten—both *for* and *by* its perversions. Heterosexualization, then, becomes an always belated rescue of child sexuality.

Klein describes how this perverse tutelage is imported into the child's observations during the scene of parental intercourse: "According to the oral- and anal-sadistic stage which he is going through himself, intercourse comes to mean to the child a performance in which eating, cooking, exchange of faeces and sadistic acts of every kind (beating, cutting, and so on) play the principal part. . . . Phantasies of the father, or of himself, ripping up the mother, beating, scratching her, cutting her into pieces, are some instances of [a] childish conception of intercourse."[61] Klein suddenly expands the scene of analysis, with a brief interpolation from the empirical world of criminal data: "I will refer here to the fact that phantasies of this nature are really carried into action by criminals, to mention only the instance of Jack the Ripper. In the homosexual relation these phantasies change to castrating the father, by cutting or biting off the penis, and all sorts of violent acts."[62]

In the same paper, Klein goes on to reaffirm the striking family resemblance she traces between sadistic childhood phantasies and what now would be called serial sex-murder; she proposes an analogy between child phantasies and their violent enactments during play, and the sensational case (from late 1924) of Fritz Haarmann, the "Butcher" or "Ogre of Hanover," who, two years before the time of Klein's writing, had been executed by decapitation for the rape, murder, dismemberment, and partial cannibalization of some twenty-seven young men.[63] "The criminal in question," Klein informs us, "became intimate with young men, whom he first of all used for his homosexual tendencies, then cut off their heads, either burnt or disposed of the parts of the body in some way or other, and even sold their clothes afterwards."[64] Drawing the intimate connection between Haarmann's crimes and the play episodes produced during Klein's analytic sessions is itself as easy as child's play: "The analogous phantasies in children which I mentioned before had in all details the same features as these crimes." Klein notes that after reporting violent phantasies concerning his father and brother, "to whom he was bound by a very strong sexual fixation," a child patient "expressed the desired mutual masturbation and other actions," and then proceeded to "cut off the head of the little doll, selling the body to a pretended butcher, who was to sell it for food. For himself, he kept the head, which he wanted to eat himself, finding it the most tempting portion."[65] The confusion that settles in here among persons, phantasies, and practices entertains the notion that the extremities of child, "pervert," and serial sex-murderer bear, at least to Klein's eyes, "the same features." Following Freud's example in his analysis of "criminals from a sense of guilt," Klein also briefly points to Nietzsche's meditations, in *Thus Spoke Zarathustra,* on the "pale criminal." But also like Freud, Klein fails to incorporate into her analysis the moment in Nietzsche, which appears above as an epigraph, that she certainly read and, we assume, just as certainly knew would undercut her diagnosis: "But thought is one thing, the deed is another, and the image of the deed still another: the wheel of causality does not roll between them."[66] By quietly and entirely eliding the question of causation, Klein confuses the relations among persons, phantasies, and practices, and thus phobically implies the conceptual interchangeability of "perverse" sexuality and sex murder. Importantly, the causal question of how the oppositions of "inside" and "outside," and "psychological" and "social," both do and do not reduce to, or determine, one another remains outside the field of interpretation.

Despite her hypothesis that such extreme forms of playacting and phantasizing are found in any child—indeed, in all "normal" children—Klein unself-reflexively contextualizes the male child's violent phantasies against the backdrop of a social scandal in which "homosexual tendencies" serve merely as an appetizer for mass murder. The mass murderer, who grows into our contemporary "serial killer," has taken up a phantasmatic residence within the child's playroom—which is also to say, sexual compulsion and serial murder have (pre)occupied the scene of Kleinian analysis. And more, the child, whom psychoanalysis compulsively transports to the primal scene of parental heterosexual intercourse, can now in hindsight be theoretically redescribed as a mass murderer in waiting. The sensational invocations of Jack the Ripper and Fritz Haarmann should not distract our attention from the rhetorical move that is being achieved in—and, I would argue, well beyond—Klein's argument. The psychoanalytic category of the "child" is conceptually subtended by a vision of perverse sexuality as repetitive, compulsive, aggressive, indeed murderous; these tendencies, streamlined through a sexual theory with nearly inexhaustible explanatory potential, are in turn reified and attached to the category of the "homosexual." The murderous "pervert," again and again, is figured as both *interior to* and *anterior to* our conception of the child, phantasmatically surrounding and overtaking any psychoanalytic profile of the "child." When Klein too easily connects the dots between violent child phantasies and adult sex crime, or when Freud frames criminal behavior and homosexual desire within the same theoretical structure, does psychoanalysis confirm or, rather, as I would argue, *betray* its best insights into the causation and formation of the psyche?

In closing, I want to make explicit my hope that, in addition to suggesting how we might disentangle the psychoanalytic knot of pervert-and-child, this essay also will complicate the ways we interpret social phenomena in which the alliance of sexuality and criminality takes center stage. I have in mind, for instance, the recent cases of child and adolescent school shootings. Were we to accept uncritically Klein's interpretive logic, we perhaps would assume that only a baby step separates the child who has violent phantasies (for Klein, this includes all children) and the contemporary child or teen who murders. Recently, Stephen Heath has offered a well-considered assessment of the ideological contradictions embedded in cultural notions of childhood and, specifically, how these contradictions inform the present "crisis" of children and violence. "Children are at risk," Heath writes, "but children also are the risk given their participation in a continuum of violence from adult to teenager to ever younger child. The child exists, frighteningly, as the victim and aggressor, and this victim-and-aggressor perception has pushed to extremes that, while they may connect with realities, also lock understanding exactly into an 'end-of-childhood' hopelessness which leaves no way out of the old irresolvable terms."[67]

Recall Guy Hocquenghem's incisive critique of the straight mind and its faith in the homophobic axiom: "Every homosexual is a potential killer."[68] In the contemporary United States, a complementary notion is slowly settling into place: "Every child is a potential killer." The child and the homosexual, each historically *objects* of social discipline, control, aggression, and (too often) outright violence, are recast or, more to the point, are ideologically reinscribed as the *agents* of social aggression and violence. But why exactly should the child and the homosexual be transformed into special categories of concern, or particularly worrisome sources of danger? The social wish fulfilled in this violent revision, the exchange of "victim" for "aggressor," bespeaks a defensive masking and displacement of heteronormative anxiety. Lauren Berlant incisively locates the origins of this straight complaint—which she names the condition of "ex-privileged heterosexuality"—in the anxiety produced by what is routinely characterized as the progressive, activist "assault" on traditional culture.[69] This rhetorical transposition of agency provides, in turn, a pretext for further and more extensive social and political interventions in the lives of children and homosexuals, all, of course, in the name of domestic safety and social welfare. With the past, present, and future of childhood permanently in danger and always at stake, who can argue, let alone resist?

Notes

I would like to thank the following colleagues and friends for their engaged, rigorous, and generous readings of this essay, through its several stages of polymorphous composition and revision: Joan Dayan, Diana Fuss, Daniel Novak, Yaakov Perry, and Erwin Rosinberg. Many thanks as well to Steven Bruhm and Natasha Hurley for their superb (and patient) editorial care.

1. Neil Postman, *The Disappearance of Childhood* (1982; repr., New York: Vintage, 1994), 85.

2. Ibid., 86.

3. Ibid., 92.

4. Sigmund Freud, *Three Essays on the Theory of Sexuality*, in *The Standard Edition of the Complete Psychological Works of Sigmund Freud*, ed. and trans. James Strachey (London: Hogarth, 1957–74), 7:171. All further quotations from Freud are from the *Standard Edition*, hereafter abbreviated *SE* and followed by volume and page numbers.

5. Jean Laplanche, *Life and Death in Psychoanalysis*, trans. Jeffrey Mehlman (Baltimore: Johns Hopkins University Press, 1976), 22.

6. Freud, *Three Essays*, 7:171.

7. Ibid., 7:171–72.

8. Teresa de Lauretis, *The Practice of Love: Lesbian Sexuality and Perverse Desire* (Bloomington: Indiana University Press, 1994), 14.

9. For an early and still very useful account of Freud's debt to narrative protocols, see Steven Marcus, "Freud and Dora: Story, History, Case History," in *In Dora's Case: Freud-Hysteria-Feminism*, 2nd ed., ed. Charles Bernheimer and Claire Kahane (New York: Columbia University Press, 1990), 56–91. Recall also the by now familiar moment in Sigmund Freud, "Case 5: Fräulein von R.," in *Studies on Hysteria*, in *SE*, 2:160–61: "Like other neuropathologists, I was trained to employ local diagnoses and electro-prognosis, and it still strikes me myself as strange that

the case histories I write should read like short stories and that, as one might say, they lack the serious stamp of science. I must console myself with the reflection that the nature of the subject is evidently responsible for this, rather than any preference of my own.... Case histories of this kind [have] ... an intimate connection between the story of the patient's sufferings and the symptoms of his illness—a connection for which we still search in vain in the biographies of other psychoses."

10. For a subtle meditation on the relation of "form" and "norm," see Lauren Berlant, "Love, a Queer Feeling," in *Homosexuality and Psychoanalysis,* ed. Tim Dean and Christopher Lane (Chicago: University of Chicago Press, 2001), 432–51.

11. Leo Bersani, *The Freudian Body: Psychoanalysis and Art* (New York: Columbia University Press, 1986), 32.

12. Paul Morrison, "End Pleasure," *GLQ* 1, no. 1 (1993): 55, 59. (This essay is reprinted, in revised form, in Paul Morrison, *The Explanation for Everything: Essays in Sexual Subjectivity* [New York: New York University Press, 2001], 54–81.)

13. Ibid., 54.

14. Ibid., 63.

15. Sigmund Freud, "Lecture XX: The Sexual Life of Human Beings," in *SE,* 16:319.

16. Ibid. Freud offers an apposite formulation in the 1920 preface to the fourth edition of the *Three Essays:* "And as for the 'stretching' of the concept of sexuality which has been necessitated by the analysis of children and what are called perverts, anyone who looks down with contempt upon psycho-analysis from a superior vantage-point should remember how closely the enlarged sexuality of psychoanalysis coincides with the Eros of the divine Plato" (7:134).

17. Freud, *Three Essays,* 7:63.

18. Sigmund Freud, "Lecture XXI: The Development of the Libido and the Sexual Organizations," in *SE,* 16:320; emphases added.

19. As Arnold I. Davidson observes, "Our experience of sexuality was born at the same time that perversion emerged as the kind of deviation by which sexuality was ceaselessly threatened." Davidson perceptively tracks the "shift from the emergence of a concept ('perversion') to the emergence of a kind of person (the pervert)," but his mention of the threat posed to sexuality by "the perversions" needs to be more concretely situated, both epistemologically and socially. In order to register how the "shift" was accomplished from "perversion" (a theological concern) to the "perversions" (sexual practices) and then to the "pervert" (a sexual identity), we need to recognize that the figure of the "child" has provided, and continues to provide, the conceptual foothold for setting forth the threat of perversion. The introduction of the "child" as the lead actor in the drama of sexual development brings the question (and the threat) of "perversion" home, while at the same time making the figure of the "pervert" both an intimate and an immediate concern. Arnold I. Davidson, "Sex and the Emergence of Sexuality," *Critical Inquiry* 14, no. 1 (1987): 41. (This essay has recently been reprinted in Arnold I. Davidson, *The Emergence of Sexuality: Historical Epistemology and the Formation of Concepts* [Cambridge: Harvard University Press, 2001], 30–65.)

20. Jonathan Dollimore elaborates the implications of the "paradoxical perverse"

in his *Sexual Dissidence: Augustine to Wilde, Freud to Foucault* (Oxford: Clarendon, 1991); see especially pts. 5 and 6.

21. Ibid., 171.

22. Ibid.,172.

23. Ibid., 183.

24. My discussion of ideological fantasy is indebted to the work of Slavoj Žižek and to its queer appropriations in the work of Lauren Berlant. See also Judith Butler, "The Force of Fantasy: Feminism, Mapplethorpe, and Discursive Excess," *differences,* 2, no. 2 (1990): 105–25.

25. Morrison, *The Explanation for Everything,* 13.

26. Jacques Derrida, *Of Grammatology,* trans. Gayatri Chakravorty Spivak (Baltimore: Johns Hopkins University Press, 1976), 146.

27. Ibid.

28. Ibid., 146–47.

29. Freud, *Three Essays,* 7:239.

30. Ibid., 7:172.

31. See Lee Edelman, "The Future Is Kid Stuff: Queer Theory, Disidentification, and the Death Drive," *Narrative* 6, no. 1 (1998): 18–30.

32. Sigmund Freud, "Lecture XXIII: The Paths to the Formation of Symptoms," in *SE,* 16:365.

33. Sigmund Freud, "Preface to Aichhorn's *Wayward Youth,*" in *SE,* 19:273. In "Analysis Terminable and Interminable," Freud regards psychoanalysis itself as an impossible profession, along with "education and government" (*SE,* 23:248).

34. The felicitous phrase "criminal continuity" is borrowed from Henry James, *The American Scene,* as cited in Mark Seltzer, *Henry James and the Art of Power* (Ithaca, NY: Cornell University Press, 1984), 14.

35. Michel Foucault, "The Dangerous Individual," in *Politics, Philosophy, Culture: Interviews and Other Writings, 1977–1984,* ed. Lawrence D. Kritzman (New York: Routledge, 1988), 128.

36. Ibid., 131.

37. Michel Foucault, *The History of Sexuality,* vol. 1, *An Introduction* (New York: Vintage, 1990), 43.

38. Here I draw from Eve Kosofsky Sedgwick's "Introduction: Axiomatic," in *Epistemology of the Closet* (Berkeley: University of California Press, 1990), 1–63.

39. Freud, *Three Essays,* 7:231, 171. The title of the section from which the second quote is drawn, "Intimation of the Infantile Character of Sexuality," provides canny psychoanalytic emendation to Wordsworth's "Ode: Intimations of Immortality from Recollections of Early Childhood." Freud's punch line, of course: "The (perverse) child is father of the man."

40. Foucault, "The Dangerous Individual," 149.

41. Ibid.

42. Ibid.

43. Ibid.

44. Melanie Klein, "Criminal Tendencies in Normal Children," in *Love, Guilt and Reparation and Other Works 1921–1945* (London: Hogarth, 1975), 170–85.

45. Ibid., 171.

46. Sigmund Freud, "Some Character-Types Met with in Psycho-Analytic Work," in *SE,* 14:333.

47. Ibid., 14:332.

48. Ibid.

49. Ibid.

50. Sigmund Freud, "On Narcissism: An Introduction," in *SE,* 14:101–2.

51. Ibid., 14:100.

52. See Judith Butler, "Contagious Word: Paranoia and 'Homosexuality' in the Military," in *Excitable Speech: A Politics of the Performative* (New York: Routledge, 1997), 103–26, for an incisive critique of Freud's theory of the superego and of the formation of conscience.

53. Klein, "Criminal Tendencies in Normal Children," 171.

54. Ibid., 170.

55. Ibid., 171.

56. Ibid.

57. Ibid., 172.

58. Ibid.

59. Ibid., 173.

60. For a brilliant queer critique of Freud's analysis of the Wolf Man, see Lee Edelman, "Seeing Things: Representation, the Scene of Surveillance, and the Spectacle of Gay Male Sex," in *Homographesis: Essays in Gay Literary and Cultural Theory* (New York: Routledge, 1994), 173–91.

61. Klein, "Criminal Tendencies in Normal Children," 175–76.

62. Ibid., 176.

63. See the Haarmann entry in Brian Lane and Wilfred Gregg, *The Encyclopedia of Serial Killers* (New York: Berkeley, 1992), 192–94.

64. Klein, "Criminal Tendencies in Normal Children," 177.

65. Ibid. For an incisive critique of how psychoanalysis figures "homosexuality" as murderous, necrophilic, and cannibalistic, see Diana Fuss, "Oral Incorporations: *The Silence of the Lambs,*" in *Identification Papers* (New York: Routledge, 1995), 83–106. In Fuss's words, "In the history of Western psychoanalytic representations of the ravenously hungry, insatiably promiscuous male invert, *gay sex has always been cannibal murder*" (84).

66. Friedrich Nietzsche, *Thus Spoke Zarathustra: A Book for All and None,* trans. Walter Kaufmann (New York: Penguin, 1966), 38.

67. Stephen Heath, "Childhood Times," *Critical Quarterly* 39, no. 3 (1997): 25–26.

68. Guy Hocquenghem, *Homosexual Desire,* trans. Daniella Dangoor (1978; repr., Durham, NC: Duke University Press, 1993), 68.

69. Lauren Berlant, *The Queen of America Goes to Washington City: Essays on Sex and Citizenship* (Durham, NC: Duke University Press, 1997), 17.

"No Trespassing": Girl Scout Camp and the Limits of the Counterpublic Sphere

Kathryn R. Kent

Marjorie opened her suitcase and took out her bugle. Swinging its cord over her shoulder, she remarked: "I suppose I really ought to be learning new calls instead of looking for trails."

"Nonsense; you don't get points for blowing the bugle."

"No, but you get smiles and maybe something better from Captain Phillips!"

"What do you mean, Marj?"

"Don't ever repeat this, Lily." Marjorie lowered her voice. "When I succeeded in blowing Reveille correctly, Miss Phillips kissed me!"[1]

This passage, from a Girl Scout novel written in the early 1920s, illuminates some of the most queerly productive aspects of Girl Scout camp: it implicitly connects the public performance of a particular task or skill with private erotic reward. Similarly, Marj and Lily's illicit conversation during rest hour highlights the movement between secrecy and revelation, ignorance and knowledge, which Marj handles as skillfully as she does her bugle.[2] She gains power by sharing her secret; she has achieved what every camper desires: through her eagerness to please and to achieve, she has been singled out for "special attention," what I call "lesbian pedagogy," by her beloved counselor, "Miss"—or is it "Captain"?—Phillips. This variability in address gestures toward what I will argue is the instability, even the total redefinition, of gender and sexuality, and the public and private performative complexities within the space of the Girl Scout camp.

Recently, there has been widespread discussion of the function of camp as an aesthetic practice, a performance, a quintessentially queer phenomenon. Yet the idea of camp as a *space, summer camp*—and in the case of the Girl Scouts, a highly routinized, geographically isolated location designed to aid in the reproduction of girls—has not been explored.[3] In this essay I attempt to begin to theorize the relationship between the Girl Scouts, usually regarded as a stable part of the faded wallpaper of white, middle-class banality, and the formation and reproduction of nascent lesbian or queer identities and identifications in the United States.

An Introduction to Girl Scouting

Girl Scout Memory

Since it is a rainy day, we are showing a movie in the lodge. We always screen the same one, a black-and-white film from the fifties on the history of Girl Scouting. I have seen it so many times that I know all the dialogue by heart. It opens with the older, distinguished-looking Agnes Mooreheadesque woman sitting on a sofa drinking tea. (One year, for my birthday, one of my Scouting friends will send me a relic, an actual piece of the film, a frame of this older woman holding her teacup, pinkie extended.) "Moorehead" narrates the film within the film, made in the early twenties, of a group of Girl Scouts and their trusty patrol leader, Margaret, a girl of great bravery and aplomb. Around me girls lie on their backs, sit cross-legged, hold hands, give back rubs, giggle and groan with boredom. I am curled up in another woman's lap, yelling out the proper responses. (Since most of the movie is a reprint of a silent film, there is tinny music, and subtitles.) Everyone reads the titles together, except for the little ones, who don't read yet. Like spectators at the Rocky Horror Picture Show, *one must cheer, boo, hiss, etc. at the appropriate moments. We watch the troop help a wayward woman organize her house and wash up her children before her soldier husband arrives home from the (First World) War. Margaret, trusty patrol leader, demonstrates her ability to "be prepared" in an emergency, when she finds the telegraph man knocked out cold in his office and uses her extensive knowledge of Morse code to call for help. At last "our founder," Juliette Gordon Low, appears and nods ever so coolly at the camera. She is*

dressed in full uniform, with a wide-brimmed hat. She looks like a male im-
personator. Or is she transgendered? She looks like a butch, her gaze so steady,
so alluring. Our heroine.

Already, in this narrative, one might recognize a reinscription of spectatorship that in some ways resembles Miriam Hansen's discussion of early
film-viewing practices. As Hansen describes it, early films were screened
as part of larger events, which often included live acts, music, and various audience-generated interruptions. Such conditions of spectatorship,
Hansen argues, prohibited the establishment of any stable, hegemonic
subject position, and instead allowed for different "horizons of experience,"
counterpublic moments of collective spectatorship.[4] One might read the
Girl Scout episode described above as a similar moment of counterpublicity. Indeed, I would argue that the Girl Scouts enables the formation of
oppositional horizons of experience even as it performs some of the most
rigidly imperialistic and antifeminist narratives of subject formation. In
the case of the film, a group of preadolescent girls feels perfectly entitled to
burst into the home of a working-class woman, take charge of her children,
and clean and reorganize her household. At the same time, this colonizing
impulse is contradicted by, even as it enables, the homoerotic scene of collective spectatorship described above.

It is this peculiar slippage between nationalist narratives of white,
middle-class femininity and queer forms of subjectivity that makes the
Girl Scouts such a suspicious and thorny subject. Many might read the
organization as simply a "partial public,"[5] an extension of the values and
politics of the industrial-commercial public sphere, a "habitus" (to use
Pierre Bourdieu's term) marked by race and class. I am interested, though,
in elucidating how, through the summer camp, it could simultaneously
become a counterpublic space for the inculcation and nurturance of (sometimes) antinationalist, antibourgeois, and antiheterosexist identities and
practices. I base my deployment (and simultaneous interrogation) of the
term *counterpublic* on the work of recent political theorists, historians, and
theorists of material culture that attempts to understand how collective,
oppositional forms of meaning/identity/representation are produced and
sustained. As such theorists describe it, the counterpublic sphere is one in
which "subordinated social groups" construct oppositional narratives of
subjectivity and resistance.[6]

But claiming counterpublicity is difficult. Determining what constitutes
disidentification or a break with the values of the public sphere, as opposed to a simple imitation of them, is always subjective, tenuous, open to
interpretation.[7] Definitions of the difference between "partial" public and
"counterpublic" spheres often rely on strictly demarcated criteria of what

constitutes political action, agency, and identity. Even as Hansen admits that it may be difficult to tell "partial" publics from "counterpublics," she, as well as Nancy Fraser, privileges an alternative public sphere as one that contains collective representations of oppositional identity, forms of visible publicity. In the case of the Girl Scouts, I argue that the line between hegemonic and subversive discourse is always unstable, and that this precariousness may itself produce queer effects.

For example, if we return to Margaret, the heroine of the film discussed above, she signifies within the space of "camp" as both a marker of shame and of distinction. To call someone a "Margaret" could indicate that this person is compulsive about rules and cleanliness, or it could mean that she is competent, strong, a butch under pressure. At least once during the season, sometimes twice, our camp would hold a "Margaret Scout" contest, and each living group or unit would field a participant, a child or counselor dressed up to imitate "Margaret." Parody or not? Similarly, the ritual screening of the film itself offered the girls and women at camp a moment of communal interaction, a chance to spend time with one's partner or cruise a new counselor, to cuddle or be cuddled, at the same time that it reinforced the imperialist values of Scouting for girls. It is precisely such queer ambivalences and performances that I examine in the rest of this essay.

The Topography of the Camp

> At school, living under the same roof, seeing each other day after day, these girls thought they knew each other well; but there is no fellowship so close as that of out-door comrades; the vastness of the sky with its millions of stars, the loneliness of the woods and of camp life, and the close association in work and play, drew them together as they would have never dreamed it possible to be drawn.[8]

Mark Seltzer's work on the "topography of masculinity" in the United States at the beginning of the twentieth century includes a detailed analysis of the ideological underpinnings of the Boy Scouts, the same underpinnings that Juliette Low would co-opt for her own purposes when founding the Girl Scouts. As Seltzer illustrates, the early proponents of Boy Scouting feared that commodity culture was "feminizing" boys. In order to combat this weakening of the body, boys must be "made into men," removed from the feminizing domestic sphere of the home and taken out into "nature," where, through the rigors of outdoor living, they would be restored to a vigorous masculinity.[9]

The Girl Scouts adapted this ideology of nature and its character-building powers.[10] But by the time I entered the organization, "nature" had acquired specific resonance. "Living in nature" became the same as "living outside the real world." A place unspoiled by urban or suburban ugliness, a place supposedly without technology, "nature" remained, as it did in the early twentieth century, a retreat both from commodity culture and from its allegedly "feminizing" effects. Yet within the counterpublic of the Girl Scout camp, "feminizing" connoted instead a release from the normative definitions of gender and sexuality placed on mainly white, mainly middle- and lower-middle-class women. At the same time, nature acted as a sort of empty signifier, a name for a space in which one could escape one's family and one's school culture, a place where one's "natural" self and "natural" attractions could surface. Thus nature and natural became interchangeable definitions, and what was "natural" at camp might be considered completely "unnatural" elsewhere.

As one of the rhetorics employed to explain intense attachments between young girls and between full-grown women (not to mention cross-generational relationships), Scouting rewrote as "natural" relationships and interactions between women that "outside the camp" might signify as "homoerotic" or "homosexual." In the "real world," people had lost the capacity for physical intimacy; in the camp, hugging, kissing, giving back rubs, and holding hands (especially on sentimental occasions, such as the last night of camp) were *natural,* produced by nature, by being one's "real" self. Thus behavior that "outside" would be pathologized or ridiculed became utterly acceptable and expected under the ideological umbrella of Scouting, so much so that intense, erotic friendships and/or sexual relationships were seen as perfectly compatible with one's heterosexual existence in the "real world."[11]

Many Scouts would be outraged to hear me call this contact "sexual," let alone "lesbian," where the term connotes any self-affiliation with collective identity. Perhaps "queer," where queer is used to include a whole host of sexual expressions excluded by the already overdetermined hetero/homosexual dichotomy, better serves as a label for these relations between women, although it would certainly not have been more acceptable to my counselors than any other "deviant" sexual label. Yet I also have encountered many women for whom "lesbian" was or has become part of their camp identity.

The rhetoric of the "natural" was also used to redefine gender identity. "Real" women were the ones who could build fires with wet wood and hike uphill for ten miles. They were independent, forthright, honorable, and butch.[12] They ran the camp, drove the vans, built the fires, and held arm-wrestling contests at the dinner table. While in the public sphere of mandatory gender binarisms, these women might have been viewed as cross-gender identified, perhaps even as transgendered, in the counterpublic of camp they were simply camp counselors.

Girl Scout Memory

When I was in high school, my brother and father devised an ingenious strategy designed to regulate my body and my sexuality. Whenever we passed a butch or transgendered woman on the street, the two of them would chortle in unison, "There goes another camp counselor." At such moments I felt a mixture of shame and anger, shame at this woman's inability to "fit in" and at my own alliance with her, and anger because, while I had no names for what my father and brother were expressing, I understood how endangered both she and I were by our identities as "camp people," as queer.

It was more difficult to express "femininity" than "masculinity," however. In fact, like much of the larger lesbian community in the United States, the Girl Scout counterpublic legitimated "butch" behavior more readily than it did "femme." But certain staff members mastered the femme role. It meant a variety of things—the ability to keep one's temper, to rival Julie Andrews in one's talent to lead songs, to quiet a whole cabin of homesick children.

Much of the camp humor and play was organized around gender transgressions, but what counted as a crossing over from one gender to another differed in the context of camp ideology. It did not simply mean "women" dressing "as men," since this distinction did not have epistimological currency within the camp. Instead, the most butch counselor would put on a dress and the femme darling would don a suit and tie, and this would be considered a cross-gendered performance.

It is tempting to read this gender play as a prototype of Judith Butler's assertion that there is no such thing as "femininity" or "masculinity," that gender is always a parody of a parody, and that such gender performance reveals this essential inessentialness.[13] This assumption was crucial to our "camp" humor and sensibility. Within the camp counterpublic, however, while parody *was* a common form of expression, there existed alongside it a strong emphasis on finding and sustaining one's "true," "natural" self. Only here, in the camp, could one truly be free. As one camp song put it, "Hiking to rainbows, sunsets and stars / Just finding out who we are." That one's identity might be "performative" was only accurate as a description of how one "survived" in the world "outside," by adopting "artificial" imitations of femininity in order to get by.

And get by one did, until the next summer started. Finding in camp a space in which their gender and sexual identities were recognized, emulated, desired, and rewarded, many of my counselors took jobs that allowed them to keep their summers free. Some were "professional" Girl Scouts (meaning they worked in the administrative structure of the local Girl Scout organization), elementary and secondary school teachers, recreation specialists (park rangers, program leaders), or seasonal employees; some were combination fruit pickers, Christmas-tree loaders, day laborers, plasma donors, and school-bus drivers.

While some of these occupations fell into the category of "traditionally female," others did not. While teaching school or running the YMCA's after-school program might be considered a middle-class occupation, many of the jobs my counselors took to support themselves in the off-season placed them firmly within the working class. Camp ideology romanticized the transiencies of seasonal wage labor: the subjugation of all employment and activities to the camp schedule (whether or not to quit one's "good" job to go back to camp is often the biggest recurring dilemma in one's life) was framed within an ethos of change, transition, movement. Many of the beloved camp songs of my childhood idealize, with a characteristic wistfulness, the vagabond, the wanderer in the wilderness, the exile. With titles like "The Life of a Voyageur," "On the Loose," and "Born for Roaming," they enforce an ideology of a gypsylike existence. For women, the realities of this hoboesque lifestyle are obviously fraught with danger. Because of the threat of sexual violence, women have never been able to ride the rails and hitchhike the way men do (although many women have done it anyway). Within the camp counterpublic, a sort of wandering could occur, as one traveled from camp to camp, summer to summer. Each season brought new friends and lovers, and then one moved on.

This romanticization of exile and transition was also a way to transform what are conventionally perceived as the isolating, devastating consequences of a queer existence, including the loss of familial support and the discriminatory practices that bar queer and transgendered people from employment. Thus the camp legitimated and reorganized what might otherwise be viewed in the bourgeois public sphere as the inability to "fit in." What might otherwise be regarded as simply a "failure" to attain the privileges and accoutrements of middle-class status, or to assume one's position in the capitalist work ethic—what my parents often referred to disdainfully as the inability to "grow up"—the camp revalued. Being "grown up," as any queer knows, means submitting to the dual claims of bourgeois normalcy and compulsory heterosexuality—getting a "real job" and getting married.[14]

Is it any wonder then, that collectively disavowing "growing up" was part of the camp philosophy (reinforced, in part, through the immense popularity of the song "I Won't Grow Up" from *Peter Pan*)? Leaving camp "for good" was thus a highly overvalued moment. At a certain point, one was regarded as being "too old" for camp. This was a personal decision, made by the individual herself. It connoted a final giving in to society, a letting go of "camp." The sense of loss one experienced at the end of every summer, as good-byes were spoken and relationships terminated, became at this moment of retirement a greater, more final loss that could never be recuperated, and each woman had a different sense of when the last summer at camp should be. Some quit in their midtwenties, others in their midthirties. Still others were persuaded to come back to camp after several years of absence. Even after they "left for good," however, many former counselors remained within a "camp network" of friends and/or lovers, returning during the summer for visits, hosting reunions during the off-season, and volunteering within the local Girl Scout organization. Thus one could maintain the camp spirit and live within the camp counterpublic long after one had retired, perhaps even for life.

All of these examples suggest that inside the ideology of the Girl Scouts an oppositional space flourished, one in which compulsory heterosexuality might be suspended, gender redefined, and one's nonparticipation in the capitalist workforce supported and justified. As I have noted above, however, there seems to be a premium placed, in much work on the public sphere, on counterpublicity as a space for those who claim a particular social identity and who assert their *right* to visibility and to representation. But what about those for whom identity politics has no urgency, or feels too dangerous, or impossible, or is simply not descriptive of their own immediacies? Is there room for a counterpublic based on practices, congregations, habits?

Furthermore, can the idea of a *counterpublic* adequately account for a space such as the Girl Scout camp, since it was precisely because the Girl Scout camp was perceived by its inhabitants as outside the "real world," a sort of "private public," that many of its collective, oppositional practices could occur? Certainly the camp functioned as a "public space" in terms of one's ability to cruise and flirt "out in the open" without fear of physical violence. As I have outlined, it also offered a space for the formulation of oppositional identity practices. Yet it was precisely because the camp was *not* "public," but in fact actively shunned publicity, that these experiences were possible. Much of the work on the utopian possibilities of the counterpublic relies, it seems to me, on the (liberal) assumption that visibility/speech itself is inherently liberatory.[15] But is the closet itself a "counterpublic" sphere? A counterprivate one? As Michel Foucault notes, "There is not one but many silences, and they are an integral part of the strategies that underlie and permeate discourses."[16]

Much of the revisionist work on the public sphere after Habermas has been based on a critique of the "private sphere" as an arbitrary, class-specific and historically specific ideology.[17] To claim the private sphere, even as a space of empowerment, is to reinscribe dangerous racist, sexist, and classist ideologies about false divisions between social spaces, to ignore that the fantasy of the abstracted, public sphere of white male citizenship in the United States exists in part because of its own "othering" of the "private" as a feminizing, racialized space, outside the realm of the "political." I am certainly not advocating a reevaluation of this particular positioning. Yet, in our urgency to abolish the idea of the private, have we lost the ability to imagine alternative, closeted spaces as sometimes just as powerfully subject forming and sustaining?

Returning once again to my memory of watching the same film over and over on rainy days, I find in this scenario a rich image for what happened at Girl Scout camp. In the darkened theater that was "camp," as long as the Girl Scout film was running, all kinds of other activities could take place among the trees and in the woods, all of them saved by the label "Girl Scout."[18] Thus camp becomes the closet of the Girl Scout public, its own, arbitrarily designated "private," whereas space within the camp repeats these layerings: there are the things one says in public versus those things that can only be spoken in private, or written in a note, the differences in how one behaves in the space of the dining hall versus how one behaves in the hidden clearing behind it. As Eve Kosofsky Sedgwick describes this phenomenon, "'Closetedness' itself is a performance initiated as such by the speech-act of silence—not a particular silence, but a silence that accrues particularity by fits and starts, in relation to the discourse that surrounds and differentially constitutes it."[19] It is these unstable relations between silence and speech, secrecy and revelation, visibility and invisibility, as well as the performance of privacy within publicity and publicity within privacy, that made camp such a richly *queer* location.

Scouting for Girls[20]

When I was thirteen, I wrote my own Girl Scout novel. My "book" made the rounds of the camp that summer, passed from camper to counselor—my own little queerzine. Later I found it simply embarrassing and put it in the back of my closet, where it lay until I began this project. The narrative describes in obsessive detail the character formation of a particular young woman, obviously modeled on myself, who is packed off to camp by her disinterested parents. It recycles a gothic plot—the main character is a girl who is always being mistaken for someone else, someone who is dead, someone who eventually turns out to be her long-lost sister. Perhaps this convention mediated the ways in which, even at thirteen, I was being "mistaken" by counselors and peers for a lesbian. The book is a blissful fantasy of an abundance of older, experienced teachers/mothers/lovers; alternatively described as "beautiful," "breathtaking," "fascinating," "talented," "athletic," "long, flowing-haired," and "short, curly-haired," these counselors take care of, instruct, punish, reward, excite, adore, and continually misrecognize and recognize a younger, femme camper.

The novel also contains scene after scene of instruction, where the protagonist "learns," in minute detail, every rule and regulation of the camp, every custom in the dining hall, every ritualized interaction, every song, every game. In the process of the heroine's instruction, the reader learns it all, too. And, as in the case of Marjorie, as the heroine masters public forms of achievement, she is rewarded with private forms of attention.

These fictionalized sites of pedagogical intensity mirror exactly the highly scripted public of Girl Scout camp life. In addition to the clearly demarcated steps up the Scouting ladder from Brownies (ages seven to nine) to Juniors (ages nine to eleven) to Cadettes (ages twelve to fourteen) to Seniors (ages fifteen to seventeen), the Scouting program also includes hundreds of badges, awards based on community service, religious service and so on.[21] All of these measures of achievement work together to ensure that a girl "becomes" a woman within a specific framework by acquiring a variety of "essential" skills.

The Girl Scout camp has its own set of progressions. Aside from the hierarchized organization of the camp staff, beginning with the camp director, moving downward through the assistant camp director, directors of various program areas, unit leaders and unit counselors, the campers themselves are also highly organized. Split first into age groups, they are further divided into interest groups (horseback, general, waterfront, trips, and so on). Once they reach Senior (high school) age they may become Counselors in Training (CITs). The dream of many young campers, the position of CIT occupies the middle ground between camper and counselor in terms of privileges and responsibilities. Yet legally CITs are still campers, meaning officially that they cannot be left alone with children and unofficially that they are off-limits for sexual encounters with counselors.

Every activity in the camp centers on progressions as well. One starts out as a beginning horseback rider, and summer after summer one improves one's riding. One learns to swim and eventually, as a CIT, earns a certificate as a lifeguard. In this way almost every increase in knowledge can be accounted for and quantitatively measured.

These progressions become part of the identities of the girls within them. Not only do the CITs and counselors memorize the characteristics of each age group as part of their training, but the girls themselves know exactly what it means to be a Brownie, a Cadette, a "canoe tripper," or a "wrangler." This allows younger campers to project themselves easily "into" older identities, to perform them, so to speak, to imitate counselors and fantasize about "being on staff." Like young girls modeling themselves after movie starlets, my friends and I dressed like staff, imitated their gestures, copied their slang, and tried to "be" them, often convincing younger campers that we "were" counselors. Not only did this involve fashion choices, it also necessitated imitating and appropriating the behaviors of counselors, often in violation of the rules.

In learning how to *be* staff, in addition to appropriating privileges and actions unique to the social structure of the camp, we were also copying, at first "unknowingly," a variety of styles of self-representation, many of which signified in the world at large as "lesbian." Cutting my hair, converting to vegetarianism, refusing to shave my legs, begging for flannel shirts and Levis and hiking boots—all these activities, much to my parents' chagrin, were often associated in the late seventies and early eighties with lesbian "subculture."

In illuminating queer and traditionally female "styles" of representation, Sedgwick values "gossip" as an important method of representing the differences that constitute one's society. As she explains it:

> I take the precious, devalued arts of gossip, immemorially associated in
> European thought with servants, with effeminate and gay men, with all
> women, to have to do not even so much with the transmission of necessary
> news as with the refinement of necessary skills for making, testing, and
> using unrationalized and provisional hypotheses about what *kinds of people*
> there are to be found in one's world.[22]

Queer-identified persons must always be aware of the people around them who may pose a threat to their physical or economic or emotional security, or who may offer erotic opportunities. "The writing of a Proust or a James," Sedgwick notes, is a project "precisely of *nonce* taxonomy, of the making and unmaking and remaking, and redissolution of hundreds of old and new categorical imaginings concerning all the kinds it may take to make up a world."[23] Or (my world) a Girl Scout camp. Just as the myriad knots to be tied, songs to be learned, and rules to be memorized themselves functioned as a kind of mapping of social space and identity, so too did the incitement to gossip and taxonomize the counterpublic/counterprivate spaces the camp provided. My novel includes numerous lessons in how to "read" scenes between women, scenes of silence, shared glances, unexplained angers, cryptic notes, desired and repelled awarenesses, scenes that require interpretation according to a varying set of codes, scenes that are predicated on established hierarchies of experience and inexperience, knowing and "unknowing," and an intricate hierarchy of influence unique to the camp and to the Scouts.[24]

For instance, much of the erotics of the exchanges of power and affection I participated in with older campers and counselors centered on convincing them to "tell" me things I wasn't supposed to know—camp gossip—which started out as questions that were fairly innocuous, such as what "Jo's" real name was,[25] how old "Leaf" was, and, as I grew older, often implicitly or explicitly revolved around the various relationships/sexual adventures of the rest of the camp—who was and who wasn't, who was doing it with whom. Lists of counselors' "real" names turned into lists identifying counselors' sexual preferences, as sexual identity became a more potent "open secret" than any other marker of identity.[26] We learned the public ways in which one indicated one was queer, too—who switched the genders of pronouns in songs, who wore a baby diaper pin on her staff tie, who sat with whom in the dining hall. With access to such well-kept and well-displayed "open secrets," my friends and I felt ourselves set apart from the rest of the Cadettes, bound together in our "Harriet the Spy"-esque conspiracy of interpretation.[27] And as we began to "taxonomize" the women around us, we could ourselves evaluate, perform, and sometimes reject their styles and mannerisms. We were in fact encouraged, through the dominant discourse of Scouting, to do so.

This "knowledge" of an adored counselor's lesbianism was often attained only after a long period of what Sedgwick describes as willed ignorance, a performance of unknowing. Of course, both the thrill and the terror that accompanied such knowledge sprang from realizing that one "knew it all along" and seeing in this moment of recognition the threat to subsume the knower—"maybe I'm one, too."[28]

Queer theory, though flourishing in recent years, still lacks models for the multiple ways in which deviant, perverse sexualities are formed and how they survive. For example, Teresa de Lauretis's work on modern lesbian subjectivity, while attempting to account for the effects of popular culture on lesbian identity, remains firmly within the psychoanalytic purview.[29] De Lauretis repeats the same old story of the construction of lesbian identity, in which a universalizing (white, middle-class) mother-daughter relationship forms the basis for a multiplicity of identities and identifications. Because of de Lauretis's inability to relinquish this model, she ends up reducing the effects of culture, ethnicity, and even, I would argue, masculinity on lesbian subject formation.

It was precisely my counselor's distance from my mother, like the camp's distance from my suburban tract home, that made her so alluring. Simultaneously, her slippage into nurturance traditionally defined as "maternal" was extremely pleasurable, but so was her adaptation of the role traditionally defined as "paternal." In fact, as I have argued elsewhere, lesbianism itself as an identity may spring in part from such historically specific, class- and race-marked moments of substitution.[30] In the late-nineteenth-century United States, the responsibility for white, middle-class, female identity formation, once sentimentally held to be solely the mother's affair,

▼ Kathryn R. Kent

became the job of other counterpublics. It is this distance and slippage between mother and other, having and being, home and camp, that seems so perversely productive, and it is a dialectic (or tria-, or quadralectic) for which psychoanalysis, with its rigidly gendered, racialized and class-delimited heterosexual family of origin, cannot begin to account.[31]

My counselors offered me multiple opportunities for identifications, identifications that, as I have noted above, were rewarded and expected within the rigid structure of the Girl Scout program. Perhaps it was this emphasis on the inherent performativity of identity that made assuming a lesbian identity feel, ironically, almost compulsory to me: when at age fifteen I began to want not only to be, but to have, my counselors, I struggled against this "recognition," not so much out of internalized homophobia (although this was certainly a player) as out of the fear that I was simply succumbing to peer pressure.

In fact, if what I believe—in essence, that I was "taught" to be a lesbian, "brought up" to desire other women—has resonance, then counterpublic spaces such as Girl Scout camp may tell us something about how gay, lesbian, and queer identities and practices have been replicated and sustained since early in the twentieth century. Perhaps some gays and lesbians, enabled by such institutionalized spaces of pedagogy, do "reproduce" themselves. This hypothesis has serious political and epistemological consequences: the terror/fantasy of gay and lesbian "recruitment" takes on new meaning in this context. With the paranoia around children and queers at an all-time high, to claim that sexual identities are "learned" or "taught" is to unleash the possibility that this knowledge could be just as easily used to justify its "unlearning" or to restrict our access to children.

Because of its emphasis on children, Scouting is in a particularly vulnerable position, as evidenced by the recent skirmishes over whether or not gay men can be Boy Scout leaders (significantly, the Girl Scouts have a nondiscrimination policy). What would it mean to really "out" the Scouts—or is that what I'm doing here?

It may be that the Girl Scouts as a space of lesbian pedagogy has lost its originary function, that other cultural locations are now able to do the work of "bringing up girls to be gay," especially in the era of Queer Nation and even Queer Scouts. This analogy between Queer Nation and the Girl Scouts raises another question, a continuous undercurrent in my discussion of a specific or universalizing lesbian pedagogy: the problematic relationship between extremely productive sites of lesbian and gay identity formation in the twenty-first-century United States and their relation to nationalism, militarism, and forms of cultural imperialism. Tomas Almaguer's critique of Queer Nation points out the dangers of a queer nationalism that enables a homogenized, singular queer identity at the expense of racial and ethnic differences.[32]

While Girl Scout camp may have been an idyllic scene of lesbian pedagogy, it, too, relied on the homogenization of identity produced by the Girl Scouts. One was always a Scout first, in the same way that much of contemporary lesbian theory, a Girl Scout camp of its own, often relies on a homogeneity of experience and privilege. Hence my discomfort at realizing I, too, was "one of them" sprang in part from the sense that I was being recruited, that I would thus have to conform to a particular set of rules and mores. The phrase "scouting for girls" epitomizes this tension; it may be interpreted simultaneously as a metaphor for the imperialist urge to reformulate individual girls into good American women and as a playful invocation of lesbian cruising. Is lesbian identity, as a set of practices, styles, and counterpublic identifications, itself a form of imperialism?

While the utopian collectivity posited by theorists of the counterpublic sphere seems both politically necessary and utterly attractive, we must not, in our eagerness to invoke radical democracy, forget those counterpublics or counterprivates for whom such moments of collectivity have no meaning, as well as those for whom *identity* is not an organizing term. Yet I would hate for my cautionary tale to be confused with something like a call for a queer rugged individualism, as it seems to me Leo Bersani's idealization of gay male subjectivity as utterly outlaw might be.[33] Many calls for anticollectivism, for gay male identity or lesbian identity as distinct, pure spaces, it seems to me, are really ways of justifying one's own misogyny, racism, classism, or AIDS-phobia, a problem that the utopian fantasy of the public sphere as a space for discursive debate among competing counterpublics seems designed to address. Yet how do theories of the counterpublic reconcile the fact that for many gay, lesbian, and queer-identified people in the twentieth century (and perhaps earlier centuries), the dramas of secrecy versus revelation, private versus public, were themselves highly eroticized, and perhaps also constitutive of such identities? Increased visibility, as Foucault reminds us, always means increased regulation, as much as it means anything else.[34] In our eagerness to co-opt and exploit the means of national, not to mention global, publicity for our own queer ends—a project in which my essay itself participates, as it "outs the Scouts"—let us not forget those for whom such performative gestures have no meaning, no erotic payoff, or too great a material cost.

Notes

For their support in and out of the Girl Scouts, I thank Alison Regan, Eve Kosofsky Sedgwick, N.W., P.T., and Jane Gaines. This essay could not have been written with-

Kathryn R. Kent

▼

186

out the encouragement/incitement of Brian Selsky, Amanda Berry, José Muñoz, and Benjamin Weaver, and the expert editing of Leslie Satin.

1. Edith Lavell, *The Girl Scouts at Camp* (New York: A. L. Burt, 1922), 54.

2. My discussion of public and private economies of revelation and secrecy relies on Eve Kosofsky Sedgwick's understanding of the powerful effects of silence and secrecy in the performative relations of discourse around the closet. See Eve Kosofsky Sedgwick, *Epistemology of the Closet* (Berkeley: University of California Press, 1990).

3. *Camp Grounds,* a recent anthology of queer writings on camp, does not include any discussion of summer camp, even as it playfully alludes to this space in its title. See David Bergman, ed. *Camp Grounds: Style and Homosexuality* (Amherst: University of Massachusetts Press, 1993).

4. Miriam Hansen, *Babel to Babylon: Spectatorship in American Silent Film* (Cambridge: Harvard University Press, 1991), 23–59.

5. In an attempt to distinguish "partial publics" from "counterpublics," Hansen, in her introduction to the work of Oskar Negt and Alexander Kluge, defines the "partial public" as one that exists inside the workings of "industrial-commercial" capitalist subject formation, does not function on an "identitarian model," and is "silent" in terms of public discourse. Miriam Hansen, foreword to Oskar Negt and Alexander Kluge, *Public Sphere and Experience: Toward an Analysis of the Bourgeois and Proletarian Public Sphere* (Minneapolis: University of Minnesota Press, 1993), xxxviii.

6. Nancy Fraser, "Rethinking the Public Sphere: A Contribution to the Critique of Actually Existing Democracy," in *Habermas and the Public Sphere,* ed. Craig Calhoun (Cambridge: MIT Press, 1993), 123.

7. For a detailed discussion of the term *disidentification* and the relations among identification, disidentification, and minority counterpublicity, see José Esteban Muñoz, *Disidentifications: Queers of Color and the Performance of Politics* (Minneapolis: University of Minnesota Press, 1999).

8. Lavell, *The Girl Scouts at Camp,* 80.

9. Mark Seltzer, *Bodies and Machines* (New York: Routledge, 1992), 149–55.

10. Ernest Thompson Seton, one of the founders of the Boy Scouts, wrote sections of the early Girl Scout handbooks; for example, *Scouting for Girls: Official Handbook of the Girl Scouts of America* (1920), 280–372.

11. For a fictional representation of precisely this phenomenon, see Judith McDaniel, "The Juliette Low Legacy," in *Lavender Mansions: 40 Contemporary Lesbian and Gay Short Stories,* ed. Irene Zahava (Boulder, CO: Westview, 1994), 242–50.

12. I use the terms *butch* and *femme* to represent two forms of gender expression evidenced by my counselors, despite the fact that few, if any, of them would have labeled themselves this way, just as many would not have identified themselves as "lesbian" or as "queer."

13. Judith Butler, *Gender Trouble: Feminism and the Subversion of Identity* (New York: Routledge, 1990), 138.

14. See Adrienne Rich, "Compulsory Heterosexuality and Lesbian Existence," in *Blood, Bread, and Poetry: Selected Prose 1979–1985* (New York: W. W. Norton, 1986), 23–75.

15. The utopian ideal of a public sphere in which multiple, and often competing, counterpublics hammer out their similarities and differences presumes not only a kind of formal equality, but also an assumption that representation and self-representation are the *paramount* political vehicles.

16. Michel Foucault, *The History of Sexuality,* vol. 1, *An Introduction* (Harmondsworth: Penguin, 1978), 27.

17. For feminist revisions of the "private sphere," see Mary P. Ryan, *Women in Public: Between Banners and Ballots, 1825–1880* (Baltimore: Johns Hopkins University Press, 1990); Linda Kerber, "Separate Spheres, Female Worlds, Woman's Place: The Rhetoric of Women's History," *Journal of American History* 75 (1989): 9–39; Gillian Brown, *Domestic Individualism: Imagining Self in Nineteenth-Century America* (Berkeley: University of California Press, 1990).

18. Cindy Patton, in analyzing the space of a supposedly "nongay" porn cinema, describes the ways the screening of "heterosexual porn" allows "straight" men to have sex with men without experiencing any challenge to their sexual identification. See Cindy Patton, "Unmediated Lust: The Improbable Spaces of Lesbian Desires," in *Stolen Glances: Lesbians Take Photographs,* ed. Tessa Boffin and Jean Fraser (London: Pandora, 1991), 233–40. Similarly, following Caroll Smith-Rosenberg, I would argue that it was precisely because of the ideology of female sexlessness in the nineteenth century that a legitimating space was created for "romantic friendships"; at the same time, the doctrine of sexlessness also maintained white, middle-class femininity as respectable, distanced from the supposed sexual improprieties of the working classes. See Caroll Smith-Rosenberg, *Disorderly Conduct: Visions of Gender in Victorian America* (New York: Oxford University Press, 1985).

19. Sedgwick, *Epistemology of the Closet,* 7–8.

20. *Scouting for Girls* is the title of one of the earliest editions of what would become the *Girl Scout Handbook.*

21. Because of the decline in enrollment among older girls, in the 1980s the Girl Scouts added another level to the progression, Daisy Scouts, who are five and six years old.

22. Sedgwick, *Epistemology of the Closet,* 23.

23. Ibid.

24. I take the term *unknowing* from Sedgwick's discussion of the performative effects of ignorance both in *Epistemology* and in her essay "Privilege of Unknowing."

25. By the time I was in Scouts, military titles had been replaced with "camp names," pseudonyms that counselors assumed for the summer, and sometimes for life.

26. My use of the "open secret" comes from D. A. Miller, who argues that secrecy functions as a space of both resistance and "accommodation," and that the "open secret," through its unstable status as both known and unknown, undermines the workings of regulatory power. See D. A. Miller, *The Novel and the Police* (Berkeley: University of California Press, 1988).

27. Louise Fitzhugh, *Harriet the Spy* (New York: Harper & Row, 1964). That Harriet is the fictional "role model" for many a queer child, and that she repeats this process of taxonomizing her world as a kind of queer reversal of adult surveillance, should come as no surprise. For a discussion of the novel and its remarkable author, see Karen Cook, "Regarding Harriet: Louise Fitzhugh Comes in from the Cold," *VLS,* April, 1995, 12–15.

28. Sedgwick, "Privilege of Unknowing," 23.

29. Teresa de Lauretis, *The Practice of Love: Lesbian Sexuality and Perverse Desire* (Bloomington: Indiana University Press, 1994).

30. Kathryn R. Kent, *Making Girls into Women: American Women's Writing and the Rise of Lesbian Identity* (Durham, NC: Duke University Press, 2003).

31. For two notable interventions into psychoanalysis, one that foregrounds and queers the "having versus being" dichotomy, see Judith Butler, *Bodies That Matter: On the Discursive Limits of "Sex"* (New York: Routledge, 1993); and Diana Fuss, "Fashion and the Homospectatorial Look," *Critical Inquiry* 18 (1992): 713–37.

32. Tomas Almaguer, "Letter to Jackie Goldsby," *Out/Look* 13 (1991): 4–5.

33. Leo Bersani, *Homos* (Cambridge: Harvard University Press, 1995).

34. Foucault, *The History of Sexuality.*

Oh Bondage Up Yours! Female Masculinity and the Tomboy

Judith Halberstam

n a 1977 punk rock classic, Poly Styrene, lead singer of X-Ray Spex, produced her classic wail of teen girl outrage: "Some people say little girls
should be seen and not heard," she whispered, "but I say . . . ," and here
she went from a whisper to a scream, "oh bondage up yours!" In her music
and in her personal style, Poly Styrene signaled her absolute refusal of the
bondage she associated with "natural femininity"; she wore Day-Glo clothes
in bright and unnatural colors and fabrics, and her teeth were encased in
heavy braces as if to signify her indifference to the injunction on girls to
be pretty or nice, sugar or spice. X-Ray Spex's songs called for liberation
from the bondage of gender and consumerism, and they did so by making
almost unbearable sounds. While few punk girls would ever lay claim to the
label "feminist," the content of their assault on conventional femininity was
often quite similar to feminist critiques of gender. However, punk allowed
for a different trajectory of rebellion than feminism did. While strong girls,

subcultural forms like punk and riot grrl have generated queer girls, often queer tomboys with queer futures. The 1970s was both the decade of punk and the decade of the tomboy film; this period witnessed the rise of feminism and the development of gay and lesbian pride; in the 1970s, we might say, great social change produced the hope that things could be different for girls. But the hope of the 1970s has not necessarily materialized into a better world for the cross-identified girl. In this essay I trace the evolution of two different models of rebellious girlhood: both have been labeled "tomboy," but one is linked securely to femininity and heterosexuality while the other is tied precariously to masculinity and queerness. Despite the rise of feminism and the recognition of the dangers posed by conventional femininity, I will argue, we hesitate to cultivate female masculinity in young girls.

The subculture of 1970s punk rock, especially in England, offered girls like me a refuge from femininity. From about the age of fourteen until the end of my grammar school days four years later, I embraced punk rock culture as if it were a life raft in the high seas of adolescence. Punk allowed me to dance wildly, dress in scruffy hand-me-downs, mess up my hair, and scowl a bit. It provided a barrier between me and conventional girlhood and gave me a loud and rebellious language for my outrage. Although it was not completely clear to me at the time, my own brand of adolescent rage was fueled by the demands made on me at school and out in the world to be a girl in conventional ways. Punk music and style countered those demands with an invitation to be different and to make sense of that difference. For many tomboys, punk was an opportunity to avoid the strictures of femininity that bound girlhood to the safety of domesticity; indeed, the ubiquitous safety pin that adorned many a punk outfit, for example, symbolized the misuse and indeed abuse of that household item. Within the outfits of punks, the safety pin was transformed from a marker of rational utility to a symbol of useless and totally unsafe fashion. Punk allowed tomboys to extend tomboyism into adolescence; punk gave us permission to be ambiguous about gender in our unisexual punk outfits, and, of course, in relation to the music, it allowed us to scream and shout and make noise and to finally be heard: "Some people say little girls should be seen and not heard, but I say . . ."

While "punk" tends to be the name we give to the rogue male who embodies a masculine refusal of socialization, when associated with girls it has a wholly different set of connotations. The punk girl marks her difference through indifference and takes her rebellion seriously as a political statement rather than just an individualistic stand against adulthood. Although punk rock of the 1970s did not really sustain extended interest in gender politics or sexual politics, it did provide a subcultural context in which girls could be boys and femininity could be totally rejected. Cultural studies of punk have not generally paid too much attention to the participation of girls. This has much to do with the fact that, as Angela McRobbie and Jenny Garber note, the very term subculture "has acquired such strong masculine overtones."[1] Accordingly, girls tend to be viewed as girlfriends or fans within the subculture rather than as agents, participants, and performers. If it is true that the term *subculture* has acquired "strong masculine overtones," then it surely makes sense to look for masculinity within girl subcultures; when girls in punk are studied, however, it is never in the context of female masculinity. The masculine girl, moreover, often functions as a lone outsider rather than as part of an elaborate subcultural group. She may be the only girl in her group to ride a motorcycle, to play boys' sports, or to dress in male clothing. In this essay I want to extend the label of punk beyond its 1970s subcultural context and make it into a marker for a particular form of tomboyism, one marked by female masculinity, noisy political rebellion, and the refusal of compulsory heterosexuality. Punk, in this essay, signifies the affirmation of masculine tomboyism.

Tomboyism usually describes an extended childhood period of female masculinity. If we are to believe general accounts of childhood behavior, some degree of tomboy behavior is quite common for girls and does not give rise to parental fears. Because comparable cross-identification behaviors in boys do often give rise to quite hysterical responses, we tend to believe that female gender deviance is much more tolerated than male gender deviance.[2] I am not sure that tolerance in such matters can be measured, or that responses to childhood gender behaviors necessarily tell us anything concrete about the permitted parameters of adult male and female gender deviance. Tomboyism tends to be associated with a "natural" desire for the greater freedoms and mobilities enjoyed by boys. Very often it is read as a sign of independence and self-motivation. It may even be encouraged to the extent that it remains comfortably linked to a stable sense of a girl identity. Tomboyism is punished, however, where and when it appears to be the sign of extreme male identification (taking a boy's name or refusing girl clothing of any type) and where and when it threatens to extend beyond childhood and into adolescence.[3]

Teenage tomboyism presents a problem and tends to be subject to the most severe efforts toward reorientation. We could say that there are at least two marked forms of tomboyism, feminine and masculine, and that tomboyism is tolerated as long as the child remains prepubescent; as soon as puberty begins, however, the full force of gender conformity descends on the girl. Gender conformity is pressed on all girls, not just tomboys. This is where it becomes hard to uphold the notion that male femininity presents a greater threat to social and familial stability than female masculinity. Female adolescence represents the crisis of coming of age as a girl in male-dominated society. If adolescence for boys represents a rite of passage (much celebrated in Western literature in the form of the bildungsroman) and an ascension to some version (however attenuated) of social power, for girls adolescence is a lesson in restraint, punishment, and repression. It is in the context of female adolescence that the tomboy instincts of millions of girls are remodeled into compliant forms of femininity.

The fact that some girls do emerge at the end of adolescence as masculine women is quite amazing. The growing visibility and indeed respectability of lesbian communities to some degree facilitates the emergence of more masculine women. But as even a cursory survey of popular cinema and literature confirms, the image of the tomboy is tolerated only within a narrative of blossoming womanhood; within such a narrative, tomboyism represents a resistance to adulthood itself rather than to adult femininity. Tomboy identities are conveyed as benign forms of childhood identification as long as they evince acceptable degrees of femininity and appropriate female aspiration, and as long as they promise to result in marriage and motherhood.

Many tomboy narratives are about the coercion of the masculine girl and the process that transforms her from boy to woman. For example, in both the novel and film versions of the classic tomboy narrative, *The Member of the Wedding* by Carson McCullers, tomboy Frankie Addams fights a losing battle against womanhood, and the text locates womanhood or femininity as a crisis of representation that confronts the heroine with unacceptable life options. While the film version, as I will discuss later, dramatizes Frankie's sense of her own freakishness in relation to the confining social relations of the American South, the novel weaves Frankie's tale quite clearly through multiple other narratives of belonging and membership. This novel is all the more remarkable for the fact that it emerged out of the repressive cultural climate of the American South of the 1950s. Carson McCullers was born Lula Carson in 1917 in Columbus, Georgia, and she grew up with a sense of her own freakishness and inability to fit the mold of conventional femininity. She was often called "weird," "freakish," and "queer," and she felt herself to be outlandish and different.[4] McCullers's girl hero Frankie Addams is similarly preoccupied with her own freakishness, which is depicted most often as a lack of commonality with other girls and sometimes as a form of female masculinity.

In the novel, as her brother's wedding day approaches Frankie pronounces herself mired in a realm of unbelonging, outside the symbolic partnership of the wedding but also alienated from almost every category that might describe her. In a haunting description of tomboy alienation, McCullers writes: "It happened that green and crazy summer when Frankie was twelve years old. This was the summer when for a long time she had not been a member. She belonged to no club and was a member of nothing in the world. Frankie was an unjoined person who hung around in doorways and she was afraid."[5] McCullers positions Frankie on the verge of adolescence ("when Frankie was twelve years old") and in the midst of an enduring state of being "unjoined": "She belonged to no club and was a member of nothing in the world." While childhood in general may qualify as a period of "unbelonging," for the boyish girl arriving on the doorstep of womanhood, her status as "unjoined" marks her out for all manner of social violence and opprobrium. As she dawdles in the last light of childhood, Frankie has become a tomboy who "hung around in doorways and . . . was afraid."

As a genre, the tomboy film, as I will show later, suggests that the categories available to women and girls for gendered and sexual identification are simply inadequate. The tomboy film dramatizes the plight of both masculine and feminine tomboys. In her novel, McCullers shows that the inadequacy of gender categories is a direct result of the tyranny of language—a structure that fixes people and things in place artificially but securely. Frankie tries to change her identity by changing her name: "Why is it against the law to change your name?" she asks Berenice.[6] Berenice answers: "Because things accumulate around your name." Without names, confusion would reign and "the whole world would go crazy." But Berenice also acknowledges that the fixity conferred by names traps people into many different identities, racial as well as gendered: "We all of us somehow caught. . . . And maybe we wants to widen and bust free. But no matter what we do we still caught."[7] Frankie thinks that naming represents the power of definition, and name changing confers the power to reimagine identity, place, relation, and even gender. "I wonder if it is against the law to change your name," says Frankie. "Or add to it . . . Well I don't care . . . F. Jasmine Addams."[8]

Psychoanalysis posits a crucial relationship between language and desire, such that language structures desire and expresses therefore both the fullness and the futility of human desire—full because we always desire, futile because we are never satisfied. Frankie in particular understands desire and sexuality to be the most regimented forms of social conformity—we are supposed to desire only certain people and only in certain ways. But her desire does not work that way, and she finds herself torn between longing and belonging. Because she does not desire in conventional ways, Frankie seeks to avoid desire altogether. Her struggle with language, her attempts to remake herself through naming and to remake the world with a new order of being are ultimately heroic but unsuccessful. McCullers's pessimism has to do with a sense of the overwhelming "order of things," an order that cannot be affected by the individual, which works through things as basic as language and forces nonmembers into memberships they cannot fulfill.

In this essay, unbelonging characterizes a queer girl identity, the punk tomboy, which can successfully challenge hegemonic models of gender conformity. I want to produce carefully here a model of youthful female masculinity that calls for new and self-conscious affirmations of different gender taxonomies, taxonomies flexible and varied enough to recognize the masculinity of young girls. The affirmation of alternative girl masculinities may begin not by subverting masculine power or taking up a position against it but by turning a blind eye to conventional masculinities and refusing to engage. Frankie Addams, for example, constitutes her rebellion not in opposition to the law but through indifference to it: she recognizes that it might be against the law to change one's name or add to it, but she has a simple response to such illegal activity: "Well, I don't care." For the tomboy, the girl with no real social power of her own, the preadult with no access to the agency required to bring about social change, power may adhere in different forms of refusal: "Well, I don't care."

I want to trace here the meanings that attach to preadult female masculinities, the logics used to explain them, and the measures taken to dispel all cross-identification during puberty. I also want to examine the ways in which youthful female masculinity articulates itself over and against the many strategies used to silence it and the ways in which a rogue or punk tomboyism might be cultivated among girls. This punk tomboyism, I will argue, constitutes a pathologized form of girl identification that parents, counselors, and psychologists find aberrant and try to repress. Social science studies of tomboyism use the feminist language of "androgyny" to refer to the versions of which they approve. Androgyny within this literature represents a healthful alternative to the excesses of gender polarization. But androgyny, I will propose, does not really describe the gender identity of the punk tomboy. When discussions of tomboyism are framed in relation to androgyny, the masculinity of the young girl is once again discounted.

While much of the scholarly work on tomboyism has appeared in social science journals, there are many different zones of representation to which one might look for alternative images of the tomboy, including children's literature, films, and TV specials. I will be drawing my examples of alternative depictions of tomboyism from a set of films made between 1953 and 1986 that constitute the genre of the tomboy film. I will also examine closely a 1995 TV special on tomboyism that proposed to examine boyish girls, their desires, and their potential futures. This program examined head-on the great anxiety generated by the prospect of lesbian futures for tomboy girls. At the same time, the researchers and interviewers in the program were unable to identify any bad effects of early cross-identification among girls. Ultimately, I will be asking questions about how we might cultivate an aesthetic of masculinity among young girls, how we might encourage punk tomboyism, and how we might theorize relations between preadult and adult female masculinity.

The Androgyny Trap

Tomboyism of a certain genre is far more common and far more tolerated than one might think. Indeed, it has become almost commonplace nowadays for at least middle-class parents to point to their frisky girl children and remark proudly on their tomboy natures. Tomboyism in such contexts usually means no more than a healthy interest in active play and a disdain for gender-appropriate clothes and toys. While a permissive attitude toward active little girls is a positive change in the parenting of girls in general, the reduction of the meaning of tomboyism to active play among girls suggests something more sinister. If *tomboy* simply means "active," then those forms of pronounced masculinity that many girls cultivate—complete male identification, lack of interest in girls and girls' activities, desire to dress in boys' clothes and play exclusively with boys as a boy—remain beyond the pale. This preadult female masculinity, in other words, is still very much outside the parameters of acceptable girl behavior. Tomboyism is tamed and domesticated when it is linked to nonmasculine girls, and this allows for a more harmful, fully pathologizing discourse to explain strong masculine identifications among preteen girls. Furthermore, excessively feminine little girls are also harmed by the generalization of the tomboy label, because when tomboy becomes a normative standard, they look pathologically bound by their femininity to weakness and passivity.

Much of the feminist psychological and sociological research on tomboyism since the 1980s has assumed that there is a nonpathological form of tomboyism that can lead to adult androgyny. Such research is founded on the recognition of the social construction of gender and assumes that gender polarization can be particularly bad for women. Articles with titles such as "Is the Traditional Role Bad for Women?" and "Dismantling Gender Polarization" mark the ill effects produced by excessive gender polarization for women.[9] Many of these studies even suggest that while gender conformity has its rewards for women early in life, women suffer from isolation and narrowed life ambitions as they grow older on account of their adoption of conventional female roles.

In much of the psychological literature, *androgyny* means some form of "mixing of masculinity and femininity" and signals flexibility in relation to gender conventions. The language of androgyny replaces an older pathologizing discourse of gender-appropriate and gender-inappropriate behaviors. One study suggests, "Research links androgyny to situational flexibility; high self-esteem; achievement motivation; parental effectiveness; subjective feelings of well-being and marital satisfaction."[10] When extended to tomboys, the notion of androgyny is often used in such studies to determine whether childhood tomboyism is an accurate predictor of adult androgyny. While of course these studies maintain a strict sense of objectivity, there is no doubt that ideologically they are committed to the production and cultivation of androgyny in both children and adults. The concept of androgyny has mixed consequences for the tomboy.

One study on "destereotyping" that used the notion of androgyny found that tomboys do not simply "reject traditionally female activities." Instead, they are flexible children who are able to "expand their repertoire to include both gender-traditional and nontraditional activities."[11] The researchers admit that earlier studies of tomboys had indeed linked the tomboy to an aversion to girls' games and female playmates and a preference for athletic activities and boys' clothing and toys, but they dismiss such data because "these defining criteria are based on atypical samples (homosexual females and genetic females masculinized in utero) compared to control samples."[12] Here we see clearly the ideological import of the emphasis on androgyny: because a high sample of women (as high as 50 percent in some studies) report childhood tomboy identification, much effort is made to de-emphasize the link between tomboyism and active male identification or, more specifically, between tomboyism and adult lesbianism, transsexualism, or hermaphroditism. Instead, the concept of adult androgyny becomes a reassurance that today's tomboy will not grow up to be tomorrow's bull dyke. The researchers who conducted this study on destereotyping conclude that "girls who are able to transcend gender-role behavior in childhood are the ones who will be most flexible and androgynous as adults."[13] They offer no explanation as to how they arrived at the conclusion that androgyny is desirable and positively linked to flexibility. But such assumptions force a pathological label on the child who eschews androgyny in favor of cross-identification. The tomboy who prefers boys' activities and clothes and rejects girls as playmates is constructed in studies such as this as an antitype for the destereotyped androgynous tomboy.

Earlier research on tomboys—research not committed to the concept of androgyny but nonetheless determined to depathologize tomboyism—also refused the notion that tomboyism is rare and abnormal. In 1977, Hyde, Rosenberg, and Behrmann, researchers at Bowling Green State University, found that 63 percent of a sample of junior high girls and 51 percent of a sample of adult women reported having been tomboys in childhood.[14] They suggest that the reasons tomboyism has been conceived of as rare have to do with links made between tomboyism and adult transsexualism and lesbianism; however, they believe that tomboyism should be viewed as "a normal, active part of female development."[15] The unfortunate effect of the normalization of the tomboy role in this study is uncannily similar to the effects of placing tomboyism within a model of androgyny: in both cases, good and bad models of tomboy identification are produced in which good tomboyism corresponds to heterosexual female development and bad tomboyism corresponds to homo- or transsexual development. In conducting their clearly feminist study, Hyde et al. rejected an earlier definition of tomboyism as "preference for the company of boys and for boys' activities" and a "persistent aversion to girls' activities and girls as playmates." Rather, they defined a tomboy as "a girl who says she's a tomboy."[16] They also suggest that "the discrepancy between the high percentages of self-reported tomboys we found and the low percentages found by Saghir and Robins (1973) may be accounted for by differences in definition."[17] They assert that particularly in regard to the rejection of other girls as playmates, the earlier definition of tomboyism forces it "a priori into being a reactive and maladaptive syndrome."[18]

While it sounds like a good idea to allow self-definition to determine who is and who is not a tomboy, if one uses that criterion, it then becomes even more important to know what the girls and women surveyed mean when they say that they do or once did identify as tomboys. Hyde and her coresearchers report that in their sample of thirty-four females entering seventh, eighth, and ninth grades who were at a summer church camp, "63% reported being tomboys currently (in response to the following item on a questionnaire: Would you say that you are sort of a tomboy?)."[19] As the survey gets more specific, we find out that tomboys differed from nontomboys in their preference for boys' games, but both tomboys and nontomboys reported their preference for trousers over dresses; the researchers downplay the differences between the two groups, noting, "Wishing to be a boy, hiding good grades, and clothes preference did not differentiate tomboys from nontomboys."[20] They seem to feel heartened that the gap between tomboys and nontomboys has narrowed, because that indicates a wide dispersion of the positive aspects of tomboy activity and perhaps also shows the nonpejorative meaning of tomboyism among girls. However, this study can also be read in a different way: we might adduce that in fact the label "tomboy" may not have meant much to this group of girls because it refers only to a high degree of physical activity and self-expression, and has been completely divorced from female masculinity. In relation to this last point, it is important to note that when and where *tomboy* becomes the general term for active girlhood, many young masculine girls may not feel comfortable expressing their desire to be boys or to play exclusively with boys. In fact, the omission of any data about the girls' masculinity leaves out important information and produces the false image of tomboyism as just an active stage along the road to adult femininity.

By contrast, Hyde et al. note that among the women they interviewed about their childhoods, "51% reported having been tomboys in childhood."[21] Contrary to the girl group, within the adult group "tomboys differed from nontomboys in terms of clothing preference, preferred sex of playmates, preferred games, wishing to be a boy, and the parent to whom they were closest in childhood and adolescence."[22] The researchers do not comment on the discrepancy between the women and the girls. While the girls would not admit to any desire to be boys, the women recalling their tomboy days did reference their desires to be boys and their strong clothing preferences. Obviously, questions must be asked about what the girls felt comfortable admitting to in the context of the study. The discrepancies between the women remembering their childhoods and the girls describing theirs may also be explained by changes in the definition of tomboyism over time. The high percentage of adult women who recalled tomboy pasts could have to do with the increased acceptance of tomboyism in the present or with changing conceptions of acceptable models of femininity. In fact, it is extremely difficult to interpret any of the results about tomboy identification without acknowledging that there may be a high degree of deception or misinformation in both the girls' self-definitions and the women's memories of self-definitions. Girls have their own functional parameters for acceptable and unacceptable degrees of boy identification, and it may well be that "tomboy" did not mean "boy identified" among them.

Sandra L. Bem, one of the most important proponents of androgyny, returns to the concept of androgyny in her later work and expresses some dissatisfaction with it. In her 1993 book *The Lenses of Gender,* Bem admits that androgyny did not live up to its early promise as a feminist challenge to gender polarization. She writes: "Androgyny inevitably focuses more on the individual's being both masculine and feminine than on the culture's having created the concepts of masculinity and femininity in the first place. Hence, androgyny can legitimately be said to reproduce precisely the gender polarization that it seeks to undercut, and to do so even in the most feminist of treatments."[23] While Bem is absolutely right that androgyny only confirms binary gender systems, she does not highlight the potentially homophobic and indeed transphobic effects of promoting androgyny. In fact, the literature on androgyny shows all too clearly that when it comes to cross-gender identifications, feminist recommendations may often actually produce homophobia and transphobia.[24] Proponents of androgyny seem to think that gender polarization is responsible for sustaining male domination and that the appropriate response is therefore to soften the contours of gender difference and argue for gender sameness. While Bem no longer proposes androgyny as the feminist solution to the problem of gender polarization, she does still argue for "gender depolarization." Since it does not seem likely that conventional gender divisions will disappear anytime soon, I would personally argue less for gender depolarization and more for gender proliferation and what we might call the deregulation of masculinity, or the extension of masculinity to nonmale bodies. Because masculinity is a sign of privilege in our society, it is much more heavily guarded than femininity. Young boys who exhibit feminine behavior are punished, not to protect femininity from male incursions but to encourage masculinity in male bodies; young girls who exhibit masculine behavior, on the other hand, are punished not only because their femininity is in jeopardy but also because masculinity has been reserved exclusively for male bodies. The fostering of youthful masculinity, therefore, can constitute a powerful assault on male privilege.

We might expect, having examined some of the "androgyny" literature and the research on the widespread nature of tomboyism, that the sociobiological research that links tomboyism to prenatally androgenized girls would make a strong case for the link between tomboyism and adult lesbianism or adult transsexuality. In his much-quoted book *Man and Woman, Boy and Girl*, John Money surprisingly holds back from such conclusions even when the evidence seems to point toward strong links between tomboyism and adult gender and sexual variance. Money studied a group of girls whose mothers had taken steroids during pregnancy to prevent miscarriage and another group of girls with female andrenogenital syndrome.[25] He distinguishes between these groups by noting that within the first group, the fetally androgenized genetic females, some "masculinization of the clitoris" occurred (meaning it was deemed too big).[26] Usually, surgical alteration of the girls' genitals would be recommended and no further treatment would be needed. In the second group, that of girls with female andrenogenital syndrome, the girl is virilized when her adrenal glands secrete androgen instead of cortisol. While it is not completely clear what the dangers of androgenization might be for girls' health, Money notes,

> because the abnormality of adrenocortical function does not correct itself postnatally, it is necessary for children with this condition to be regulated on cortisone therapy throughout the growing period and, indeed, in adulthood also. The regulation is imperative to prevent growth and maturation in childhood which is too rapid, too early, and too masculine. Otherwise the physique would simulate that of normal male puberty, but eight to ten years ahead of the normal time of male puberty. Of course, masculine

puberty in a child living as a girl is unsightly and wrong. In later years, a girl does not desire to be hairy, deep-voiced and masculine in appearance, for which hormonal regulation on cortisone must be maintained.[27]

We do not know from this paragraph what the effects of prolonged cortisone therapy might be on the health of a girl.[28] Furthermore, while obviously one would not want a girl to go through puberty prematurely, Money's comments on the effects of virilization on girl bodies are oddly unscientific. Masculine puberty for a girl is "unsightly and wrong," he tells us, and he further assumes that no woman would want to grow up to be "hairy, deep-voiced and masculine." Since we all know women who are hairy, women who are deep-voiced, and women who are masculine, or all three, it becomes apparent that much of the impetus for this research is the maintenance of dimorphic gender despite the proliferation of hybrid genders in "nature."[29]

In his comments about the psychosexual development of these girls, Money examines them for "tomboyism," which he defines according to a list of activities and preferences such as "clothing and adornment," "childhood sexuality," and "maternalism." Money reports that most of the women in both groups in his study had strong tomboy identifications in childhood. But he also notes, in relation to the prenatally and androgenized girls, "It is of considerable importance that there were no indications of lesbianism in the erotic interests of the fetally androgenized girls, nor in their controls."[30] For the other group he reports some incidence of homosexual fantasy but no lesbian identification or transsexuality. As Ann Fausto-Sterling has argued convincingly, much of the reclassification effort directed at intersexuals has to do with the challenge they pose to binary gender systems and compulsory heterosexuality. It is quite clear that Money's scientific research on intersexuals uses tomboyism as a benign form of childhood virilization that the girl is expected to outgrow. Money has no real investment in learning about potential cross-gender identification made by the girls or homoerotic desires that they may actively cultivate.

There is a sense of the absurd in some of Money's analysis that underscores the effort made by scientists to force irrational and multigendered behaviors into a binary gender system. For example, Money provides an index of tomboy behavior designed to summarize the category definitively; he lists formulas such as "the ratio of athletic to sedentary energy expenditure is weighted in favor of vigorous activity, especially outdoors" (in other words, tomboys tend to be sporty and like to play hard) and "rehearsal of maternalism in childhood dollplay is negligible" (basically, tomboys have no interest in playing mommy).[31] He follows this up with the observation that tomboys do not rule out the prospect of motherhood in the future,

▼ Judith Halberstam

they just do not become too excited by it. He gives a precise prediction: "The preference, in anticipation, is for one or two children, not a large family." Finally, my favorite tomboy characteristic as summarized by Money falls within the category of self-adornment. He tells us first that the tomboy favors utility over adornment and prefers slacks and shorts as far as clothing goes, but then in relation to makeup, Money categorically asserts that the tomboy's "cosmetic of choice is perfume." This attempt to produce a definitive index of tomboy behavior and dislikes both homogenizes the category and makes the tomboy sound pathological in relation to this set of desires. It also creates a firm sense of the predictability of tomboy behavior, and therefore lends credibility to Money's assertion that there were no traces of lesbian identification among the group he studied. The production in the social scientific and scientific research on tomboyism of such things as "tomboy indexes," "sex-role inventories,"[32] and "destereotyping measures" almost invites parody, if only because such behavioral models take themselves so seriously. One only has to refer back to one's own childhood in order to produce counterexamples. Clearly, the emphasis on explaining tomboyism, and doing so in highly detailed ways, makes tomboyism into an abnormal model of childhood development because of the scrutiny it endures. Imagine, for example, a "macho index" that might be developed and applied to young boys who show early signs of antisocial behavior (fighting, dominating conversations, rudeness, bullying). If scientific researchers spent time and money trying to evaluate whether a "macho boy syndrome" exists that may serve as a predictor for adult sexually abusive behavior or violent personalities, boys who fight a lot or act out aggressively would grow up thinking there is something very wrong with them (and there may well be). In other words, scientific attention can produce self-censoring among kids and adult scrutiny of otherwise normal childhood behavior.

A TV special on tomboys that aired in 1995 makes clear some of the dangers of scientific observation of active and masculine-identified girls. In a surprisingly evenhanded program produced for the newsmagazine *Dateline NBC*, the topic of tomboyism is presented in relation to the vexed issue of its predictive value for adult sexuality.[33] The program, titled "Sugar and Spice," focuses on a long-term study of tomboys being carried out by behavioral scientists at Northwestern University. The researchers, Michael Bailer and Sherry Berenbaum, claim to be collecting data on tomboy behavior by observing and videotaping a hundred girls ranging in age from four to nine "who do everything a typical boy does." The scientists want to find out, among other things, how many of these little girls will grow up to be lesbians (no mention is made of their interest in how many might turn out to be transsexual). In the program, one of the scientists suggests that 10 percent of tomboys become lesbian identified. The two girls featured in the program respond to the questions of an extremely feminine interviewer (Victoria Corderi), who also interviews their parents. One girl, Simone, age eight, who plays only with boys and wears boys' clothes, tells the interviewer that she really likes to wear ties, "especially with my suit." Simone shows no signs of shame about her gender identity in the short interview segments, but when her mother speaks to the interviewer, she gives clues as to how Simone has been subtly pushed away from certain forms of boy identification. The mother recalls that Simone used to like to refer to herself as a boy and for a while would only wear boys' underwear. Simone's mother admits that this disturbed her and that she had expressed her distress to her daughter. Simone no longer says that she is a boy or expresses a strong preference for boys' underwear. This suggests that Simone has been trained out of certain extreme forms of male identification.

Both Simone and the other tomboy, Jackie, tell the interviewer that they hate playing with dolls, and both say that they tear the heads off dolls if asked to play with them. Simone's masculinity seems quite developed, and she boldly told tells the interviewer to refer to her as "handsome" rather than "pretty." Both girls are articulate about their tomboy habits and seem comfortable speaking about them; Jackie in particular seems to take a certain pleasure in the attention her behavior has garnered. Again, it is unclear how much the experience of being observed plays into these girls' ability to articulate their gender identities. In one interesting segment of the program, the interviewer brings the four parents of the girls together and asks them how they feel about their children being subjects in a project on sexual preference. The parents admit that this is the first time they have been made aware of the study's link between tomboyism and lesbianism, and Jackie's parents admit to being a bit disturbed. Simone's parents, on the other hand, are not perturbed at all. They admit that they had considered the possibility that Simone might grow up to be a lesbian and they articulate a high degree of tolerance in relation to this possibility. While it is encouraging that at least some parents of tomboys evince no real anxiety about possibly queer adulthoods for their children, the interview with the parents does suggest that the researchers themselves expect parents to resist connections between tomboyism and lesbianism. The researchers had apparently not told the parents that their study focuses in part on the development of sexual preference. Nor had they shared the information about the high incidence of lesbianism among tomboys.

Potential problems arising from such a research project are predictably not articulated within the program as the danger of producing homophobia. Rather, in an interview with feminist Ann Roiphe, the program suggests that such research is most threatening to the development of a strong model of heterosexual womanhood. Roiphe tells the interviewer that she worries that the information produced in the study could be used by future parents to "limit their girl children's lives" and to "intimidate women." She states, "I think that the fact that there is such a study tells us that people are afraid that strong girls will make strong women and that strong women don't make good wives and mothers, they won't be heterosexual and of course this is completely absurd." While Roiphe may well be correct in assuming that the study provides evidence of considerable cultural anxiety around the meaning of cross-identifications among girls, she takes an oddly conservative line on the adult futures of these girls. Her fear is that people will disassociate female heterosexuality from tomboy behavior, and, rather than argue that we should welcome the possibility of lesbian futures for tomboys, she asserts that tomboyism should be seen as perfectly consistent with being a future wife and mother. Roiphe's strategy of encouraging us to see tomboyism as a normal part of female development, like the androgyny studies and the scientific studies, is an attempt to depathologize tomboyism not by affirming girl masculinities and lesbianism but by making links between tomboyism and "normal" heterosexuality. By using Roiphe as the sole critic of the study and by not interviewing any adult lesbians, this program inadvertently turns the viewer's attention away from the crucial topic of sexual tolerance and gender variance and back to the issue of how to channel all childhood behavior into the safe havens of heterosexual domesticity. "Sugar and Spice" ends optimistically by claiming that neither the researchers nor the parents want to try to change the tomboys, but it leaves us in doubt as to whether any of these masculine girls will be allowed to extend their boyish ways into adolescence.

Within the context of social psychology and behavioral science, the development of normalizing models of female development and the cultivation of models of androgyny are far preferable to the gender-polarized alternatives that associate men and masculinity with all things good and active and women and femininity with all things bad and passive. Psychological models of sex roles, for example, have tended to define masculinity and femininity along the lines of familial roles and have made a distinction on this basis between masculine instrumentality and feminine expressiveness.[34] Within such strict models of gender, girls in particular are likely to be punished for nonconformity because the rules of feminine behavior are so much more confining than the rules of masculine behavior. But it is important that we not replace one set of gender prescriptions with another. Basically, as long as we define gender in terms of a binary system there will be boys and girls who cross-identify. It seems important that we find ways of depathologizing cross-identification rather than simply promoting gender mixing as a healthful alternative. There most definitely are many young girls who identify as boys, enjoy boys' games, play with boys' toys, prefer boys' clothes, and who, as preadolescents at least, reject the company of other girls. If *tomboy* becomes a generalized term for an active girlhood, then these cross-identifying children are once again cast in the role of deviant and are viewed as abnormal and atypical. As I suggested earlier, since the literature makes a huge distinction between normal and abnormal tomboyism, we might want to give this cross-identifying and indeed "rogue" form of tomboyism another name: I am calling it *punk tomboyism*.

The Rogue Tomboy

There is a long literary and cinematic history that celebrates boys as outsiders. James Dean *(Rebel Without a Cause)*, Matt Dillon *(The Outsiders)*, Johnny Depp *(Edward Scissorhands)*, Christian Slater *(Pump Up the Volume)* all represent the power of the sullen and recalcitrant white youth who says no to paternal authority. James Dean has pouted his way into the hearts of several generations of bad boys and girls, but there is simply no cinematic girl equivalent for the rebel icon. When a girl does rebel on film, it is usually by running off with a boy rather than by refusing heterosexual courtship or renouncing femininity altogether. Boy rebellion as exhibited by a Brando or a Brad Pitt is accompanied by motorbikes and guns, sexy indifference to authority, a violent but maverick sensibility; girl rebellion as exhibited by a Sissy Spacek or a Juliette Lewis represents only precocious sexual knowledge, rejection of the father for the boyfriend, too much makeup, and other markers of dangerous femininity. Indeed, the recent spate of killer-girl movies *(Heavenly Creatures, Fun)* might be seen as one alternative to the depiction of girls as helpless, passive, and trapped within powerless models of femininity. These killer-girl films represent girlhood as a tenuous balance between rage and hysteria that could erupt at any moment into violent outrage.

While few if any contemporary girl films focus on the masculine tomboy, a number of tomboy films made from the late 1950s to the early 1980s examine the forms and contours of tomboy rebellion.[35] To a certain extent, the tomboy film is an offshoot or variation of another more mainstream genre, the boy film. Hollywood, as we know, loves stories about little boys. It doesn't really matter what the little boys are doing; they might be growing up or refusing to, bonding with a pet or torturing it; they could be playing with aliens, struggling to get by without a father or a mother or both; they might be good or evil, smart or impaired, left home alone or reunited with a family. The timeless popularity of the boy movie suggests that the transformation of boy into man is endlessly interesting to this culture. Predictably enough, there seems to be little or no interest in girls in Hollywood unless they are becoming the sexual objects of male desire. But this has not always been the case, and indeed the girl movie has not always been such a debased category.

In *Hollywood Androgyny*, Rebecca Bell-Metereau suggests that "the popularity of the tomboy reached its peak in the years after the Second World War," pointing to films like *National Velvet* (1944) and *Pat and Mike* (1952) as examples.[36] I think it is fair to say, however, that the heyday of the tomboy film was the 1970s and 1980s, when a plethora of films were made featuring butch, wisecracking, aggressive little tykes like Jodie Foster (*Foxes,* 1980, and *Alice Doesn't Live Here Anymore,* 1974), Tatum O'Neal (*Paper Moon,* 1973), and Kristy McNichol (*Little Darlings,* 1980). These movies made girlhood interesting and exciting and even sexy. They also, of course, tended to imagine girlhood as tomboyhood.

In the 1970s and 1980s, the effects of the rise of feminism in the 1960s were finally beginning to affect child rearing. Tomboyism flourished in a climate of liberal parenting where parents were questioning sex-role orientation and challenging the conventional wisdom about girls and boys. Within such a climate, feminists and others may well have thought that change begins at home and that the way to intervene most effectively in the seemingly concrete and rigid societal standards for female behavior (and misbehavior) was to bring up children differently. In the 1970s, moreover, there was finally a visible gay and lesbian community in the United States, and in the wake of the Stonewall rebellion, many "gay power" groups sprang up across the country.[37] Of course, as gays and lesbians became more visible throughout the decade, the effects of that visibility changed. While at first queer visibility offered the promise of some kind of proliferation of sympathetic representations of gays and lesbians, as I showed earlier, the tomboy within a public psychologized discourse on homosexuality threatened to become the precursor to queer adulthood. Tomboy films featuring masculine girls faded from view by the end of the 1980s, partly on account of the implicit link between tomboys and lesbians. Nowadays, the few tomboy films that appear *(Harriet the Spy,* 1996, for example) have to feature properly feminine girls. Indeed, a 1997 remake of *The Member of the Wedding* as a made-for-TV movie featured the feminine actress Anna Paquin as Frankie Addams.

In the early 1970s, child stars such as Tatum O'Neal, Kristy McNichol, and Jodie Foster regularly played spunky tomboys with attitude and smarts; there were also, by the end of the decade, teen actresses such as Robin Johnson and Pamela Segall, who portrayed the anguish of adolescence within an oddly gendered body. "They're gonna see who I am," shouts Robin Johnson as Nicky in the classic punk girl movie *Times Square* (1980). Her desire to be seen as something or someone other than a presexual woman propels her on a rocky search for fame that takes on heroic proportions. And, like the tragic hero, she suffers for her ambition. *Times Square* features two girls on the run from parents, the law, and boys. To the accompaniment of a fine punk-influenced sound track, Nicky and Pammy very specifically aim their attack at the media. Their signature act of rebellion is to throw TVs off the tops of buildings. This image of two wild girls—Thelma and Louise for juniors—destroying televisions is a perfect representation of girls bashing back loudly, angrily, and violently against their invisibility. It is also a perfect image of the two types of tomboyism that I have identified here and their different trajectories. Nicky is male identified, takes a male name, and aspires to be a rock star. Pammy is also rebellious; she struggles with the parameters of conventional femininity, but she is not masculine. The two girls are involved in a beautifully nuanced teenage butch-femme dynamic, but explicit lesbian content was edited out of the film.[38]

The original tragic hero of adolescent growing pains, as I mentioned earlier, is Frankie Addams as played by Julie Harris in *The Member of the Wedding* (1952). Fred Zinnemann's adaptation of Carson McCullers's novel perfectly captures the balance between comedy and tragedy in this story. The set is sweaty and claustrophobic and the camera stays almost exclusively in the hot confines of the family kitchen. In one of the few outside scenes, Frankie runs onto the porch to greet the girls in the neighborhood girls' club. "Am I the new member?" Frankie demands urgently as the girls march through her yard. The camera moves back and forth between the real girls, the emblems of true femininity, and the ragtag tomboy Frankie who awaits their answer. "No," answers one particularly groomed girl, "you're not the new member." But of course Frankie has never been and will never be a member, has never belonged, and will never succumb to the pressure to be a heterosexual and feminine girl.

This film version of *The Member of the Wedding* draws attention to the clubby nature of gender: Ethel Waters reminds Frankie of the definition of a club: "There must be members and nonmembers." Waters's character, Berenice, also articulates membership in relation to racial relations in the South in the 1950s, and the film and the book strenuously link racial oppression to gender oppression within the matrix of prejudices that characterized the South in the 1950s. While unbelonging is obviously a historical legacy for blacks in the South, the nonmembers of the club of white girls are the tomboys and pre-butches, the not-girls who struggle to make gender fit and who attempt to squash their angular and flat bodies into the curves of naturalized femininity. Failure to assimilate to the demands of femininity, of course, spells trouble for the tomboy by imagining a queer future for her butch body. *The Member of the Wedding* emphasizes the tragic nature of the tomboy quest and quietly confines the tomboy to a past better forgotten and left behind; the tomboy's tragedy is to be forced to blossom into a quiescent form of young adult femininity. In *The Member of the Wedding*, the tomboy is also paired up with a more feminine girl. While in *Times Square* Nicky is paired up with the little rich girl Pammy, in *The Member of the Wedding* Frankie fantasizes about Mary Littlejohn. The novel suggests, however, that as Frankie cannot have Mary, she must become her. Thus the lesbian bond between the girls is transformed from desire into identification.

Thirty years after the release of *The Member of the Wedding,* the tomboy couple shows up again in *Little Darlings,* starring Tatum O'Neal and Kristy McNichol. McNichol and O'Neal play the opposite ends of tomboyism in this film about a group of girls spending the summer together at Camp Little Wolf. McNichol plays Angel Bright, a fatherless girl from the wrong side of the tracks whose mother smokes and wears sexy dresses and drives a big American car. Angel is a tomboy in an Oedipally inflected relation to her mother; she swaggers around the neighborhood in denims, beating up boys. O'Neal plays a motherless rich girl, Ferris Whitney, whose father is somewhat negligent and drives her to camp in a big Rolls-Royce. The names of the girls suggest the archetypal opposition they represent. Angel Bright is the white-trash devil child who turns out to have a heart of gold, and Ferris reveals an inner toughness (Ferris might refer etymologically to "iron") that is only superficially covered over by her rich and snotty exterior. McNichol as Angel performs a truly butch tomboy, and while Ferris wears masculine clothing at the beginning of the film, her tomboyism develops as a wholly feminine form of rebelliousness.

Angel and Ferris are immediately linked by the other girls at camp as different kinds of outsiders. In a classic bathroom confrontation scene, the pretty girl of the group asks Angel and Ferris whether they are still virgins. "I think guys are a pain in the ass," intones Angel. Another girl snickers, "They are probably lezzies," and Ferris responds quickly: "*She* may be but I am straight!" Significantly, Angel does not deny the charge of lesbianism. Instead, she defiantly makes a grab for the older girl's breasts and wrestles with her. Although the rest of the film degenerates into a competition between Angel and Ferris over who can lose her virginity first, the bond between Ferris and Angel is nicely established in this central scene. While in women's prison films the bathroom tends to be the scene of torture and sexual assault, in tomboy films the bathroom, with its woman's sign on the door and its mirror-covered interior, becomes an active gender zone. Females are literally divided up here into women and girls, girls and not-girls, straights and dykes. Kristy McNichol's tough stand in this bathroom scene echoes Julie Harris's outrage against the girls who exclude her from their neighborhood club. And Tatum O'Neal's role as the nonmasculine tomboy reprises an earlier tomboy role she played in *Paper Moon.*

In the comedic tomboy film *Something Special* (1986), the tomboy narrative plays in and through a narrative of hermaphroditism.[39] In this odd movie, a tomboy is granted her deepest and darkest wish one night when she wakes up with something very special—a penis. Milly Niceman (played by Pamela Segall) changes her name appropriately to Willy and attempts to acclimate herself to boyhood. Gender trouble in this made-for-TV movie comes in the form of family pressure to be one of two available genders. Mr. and Mrs. Niceman confirm the doctor's opinion that Willy must choose a gender and stick with it. Willy asks pragmatically, "Can't I be both?" Mr. Niceman explodes with outrage and says, "There will be no girlish boys and no boyish girls in this house!" While this scene is humorous in the way it depicts a struggle between the parents as they try to convince their child that he or she must pick his or her "side," it is troubling in the way it resolves the problem of intersexuality or transsexuality by abjecting gender ambiguity. It is in-betweenness (not androgyny but the active construction of new genders) here and elsewhere in the history of tomboys that inspires rage and terror in parents, coworkers, lovers, and bosses. As soon as the tomboy locates herself in another gender or in an affirmative relation to masculinity, trouble begins and science, psychology, family, and other social forces are all applied to reinforce binary gender laws. As Willy, Milly Niceman is at first lulled into the pleasures of boyhood: clothing, new freedoms, new privileges. However, the film reverses its originally transgressive premise by creating a rather predictable obstacle to the transition Willy seems to be making with no trouble from female to male. Suddenly, Willy is forced to confront the fact that his best male friend is also the object of his desire, and while he may have changed sex, he has not escaped compulsory heterosexuality. With the specter of homosexuality looming in the not-too-distant future, Willy wishes to return to his girl self and gender normativity is restored.

The tomboy film has long since disappeared as a distinct genre, and it is worth asking why. Where are the next generation of girl actors, sassy girls playing tough tomboys and pushing the limits of compulsory femininity? And what exactly is the threat of the little girl film and the tomboy aesthetic? One can only speculate, but it seems reasonable to suppose that the tomboy movie threatens an unresolved gender crisis and projects or predicts butch and transgender adulthoods. There is always the dread possibility, in other words, that the tomboy will not grow out of her butch stage and will never become a member of the wedding. Today we have only boy movies (think of *Free Willy*) and the girls are relegated to roles as dumb sisters, silly crybabies, and weak playmates. Quite obviously, Hollywood sees tomboy films as a queer cinema for preteens. Boys can be shown bonding, hiking together, fighting, discovering dead bodies, killing people, killing each other, but even the suggestion that girls might be shown doing similar things raises the specter of the dyke. Girls in films tend to fight each other for boys *(Heathers)* or for older men *(Poison Ivy)* or just fight. They do not bond, they do not rebel, they do not learn, they do not like themselves, and, perhaps most important, they do not like each other. In the rogue tomboy films, rebellious girls are locked into intense tomboy bonds, and one girl often plays a butch role to the other girl's femme. Both these forms of queer tomboyism may threaten queer futures, but it is the masculine tomboy who is singled out for the severest forms of social reorientation.

Conclusion

Current research on tomboyism allows for the possibility that a high percentage of tomboys may well grow up to be lesbians. Much of the information circulating on tomboyism seems profoundly unclear about how researchers and parents should think about the relation between adult lesbianism and childhood tomboyism, and a variety of strategies have been used to temper the threat of queer adulthoods. The androgyny model presumes that gender polarization is counterproductive and sees tomboyism as a useful way of opposing social mandates to adhere to gender protocols. The androgyny literature, however, tries to downplay the possibility of strong tomboy cross-identification or masculinity. Scientific research on intersexed girls tends to channel all ambiguous bodies into binary genders and has no interest in promoting the gender variance and multisexuality made possible by such bodies. In cultural arenas, the tomboy narrative tells of the pain of tomboyism and the trials and tribulations of the tomboy who refuses to grow up, and some films and novels offer alternative models of queer youth.

In this essay I have tried to offer an alternative model of the tomboy, one that rejects androgyny and binary gender systems, revels in girl masculinity, and encourages queer adulthoods (homo- or transsexual). The punk tomboy defies conventional gender paradigms and should be congratulated for her clear efforts to remake childhood gender. Punk tomboys like Nicky in *Times Square*, Frankie in *The Member of the Wedding*, Angel in *Little Darlings*, Willy in *Something Special*, and Simone and Jackie in the TV program "Sugar and Spice" all offer unique challenges to the Victorian notion that little girls should be seen and not heard and the current sense that little girls can be boys as long as they grow up to be heterosexual women. To such popular wisdom, the punk tomboy offers her own unique response: "Oh bondage! Up yours!"

Notes

Many thanks to Gayatri Gopinath, who read and commented on many different drafts of this essay. Some of my discussions of tomboy movies are drawn from the clip show "Looking Butch: A Rough Guide to Butches on Film," which was cocurated with Jenni Olson and also appears in my book *Female Masculinity* (Durham, NC: Duke University Press, 1998).

1. Angela McRobbie and Jenny Garber, "Girls and Subcultures" (1975), in *The Subcultures Reader*, ed. Ken Gelder and Sarah Thornton (London: Routledge, 1997), 114.

2. Most of the literature on tomboys and sissy boys makes this claim. The classic reference for the continued intolerance of sissy boys is Richard Green, who claims that the term *sissy boy* is always used as an insult, whereas *tomboy* is not. He also argues that tomboyism is a common stage within female development and most women simply pass through it unscathed and outgrow it. Green's argument is devised to support his claims regarding the "management" of the "sissy boy syndrome." See Richard Green, *The "Sissy Boy Syndrome" and the Development of Homosexuality* (New Haven, CT: Yale University Press, 1987); Richard Green, *Human Sexuality: A Health Practitioner's Text* (Baltimore: Williams & Wilkins, 1975), 29–31.

3. For more on the punishment of tomboys, see Phyllis Burke, *Gender Shock: Exploding the Myths of Male and Female* (New York: Anchor, 1996). Burke analyzes some recent case histories of so-called gender identity disorder (or GID) in which little girls were carefully conditioned out of male behavior and into exceedingly constrictive forms of femininity.

4. Virginia Spencer Carr, *The Lonely Hunter: A Biography of Carson McCullers* (New York: Doubleday, 1975), 29–31.

5. Carson McCullers, *The Member of the Wedding* (1946; repr., New York: Bantam, 1973), 1.

6. Ibid., 107.

7. Ibid., 113.

8. Ibid., 15.

9. See R. Helson, "Is the Traditional Role Bad for Women?" *Journal of Personality and Social Psychology* 59 (1990): 311–20; Sandra Lipsitz Bem, "Dismantling Gender Polarization and Compulsory Heterosexuality: Should We Turn the Volume Up or Down?" *Journal of Sex Research* 32, no. 4 (1995): 329.

10. Shawn Meaghan Burn, A. Kathleen, and Shirley Neverend, "Tomboyism and Adult Androgyny," *Sex Roles* 34, nos. 5–6 (1996): 419–29.

11. Pat Plumb and Gloria Cowan, "A Developmental Study of Destereotyping and Androgynous Activity Preferences of Tomboys, Nontomboys, and Males," *Sex Roles* 10, nos. 9–10 (1984): 703.

12. Ibid., 704.

13. Ibid., 711.

14. Janet S. Hyde, B. G. Rosenberg, and Jo Ann Behrmann, "Tomboyism," *Psychology of Women Quarterly* 2, no. 1 (1977): 74–75.

15. Ibid., 75.

16. Ibid.

17. Ibid.

18. Ibid.

19. Ibid., 74.

20. Ibid.

21. Ibid.

22. Ibid., 76.

23. Sandra L. Bem, *The Lenses of Gender: Transforming the Debate on Sexual Inequality* (New Haven, CT: Yale University Press, 1933), 125.

24. Indeed, the feminist opposition to both gender polarization among lesbians (butch/femme) and transsexuality provides ample evidence of just such a historical conflict between feminists and queers over the cultural and political implications of extreme cross-identification. See Janice Raymond, *The Transsexual Empire: The Making of the She-Male* (Boston: Beacon, 1979); and Sandy Stone's critique of Raymond in "The 'Empire' Strikes Back: A Posttranssexual Manifesto," in *Body Guards: The Cultural Politics of Gender Ambiguity*, ed. Julia Epstein and Kristina Straub (New York: Routledge, 1993), 280–304.

25. John Money, *Man and Woman, Boy and Girl* (Baltimore: Johns Hopkins University Press, 1972).

26. It is important to know that the parameters of normal clitoral size are extremely narrow, and many girls not exposed to steroids prenatally may also be deemed irregular in relation to large clitorises. Doctors have been quite comfortable until recently with cutting the clitoris to "normalize" its appearance. See Suzanne Kessler, *Lessons from the Interesexed* (New Brunswick, NJ: Rutgers University Press, 1998).

27. Money, *Man and Woman, Boy and Girl*, 97.

28. In her analysis of Money's studies, Sandra L. Bem suggests that "because of either their continuing need for surgery or their continuing cortisone therapy or both, all twenty-five of the fetally masculinized girls were, in a sense, chronically ill during some part of their childhood." Bem, *The Lenses of Gender*, 26.

29. See Ann Fausto-Sterling, "The Five Sexes: Why Male and Female Are Not Enough," *The Sciences* (March/April 1993): 20–24. Fausto-Sterling examines the surgical interventions made by modern medicine on the intersexed body and concludes: "Society mandates the control of intersexed bodies because they blur and bridge the great divide. Inasmuch as hermaphrodites literally embody both sexes, they challenge traditional beliefs about sexual difference: they possess the irritating ability to live sometimes as one sex and sometimes as the other, and they raise the specter of homosexuality" (24).

30. Money, *Man and Woman, Boy and Girl*, 102.

31. Ibid., 10.

32. See Sandra L. Bem, "The Measurement of Psychological Androgyny," *Journal of Consulting and Clinical Psychology* 42, no. 2 (1974): 155–62.

33. Deborah Copaken (producer) and Billy Ray (editor), "Sugar and Spice," *Dateline NBC*, April 14, 1995. My thanks to Larry Gross for copying and sending me a tape of this program.

34. For a discussion of such sex-role definitions, see Ellen Piel Cook, *Psychological Androgyny* (New York: Pergamon, 1985).

35. Rebecca Bell-Metereau, *Hollywood Androgyny* (New York: Columbia University Press, 1993), creates a tomboy category, but this is within a chapter on "male impersonation"; she links the tomboy to the "female cross-dresser who acts as a buddy" (95). I do not see the tomboy as either a male impersonator or a cross-dresser but as a preadolescent gender within which the adult imperatives of binary gender have not yet taken hold. Bell-Metereau also stops her summary of tomboy movies with *The Member of the Wedding,* and many tomboy films were yet to come after this film was made in 1952.

36. Ibid., 96.

37. See John D'Emilio and Estelle Freeman, *Intimate Matters: A History of Sexuality in America* (New York: Harper & Row, 1988), 319.

38. For more on the fascinating production history of *Times Square,* see Jenni Olsen, *The Ultimate Guide to Gay and Lesbian Film and Video* (New York: Serpent's Tail, 1996).

39. This film, which was directed by Paul Schneider, was also released as *Willy/Milly* and *I Was a Teenage Boy.*

Tongues Untied: Memoirs of a Pentecostal Boyhood

Michael Warner

I was a teenage Pentecostalist. Because that is so very far from what I am now—roughly, a queer atheist intellectual—people often think I should have an explanation, a story. Was I sick? Had I been drinking? How did I get here from there? For years I've had a simple answer: "It was another life." If you had spent adolescence passing out tracts in a shopping mall, you might have the same attitude. My memory gives me pictures of someone speaking in tongues and being "slain in the spirit" (a Pentecostalist style of trance: you fall backward while other people catch you). But recognizing myself in these pictures takes effort, as though the memories themselves are in a language I don't understand, or as though I had briefly passed out.

Once, when I said, "It was another life," someone told me, "That's a very American thing to say." And it's true; a certain carelessness about starting over is very much in the national taste. On average, we afford ourselves a great deal of incoherence. Americans care about the freedom not only to have a self, but to discard one or two. We tend to distrust any job—peasant, messiah, or queen, for example—that requires people grown specially for the purpose. We like some variety on the résumé (though not necessarily a degree from Oral Roberts University, as in my case). We like people who take you aside, very privately, and whisper, "I'm Batman." In fact there's an impressive consistency on this point in the national mythology, from Rip Van Winkle to Clark Kent and Samantha on *Bewitched*.

Still, even allowing for the traditional naïveté and bad faith that is my birthright as a citizen of this, the last of history's empires, I have never been able to understand people with consistent lives—people who, for example, grow up in a liberal Catholic household and *stay* that way; or who in junior high school are already laying down a record on which to run for president one day. Imagine having no discarded personalities, no vestigial selves, no visible ruptures with yourself, no gulf of self-forgetfulness, nothing that requires explanation, no alien version of yourself that requires humor and accommodation. What kind of life is that?

For us who once were found and now are lost—and we are legion—our other lives pose some curious problems. Is there no relation at all between our once and present selves, or only a negative one? Is there some buried continuity, or some powerful vestige? In any case it would be hard to imagine a more complete revolution of personality. From the religious vantage of my childhood and adolescence, I am one of Satan's agents. From my current vantage, that former self was exotically superstitious. But I distrust both of these views of myself as the other. What if I were to stop saying "It was another life"? What if that life and this one are not so clearly opposed?

Of course, my life in the bosom of Jesus influenced me; but what interests me more is the way religion supplied me with experiences and ideas that I'm still trying to match. Watching Kathryn Kuhlman do faith healing, for example, didn't just influence my aesthetic sense for performance and eloquence; it was a kind of performance that no one in theater could duplicate. Religion does things that secular culture can only approximate.

Curiously enough, considering that fundamentalism is almost universally regarded as the stronghold and dungeon-keep of American anti-intellectualism, religious culture gave me a passionate intellectual life of which universities are only a pale ivory shadow. My grandfather had been a Southern Baptist preacher in North Carolina mountain towns like Hickory and Flat Rock, but my family migrated through various Protestant sects, including Seventh-Day Adventists, winding up in the independent Pentecostalist congregations known as "charismatic." We lived, in other words, in the heart of splinter-mad American sectarianism. In that world, the sub-denomination you belong to is bound for heaven; the one down the road is bound for hell. You need arguments to show why. And in that profoundly hermeneutic culture, your arguments have to be *readings:* ways of showing how the church down the road misreads a key text. Where I come from, people lose sleep over the meanings of certain Greek and Hebrew words.

The whole doctrine of Pentecostalism rests on the interpretation of one brief and difficult passage in the book of Acts. The apostles have been sitting around with nothing to do: "And there appeared unto them cloven tongues like as of fire, and it sat upon each of them. And they were all filled with the Holy Ghost, and began to speak with other tongues, as the Spirit gave them utterance." In the late nineteenth century, certain Americans decided you not only could but should do the same thing. In 1901, for example, Agnes Ozman of Topeka, Kansas, asserted that after being filled with the Holy Ghost she spoke and wrote Chinese for three days. (The Paraclete's literary tastes seem to have changed; nowadays people who speak in tongues favor a cross between Hebrew and baby talk.)

Pentecostalism interprets this verse as a model to be followed mainly because of another verse that comes a little later, in which Peter tells passers-by to be baptized and "receive the gift of the Holy Ghost." My mother, my brother, and I, like other Pentecostalists, accepted an interpretation in which "the gift" means not the Holy Ghost himself (i.e., "receive the Holy Ghost as a gift"), but the glossolalia given by him/it (i.e., "receive incomprehensible speech from the Holy Ghost as a gift"). We were known as "charismatics" because of this interpretation of the word *gift* (charisma); on the basis of this one interpretation my family was essentially forced out of our Baptist church. But only after a lot of talk about the texts and their interpretation. Throughout my childhood and adolescence, I remember being surrounded by textual arguments in which the stakes were not just life and death, but eternal life and death.

When I was fifteen or so, my family moved to Tidewater, Virginia, in part to be closer to the great revival led by the then obscure Pat Robertson. There, we went to special Bible study sessions for charismatics, held in the basement of a Lutheran church on nights when the room wasn't needed by Alcoholics Anonymous. (The Lutherans were the only Protestants in town who cared so little about theology that their scorn for us was only social rather than cosmic. For just this reason, of course, we regarded the Lutherans with limitless contempt, while in their basement we studied the grounds of their damnation.) The leader of these Bible study groups was a brilliant and somewhat unsettled man who by day worked as an engineer for International Harvester and by night set up as the Moses Maimonides of the greater Tidewater area. He had flip charts that would have impressed Ross Perot. He also had a radical argument: God could not possibly be omniscient. The Old Testament, he said, clearly showed God acting in stories, stories that, like the concept of free will itself, made no sense unless God doesn't know the future. If God does know the future, including your own decisions, then narrative time is illusory and only in farce can you be held responsible for your decisions. (Like most modern fundamentalists, he was deeply committed to a contract ideal of justice.)

Every Wednesday night without fail, as this man wound himself through an internal deconstruction of the entire Calvinist tradition, in a fastidiously Protestant return to a more anthropomorphic God, foam dried and flecked on his lips. For our petit-bourgeois family it was unbearable to watch, but we kept coming back. I remember feeling the tension in my mother's body next to me, all her perception concentrated on the desire to hand him the Kleenex that, as usual, she had thoughtfully brought along.

Being a literary critic is nice, I have to say, but for lip-whitening, vein-popping thrills it doesn't compete. Not even in the headier regions of Theory can we approximate that saturation of life by argument. In the car on the way home, we would talk it over. Was he right? If so, what were the consequences? Mother, I recall, distrusted an argument that seemed to demote God to the level of the angels; she thought Christianity without an omniscient God was too Manichaean, just God and Satan going at it. She also complained that if God were not omniscient, prophecy would make no sense. She scored big with this objection, I remember; at the time, we kept ourselves up-to-date on Pat Robertson's calculations about the imminent Rapture. I, however, cottoned on to the heretical engineer's arguments with all the vengeful pleasure of an adolescent. God's own limits were in sight: this was satisfaction in its own right, as was the thought of holding all mankind responsible in some way.

Later, when I read Nietzsche on the ressentiment at the heart of Christianity—the smell of cruelty and aggression in Christian benevolence—I recognized what that pleasure had been about. In my experience, ressentiment wasn't just directed against Power. It was directed against everything: the dominant cadres of society, of course, parents, school, authority in general; but also God, the material world, and one's own self. Just as the intellectual culture of religion has an intensity that secular versions lack, so also Protestant culture has an intricate and expressive language of power and abjection that in secular life has to be supplied in relatively impoverished ways. The world has not the least phenomenon that cannot, in Christian culture, be invested both with world-historical power and with total abjection. You are a soldier of the Lord, born among angels, contemplated from the beginning of time and destined to live forever. But you are also the unregenerate shit of the world. Your dinner-table conversation is the medium of grace for yourself and everyone around you; it also discloses continually your fallen worthlessness. Elevation and abasement surround you, in every flicker of your half-conscious thoughts. And the two always go together.

People often say, as though it's a big discovery, that Christians have a finely honed sadomasochistic sensibility. But this doesn't come close to appreciating religion's expressive language for power and abjection. The secular equivalents, such as Foucauldian analysis, have nothing like the same condensation. I realize this every time I read Jonathan Edwards:

> The sun does not willingly shine upon you to give you light to serve sin and Satan; the earth does not willingly yield her increase to satisfy your lusts; nor is it willingly a stage for your wickedness to be acted upon; the air does not willingly serve you for breath to maintain the flame of life in your vitals.... And the world would spew you out, were it not for the sovereign hand of Him who hath subjected it in hope.... The sovereign pleasure of God, for the present, stays His rough wind; otherwise it would come with fury, and your destruction would come like a whirlwind, and you would be like the chaff of the summer threshing floor.

You almost expect the next paragraph to be a manifesto for ecofundamentalism. Not even the final paragraphs of *The Order of Things* contain a more thorough distrust of everything in the human order. American religion has lost much of that antihumanism, even in the fundamentalist sects that rail against the "religion" of secular humanism, but they retain the imagination of abjection. And the abjection can be exquisite:

> The bow of God's wrath is bent, and the arrow made ready on the string, and justice bends the arrow at your heart, and strains the bow, and it is nothing but the mere pleasure of God, and that of an angry God, without any promise or obligation, at all, that keeps the arrow one moment from being made drunk with your blood.

In the film version the role of *you* will be played by a trembling and shiftless Keanu Reeves. Stuff like this can displace almost any amount of affect because of the strobe-light alternation of pleasure and obliteration: "It is nothing but His mere pleasure that keeps you from being this moment swallowed up in everlasting destruction." *Nothing but pleasure,* indeed. When I read this my blood heats up. I can hardly keep from reading it aloud. (Maybe that comes from hanging out with Oral Roberts.) The displacement and vicarious satisfaction provided in consumer culture is, by contrast, low-budget monochrome.

About the same time that we were going to hear the holy prophet of International Harvester, my mother made a new church friend, Frankie. Frankie was very butch. She was sweet to me, but visibly seething toward most of the world. Her sidekick Peggy, however, was the devoted servant of everybody, making endless presents of macramé before finally opening her own macramé store in a strip mall. Frankie, Peggy, and my mother belonged to a circle of women who held Bible studies in one another's living rooms (furnished in Ethan Allen early American, most of them), swapped recipes, came to each other in trouble, and prostrated themselves in the power of the Holy Spirit together.

I remember watching the way they wept together, their implicit deference to Frankie, their constant solicitation of one another's sufferings. Most of them worked. All were unhappy in the family dramas to which they nevertheless held absolute commitments. None of them liked her lot in life. They would pray in tongues while vacuuming the shag carpet. When the bills could be paid, it was because Jesus provided the money. In church, weeping in the intense but unfathomable love of Jesus, they repeated certain gestures: head slowly shaking no, eyes closed above damp cheeks, arms stretched out in invisible crosses, the temporarily forgotten Kleenex clenched in the hand. (Because Pentecostalists exalt weeping and catarrh so much, I still associate the smell of tissue with church.)

At the time I remember thinking that this social-devotional style, in which I was often a half-noticed participant, had a special meaning for these women. Not that it was a mere displacement or substitute for an articulate feminism; my mother and her friends felt, I'm sure, that Jesus spoke to them on more levels, and deeper ones, than did the feminism they had encountered. But certainly the redemption of Jesus compensated sufferings that were already framed by women's narrative. Think about the consequences of having fundamental parts of your life—gender, especially—filtered through fundamentalism's expressive language of power and abjection. In their descriptions of the love of Jesus—undeserved, devastating benignity—one heard always the articulation of a thorough resentment of the world and themselves, but also of hitherto unimaginable pleasures, and of an ideal that was also an implicit reproach against their social world. It was not lost on me that we migrated to more extreme versions of Protestant fundamentalism as my mother saw more and more clearly her dissatisfaction with the normal life to which she was nevertheless devoted. Even now, her sons have left home, three husbands have been reluctantly divorced, her friends have parted ways, and she's had to go back to teaching school—but Jesus still pays the bills.

C. S. Lewis once complained that English pictures of Jesus always made him look like an adolescent girl; I think this was and is part of the appeal, for me, for my mother's friends, *and* for Lewis, whose desire for a butch deity said more about his own queeny tastes than about the Jesus we continue to reinvent. As Harold Bloom has pointed out in his recent book *The American Religion,* many American Protestants, particularly Southern Baptists, have essentially reduced the trinity to Jesus. "He walks with me, and he talks with me, and he tells me I am His own," as we always sang. During this hymn, I would look around to make sure no one noticed that these words were coming, rather too pleasurably, from my mouth.

Jesus was my first boyfriend. He loved me, personally, and he told me I was his own. This was very thrilling, especially when he was portrayed by Jeffrey Hunter. Anglo-American Christian culture has developed a rich and kinky iconography of Jesus, the perma-boy who loves us, the demiurge in a dress. Here, for example, is Emerson's Divinity School Address of 1838: "Jesus Christ belonged to the true race of prophets. He saw with open eye the mystery of the soul. Drawn by its severe harmony, ravished with its beauty, he lived in it, and had his being there. . . . He said, in this jubilee of sublime emotion, 'I am divine.'" Well, it's fun to exclaim, "I am divine," and Emerson's point is that we all should. But he does some extra fantasy work in this picture of Jesus the happily ravished, Jesus the perpetual jubilee of sublime affect. Jesus, it seems, is coming all the time. This wouldn't make him good for much *except* being a fantasy boyfriend. With spikes in him.

Since the early days of Methodism, of course, it has been commonplace to see enthusiastic religion as sexual excess. In a characteristically modern way, writers such as Lacan and Bataille have regarded all religion as an unrecognized form of sexuality. Bloom, in *The American Religion*, writes that "there is no way to disentangle the sexual drive from Pentecostalism." He calls it "sadomasochistic sexuality," "a kind of orgiastic individualism," a "pattern of addiction," "an ecstasy scarcely distinguishable from sexual transport."

There's something to this, but I worry about putting it like that. You can reduce religion to sex only if you don't especially believe in either one. When I learned what orgasm felt like, I can't say that the difference between it and speaking in tongues was "scarcely distinguishable." It seemed like a clear call to me. And the two kinds of ecstasy quickly became, for me at least, an excruciating alternative. God, I felt sure, didn't want me to come. And he always wanted to watch.

The agony involved in choosing between orgasm and religion, as I was forced to do on a nightly basis, is the sort of thing ignored by any account that treats religion as sublimated, displaced, or misrecognized sexuality. At the beginning of *Two Serious Ladies*, the great Jane Bowles novel, one little girl asks another to play a new game. "It's called 'I forgive you for all your sins,'" she says. "Is it fun?" asks the other. "It's not for fun that we play it, but because it's necessary to play it." This, undoubtedly, is just why religion is so queer; it's not for fun that we play it.

What I think critics like Bloom are trying to say, against their own anerotic reductivism, is that religion makes available a language of ecstasy, a horizon of significance within which transgressions against the normal order of the world and the boundaries of self *can be seen as good things.*

Pentecostalists don't get slain in the spirit just by rubbing themselves, or by redirecting some libido; they require a whole set of beliefs about the limitations of everyday calculations of self-interest, about the impoverishment of the world that does not willingly yield its increase to satisfy your lusts. In this way ecstatic religions can legitimate self-transgression, providing a meaningful framework for the sublime play of self-realization and self-dissolution. And once again, the secular versions often look like weak imitations. Only the most radical theories of sexual liberation (Marcuse's *Eros and Civilization,* for example) attribute as much moral importance to self-dissolution as fundamentalist religion does. (And nobody believes them anymore.) Simple affirmations of desire, by contrast, don't supply a horizon of significance at all. The bliss of Pentecostalism is, among other things, a radical downward revaluing of the world that despises Pentecostalists. Like all religions, Pentecostalism has a world-canceling moment; but its world-canceling gestures can also be a kind of social affirmation, in this case of a frequently despised minority. I suspect that the world-canceling rhetorics of queer sexuality work in a similar way. If you lick my nipple, the world suddenly seems comparatively insignificant. Ressentiment doubles your pleasure.

Both my moral, Christian self and my queer, atheist one have had to be performed as minority identities. What queers often forget, jeopardized as we are by resurgent fundamentalisms in the United States, is that fundamentalists themselves are not persuaded by "moral majority" or "mainstream values" rhetoric; they too consider themselves an oppressed minority. In their view the dominant culture is one of a worldliness they have rejected, and bucking that trend comes, in some very real ways, with social stigmatization. For instance, as far as I can make out, Jehovah's Witnesses believe in almost nothing *but* their own minority status and the inevitable destruction of the mainstream.

The radical Protestant and quasi-Protestant (i.e., Mormon) sects in this country have helped, willingly or not, to elaborate minoritarian culture. Left political thought has been remarkably blind to this fact. Most of us believe, I think, that we are in favor of all oppressed minorities, and that you can tell an oppressed minority because the people concerned say that's what they are. Who gets to say, and by what standards, that Pentecostalists, or Mormons, are not the oppressed minority they claim to be? This is not a rhetorical question.

One way that fundamentalists have contributed to the culture of minority identities is by developing the performative genres of identity-talk. Sentences like "I'm Batman" or "We're here, we're queer, get used to it" take for granted a context in which people are accorded the power of declaring what they are. In the world of Southern Baptists and charismatics, people practice a genre known as witnessing, in some ways the ur-form of all modern autobiographical declarations. Witnessing might mean telling a conversion narrative or a miracle narrative in church, but it also might mean declaring yourself in suburban shopping malls. It is the fundamentalist version of coming out, and explained to the budding Pentecostalist in much the same language of necessity, shame and pride, stigma and cultural change.

In writing all of this, of course, I am stuck between witnessing and coming out. One of the most interesting things about the gap between religious and secular culture is that no matter which side you stand on, conversion or deconversion, the direction seems inevitable. Religious people always suppose that people start out secular and have to get religion. People like me don't secularize: we *backslide*. Of course, I have slid back to places I never was or thought of being, and it may be to halt this endless ebb that my mother has recently begun trying out a new paradigm: she's willing to consider me as having a lifestyle. I might prefer backsliding, but the concept of an alternative path marks progress in our relations. Meanwhile, those of us who have gotten over religion find ourselves heir to a potent Enlightenment mythology that regards religion as a primitive remnant, a traditional superstition. This has been the opinion not only of thinkers with very little religious imagination, like Marx and Freud, but even those who have given us our most profound analyses: Nietzsche, Weber, Durkheim, Bataille. (William James is a rare exception.) It's almost impossible to broach the subject of religion without taking the movement of this narrative for granted. To be secular is to be modern. To be more secular is to be more modern. But religion clearly isn't withering away with the spread of modern rationalism and home entertainment centers. In a recent Gallup study 94 percent of Americans said they believe in God. Better still: 88 percent believe that God loves them personally. Yet this is the country that has always boasted of *not* having a feudal past, of being the world's most modern nation. It's enough to make you ask: Are we sick? How did we get here from there?

I'm as secular and modern as the next person, but I doubt that these statistics indicate a residue of pre-Enlightenment superstition. And I don't think that my own personal incoherence is entirely of the linear and progressive type. Even to raise the subject of personal incoherence, identity, and rupture is to see that, in a way, the secular imagination and the religious one have already settled out of court. For both the notion of having a rupture with your self *and* the notion of narrated personal coherence are Protestant conventions, heightened in all the American variants of Protestantism. No other culture goes as far as ours in making everything an issue of identity. We've invented an impressive array of religions: Mormon, Southern

Baptist, Jehovah's Witness, Pentecostalist, Nation of Islam, Christian Science, Seventh-Day Adventist—every last one of them a conversion religion. They offer you a new and perpetual personality, and they tell you your current one was a mistake you made. They tell you to be somebody else. I say: believe them.

Guy Davenport's Pastorals of Childhood Sexuality

Andre Furlani

"Shall I say it, provided that I don't get throttled for it?" Montaigne asks in his essay on sexuality, "Sur des vers de Virgile." "It seems to me that love is not properly and naturally in its season except in the age next to infancy."[1] Urging that repression issues in ignorance and concupiscence, Montaigne recommends the allowance to youth of "a taste of the quick" and of freedom from the scrutiny and strictures of monitors. The precocious Bordeaux characters of Guy Davenport's novella "On Some Lines of Virgil" read Montaigne's essay, but scarcely need to take hints from their city's renowned former mayor. Youths impart to one another the techniques of masturbation, share each others' lovers, and introduce prepubescent siblings to their orgies. Jonquille, a teenage paleoethnobiology student, relieves Jolivet, the story's fourteen-year-old narrator, of his virginity and orchestrates the revels of their Fourierist *petite horde*, made up of young adolescents and Jolivet's twelve-year-old brother, Victor. Camping by a river where members of the horde experiment with masturbation and oral sex, Jolivet asks his girlfriend, "How far do we go? . . . That's our affair, Jonquille said with authority. Shove the strawberries closer, she added. What pleases us, that's what we'll do."[2] The reply echoes the famous call for free love in the first chorus of Tasso's pastoral drama *Aminta, "S'ei piace, ei lice"* (If it pleases, it's permitted).[3]

Distinctions of age or sexual orientation are never drawn in Davenport's stories of childhood and youth, consent alone determining sexual relations; persuasion is not used, force never applied. The radical premise is that youths as young as Victor are potentially mature enough to exercise such autonomy, monitored from a distance by loving, liberal parents. Jolivet teaches techniques of masturbation to his younger brother, who soon masturbates Jonquille, who fellates Jolivet's pal Michel, who makes love to all three. Later they do much the same for their friend the crippled beggar Marc Aurel. "I have no defense of my fictions," Davenport told me in a letter dated September 7, 1999. "I'm aware that I'm imagining a morality transcending practically all present cultures. Hence my interest in Fourier's 'calculus of the passions.'" Davenport's stories locate a source of the radical innocence of children in their embryonic sexuality.

Davenport's bucolics, however, depends on a recognition of its status as fantasy, made conspicuous by a flaunted artifice. Such artifice allows him to explore proscribed areas of childhood sexuality, but also to confine it outside the norms such fiction would challenge. The unlikely shepherds of Theocritus and Virgil compose cosmopolitan verse; the unlikely youths of "Virgil" tour Magdalenian cave sites in the nearby Dordogne as knowledgeably as archaeologists and read Montaigne's Latin quotations without a crib. The pastoral conventions insulate the narrative, so that a description of a Hellenistic pastoral poem applies equally to the story itself: "These are not real boys in the poem, but porcelain figurines in a neoclassical tradition, like Virgil's and Theokritos's shepherds and girls. They are imaginary. The wine, however, and honey are there."[4] Davenport's neoclassical porcelain imposes on his realism an overt formal and thematic artifice. Divided into seventy-five five-part sections of isometric paragraphs (each four lines long), the form of "Virgil" enforces rigorous constraints on its emancipatory narrative. The story is organized like many of Davenport's paintings and several other of his fictions (including "Au Tombeau de Charles Fourier") on a grid structure, and thus is as arbitrarily and severely structured as Marianne Moore's syllabic stanzas. Like Montaigne's essay, the story is a serpentine patchwork of citations, translations (e.g., of Rimbaud's "Tête de Faune"), observations and anecdotes coiled around the theme of emerging sexuality, but like a classical pastoral it observes strict conventions. The laboriously parceled paragraphs confine the anarchic erotic idylls they contain. The isometric construction of the story advertises its artifice, while its characters exercise imaginative liberties. Before an orgy with Marc and Michel, Jolivet says to his brother, "You must remember none of this happened, understand?"[5] The challenge is put squarely to both Victor and the reader.

A painter as well as a writer (a monograph devoted to his paintings and drawings has been published),[6] Guy Davenport has published eight books of fiction and two of verse, in addition to several volumes of Greek translations; studies of Balthus, Pound's *Cantos*, Homer, and still-life painting; and three volumes of essays. Few contemporary American writers have made so radical an inventory of the potential of childhood and youth. Adapting Fourier to Freud, Davenport has employed diverse experimental means to rehearse, with arresting candor, the manifold vitality of precocious sexuality. Not since Randolph Bourne, who died in 1918, has an American writer so fervently and articulately insisted on childhood and youth as specific social classes of revolutionary potential. In Davenport's work the young are invited to view themselves as a subordinated social group, enriched by a tragic legacy that can instigate their enfranchisement. Davenport's frank, learned, and lyrical stories disengage childhood sexuality from the commercial kitsch of much youth culture, from puritanical censure, the cynicism of camp, and the theoretical straitjackets of both social constructionism and biological determinism. He imagines instead an arcadian margin where children are granted an autonomy they are schooled to maintain in a spirit of idealism. From his utopian fictions emerge various versions of preadolescent sexuality: as a bucolic interval, as the core human experience, as an idyll the adult must endeavor to recover, as a means of interrogating ideologies, as a stage of vitality primitive to the mature conceptualizations of taboos.

"I'm boss in my own pants," the pubescent artist's model Mikkel tells the young sculptor Gunnar in "Gunnar and Nikolai."[7] The pubescent brothers Adam and Peter in "Concert Champêtre in D Minor," unembarrassed foragers in nascent sexuality, decorate their bedroom with a Dutch poster repeating the same slogan: "BAAS IN EIGEN BROEKJE, depicting two naked blond handsome well-formed frank-eyed boys, one with an arm over the other's shoulders, both prepubescent but with incipient hopeful microfuzz apparent. Their father said it was their assurance that somewhere somebody understood how things are."[8] Like Janusz Korczak in Poland and, earlier, Kate Douglas Wiggin in New England, Davenport affirms the right to childhood, but extends the right into the sexual sphere. In contrast to such revisionist historians as Philippe Ariès, Davenport reserves for childhood a space beyond social construction. Ariès has argued that, conceptually at least, childhood scarcely existed prior to the Renaissance, and indeed did not become a discrete cultural category until the nineteenth century.[9] For Davenport, rather, childhood is not a category but an authentic developmental phase that we are only beginning to discover. In *A Balthus Notebook*, he identifies childhood as one of modernity's great discoveries—excavations, his rhetoric suggests:

> The Enlightenment, removing encrustations of convention from human nature, discovered the durée of childhood as the most passionate and beautiful part of a lifetime. (In Plutarch's *Lives,* no childhoods are recorded.) Rousseau, Blake, Joshua Reynolds, Gainsborough, Wordsworth.
>
> By the Belle Époque, children (in a pervasive, invisible revolution) had come into a world of their own for the first time in Western civilization since late antiquity, and we begin to have (in Proust, in Joyce) dramatic accounts of their world as never before.[10]

Davenport recommends the paintings of Balthus in part for their idealization of childhood sexuality. The pubescent girl, he asserts, is the painter's "symbol of spirit integral with matter."[11] This does not make her any less sexual. "Balthus's girls are sexy, charming, French adolescents painted with a fresh seeing of the human body, with humor, with wit, with clarity, and with an innocence that we can locate in adolescent idealism itself rather than in an obsession."[12]

Davenport is too ardent an admirer of Blake and Wordsworth to relinquish entirely the metaphysical categories of innocence and idealism. For James R. Kincaid, neither term is helpful, and both "child" and "pedophile" are social constructions derived from the Victorian eroticizing of the child. Writes Kincaid, "Innocence is not, as we said, detected but granted, not nurtured but enforced; it comes at the child as a denial of a whole host of capacities, an emptying out."[13] Davenport, by contrast, sees in Balthus "a stratification that zones off children from adults (reminiscent of Rousseau's distinction between noble savagery and civilization) and assigns a native creativity and intelligence, along with a radical innocence, to children."[14] Such a privileging of childhood is equally discernible in Davenport's fiction.

Kincaid rejects most stereotypes of childhood, as of pederasty. Among the "host of capacities" of children is the sexual. He argues that a sublimated erotic interest in children pervaded Victorian culture and persisted in the twentieth century, leading to the criminalization of "child-loving." The "utopian and revolutionary" aim, as he calls it, of his book *Child-Loving: The Erotic Child and Victorian Culture,* is to reposition sexual attitudes toward children, who are "being assaulted" by societal protections.[15] He advances "a form of sexual thinking that abandons fixed categories in favor of a scale of dynamic and relativistic measure of a shifting range of possibilities." He recognizes, however, that "there are some categories whose fixity we are unwilling to regard as negotiable."[16]

In contrast to Davenport, Kincaid is suspicious of efforts to reconceptualize child-loving as a potentially utopian "melting down" of gender and age differences and of the "oppositional terms" in which sexuality is understood.[17] And although both view power as the primary threat to children and to the exercise of autonomy, Kincaid doubts that children's sexuality can be realized outside the coercive forces of adult power. Kincaid's summary of Stevi Jackson's utopian position, which consists in the faith that this is possible, suggests Davenport's own view:

> If we then proceed to dissolve the association of sex with power we have made the problem itself seem both unnatural and insoluble. Noting all this does not, of course, naturalize pedophilia, much less justify it. But it does suggest that our resistance to child-love helps ensure the perpetuation of the activity. Child-love, in this figuring, is an attempt to fly free from power, to fly by the nets created by our way of catching meaning.[18]

All of Davenport's fiction about childhood sexuality takes place in the space cleared by Kincaid's quite skeptical *if.* The fiction imagines the suspension of all coercive mechanisms in a ludic space that is bucolic and utopian. In the novel-length story *Apples and Pears,* for instance, a Dutch philosopher finds himself applying some of the principles of the early-nineteenth-century French utopian Charles Fourier, launching a commune out of a De Stijl townhouse in downtown Amsterdam during the nuclear arms buildup in 1981.

In the house assemble reformed strays, family, friends, and their children. The philosopher Adriaan van Hovendaal is an avuncular mentor, a "Pythagorean Calvinist" who rescues teens from squalor and profligacy with financial support, encouragement, and affection.[19] Like Fourier, he recognizes no noncoercive sexual perversions. The nineteen-year-old painter Sander (whose own rescue furnishes the plot of Davenport's earlier story "The Death of Picasso"), preparing Fourierist canvases for his first gallery exhibition, is involved incestuously with his sister Grietje (they hope to have children), is sexually involved with an illiterate adolescent vagrant whom the commune is educating (he eventually becomes Sander's apprentice), and is in love with the standoffish Adriaan, who rarely gratifies the painter's desire. Around them in the unpartitioned townhouse scamper two pairs of pubescents whose erotic experiments with each other are condoned. The kids are about the same age as Catherine and Heathcliff (Balthus illustrated an edition of *Wuthering Heights*),[20] but they at least do not have to escape to the heath and into the lacunae of Victorian fiction to fulfill their passion. Adriaan's pleasure in them is voyeuristic only, extending little further than giving them sexual advice.[21] Nuclear arsenals, the surrogate wars of the Cold War superpowers, child neglect and child abuse, homophobia and consumer greed, not the sexual impulses of children and teens, are the perversities bewailed in *Apples and Pears.*

Fourier provides one framework for the establishment of such rights, and Adriaan quotes him frequently in the notebook that makes up *Apples and Pears.* All children are geniuses in the utopia of Charles Fourier. At three years old their predilections and aptitudes, scientifically categorized according to some eight hundred types, are carefully cultivated. Believing that God rules by attraction rather than constraint, Fourier views all passions as good; hence education involves simply the development of drives that children already exhibit. The result is an exponential increase in talent: "Eight hundred randomly chosen children could provide the germ of all perfection that the human spirit can attain to. Each one, that is, will be naturally endowed with abilities sufficient to equal some outstanding historical figure, such as Homer, Caesar, Newton, etc."[22]

No normative sexuality prevails in Fourier. Any desire can be harnessed to foster social harmony and economic prosperity. Repressive civilization had, in Fourier's view, transformed potentially useful sexual manias into vicious and harmful perversions. "Attractions are proportional to the destinies," Fourier argues; "all the impulses of attraction, which are ridiculed because they seem bizarre, are usefully coordinated in the societary mechanism, and will become as precious as they are useless and harmful in the sub-divided or family system."[23] The divine law of passionate attraction rules what he calls his "New Harmony," where love is regarded as an index of Providence and the chief source of beneficial social cohesion. From puberty on, youths are recruited into Fourier's *nouveau monde amoureux,* in which homosexuality, pederasty, "Sapphism," and compound unions all have a welcome place in the establishment and maintenance of harmony.

Davenport gives to his stories the full sexual emphasis that Fourier viewed as the necessary precondition for a utopian project. Charles Fourier "designed his Harmony to preserve the liveliness of the child into old age," Davenport writes. "He saw no reason why it should drain away."[24] The fortunate in Davenport's stories go back and become children. In several linked stories in *The Jules Verne Steam Balloon,* the classics master Hugo heeds the call when Franklin, pubescent brother of his lover Mariana, plays Cupid between them.[25] As does the Dutch philosopher Adriaan, the protagonist of four stories, whose Freudian wound, associated with the loss of an adored childhood playmate, is healed once he becomes the custodian of an informal Fourierist sodality of uninhibited teenage mavericks, who ground his deracinated metaphysics in the body. In "Wo Es War, Soll Ich

Werden," the teacher Holger is similarly delivered by Franklin's pubescent mate, the prodigy Pascal.

In "The River," Davenport charts the progress of eros from childhood to pubescence. Narrated by the Danish boy Adam, the story is punctuated without commas or semicolons, conveying a childhood intelligence still overwhelmed by the experiences it verbalizes. He recounts a bucolic excursion with his agemate Christian and the adolescents Rasmus and Sven. The older pair wrestle, swim, repeat Pythagorean number lore, and invoke the ideals of classical Greek sexual license, but while Sven is unreservedly "pagan," Rasmus yearns to achieve the puritan self-mastery of the fabled members of the Theban Band, Epameinondas and Pelopidas (who are the main characters of Davenport's retelling of Plutarch's *conte philosophique*, "The Daimon of Sokrates"). It is into this austere code of passionate friendship that Rasmus intends to initiate the boys. Sven explains to them that, according to Rasmus, "friends should be brotherly like Epameinondas and Pelopidas and when they are together have only pure thoughts even when they're wrestling or in the one sleeping bag breathing in each other's ear unhampered by underwear or pajamas."[26] Sven neither accepts the need for such restraint nor believes in its feasibility. In the story's sequel, "Concert Champêtre in D Minor," Rasmus explains his relationship with Sven to Adam and Christian: "He thinks sex is the important thing about us, and I think that love and trust are, and only when the two are in sync do I love him the way he wants to be loved. We have to swap selves to do it."[27] Seeking a compromise between hedonism and abstinence, Rasmus in "The River" seats the nude Adam and Christian facing each other, instructing them to gaze into each other's eyes.

> Hug if you want to and kiss if you want to and it's fine if your dicks rear up according to nature. I thought this up for Sven and me summer before last when we were on a trail in a larchwood in Norway. We looked into each other's eyes for how long who knows for time stops. I figured it out. A long togetherness with a promise to each other to let the craving build and build and not give in.[28]

His skepticism encouraged by Sven, Adam comments, "And it was only fair to say that they do give in when they're both out of their minds and Rasmus mopes the next day about lack of character and about Pythagoras's noble soul."[29] The story ends with Adam and Christian's Pythagorean embrace dissolved when their elders return from a swim in the river.

Making allusions to the sexual customs of the Inuit of Greenland, colonized by the Danes, "The River" finds impetus for its treatment of prepubescent sexuality not only in the ancient Greeks but in modern aboriginals. Davenport borrows the sexual morality of such stories from the Inuit anthropology of the Dane Peter Freuchen, whose work challenges most Western sexual taboos. Attaching no shame to sex, Freuchen's Inuit are polygamous, forming extramarital bonds without censure and reserving opprobrium only for clandestine or dishonest unions. Most sexual practices are tolerated when not concealed. Although homosexuality, incest, and bestiality are avoided, they are tolerated when not concealed. Pubescents in larger communities congregate at the Young People's House to "sleep together just for the fun of it, with no obligation outside of that certain night. Nobody takes offense at this practice."[30] Children are meanwhile especially cherished (to strike them incurs dishonor) and are integrated into mature routines. This extends to sexual experimentation: "Toddlers of both sexes are encouraged to play together with a freedom that would outrage a mother in America, and the game of 'playing house' can—among Eskimo children—assume an awfully realistic appearance."[31] Females marry very young, usually much older males: "Eskimo girls marry so very young that a girl will often continue to play with the other children right up to the time of her first pregnancy. A boy, on the other hand, has to hunt well for many seasons before he has accumulated enough property to establish a home."[32]

In Davenport's stories, many of which take place in Denmark, the young are equally independent and sexually active members of a permissive society. The boxcar of "The Lavender Fields of Apta Julia" and the meadow of "The River" provide a refuge for sexual adventure resembling the igloo reserved for the trysts of Inuit youths. The devotion, magnanimity, and frankness generated in such conditions translate into an outraged response to the mature values of American culture. Several of Davenport's stories situate the utopian possibilities of childhood autonomy in menaced proximity to the inherited culture, characterized in terms of cupidity, ignorance, hypocrisy, and violence. The utopian conception of childhood implicitly assails the ideologies that prevent it from being realized.

This is, of course, itself an ideology, a transformative one derived from some of the precursors I attempt to sketch in this essay. Davenport, however, shares with his most cherished precursors (including Fourier and, as will now be seen, Randolph Bourne and Janusz Korczak) the assumption that this utopian stratification of childhood conforms with transcendent laws of human nature. He follows Fourier in accepting the paradoxical need for normative frameworks within which to foster in children traits regarded as essential. Although any utopia is a social construction, Fourier claims that within his New Harmony universal, transhistorical imperatives would be realized—hence the profusion in Fourier of organicist metaphors, many of which Davenport adopts. The aim is the restoration of human nature in an arcadia regained rather than its reformation in a New Jerusalem.

In his mobilizations of childhood and youth as a discrete and oppressed social class, Davenport is preceded by the American literary radical Randoph Bourne. In *Youth and Life*, Bourne anticipated Vietnam-era student radicalism by protesting the older generation's coercion of the young: "They kill his soul, and then use the carcass as a barricade against the advancing hosts of light. They train him to protect and conserve their own outworn institutions when he should be the first, by reason of his clear insight and freedom from crusted prejudice, to attack them."[33] (Not surprisingly, Bourne was, like Fourier, rediscovered during the generational conflict and sexual revolution of the 1960s.)

In youth preserved from the depredations of puritanical conformity Bourne locates the germ of radical social reform. Scoffing at the notion of the wisdom of age, Bourne argues that the young "have all the really valuable experience."[34] Morality is acquired not through prudence and sober precept but through "moral adventure," audacity and susceptibility. The coercive logic behind the exaltation of the child's "innocence" is exposed and vilified. Education should consist not in moral instruction but in the stimulation of an uninhibited curiosity. "If his mind and body are active, he will be a 'good' child, in the best sense of the word."[35] The influence of elders must inevitably be pernicious, an imposition of stifling ancestral values legitimated strictly by pedigree. The largest channel of self-discovery is not reached through obedience to adult admonition but through emulation of friends.

Sexual desire complements other forms of curiosity, and thus Davenport's fiction realizes the erotic implications of Bourne's belief that the virtues of childhood are not in "the moral realm" where adults strive to confine them: "Discarding the 'good' child, then, we will find the virtues of childhood in that restless, pushing, growing curiosity that is characteristic of every healthy little boy or girl."[36] For Bourne, virtue issues from an ardent curiosity for the data of the material world, leading to the acquisition of powers of judgment indispensable to the expansion of one's moral sympathies. Davenport does not hesitate to identify such ardor with eros. "It is the kinetics of desire that creates the euphoria of loving and of learning, of being alive," Davenport observes in his review of Anne Carson's *Eros the Bittersweet*. "We want to nibble our beloved's ear, to master the Pythagorean theorem; what we are really doing is defying entropy and moving into the mind's capacity for synergy. . . . A sense of wonder lost since childhood returns."[37] The pubescent and adolescent characters of "The River" and "Concert Champêtre" make love and solve mathematical equations interchangeably. The erotic experimentation obliquely implied by Bourne's advocacy is boldly acknowledged in such stories.

In stories like "The River" the youths operate in a theater of moral adventure, guided by the exhilarating sensation of a new responsibility for one another, insulated from both adult culture and commercial youth culture.

In "Gunnar and Nikolai," Davenport in a sense fuses Bourne's emancipatory program for youth with the attempt to establish a childhood utopia among the Jewish orphans of pre–World War II Poland. The promising young Danish sculptor Gunnar hires a pubescent model to pose for an Ariel and a King Matt, the latter the hero of Janusz Korczak's children's novel *King Matt the First*. The child king, who yearns to become the king of all children, endeavors to make a social class of children and to reform the world by establishing trust and cooperation between elders and minors. Defeated militarily by treacherous neighboring monarchs, Matt is poisoned with sleeping gas and later marched past ridiculing gawkers to his execution. Only the commuting of the sentence distinguishes Matt's fate from that of Korczak and the inmates of the Warsaw Jewish orphanage he directed. The pediatrician, educator, and writer chose on the morning of August 6, 1942, to accompany his 192 wards to Treblinka, where they were locked in sheds and murdered with carbon monoxide.[38] The model, who has switched identities with his dear friend in order to earn money posing for Gunnar, tells his pal Nikolai in their tree house, "There was a day when the Germans took all the kids and Korczak and a woman named Stefa to die at Treblinka, and they all marched through the streets to the cattle cars. I'm to be the boy that carried their flag, the flag of their republic, the orphanage."[39]

Korczak's orphans participated in the administration, rule, supervision, and responsibilities of Dom Seriot (House of Orphans). Inspired by the pedagogical philosophy of Pestalozzi, Korczak sought to accelerate maturation by instilling an early sense of personal responsibility and by exposing children to the challenges of real experience. In his tract "The Child's Right to Respect," he urged more autonomy for children and assailed the puritanism that idealizes the "pure" child at the expense of chastising the sexuality of the "bad" one. He detected in moral codes an imposition on the nature of children. "The teacher's job is to let him live, to let him win the right to be a child," Korczak asserted.[40]

"There is no such thing as a pure child," Korczak claimed. "Oh, but how quickly does the child free and cleanse himself."[41] "Gunnar and Nikolai" ends with Mikkel's confession of his ruse, received by an astonished Gunnar without recrimination. They pass the evening getting to know each other on this firmer footing. When Gunnar's lover phones the next morning, Mikkel congratulates her on being pregnant and Gunnar explains that he and Mikkel are in bed together: "Oh yes, you know what boys are like. Disgraceful, yes, and frowned on by psychologists and the police, but lots of fun. The clergy are of two minds about it, I believe. Actually, he went to sleep while we were talking about how friendly it was sharing a bed." "None of last night happened, you know?" Mikkel adds.[42]

The nonexistence of the Danish boarding school where "Wo Es War, Soll Ich Werden" takes place is the novella's most salient element, as the teacher Holger reminds the pupil Pascal, "There is decidedly no such place as NFS Grundtvig. Never was."[43] The school is really a remote Fourierist phalanstery, where every pupil has realized his or her genius by the age of ten. Pascal has already had a scientific article accepted by a prestigious academic journal and has been offered a university post on its basis; the Icelander Holger is pursuing advanced botanical research on Arctic mosses and fossil flowers. He realizes himself, however, through contact with the school's twelve-year-old prodigy. The characters, corresponding to the behavioral types anatomized by Fourier, are "united by a shared taste for the exercise of a particular function."[44] The school into which the group is integrated is a *série passionelle,* each of which is characterized by some variety of a generic enthusiasm. Every penchant has its use in such a series, in which even rivalry, intrigue, and other forms of discord are treated as indispensable. As in Fourier, education comes through experience much more than through lectures. Elective kinships are privileged over family ties, and evil is presented as privative, not inherent but emerging out of specific and correctable social conditions. Friction rather than sin besets the characters and is not demonized as an insurmountable obstacle to happiness. The novella indeed begins with two school fights, the origin of which is the dissolution of a pubescent ménage à trois. The passionate friendship of Pascal and the day student Franklin, seemingly strengthened by the admission into their fellowship of Alexandra, is soon ruptured when Franklin and Alexandra exclude Pascal, who finds refuge in Holger.

Although initially a reticent Nick Adams sort who camps alone and practices an austere cult of precision, Holger is encouraged by the young classics master Hugo to retrace the genius of childhood through his attachment to Pascal. In the reminders of childhood sexual stirrings, Holger detects a buried vein of his identity—hence the novella's title. In *New Introductory Lectures on Psychoanalysis,* Freud claims as the intention of psychoanalysis "to strengthen the ego, to make it more independent of the superego, to expand its field of perception and to extend its organization, so that it can appropriate new pieces of the id. Where id was, should ego come to be."[45] *Wo Es war, soll Ich werden.*

Davenport retains the axiom but reads through the specialized terminology to the opacity of the original German. Hugo tells Holger:

> You were interested in Freud's enigmatic statement that where it was, there must I begin to be. The oyster makes a pearl around an irritant grain of sand. Nature compensates. . . . That is, one source of strength seems to be weakness.

—Surely not, Holger said. That sounds like the suspect theory that genius is a disease: Mann's paradox. It's romantic science, if science at all.

—No no, Hugo said. Freud meant that a wound, healing, can command the organism's whole attention, and thus becomes the beginning of a larger health.[46]

Holger eventually surmises that in his life the *Es* of Freud's formula was a childhood sexual encounter with a blind Icelandic folksinger who resembled Walt Whitman, but Hugo conjectures that the source is an earlier and intensely vivid memory, of his penis being dried or fondled after a bath in his infancy. Childhood becomes an idyll maturation must recover if the adult is to thrive. Holger rescues Pascal from heartbreak, while Pascal rescues Holger from a strain of puritanism Randolph Bourne viewed as the chief menace to the "experimental life" practiced so audaciously at NFS Grundtvig.

Pascal's overtures and Hugo's growing receptiveness culminate in a camping trip that, unlike that of Florent and Jens in "O Gadjo Niglo" (see below), affirms their mutuality. In a school of ménages à trois, of young couples and pubescent homoerotic fellowships, their association is welcomed. Like Davenport's other older lovers, Holger observes strict propriety and instigates nothing. Pascal first brings him flowers and, playing Alcibiades to his Socrates, later slips into his sleeping bag. An ellipsis implies that Pascal receives a warmer welcome.

"O Gadjo Niglo" is, in contrast to "Wo Es War, Soll Ich Werden," partly about the failure to maintain that delicate mutuality. The story is unique among Davenport's stories for destroying the utopian illusions its characters project. As in James Kincaid's analysis, power relations mar even the most tenderly reciprocal of attachments. While "Wo Es War, Soll Ich Werden" is set in a contemporary liberal utopia where enemies reconcile and prejudices gain no foothold, "O Gadjo Niglo" is set in a nineteenth-century Lutheran Sweden of sexual and racial stereotypes from which the protagonists cannot fully escape.

The most explicit and provocative of Davenport's stories, "O Gadjo Niglo" is also one of the most "classical": a first-person retrospective narration in the vein of psychological realism, related chronologically and without Davenport's characteristic bricolage of decontextualized citations or Steinian section titles. Its one structural idiosyncrasy, the omission of commas, colons, and semicolons, is rendered inconspicuous by Davenport's beautifully pitched and rhythmic prose. As in "The River," the sparsely punctuated prose reveals the artless spontaneity and innocence of its gifted but bewildered young narrator.

Whereas "The River," however, describes only the initiation and splendor of adolescent homosexual ardor, "O Gadjo Niglo" pursues as well its checkered progress. The pubescent narrator Jens, being raised in his grandmother's country house and privately educated, befriends the abused Tarpy, the bastard child of a vicious miller. Jens belongs among Davenport's cast of precociously intelligent youths, independent, curious, and a budding naturalist. Tarpy belongs among the writer's *hommes sauvages:* lusty and uncouth, but also alert, candid, and secretly gentle. They make an exchange of their distinctive qualities. Jens resolves to educate the wild child:

> I would teach him botany and algebra. I would write Pa and tell him that Tarpy the miller's bastard son is not an idiot as people say. That I have given him a bath and some of my clothes and am teaching him subjects. After I teach him to read and write. That he is really clever and deserves better than to live with old Sollander who is an ignorant man and beats him without cause.[47]

Disapproving of the relationship, Tarpy's father later commits his son to an institution, precipitating Jens's breakdown just as a young tutor arrives. Here begins the story's second conversion narrative. Like many of the mentors in Davenport's fiction, Florent is liberal, cerebral, spartan, and hale. He takes the youth nude bathing, teaches him geology and physical exercise, and takes him camping. The camping trip first crowns Jens's recovery, then shatters it. Jens is a young teen, Florent appears to be an ephebe: "Though he was not yet a man . . . he was no longer a boy."[48] Florent's custodial role nevertheless underscores the gap between them. Like the guardian in Henry James's *Watch and Ward,* who falls in love with his young charge, this hierarchy does not prevent him from taking the youth as a lover.

Their tent becomes a sanctuary and conduit to a proscription-free parallel world. Davenport indicates through several strategies the inaccessibility, yet teasing proximity, of this idyllic territory. On the one hand, this is a Thoreauvian excursion requiring only camping gear, made entirely on foot. On the other hand, the region is remote, for the story takes place near a Swedish coast some time in the nineteenth century. The intellectual sophistication of Jens further disrupts the realistic illusion. He decorates his room with a picture of von Humbolt and Boupland in the Amazon, studies Agassiz and petroglyphs, reads Canot's *Natural Philosophy,* and can identify plants by their Linnaean binominals. All of these elements are characteristic of Davenport's pastorals. Unusual here, however, are the anguished scruples of the older companion and the failure to maintain the passionate tie. Florent fears—rightly, as events confirm—that the attachment is risky. From mutual masturbation the pair graduate to fellatio:

He said he thought we had gone too far. Was it wrong? It was wrong in that a game we played for the lust of the flesh might become a bond which we could only break along with our hearts. You have already had your heart broken.

    With Tarpy.

He would have to go away in less than a month. I said I thought I understood. I wasn't sure. He mentioned the world. Its disapproval. And added that for the moment the world around us was but rain. Lovely rain. Cozy rain.[49]

The rain becomes an index of the futility of efforts to maintain the illusion of a "game" and of their seclusion from the "world." Later, following their rift, the difficulty of the hike back is only exacerbated by the steady rain.

Their bliss in exploring the countryside and each other overrules such reservations. Although Florent invokes Patroclus and Achilles, and Jens the ideal of *bon ton,* the tutor is not altogether deceived: "Florent said that I could have fooled him. He thought we were two randy boys who had found it convenient to invent the pagan world again for their particular use and delight."[50] The melancholy paradox of the story is that both are equally correct. Fourier, *The Iliad,* classical pastoral—these are summoned both as ideals and as expedients.

Eventually Jens thinks he detects Tarpy in a Gypsy caravan. Florent, however, is unconvinced, and moreover fears the Gypsies. When Florent tries physically to restrain him from running after Tarpy, "I hit him as hard as I could with the sharp of my elbow against the mouth."[51] Here is a rivalry between an adult and a youth for the loyalty of another youth. As Jens risks his safety to reunite with Tarpy, Florent learns how faint has been his own influence, and how limited their fellowship. Separated by age and the power relations age enforces, Florent and Jens have no secure basis for an attachment. Disenchantment and remorse follow.

Jens faces a parallel reversal. Tarpy, who speaks Romany, wears Gypsy dress, and is in the company of two friends, refuses to recognize him. An old man tries to console Jens:

Gadjo! he laughed. You have known our golden-haired *niglo*? He is now a rom. Forgive him he cannot to you come back. . . . The *gadji* beat him and starved him. We are better people. He has now mother and father. Like you he has a brother. He raised his hand. And there was Florent.[52]

It is Florent's despair that he forfeited the dignity and safety of a strictly fraternal tie. Despite darkness, rain, and cold, Florent resumes the marred hike, tramping ahead silently. The arduous trek becomes a miserable expiatory pilgrimage. After three such days they agree to return home. "We were tired of each other's company."[53]

The day after their return, Florent abruptly departs, but not before Jens catches up with him, waiting alone for the coach. "He turned when I was near and about to call his name. He walked up to me expressionless and hugged me as tight as he ever had. *Forgive me* he said so quietly at my ear that I had to think what he had said. Forgive you?"[54] Unlike Tarpy, Florent here acknowledges Jens. His expression impassive while he embraces Jens passionately, Florent embodies the conflicts of a tender yet taboo affection. And while Jens must have felt himself chastised during the bitter sequel to their intimacy, he now learns that he is not the object of Florent's animosity, but Florent himself, who blames himself for having promoted intimacy. He is the only such character in Davenport, forced to confront the negative repercussions of pederasty and lacerated by guilt so tortured as to compound his victim's dismay.

But is Jens a victim? The youth does not understand Florent's appeal for forgiveness, and the story suggests that Florent is guilty not of sexual misconduct but of misplaced conscience. Florent appears first jealous, then sullen, and finally disloyal. He retreats into the very Lutheran morality that their affection had taught them to defy, and in so doing increases rather than mitigates the injury to Jens. Florent had fancied that Jens's passion for him supplanted the previous erotic tie, which Tarpy's reappearance contradicts, and he had imagined that his own passion for Jens is corrupting, which Jens's narrative belies. The transgression consists in his abrupt revocation of his affection.

At the end of the story Jens has lost Tarpy, the grandmother who raised him has died, and Florent has returned to the university. "I saw him once afterwards at the university but we did not speak."[55] The contrast with Tarpy is poignant: the lonely, abused orphan is now the adopted son of a warm extended family. Jens is meanwhile Davenport's most desolated protagonist. Jens's office is to withhold reproach and resign himself to loss. "Forgive him he cannot to you come back," the Gypsy elder had told him. *"Forgive me,"* Florent had begged. As its candor, equanimity, and absence of reproof testify, Jens's story extends forgiveness, but the youth's ardor, trust, generosity, and loyalty, which (as often occurs in Davenport) a companion might have fostered and directed toward high moral and intellectual ends, is instead confined to such luckless renunciations.

For all the sanction Davenport gives to a freely exercised sexuality beyond the utilitarian strictures of ethical categories, he refuses to jettison ethics. A moral dividend is paid to those whose intellectual growth coincides with sexual exploration. Davenport regards the two as inseparable. This view derives ultimately from Walt Whitman's belief in the redemptive character of "camaraderie" or "adhesiveness," which in "Democratic Vistas" the poet presented as both necessary to the maintenance of American freedoms and the means to suppress the materialism and individualism he believed jeopardized these.[56] For Davenport, sexual curiosity, which children exhibit in abundance, is both a splendor to be cherished for its own sake and one signal expression of a wider receptiveness. It is a mode of knowledge inevitably and of ethical knowledge properly.

Davenport is consequently surprisingly conservative, placing sexuality back into the sphere of the normative, indeed finding in it a mode of secular redemption conforming again to Fourierist precept. When, in *Apples and Pears,* the Fourierist Dutch philosopher Adriaan establishes a microphalanstery with the help of a reformed teenage profligate, his sister, a pair of pubescent couples, and a rehabilitated stray, it is, pointedly against the background of the escalating arms race, "to breed meanness out of human nature."[57] The sodality certainly breeds it out of its own, finding a mode of permissiveness inseparable from mutual respect and collective responsibility.

Uninhibited "passionate attraction" was for Fourier not merely a good for its own sake but a social ideal and finally the structural principle of the very cosmos.[58] Fourier's autarchic utopia is governed by the associative—*sociétaire*—principle, of which sexual association is the epitome. Pleasure here is exuberantly instrumental, for the universal law of passionate attraction proceeds from God,[59] who uses our petty vices as instruments not to plague us but to secure for us the blessings of a benign Providence. With a deistic conviction, to which Newton's science had seemingly lent credence, that the cosmos is a divinely ordained harmony, Fourier declared "the unity of system" from which to seek the divinely ordained social code: "This implies the use of attraction, which is the known agent of God, the mainspring of the social harmonies of the universe, from those of the stars to those of the insects."[60] Although Davenport dispenses with an anthropomorphic Creator, he follows the pre-Socratics (one of his first books includes a full translation of the fragments of Heraclitus, and one of his earliest stories is "Herakleitos")[61] in holding that the universe is a harmony.

"Pedophiliac figurations situate the child at a distance impossibly remote and in a focus impossibly blurred," James Kincaid contends, "but such an image really allows the adult to leap into this blur, somehow without cancelling the desire—and, what is more crucial, without capturing or cancelling the child who was originally there."[62] Davenport's Fourierist idylls of a utopian Scandinavia achieve this quality of distance and blur, where adults recover a degree of childhood vitality without dislodging children themselves, who maintain their alterity. Davenport is close to the Balthus he admired because "he is never vulgar, never paints in the vernacular."[63] Praising, in his preface to *The Drawings of Paul Cadmus,* the candor and freedom from taboo of the artist's nudes, Davenport notes, "Practically all of Cadmus has an air of saying, *'This, too, can be shown.'*"[64] Davenport's fiction hazards the censure of puritanisms both liberal and conservative in order to say that childhood sexuality too can be shown.

While American sex educators have been reduced, since feminist sexual conservatives and the religious right made common cause during the Reagan presidency, to defining sex as a "risk behavior," preaching abstinence and omitting reference to pleasure, Davenport's youths flourish in environments where the exploration and expression of their sexuality are neither denied nor suppressed. In Davenport's stories, protection of the interests of minors proceeds in concert with respect for their choices, including their erotic choices. In *Harmful to Minors,* which Davenport praises in a *Harper's* review, Judith Levine asserts that "sex is not harmful to children. It is a vehicle to self-knowledge, love, healing, creativity, adventure, and intense feelings of aliveness. There are many ways even the smallest children can partake of it. Our own moral obligation to the next generation is to make a world in which every child can partake safely, a world in which the needs and desires of every child—for accomplishment, connection, meaning, and pleasure—can be marvelously fulfilled."[65] The idealism of this apostrophe marks a continuity with Davenport's fiction. In the guise of pastoral utopias, many of Davenport's frankest stories simply imagine the fulfillment of such impulses.

Notes

1. "Le diray-je, pourveu qu'on ne m'en prenne à la gorge? l'amour ne me semble proprement et naturellement en sa saison qu'en l'age voisin de l'enfance," in Michel de Montaigne, *Oeuvres Complètes,* ed. Albert Thibaudet and Maurice Rat (Paris: Gallimard, 1962), 874.

2. Guy Davenport, *Eclogues* (San Francisco: North Point, 1981), 200.

3. Torquato, Tasso, *Aminta,* ed. Luigi Fassó (Florence: Samsoni Editore, 1962), 26.

4. Ibid., 236.

5. Ibid., 217.

6. Erik Anderson Reece, *A Balance of Quinces: The Paintings and Drawings of Guy Davenport* (New York: New Directions, 1996).

7. Guy Davenport, *A Table of Green Fields* (New York: New Directions, 1993), 25.

8. Guy Davenport, *The Hunter Gracchus* (Washington, DC: Counterpoint, 1996), 62–63.

9. See, for example, Philippe Ariès, *Centuries of Childhood: A Social History of Family Life,* trans. Robert Baldick (New York: Knopf, 1962).

10. Guy Davenport, *A Balthus Notebook* (New York: Ecco, 1989), 24.

11. Ibid., 80.

12. Ibid., 59.

13. James R. Kincaid, *Child-Loving: The Erotic Child and Victorian Culture* (New York: Routledge, 1992), 73.

14. Davenport, *A Balthus Notebook*, 9.

15. Kincaid, *Child-Loving*, 10.

16. Ibid., 189.

17. Ibid., 14–15.

18. Ibid., 210.

19. Guy Davenport, *Apples and Pears* (San Francisco: North Point, 1984), 254.

20. Reproduced in Sabine Rewald, *Balthus* (New York: Metropolitan Museum of Modern Art and Abrams, 1984), 161–66.

21. Kincaid quotes Kinsey's *Sexual Behavior in the Human Male:* "Older persons are the teachers of younger people in all matters, including the sexual. . . . Without help from more experienced persons, many pre-adolescents take a good many years to discover masturbatory techniques that are sexually effective." *Child-Loving*, 186.

22. Charles Fourier, *The Theory of the Four Movements*, trans. Ian Patterson (Cambridge: Cambridge University Press, 1996), 86–87.

23. Charles Fourier, *The Utopian Vision of Charles Fourier*, ed. and trans. Jonathan Beecher and Richard Bienvenu (Boston: Beacon, 1971), 268.

24. Guy Davenport, *The Geography of the Imagination* (New York: Pantheon, 1981), 77.

25. Guy Davenport, *The Jules Verne Steam Balloon* (San Francisco: North Point, 1987).

26. Davenport, *The Hunter Gracchus*, 51.

27. Ibid., 79.

28. Ibid., 55.

29. Ibid.

30. Peter Freuchen, *Peter Freuchen's Book of the Eskimos*, ed. Dagmar Freuchen (New York: World, 1961), 122.

31. Ibid., 121.

32. Ibid.

33. Randolph Bourne, *Youth and Life* (Freeport, NY: Books for Libraries, 1967), 253.

34. Ibid., 12.

35. Ibid., 70. Bourne is the subject of Davenport's composite painting *War Is the Health of the State* (see color plate in Reece, *A Balance of Quinces*, 82). Its Nietzschean title quotes Bourne's posthumously published critique "Unfinished Fragment on the State." Its images are organized on an asymmetrical grid dominated by Bourne, whose deformity contrasts with the beauty of a nude adolescent, the face of a pretty child, the neolithic Swedish petroglyph of a shaman, Brancusi's *Muse*, and a caricature of Bourne's inspiration, Nietzsche. The painting suggests the erotic implications of Bourne's views.

36. Bourne, *Youth and Life*, 62–63.

37. Davenport, *The Hunter Gracchus*, 140, 141.

38. For more on this, see Betty Jean Lifton, *The King of Children: A Biography of Janusz Korczak* (New York: Farrar, Straus & Giroux, 1988); Yitzhak Perlis, "Final

Chapter: Korczak in the Warsaw Ghetto," in *Janusz Korczak: The Ghetto Years,* trans. Jerzy Bachrach et al. (Tel Aviv: Ghetto Fighters House, 1983).

39. Davenport, *A Table of Green Fields,* 29.

40. Janusz Korczak, *When I Am Young Again and The Child's Right to Respect,* trans. E. P. Kulawiec (Lanham, MD: University Press of America, 1992), 184. Davenport has painted Korczak as the gray, emaciated inmate of the Warsaw ghetto, his gentility encountering its monstrous contrary in a pendant where the lower black field designated "Treblinka" begins to overtake the blue one designating "Korczak." See Reece, *A Balance of Quinces,* 136–37.

41. Korczak, *When I Am Young Again,* 181.

42. Davenport, *A Table of Green Fields,* 60, 61.

43. Guy Davenport, *The Drummer of the Eleventh North Devonshire Fusiliers,* (San Francisco: North Point, 1990), 108.

44. Fourier, *The Utopian Vision,* 225.

45. Sigmund Freud, *Neue Folge der Vorlesungen zur Einführung in die Psychoanalyse* (Frankfurt: Fischer Verlag, 1998), 81; my translation.

46. Davenport, *The Drummer,* 61.

47. Davenport, *A Table of Green Fields,* 111.

48. Ibid., 120.

49. Ibid., 130.

50. Ibid., 152.

51. Ibid., 138.

52. Ibid., 142. The affectionate pet name *niglo,* which signals Tarpy's defection, means "gentile hedgehog."

53. Ibid., 144.

54. Ibid., 145.

55. Ibid.

56. Adhesiveness, Whitman asserts in "Democratic Vistas," is "the most substantial hope and safety of the future of these states." Walt Whitman, *Specimen Days and Collect* (Glasgow: Wilson & McCormick, 1883), 247. The poet is a character in Davenport's rewriting of Theocritus's Carmen V, "Idyll" (in *Eclogues*), and the subject of several adulatory essays by Davenport, including "Whitman" (in *The Geography of the Imagination*), "Walt Whitman and Ronald Johnson" (in *The Hunter Gracchus*), and "Endlessly Talking" (in *Harper's,* July 2001, 78–82).

57. Davenport, *Apples and Pears,* 235.

58. See Fourier, *The Utopian Vision,* 228–32.

59. See Fourier, *The Theory of the Four Movements,* 55.

60. Fourier, *The Utopian Vision,* 210.

61. See Guy Davenport, *Herakleitos and Diogenes* (San Francisco: Grey Fox, 1979), which is also incorporated into *7 Greeks* (New York: New Directions, 1995); and "Herakleitos," included in *Tatlin!* (New York: Scribner, 1974) and *Twelve Stories* (Washington, DC: Counterpoint, 1997).

62. Kincaid, *Child-Loving,* 196.

63. Davenport, *A Balthus Notebook,* 85.

64. Guy Davenport, *The Hunter Gracchus,* 295.

65. Judith Levine, *Harmful to Minors: The Perils of Protecting Children from Sex* (Minneapolis: University of Minnesota Press, 2002), 225. In his review, Davenport hails Levine for "leading with her chin against a formidable army of upholders of biological ignorance and as transparent a taboo as any known to anthropology." See "New Books," *Harper's,* August 2002, 66.

Theory *a Tergo* in *The Turn of the Screw*

Eric Savoy

> Sexuality is essentially the violence of its own non-simplicity. . . .
> Sexuality *is* rhetoric, since it essentially consists of ambiguity: it is
> the coexistence of dynamically antagonistic meanings. Sexuality is
> the *division and divisiveness of meaning*: it is meaning *as* division,
> meaning *as* conflict.
>
> —*Shoshana Felman, "Turning the Screw of Interpretation," 1982*

> It's just your *cavity* needs a little *fillin'*.
>
> —*"Long John Blues," Tommy George, 1948 (as sung by Bette Midler)*

I t is "the greatest social panic of our time," asserted Margaret Wente, a columnist for the *Globe and Mail,* Canada's national newspaper, in a story about inconclusive investigations of alleged sex crimes against children that ran in January 2001.[1] Not infrequently, such cases are prosecuted on the basis of puzzling things that children say—things that, while potentially incriminating, have dubious meanings and are interpreted very differently by the child-welfare and criminal justice systems. Evidently, social panic escalates in response to the general instability of the grounds of suspicion. Because these "grounds" continually expand—voraciously annexing more and more of what might count as evidence or symptom—but paradoxically shrink in terms of verifiable history, the cultural agenda of suspicion itself becomes suspect, invites analysis. As James R. Kincaid suggests, "As a category created but not occupied, the child could be a repository of cultural needs or fears not adequately *disposed* of elsewhere."[2] While Kincaid's subject is the Victorian child, there are strong continuities between the anxious investments in childhood sexual "purity" at the end of the nineteenth century and at the turn of the twenty-first. In its dilation of the epistemic "ground" for reconstructing a plausible history of the sexual abuse of children and the difficulties that attend such a historiography, Henry James's 1898 novel *The Turn of the Screw* charts with remarkable clarity the anxieties and bafflements of our own time. It examines in particular the uncertain nature of evidence that generates suspicion, the spiraling of suspicion into panic, the inability of panic to produce a narrative of origin and consequences—in short, a precarious and incoherent dynamic of investigation and a regime of "knowing" that is in no way outdated or superseded. In the argument that follows, I shall track the rhetorical circuits of suspicion in James's gothic tale, its specific narrative *disposition.*

Suspicion arises from the pursuit of highly ambiguous, connotative signs and in turn generates a supplementary figurative lexicon. To speak of the rhetoric of suspicion in Jamesian narrative is, inevitably, to address the function of poetics, for the hermeneutic enterprise is contained by a claustrophobic matrix as suspicion generates repression and repression returns in uncanny, figurative ways. The protocols of connotation—an indirect mode of discourse that points suggestively toward, but can never coincide with, referential certainty—result in a certain dislocation, or dis-position, of narrative authority. For once connotation establishes itself as the master trope of traumatic historiography, pulling everything into its circuitous orbit around the unverifiable, narrative suffers traumatic occlusions arising from a predisposition to return obsessively to—that is, to reposition—suspicion.

The Turn of the Screw dramatizes the perverse pleasures of suspicion in its opening frame. Douglas's inability or reluctance to describe the subject of the governess's manuscript—his tantalizing, drawn-out promise that "nothing at all that I know touches it. . . . For dreadful—dreadfulness. . . For general uncanny ugliness and horror and pain"—prompts a woman in his audience to exclaim, "Oh how delicious!"[3] The imminent prospect of savoring the unsavory depends entirely on the centrality of the traumatized child in the ensuing story, and Douglas approaches the interlinearity of horror and titillation with an exquisitely seductive calculus. Conceding that appearance of "Griffin's ghost," the subject of the preceding tale, before "the little boy, at so tender an age, adds a particular touch," he proceeds to up the ante: "If the child gives the effect another turn of the screw, what do you say to *two* children—?" (1). Douglas's promises have his audience salivating, already installed in the exciting circuits of suspicion; moreover, his teasing indirection about the precise grounds for suspicion in the thematics of the story anticipates the obliquities of the governess's narrative, which dilates suspicion in proportion to the recessive nature of its traumatic ground.

Indeed, *The Turn of the Screw* exceeds in perplexing ways the parameters of the "ghost story": while the spectral presences of Peter Quint and Miss Jessel figure forth the historical shadow of some obscure crime—Quint, the governess-narrator learns "with a sudden sickness of disgust," was "much too free . . . too free with *my* boy" (25)—the implicitly pederastic, connotatively pursued nature of this crime withdraws from narrative grasp. Yet the story, like the narrative with which it can never entirely coincide and like the ghost of Peter Quint, "hungrily hover[s]" (44) as the governess reconstructs "just the sinister figure of the living man" who, in life, was characterized by "secret disorders, vices more than suspected" (27). It is worth entertaining at the outset the question of what particular episteme governs the discernment of a "disorder" or "vice" that is "more than suspected" but never attains nomination. Indeed, *The Turn of the Screw* is a sustained exploration of the "sinister" figurative process that attends the arousal of horrified suspicion of a child's sexual precocity: the ghosts are spectacular figures that recur after the governess has turned the interpretive screw of connotation to an unbearable point—the various moments in which she "com[es] into sight of subjects before which [she] must stop short" (49). If suspicion is generated by the gap between seeing and knowing, then James's gothic visual economy—its reiterated turns from connotation to prosopopoeia—constitutes the ghosts as the stubbornly irrepressible "real," the historical trauma that compels the governess's recourse to symbolic condensation yet resists the reach of the symbolic. The story, then, "hovers" at bottom, emerging only sporadically in the field of arcane poetics, for whatever the governess "had seen, Miles and Flora saw *more*—things terrible and unguessable and that sprang from dreadful passages of intercourse in the past" (51).

The governess's project is to construct a case history of the children—of Miles particularly, since he is installed from the outset as the most alarmingly troubled, as the child with the most suspicious recent history. *The Turn of the Screw* is organized around the governess's persistent return to the receding array of questions occasioned by Miles's suspension from school: What did he do at school that warranted expulsion? What happened before he went off to school? What is the connection between that remote time, when he was at the mercy of Peter Quint and Miss Jessel, and his more recent, scandalous past? While James's pursuit of the signs of this history is resolutely deconstructive, a deconstructive tracking alone will not take us very far into the "something" that occupies what Cathy Caruth terms "a locus of referentiality," a "something" that, because of "its very unassimilated nature—the way it was precisely *not known* in the first instance—returns to haunt the survivor later on."[4] Rather, deconstructive poetics are framed by James's psychoanalytic matrix, for the governess, like Freud in the "Wolf Man" case history, attempts to focalize the indexical quality of her grounds for suspicion on a primal scene, an original trauma that would explain subsequent history in terms of narrative continuity from a clear beginning. And as in Freud's case study, the governess's reconstructions project, and their credibility turns upon, a *coitus a tergo*—not in this case a scene of sexual penetration from behind that the child witnessed and understood, in his identification with the mother, as a threat of castration, but rather one in which the child was himself the object of Quint's predation. For my purposes, another vitally important congruence between these "case histories" has to do with the abundant narrative recircling that attenuates the approach to the primal scene: the governess's meditations suggest a deep and anxious awareness that her projection of the sodomitical scene laminates her "going behind" obscure evidence, her interrogations, to the "horror" of the original act of "going behind"; both are violations of "innocence." This anxiety takes a peculiar turn in *The Turn of the Screw*, for, as I shall demonstrate in due course, the complexities and occlusions that mark the governess's case history of Miles raise intriguing questions about her own. Most horrible for the governess is her uncanny recognition of Peter Quint in moments that point to the most stubbornly recessive "story" that lies behind this story—the governess's own sexual history and its congruence with Miles's.

Recent queer-theoretical approaches to *The Turn of the Screw* have situated Jamesian gothic in relation to the knowledge effects of the Wilde trials of 1895. John Fletcher argues that the trials' process of homosexual and pederastic "consolidation, specification and implication" produced a new type of "closet-work" because "the queer or merely odd, the . . . bachelor becomes a candidate for . . . suspicion." The new rigors of "self-policing" turn the bachelor into a "subject of self-regulating self-division" that produces "various moments of the uncanny in the field of sexual self-definition"; the uncanny emerges in narratives of what Fletcher calls "homospectral panic."[5] Fletcher locates sodomy in *The Turn of the Screw* within the dynamic of heterosexual repression: "The Master as the forbidden object of the governess's desire is replaced by two substitutes[,] the sublimatory figure of little Miles . . . and the haunting, predatory Quint. . . . Her displaced and negated desire for the Master feeds into the fantasy of a same-sex, pederastic scene between [Quint] and the boy."[6] In referring his excellent model of "homospectrality" to thwarted heterosexual desire, Fletcher implies that the governess, as Kincaid would have it, *disposes* of needs and fears that are elsewhere unaddressable; this, I think, is a form of *critical* disposal that evades the narrative disposition of Jamesian gothic.

Eric Haralson offers a more prescient historicization in claiming that "the tale is an allegory of sexual panic—a very real allegory of the *fin-de-siècle*," for *The Turn of the Screw*, like the Wilde trials that stand solidly behind it, rests "on the fulcrum of not only age disparities but social distinctions between the well-heeled defendants and the working-class adolescents who sometimes served their 'unnatural lust'—'our boys,' in the parlance of the tabloids."[7] James's tale reversed the age and class specificity of pederast and victim, but nonetheless, "his narrative absorbed both a vocabulary and an implicit etiology of male homosexuality, connecting the plot with a specific institutional history of Victorian England."[8] Fletcher and Haralson are entirely correct to install the Wilde trials and their episteme of scandal as the historical trauma that haunts *The Turn of the Screw*. However, their suggestions about the queer field and subject matter of Jamesian gothic leave unaddressed both the narrative unfolding of a specific poetics of haunting and the function of this poetics within the uncanny pressure of suspicion. I turn, therefore, to the queer formalism of *The Turn of the Screw*.

History, Adumbrated

"If the ghosts of *The Turn of the Screw* are not real, certainly the controversy over them is," observed John Silver in 1957, at the historical midpoint between the tale's publication in 1898 and our own analytic moment.[9] Although deconstructive, psychoanalytic, and queer-theoretical schools have generated increasingly complex readings of Henry James's gothic puzzle, the tale's notorious recessiveness—its discretions, obliquities, and intricate evasions—continues to thwart critical consensus; the more extensive and detailed the scholarship, the sharper the irony of Ned Lukacher's opinion that "the task of reading James is one of remembering that although there is a right track, we are not going to be on it."[10] To put this another way, *The Turn of the Screw* is a prime example of nineteenth-century fiction's invention of ludic, deconstructive textual pleasure *avant la lettre;* as James concedes in his preface to the New York edition, hermeneutic bafflement is both the goal of his narrative technique and the drama enacted in the story. "Only make the reader's *general* vision of evil intense enough ... and his own experience, his own imagination ... will supply him quite sufficiently with all the *particulars*."[11] The binary relation of James's adjectives consigns to the "general" the overall gothic effect of narrative technique—the rousing of readerly anxiety that desires to focus its suspicions—and to "particulars" the verifiable happenings that constitute "content" and thus ground suspicion. It is entirely typical of James's critical discourse to propound *at length* the particulars he will not go into. This extensive list of what will not be found resonates, in a supplementary fashion, with the warning proffered by Douglas that "the story *won't* tell ... not in any literal vulgar way" (3). For James promises that his atmosphere of "portentous evil" will be "saved" from "the drop, the comparative vulgarity, inevitably attending ... the offered example, the imputed vice, the cited act, the limited deplorable presentable instance"; it will not "shrink to the compass of some particular brutality, some particular immorality, some particular infamy."[12] Even for Henry James, this is a lot of eschewal and refraining, a considerable extent of nothing: "my values," he insists, "are positively all blanks."[13]

To embark on any track into *The Turn of the Screw* and its long critical heritage, it is instructive to begin by attending to James's key word for his narrative technique and teasing out its implications: "My idea," he claims, is "the lively interest" of "a process of *adumbration*."[14] Like much of James's critical lexicon, "adumbration" comes from the language of painterly practice; according to the *OED,* "to adumbrate" means "to shade (a picture), to represent the shadow of (anything), to give a faint indication of." Adumbration, by extension, denotes "shading in painting, representation . . . of a shadowy figure" and, most tellingly, "overshadowing, shade, obscuration." In the visual arts, adumbration procures a certain depth, a richness of tone, and an extension of perspective, but to envelop the represented object in shadow is not to obliterate the object itself. James's revision of the critical term—its significance in his artistic calculus that privileges the general over the particular particulars that will not be particularized— provides the very matrix of his narrative's recessiveness. We see this over and over again in the governess's fainthearted attempt to convert what she sees into what she might possibly know, a process that inevitably adumbrates and ensures the recession of the history of the goings-on at Bly: for if her "monstrous ordeal" demands "only another turn of the screw of ordinary human virtue," any attempt at the perilous transition from uncertain seeing to an unspeakable speaking would entail but "a new plunge into the hideous obscure" (77). The constant refusal of this tale to name or to come to terms and its concomitant, reiterated turning of the hermeneutic screw generate a spectral adumbration of the titular metaphor in James's preface, where he explains that the tale's "excursion into chaos . . . *return[s] upon itself.*"[15]

Shoshana Felman deftly analyzes the metaphorical implications of the turning of a screw—under which the "text is organized as a veritable *topography of turns*"[16]—to provide the classic deconstructive geometry of the Jamesian signifier's deferral of the signified's punctual grasp. Obscure incidents in the tale are never closed, never accounted for, "since the movement of the screw constitutes in fact not a circle but a spiral which never closes: . . . the spiral consists of a series of repeated circlings in which what turns is indeed bound to *re-turn*, but . . . only returns so as to *miss* anew its point of departure, to miss the closing point, the completion (or perfection) of the circle."[17] Felman's account of James's narrative temporality— the inconclusive turn toward a referential meaning on the far side of language that returns, as James suggests, upon itself, in a spiral of hermeneutic occlusion—explains the suspension of resolution characteristic of gothic suspense. However, a certain rigidity in Felman's deconstructive template and a reluctance to move beyond the self-referential circlings of the Jamesian intratext yield a critical confinement that one might say "misses anew" the historically specific poetics of fin de siècle gothic discourse, a poetics of the indexical and the connotative that locates its occult, textual suspensions in the field of unspeakable sexuality. Consider, for one thing, that the specters that haunt *The Turn of the Screw* arise not immediately from the ghostly play of referential indeterminacy but rather from the narrative's traumatic prehistory, which, however ambiguous its reconstructive potential, endures *as* traumatic history. It is a "something" that merits closer investigation—an inquiry into the poetics by which the shadow cast by the story's recessive origins over the narrative's present is obliquely legible—rather than the "nothing" that deconstruction consistently yields.

Consider, too, the logistical problem inherent in Felman's analysis of the inclusive spiral of returnings generated by the metaphorical screw: her claim that "the screw . . . by the very gesture of its tightening, while seemingly filling the hole, in reality only makes it deeper" misses the point that the screw has a point, and that point works according to very precise physics—both an actual point, which generates the pressure necessary to tighten, and the point of its very efficacy, which is to tighten by exerting pressure.[18] A screw that does not tighten—that does not eventually close in on its ultimate point—must be understood as failing in its very point. I agree entirely with Felman's structural geometry of narrative recircling, but I would particularize it: *The Turn of the Screw* is indeed organized under the spiral of re-turning, but that spiral *narrows in its diameter* as the governess's interrogations of the prehistory of Bly circle ever more closely around particular possibilities, arriving finally at a point. For the governess ultimately confronts Miles to press the point directly: if he "said things" at school, "what *were* those things?" (83–84). By this point, such "things" are inextricable from Miles's relationship with Peter Quint, from an obscurely coherent pederastic history. Felman's model of a screw that turns inconclusively and loosely misses the logistics of the screw, and of the tightening of the suspenseful pressure that is the point of the gothic; rather than discern the evasions of James's own commentary on the tale, she underwrites them, and thus ironically participates in the Jamesian project of adumbration.

Leo Bersani points out that James's "discussion of his books almost only in terms of their technical ingenuities" amounts to "his refusal 'to go behind' technique to 'meanings.'"[19] "Going behind" is, of course, the critical exercise of tracking cultural meaning, and a century of grapplings with

The Turn of the Screw suggests that the track has proved to be a labyrinth, less a movement toward verifiable certainty than a function of the theoretical imaginary, seeking an elusive "thing" that sustains and renews critical desire. James has great fun with critical impossibility in his 1896 tale "The Figure in the Carpet," in which an eager critic comes up against the refusal of a celebrated and "difficult" author, Hugh Vereker, to articulate his governing intention: the author teases the critic by claiming that "the order, the form, the texture of [his] books will perhaps some day constitute for the initiated a complete representation of it." When the critic laments that authorial discourse "about the initiated" would require some specificity— "there must therefore, you see, be initiation"—Vereker returns, "What else in heaven's name is criticism supposed to be?"[20] Every school of critical theory approaches the Jamesian text in the confidence of its own superior initiation, determined to illuminate the text by "going behind" its formal obscurities to explain what it is really doing, how it is really organized, what it really means. James anticipates this when Vereker observes that critical perplexity arises "only because you've never had a glimpse of it [Vereker's recurring 'it' denominates his artistic intention]. If you had had one the element in question would soon have become practically all you'd see."[21]

I embark on my own exercise of going behind *The Turn of the Screw*— my attempt to locate a very specific "something" in the topography of its ever-narrowing spiral of narrative returns—by admitting that I've taken the bait that Vereker offers: my own initiations in a queer formalism that attempts to go beyond deconstructive eschewals and refrainings generate an uneasy knowledge that my "glimpse" of what "it" might be will coalesce into "practically all [I'll] see." However, if the critical matrix of "initiation" operates along the lines of James's visual metaphor—by which a "glimpse" inaugurates an interpretive chain that provides the totality of what one "sees"—then it is remarkably congruent with the reconstructive drama enacted in the text, whereby the governess's job is to go behind the spectral evidence at Bly to locate and to explain the children's particular and highly traumatic "initiation." For this is what happens in *The Turn of the Screw*: the governess is initiated into the "hideous obscure" when she receives a letter from the children's uncle enclosing another letter from Miles's school that refuses to allow him to return. The plot of the tale is organized around the governess's return to the perplexing question of the impossibility of Miles's return: "Is he really *bad*? . . . They go into no particulars. They simply express their regret that it should be impossible to keep him. They can have but one meaning . . . That he's an injury to the others" (10).

The questions of Miles's "badness," of the ways in which his presence might be injurious to other children, and of precisely what happened that made him so constitute the plot as a chain of baffled interrogations, for the very *partiality* of the governess's investments in heteronormative models of childhood, and of her initiation into late-Victorian configurations of knowledge as sexual knowledge, makes her hesitant to interpret the evidence that she locates in her perseverated returns to Miles's initiation into "badness." The governess, then, is a failed reader who requires the supplement, or perhaps the finely baited trap, of critical intervention: the suspense of the tale arises almost exclusively from her inability to move from seeing to knowing to articulating. The prolongation of the exquisite pleasure of gothic suspense might be said to require these two forms of suspension, one arising from the repression of conclusive interpretation (when evidence points to "exactly the particular deadly view I was in the very act of forbidding myself to entertain"; 36), the other from the repression of speech (she rehearses "the manner in which I might come to the point," but "always broke down in the monstrous utterance of names"; 51).

In the argument that follows, I shall elaborate the "point" at which the governess cannot discursively arrive. The occluded end point of her reconstruction of the goings-on at Bly, the prehistory of her own narrative—which accrues a stubborn particularity in the ever-narrowing, increasingly focalized, circuits of return to the question of Miles's "badness"—is a scene of sodomitical pederasty. Rich in explanatory potential, it has precisely the historical status and the narrative function of the Freudian primal scene in a text that requires to be approached as "The Case History of Miles X." Like the classic example of the primal scene—that reconstructed by Freud in the "Wolf Man" case history—it is generated by a speculative historiography that requires an absolute origin in order to fulfill the imperatives of story, but that can assemble that origin only by reading the symptom, the evidence, the sign, as an allegorical index that points, obliquely, to a hypothetical referent. In the historical field of fin de siècle pederastic homosexuality, I understand the allegorical index as operating under the protocols of connotation as conceptualized by D. A. Miller. In contrast to the self-sufficiency and self-evidence of denotative language, connotation seeks, as Miller explains, "corroboration," but "find[s] it only in what exhibits the same need." Therefore, once the connotative spiral has been initiated, it "tends to light everywhere, to put all signifiers to a test of their hospitality." If connotation invites a reading practice that is rather like mathematical set theory—sorting out what belongs and the basis for belonging—then it remains oblique, "allowing homosexual meaning to be elided even as it is also being elaborated." Moreover, if connotation yields a homosexual thematics "held definitionally *in suspense* on no less a question than that of its own existence," and if it constructs "an essentially insubstantial homosexuality," it nonetheless tends "to raise this *ghost* all over the place."[22]

Miller's tropological account of connotation as a spectral, suspenseful haunting—as a process of converting the sign to a shadowy index that yields referentiality as a ghost effect—is highly resonant with both James's poetics of "adumbration" and, of course, the plot of *The Turn of the Screw*, in which the ghosts of Peter Quint and Miss Jessel appear *after* the governess has tightened the screw of interpretation by narrowing the diameter of plausibility that circles around the question of traumatic origin. To focalize the *point* of her investigations, she employs connotation in a variety of ways and in various scenes. Connotation, as we shall see, isn't simply one thing: it turns not only on speech acts that are, queerly, both pointed and evasive and that accrue referential persuasiveness through sheer accumulation, but also on tropes associated with the spectral gothic, and indeed on patterns of syntax, which include breaks, gaps, hesitations, and tentative progressions. The analytics of queer formalism are essential, I would suggest, for understanding the topography of ever-narrowing turns toward oblique clarification in the temporal organization of *The Turn of the Screw;* moreover, this species of formalism is inextricable from the lamination, the interlinearity, of several kinds of "goings-behind" that are basic to the tale's cultural project. These include the refusals of James's prefatory explanations, the governess's retrospective meditations, and the procedures and the goals of the critical industry, all of which culminate—find their end point and their absolute origin—in the sodomitical scene in the Case History of Miles X, an unnarrated, unnarratable, historical event that demands to be witnessed in direct proportion to everybody's horror at arriving there. For the governess, as Ned Lukacher reminds us, "is trying to remember something that everyone else is trying to forget."[23]

Critical reorientation might take the measure of the *formal* blockages to "remembering" by attending to a couple of neglected passages that reveal much about the determination of the governess's analytic enterprise. The first occurs immediately after the governess has caught Miles out of doors in the middle of the night, gazing up at the tower where she first saw the ghost of Peter Quint. Convinced that Miles too has been in communication with the ghost, and has crossed certain boundaries, she resolves "to put it to him":

"You must tell me now—and all the truth. What did you go out for?"

. . . "If I tell you why, will you understand?" My heart, at this, leaped into my mouth. *Would* he tell me why? . . . "Well," he said at last, "just exactly in order that you should do this."

"Do what?"

"Think me—for a change—*bad!*" . . . It was practically the end of everything.

I met his kiss and I had to make, while I folded him for a minute in my arms, the most stupendous effort not to cry. He had given me exactly the account of himself that permitted least *my going behind it.* (45; final emphasis added)

The obvious irony that Miles should want the governess to think him "bad," "for a change," when she has entertained no other suspicion since his return to Bly and her receipt of the school's obscure letter of dismissal, is compounded by Miles's attempt to restrict the meaning of the "bad" child to harmless high jinks, disobedience, and a certain willfulness, and thus to preempt other possibilities. In other words, and in a further irony, it is precisely Miles's self-presentation as the *good* child, the innocent child, that blocks the governess's determination "to go behind" to a darker "account of himself." Miles's aptitude for defensive deflection, his subversion of a re-iterated attempt to "go behind," returns after he has raised the question of when he will return to school. The governess renews her attempt to go be-hind, to establish a clear story of what transpired at school that occasioned his dismissal. "Never, little Miles—no never—have you given me an inkling of anything that *may* have happened there" (61), she points out as a prelude to her arrival at a literally ambiguous—that is, two-pointed—question:

I waited a minute. "What happened before?"
He gazed up at me again. "Before what?"
"Before you came back. And before you went away."
For some time he was silent, but he continued to meet my eyes. "What happened?" (62)

These four lines of dialogue contain, in miniature, the entirety of the narrative project of *The Turn of the Screw*—the governess's attempt to re-construct the prehistory of traumatic sexual initiation at Bly—as well as its formal structure of circular return, the very occlusions of which point to a particular something, an "anything that *may* have happened." The gov-erness's simple, three-word question, totalizing in its compass, recasts her project of temporal reconstruction of "going behind" to reach explanatory origins as a matter of "before," which holds the double sense of the histori-cally "prior" poised alongside the present, as in "before one's eyes." It is an invitation to bring the "behind" (in both the historical and the anatomical senses) to articulation, to presence, in the conjoining of the behind in the narrative spectacle "before" the inquisitorial gaze. The governess's question is subsequently particularized and redirected to two discrete historical happenings; her implicit point is that what happened "before [Miles] came back" (i.e., at school) requires a cause-and-effect narrative connection to what happened "before [he] went away (i.e., in his earlier childhood at Bly). Miles's strategy of resistance is literally to fragment the governess's initial question, to return it to her in pieces. The frustration of the governess's attempt at reconstruction by a very specific moment in, and type of, the circuits of return justifies James's observation that the tale's "excursion of chaos . . . returns upon itself," which I noted above. More immediately, is this further instance of Miles's willfulness to be understood as innocence, as innocuous, playful perversity, or as his attempt to "adumbrate"—to short-circuit—the imminent revelation of a more insidiously perverse history by playing dumb? We can answer this question only by situating this moment of pointed, pointless circumlocution within the longer, and narrowing, spiral of other forms of connotative, indexical reconstruction.

History as Case History: Miles X

I shall return to track and to particularize the web of connotative discourse through which James inflects—or, rather, refracts—the story of what happened in the early days at Bly, the queerly recessive story of preadolescent sexuality. First, however, I shall entertain questions that go behind the general *emplotment* of *The Turn of the Screw*, its ever-narrowing spiral of return to the pederastic scene that simultaneously closes in on revelation and defers it: Why is Miles such a recalcitrant subject of the governess's persistent analysis? And under what restraining order, compelling her to retreat from the "monstrous utterance of names," does the governess operate? In structural terms, the governess's story unfolds as a supplement of reading initiated by the nondisclosure of the reason for Miles's dismissal from school in the headmaster's letter: as Shoshana Felman points out, the story's "very *telling* involves the non-possession of its beginning," for "it is not what the letters *say* which gets the story started, but what they *don't say*." Moreover, "it is precisely *because* the letters *fail* to narrate, to construct a coherent, transparent story, that there is a story at all. . . . Narrative, paradoxically, becomes possible to the precise extent that a story becomes *impossible*."[24] Felman's deconstructive point is that the governess's narrative movement toward an "impossible" and nonexistent story is in turn governed: "Thus it is that the *whole* course of the story is governed by the *hole* in a letter."[25] As I have had occasion to remark earlier in this essay, Felman's work—which stands, in my opinion, as the most acute, informative, and prehensile excursion into the chaos of *The Turn of the Screw*—is a remarkable instance of the blindness that attends and interlines spectacular critical insight. I would like to tease apart the deconstructive sutures of her totalizing argument by aligning her homonyms and fleshing out their astonishing resonance—or, to state the matter less elegantly, to put the "hole" back into the "whole course" of narrative design. For, as I have argued above, the "hole" is not an ontological nothing: it speaks to us with astonishing, if distinctly oblique, clarity. Let me attempt, then, to put a tongue to this hole.

If the "hole" is a critical metaphor that intentionally points to the suppressed content of the headmaster's letter, the recessive prehistory at Bly, the gaps in the narrative, and the governess's thwarted or repressed conclusion, then these various *formal* deployments of the term can be understood as a perseverated recircling around the anatomical "hole" that is both the site of traumatic initiation and, consequently, the occluded, nonpossessed "beginning" that initiates the circumlocutions of the story's "very telling." That anatomical hole is—if one follows this narrowing spiral of reasoning—Miles's anus, the very unspeakability of which prompts Douglas's warning that the story *"won't* tell" in what we might now understand as a particularly pointed "vulgar way." It is striking that criticism has been so reluctant to trace the signifying chain of the "hole" to its eminently plausible origin in the narrative's prehistory of traumatic sexual initiation. To invoke the signifier as a metaphor for the formal dynamics of textual indeterminacy but to resist reading its obvious *informal* import suggests that the history of criticism on *The Turn of the Screw* is bound by the ostensible Jamesian contract of delicacy and reticence—itself a critical lie—and by the governess's overdetermined scruples. It may be that the deployment of the concept of the "hole" in various forms of structural analysis constitutes a return of the repressed, from the critical unconscious, of a homonymic shadow that turns, inconclusively, around an anatomical meaning that, dimly perceived, must be disavowed. In any case, such assiduous avoidances reflect what Ross Posnock has diagnosed as "the cramped aura of sanctity [that] has grown up around what might be called James's cultural presence" and lend relevance to Michael Moon's insistence that "the queerness—the daring and risky weirdness, dramatic uncanniness, erotic offcenteredness, and unapologetic perversity—of James's writing continues to demand to be addressed."[26]

"Erotic offcenteredness" is a compelling term in the new critically queer lexicon. It connotes an erotic thematics on the margins of heteronormative sexualities, an indirect or indexical mode of representation, and both a hermeneutics and an epistemology—enacted within the text and also by its readers and critics—that somehow miss the mark. If it suggests, as a diacritical term, that both interpreters of Jamesian fiction and interpretants within them say more than they know and know more than they say, then "offcenteredness" provides a useful model for grasping the governess's tellingly "inept" efforts at focalization. At an early point in her adventure—after she has had her first sighting of the ghost of Peter Quint, but before she has identified him or read his return as a sign or shadow of Miles's past—the governess contemplates the tension between the general volubility of her companionable pupils and their particular reticence about their lives prior to her arrival at Bly, for "there was one direction, assuredly, in which these discoveries stopped: deep obscurity continued to cover the region of the boy's conduct at school" (18). In order to go behind the governess's musings on the children's silence—spatially, if not temporally—and to approach it from off center and awry, it is helpful to consider not what obscurity "covers," but rather what covers obscurity. As the governess brings Miles into perspective, she positions him with his back—that is, both his temporal anterior and his physical posterior—to the wall, with important consequences for the model of historical reconstruction she will deploy:

> They were like those cherubs of the anecdote who had—morally at any rate—nothing to whack! I remember feeling with Miles in especial as if he had had, as it were, nothing to call even an infinitesimal history. We expect of a small child scant enough "antecedents," but there was in this beautiful little boy something extraordinarily sensitive, yet extraordinarily happy, that, more than in any creature of his age I have seen, struck me as beginning anew each day. He had never for a second suffered. I took this as a direct disproof of his having really been chastised. If he had been wicked he would have "caught" it, and I should have caught it by the rebound. I should have found the trace, should have felt the wound and the dishonour. I could reconstitute nothing at all, and he was therefore an angel. (19)

In two senses, Miles is constructed as a boy without a behind: he possesses, on the face of things, "nothing to whack" and nothing that would constitute "even an infinitesimal history." All of the governess's defenses are on high alert, because she is anxious to normalize things at Bly after her unsettling experiences of apprehending a mysterious intruder and her receipt of the news from Miles's school, events that she cannot yet connect. It is interesting, and supremely telling, that at the outset the governess, like the critics who will follow her, invests in one hole—the impenetrability of Miles's "antecedents"—at the expense of that other more literal hole, the anus and its attendant backside, which, as the site of childhood erotic pleasure, transgression, and possible origin of the history she is momentarily determined not to know, must be disavowed through a hyperbolic chain of images. Once set in motion, hyperbole circulates and recircles around "nothingness" in a dizzying spiral toward the utterly implausible: because Miles is represented initially as having no backside, he is exempt from punishment; because he is exempt from punishment, he has no history—like Peter Pan, he begins "anew each day"—and therefore has not suffered; because he has not suffered, he has never been chastised for "wickedness"; because he has not been wicked, he is "therefore an angel." If the persistent problem in *The Turn of the Screw* is Miles's recalcitrance, it arises at least in part because of the hyperbolic preteritions of the governess's initial focalization of him. It is striking, too, that the critical problem I pointed out above—the reluctance to trace the "holes" in letters, narrative gaps, and referentiality back to the sexual anatomy—is anticipated, indeed prefigured, in the governess's figurative language. For the point of her operation is to *laminate* historiographical formalism and the literal anatomy of sexual trauma in a discourse that permits the former to cover the latter: the governess's discourse ironically dilates the hole in history by metaphorically, hyperbolically, frantically foreclosing the sexual anatomy as the very site of that history. That is, she recuperates "history" as a task of reconstruction, of filling in the gaps, yet that task conveniently, and ironically, precludes a return to the anus as traumatic origin. *This* is what "covers" obscurity.

To take a further turn that is but a re-turn, I would point out that the governess's claim to have caught no "rebound" of Miles's "wickedness," to have "found [no] trace," is belied by the traces of her figurative language that cannot *quite* be assimilated into hyperbole's totalizing transfiguration of "angelic" Miles. This residue is to be located at the beginning and the end of the governess's focalization, and it disturbs her comfortable picture by running counter to it. Bearing in mind that the governess represents Miles—in the course of her images analyzed above—as angelic because, ultimately, he has no arse, the strenuousness of her negations locates a connotative "something" in her series of nothings. Miles's gentleness, she begins, "never made him a muff" (19)—that is, a sissy or an effeminate, queer boy. Now, I won't start in on other, specifically feminized and sexual meanings of the word "muff" because it is difficult to establish their historicity. However, it is intriguing that the governess's sequential observations that Miles wasn't a muff and he had no backside (that is, from her point of view he had nothing to punish, nothing to give pleasure, no place of sexual transgression) bring Miles into focus very much below the waist. Then, as we have seen, her peroration laminates the disavowal of one hole to the recuperation of another, historical one: it culminates in another telling negation, that had Miles had a backside and an attendant, antecedent history of wickedness, she "should have felt the *wound* and the *dishonour*." It is plausible to make the connections the governess claims she cannot "trace": if I am on the right track, Lukacher's warning notwithstanding, then the backside and its anus are precisely the wound—the wound of traumatic initiation into sexuality, of shame, of premature knowledge, of a further spiral of "initiations" at school, and consequently the "dishonour" of expulsion.

Millicent Bell argues that the governess is driven by an "absolutist obsession" and consequently must be imagined as "the writer of a Calvinist romance which shifts alternately from a view of Bly as a garden of innocence to one which perceives it to be permeated by corruption." Within this binary logic, the governess "knows no middle ground, recognizes no human mixtures."[27] Her resolution to go behind Miles's silence and yet to avoid preadolescent sexuality altogether—an avoidance determined, perhaps, as I shall explain in due course, by her own "case history," which uncannily resembles Miles's—justifies Bell's observation, for the governess carefully installs Miles in an oppositional remove from the world of nasty little boys: her "conclusion bloomed there with the real rose-flush of his innocence: he was only too fine and fair for the little horrid unclean school-world" (18). The governess's division between the "fair" and the foul invites deconstruction, for it turns upon the trope of the "rose-flush," or the blush, which is one of James's most queerly ambiguous images. Far from stabilizing any "real . . . innocence," the image tends to coincide with its abjected opposite, with what the governess understands as the "unclean." It functions not so much to put "innocence" under erasure as to trace a temporal process by which innocence gives way to knowledge, the stages of which are impossible to demarcate. To understand the functions of this notoriously restless metaphor, it is helpful to measure the congruity and the intertextual resonance between the predicament of the governess and that of Pemberton, her pedagogical colleague in James's 1891 story "The Pupil," in his sounding of Morgan Moreen.

When Pemberton tries "to figure to himself the morning twilight of childhood, so as to deal with it safely, he perceived that it was never fixed, never arrested, that ignorance, *at the instant one touched it,* was already flushing faintly into knowledge, that there was nothing that at a given moment you could say a clever child didn't know."[28] The metaphor of childhood as an opening rose, like that comparing childhood to the dawn, denotes the temporality of the always-already, and thus undermines any comforting opposition between ignorance and knowledge, innocence and whatever the historical moment installs as its opposite. And if these metaphors *connote* a somatic affect that is, undecidably, either the blush of innocence or the flush of shame (or, more likely, both), that locates the sexual consciousness of childhood on the visible body, then it isn't surprising that Pemberton's trope includes a spectral hand that "touches" the child's body. Spectral, I suggest, because the "one" who touches necessarily hovers in the figurative construction between presence and absence; operating under the logics of synecdoche, the impersonal pronoun "one" gestures toward a recessive agent, a human figure whose touching hand materializes indistinctly and remains a matter of speculation. This passage from "The Pupil" is a useful supplement, then, precisely because it resonates with the governess's *adumbration* of sexual initiation as a historical shadow, as a ghost effect in the recesses of her figurative language. To meditate on these connotative recesses is, then, to go behind—in this case, to go behind the tropes of *The Turn of the Screw* to their striking prefiguration in an earlier moment in James's queer lexicon.

Talking of ghost-effects of figure and of the spectral hovering of synecdochic hands requires, in turn, a revisionist critical grappling with the actual specters that return to haunt Bly. For ghostly visitation is the gothic narrative process by which the adumbrations inherent in the governess's tropic discourse acquire a paradoxical *literalness*. To put this another way, the ghosts of Peter Quint and Miss Jessel are a turning outward, a return to visibility, of the recesses of the governess's speech acts; they dramatize also the uncanny return of her repression of Miles's backside as the erotic locus of his troubling history. In James's emplotment of the governess's narrative, it is surely significant that the apparition of Peter Quint makes his initial return immediately *after* the governess receives the mysterious letter from Miles's school, *after* she has reached general conclusions about what transpired there, and *after* she has been initiated into the spiral of circuitry that she later describes as "the more I see in it the more I fear" (30). In order to fear, it is necessary to see, or at least to imagine seeing, and as I have argued, the augmentation of gothic suspense is a function of the suspended historical significance, the adumbrated referentiality, of the ghosts' (in)explicable, persistent return. One might argue that the ghosts are connotation writ large, that they accrue in rather circular fashion as a sustained act of prosopopoeia that *is* the essential gothic story of *The Turn of the Screw*: circular because they arise *from* the connotative quality of the fragmentary historical evidence, and they *generate* more connotative interpretive discourse from which they arose. Indeed, the ghosts are entirely supplementary to the letter from Miles's school—and vice versa—for their interpretation collapses into a single project of connotative projection.

In making this argument, I follow Felman's insistence that *The Turn of the Screw*

> is organized around a double mystery: the mystery of the letters' content and the mystery of the ghosts. . . . On the one hand, then, the ghosts—which are, by definition, "horrors" ("What is he? He's a horror" [22]; "the woman's a horror of horrors" [31])—are as *mute*, that is, as *silent* as the letters. And on the other hand, the letters themselves, through their very silence, point to "horrors": "My fear was of having to deal with the intolerable question of the grounds of his dismissal from school, for that was really but the question of the *horrors gathered behind*" [55].[29]

Yet just as innocence in Jamesian fiction is never authentic, silence is never actually silence: if the silence of the letter corresponds to the silence of the ghosts, as Felman correctly points out, then the point is *not* silence per se, but rather another mode of obscurity that seeks to "cover" and whose cover is disrupted by connotative poetics from the outset around the letter's and the ghosts' interlinearity.

Immediately upon the governess's receipt of the letter from Miles's school, three things happen in quick succession that establish the protocols of her subsequent historiography; all three arise in her conversations with Mrs. Grose, yet each is a specific method of interrogation, of circling back in time to establish plausible explanation, that manages defensively to retreat or to stop short. These protocols include the nomination of Miles's transgressions by the production of increasingly pointed connotative language; the governess's reiterated, obsessive attempt to go behind Mrs. Grose's reluctance to describe Miles's "badness"; and a mode of syntactic *irresolution* in which the sentence breaks off in midpoint, called aposiopesis, which performatively signals the fainthearted hermeneutic that backs off when it comes too close. Although these habits overlap to a considerable extent, I shall consider each in turn.

The governess represents the letter as "simply express[ing] their regret that it should be impossible to keep him" and proceeds immediately to fill in the missing explanation: "'They can have but one meaning' . . . to put the thing with some coherence . . . I went on: 'That he's an injury to the others'" (10). This is a vitally important moment of discursive condensation: in restricting the ground of explanation to "*one* meaning," and in locating that singularity as "injury," the governess uncannily tells more than she can know at this point; in naming undisclosed history as "injury," she *inaugurates* the hermeneutic spiral at its widest diameter and will in due course *narrow* the circumference of injury with nominations that grow more pointed in exact proportion to their oblique elaboration. Moreover, if the singularity of meaning as "injury" seems rather general and wide open, raising more questions than it answers, it also accrues a certain ominous specificity from the outset precisely through the indexical gesturings of connotation. The governess's conclusion that Miles is injurious to others installs the episteme of dirt, disorder, and spreadable disease (remember that she understands the school-world as "horrid" and "unclean"), which she will immediately turn to particularize in more pointed sexual ways. More important, the matter of "injury" invites the question of origin, which in turn necessitates historical retrospection, and in so doing, it points to the "wound" or the sexualized backside of history, the preterite that the governess will, as I have demonstrated, subject recalcitrantly to preterition.

In the second phase of the hermeneutic protocol, the governess negotiates with the reticence of Mrs. Grose to establish the evidence of Miles's "badness." Here, too, a spiral of return is inaugurated: while the governess seeks, in this conversation, to frame her nomination of "injury" within historical testimony, she initiates a series of conversations that will circle ever more particularly around the etiology of pederastic injury. This etiology accommodates a slippage between Miles as one who has injured and Miles as one who has been injured. This spiral *contains* the hermeneutic spiral of reconstruction, but it also *sustains* the very emplotment of *The Turn of the Screw*, for whatever connotative evidence is generated by the narrative, it leaks out almost exclusively in these scenes of interrogation and confrontation. These scenes, in short, are the high points of the drama, and their return marks the signposts of the governess's ever-narrowing circling around the backside of explanation. If these scenes, cumulatively, represent a going-behind of Mrs. Grose's discursive avoidances, their habit of peregrination is cast from the outset, presently, when the governess begins by *returning* to clarify something that Mrs. Grose has (not) said:

> I began to fancy she rather sought to avoid me. I overtook her, I remember, on the staircase . . . and at the bottom I detained her, holding her there with a hand on her arm. "I take what you said to me at noon as a declaration that *you've* never known [Miles] to be bad."
>
> . . . "Oh never known him—I don't pretend *that*."
>
> I was upset again. "Then you *have* known him—? . . . You mean that a boy who never is—? . . . But not to the degree to contaminate—"
>
> "To contaminate?"—my big word left her at a loss.
>
> I explained it. "To corrupt." (11)

Situated at the architectural "bottom" of the staircase, the descent of which suggests—is it too obvious a symbol to point out?—the governess's determination to arrive at an explanation at the bottom of childhood's history, this confrontation yields a discourse that specifies injury as contamination and contamination as "corruption." The governess's "not to the degree to" is ineffectual; it is merely a reluctance to accept what she has interpreted. It seems highly unlikely that, in the 1890s context of regulation and surveillance of children's bodies, "corruption" could contain anything other than a sharply sexual meaning. If so, then the architectural bottoms in houses, which lend a spatial imaginary to the temporality of history's occluded bottom, index connotatively the anatomical bottom, the violation of which incarnates corruption. Once again, connotation operates queerly, both to condense a spectrum of meanings along which reading must slide toward the spectral shadow of "what happened" and to obviate more "gross" nominations.

Aposiopesis, the third of the governess's protocols of circularity, makes its suspensions of interlocution felt in the passage I have just explored. It operates in several ways: sometimes it is an abrupt arrest of speech, a breaking off in order to break the unbearable point; at other times, it acts as an invitation for the interlocutor to come to terms. Invariably, it escalates in direct proportion to the narrowing of focalization and the imminence of a revelation of a "behind" that is always already disavowed, but with equal invariability it proves ineffectual in halting the progress of connotative spin. In this case, the governess attempts to go behind Mrs. Grose's inconclusive impressions of Miles's "badness" by inquiring about her pedagogical predecessor, Miss Jessel:

> The next moment I had lost my impression of [Mrs. Grose's] having said more than she meant; and I merely asked what I wanted to know. "Did *she* see anything in the boy—?"
>   "That wasn't right? She never told me."
>   I had a scruple, but I overcame it. "Was she careful—particular?"
>   . . . "About some things—yes."
>   "But not about all?" (12)

Having already arrived, hesitantly, at a singularity of historical meaning that is articulated as "contamination" arising from "corruption," the governess now turns—in a movement that will have enormous consequences for the ensuing narrative—to supplement the interpretation based on *reading,* on filling in the hole in the letter, to one based on *seeing.* In this moment, the governess must project the act of visual witnessing onto the previous governess, who is, in some sense, her double, the agent responsible for knowing; she will soon, in due course, have ample visual testimony of her own, arising—as I have indicated—from the gaps in the letter and her own engagement in connotative reconstruction that coalesces uneasily between the desire to know and the fear of knowing. I suggest that everything that is subsequent in the governess's adventure *turns* upon the imperative of seeing that is here deferred—that is, referred to the previous governess and arrested by her aposiopesis. Moreover, her shrinking desire to locate "corruption," reflected in her return to a generalized "anything *in* the boy," meets an equally general deflection—an anything that "wasn't right"—and an abrupt closure, for whatever the earlier governess saw, she "never told." In a final going-behind from what her predecessor *saw* to what she *was,* the governess laminates the imperative of seeing "corruption" to the inevitable question of the origin of corruption in its agents, perpetrators, and accomplices. Miss Jessel could not have seen "anything" because she was doing or not doing "something." The function of aposiopesis in this initiatory moment, then, is to open a hole in discourse that will be filled in by the governess's own entry into the visual economy of historical corruption.

Once again, D. A. Miller's model of connotation's further reaches is helpful in grasping the logistics of a gothic visual economy—a tropics of the spectral—by which the return of the repressed "backside" finds its narrative course. According to Miller, "Every representation that shows homosexuality by connotative means alone will thus be implicitly haunted by the phantasm of the thing itself, not just in the form of the name, but also, more basically, as what the name conjures up: the spectacle of 'gay sex.' Whenever homosexuality is reduced to epistemology, to a problem of *being able to tell*, this will-to-see never fails to make itself felt."[30] Because the governess's sightings of Peter Quint's ghost are a consequence of her soundings of the letter from school, the ghost's materialization permits a *narratable* "haunt[ing] by the phantasm of the thing itself"—the missing referent— that is subject to the conventions of gothic suspense. Yet Miller is entirely correct to describe this "haunting" as "implicit," for the ghost—a strikingly literal mode of haunting—cannot enable connotation to transcend its "dusky existence for [the] fluorescent literality" that is denotation;[31] rather, the ghost's literal initiation of the visual economy that *is* the supplement of the governess's reading is always already bound by the figurative contract of the connotative spiral.

If the governess comes face-to-face with "history" in her encounter with the ghost, then the ghost itself arises from the gap in nomination that is aposiopesis; having spun the discourse of "contamination" and "corruption" as the theme of her historiography, the governess now finds a face and a body to personify that history because the circuits of the figurative take a further turn toward prosopopoeia. As Paul de Man suggests, "prosopopoeia is hallucinatory," for "to make the invisible visible is uncanny"; moreover, while prosopopoeia renders indeterminate the "distinction between hallucination and perception," it also, and consequently, "undoes the distinction between reference and signification."[32] Hence Miller's point that the "thing itself" haunts uncannily but implicitly: what the ghost "means" is the return of the repressed backside of history, but *how* it means involves the escalating pointedness of connotation as adumbration. If the entrance of the ghost does not quite dispel the occlusion of history, it nonetheless renders history more proximate; it entertains what Miller describes as a "closer, more nearly causal connection to gay male sex." In effect, the materialization of the ghost "means" that we are "put in the position of being *just about to see* what we are waiting for; and the desire for the spectacle of gay male sex is intensified accordingly into that pleasurably (because all but unpleasantly) prolonged state of expectation we call suspense."[33]

It will come as no surprise that the governess's coming closer to the historical "thing" is attended by attenuation, nor that this attenuation is a function of James's complex tropic framing, a procedure that interlines the psychodynamics of repression's return with specific rhetorical tricks. For if Peter Quint's ghost materializes through the holes in discourse that are the aposiopetic suspensions of nomination, the ghost itself—"as definite as a picture in a frame" (16), the governess avers—is a prosopopoeic figure framed by the figurative maneuvers of distinctly irresolute similes. The time of her meditation on the letter's import is described as a period of "stillness" and "hush in which *something* gathers or crouches. The change was actually like the spring of a beast" (14; emphasis added). James's simile attempts to denote the suddenness and dramatic "change" of the ghost's "spring," yet prosopopoeia accrues temporally *in* the very "hush," the very silence, that is the letter's nondisclosure and the governess's stopping short. Clearly, the "something" that "gathers" arises from and speaks to the history that has been preterited through connotation's evasions. This "some*thing*" coheres as prosopopoeia when the governess anticipates that "some*one* would appear there at the turn of a path," and indeed her "imagination had, in a flash, turned real. He did stand there" (15). Never mind that the governess had hoped to see her employer, the children's uncle, with whom she is infatuated, for James ironizes this desire by presenting not the heteronormative possibility, but rather the figure who portends a darker fulfillment—knowledge of what has lurked behind the heterosexual surface of things. This irony is compounded when the governess recognizes "the figure I had so often invoked" (15): she continues to misrecognize the "figure" whom she has sought, "invoked" speculatively, as the agent behind Miles's initiation into "badness." Yet this misrecognition contains the seeds of subsequent recognition, for the governess will make precisely that connection in her next apparitional encounter and thus install in the historically real what she has conjured here through prosopopoeia's uncanny suspension of sign and referent.

This suspension is framed, (in)conclusively, by the simile that is James's closing frame for the uncanny return implicit in the governess's act of seeing: "I saw him," she claims, "as I see the letters I form on this page" (16). Once again, the comparative logistics of simile are undermined by the terms of comparision and their temporal origins, for if the intent is to insist upon the equal and literal legibility of things seen, the "letters" that she actually sees and "forms" in the present do not address a present "presence"; rather, they reconstitute a "form" that, as I have demonstrated, marks the incarnation, a will-to-see, of an anterior gap in discourse. The point of the prosopopoeic supplement *is* to supplement, to extend the circuits of interpretation from letters on pages into a gothic visual economy. It would seem that the efficacy of prosopopoeia turns ultimately on the queer fracturing of simile's representational contract. To circulate this argument in theoretical terms, I return figural suspension to Miller's point about narrative suspense, of being "just about to see" what the narrative can never directly represent, for the narrowing focalization of the governess's connotative hermeneutic will be saved, *just in time,* from time's ultimate revelation. If prosopopoeia, then, marks a turn that tightens the diameter of the interpretive spiral, it too functions like connotation as "the *sign* of gay sex [that] tends in some degree to become [and to remain] an *index* of it."[34]

At Bottom

Let me stand back from this tortuous analysis to refresh the overarching questions that I posed at the outset of the preceding section of my argument: we have seen that the recalcitrance of Miles's case history is a function of the discourse that tracks it, for the "horrors gathered behind" his mysterious dismissal from school point in turn to other adumbrated "horrors," all of which terminate at an anatomical "behind" at which the narrative cannot bear to arrive. This "tracking" discourse remains suspended not only between fascination and fear, but also *within* a tropics of reconstructive image that invites deconstruction, that focuses *in* only to stop short in the indexical moment. Moreover, if the will to interpret holes in discourse generates more holes in the connotative spiral, the will-to-see emerges as an uncanny mode of figuration that can proximate history only approximately, bound up as it is in the tropic matrix that engenders it. But my other question has to do with the restraining order under which the governess performs her office of analysis and surveillance: Apart from the cultural milieu that resists the sexuality of children, what is it about the governess that overdetermines her paradoxical predicament of suspension, of recognition and assiduous avoidance? Critical accounts of the governess have shied away from psychoanalysis ever since Edmund Wilson argued that she is "a neurotic case of sex repression, and . . . the ghosts are not real ghosts but [her] hallucinations";[35] this had dire consequences for criticism, as generations of critics divided along the binary positions that Wilson set up, debating the evidence of ghosts' "reality."

While it is difficult to establish the governess's own "case history" with any degree of certainty, given that we know practically nothing about this character prior to her arrival at Bly, her narrative embeds fleeting suggestions that point to some traumatic event in the dim recesses of her childhood. Whatever this "something" might be, it coheres in a manner remarkably congruent with Miles's situation and ought to be understood as a further historical adumbration, as a shadow cast over the governess's circuitous attempt to come to terms with Miles. On her very first night at Bly, she listens closely "in the fading dusk . . . for the possible recurrence of a sound or two . . . that [she] fancied [she] heard. There had been a moment when [she] believed [she] recognized, faint and far, the cry of a child" (7–8). This could be dismissed as a strategy of gothic prefiguration, but such dismissal would be premature: a few days later, while the governess ponders the import of the headmaster's letter, she chooses (as we have seen) to regard Miles as an "angel," for such a view "was an antidote to any pain"; intriguingly, the "pain" of Miles's possible history is folded into her claim that she "had more pains than one," occasioned by her "receipt in these days of disturbing letters from home" (19). Multiple "disturbing letters," the contents of which are suppressed by the narrative, do not necessarily imply the same thing, but their temporal alignment and the resonance of one story of pain with another are surely suggestive: it is another coalescent moment in an emerging congruity. Such congruity is brought retrospectively into sharper focus when, immediately after this passage—and, more important, immediately after her construction of Miles as the boy with no "antecedents," the boy without a behind—the governess has her second encounter with Peter Quint's ghost.

This second visitation is the most chilling moment in the entire narrative, not simply because Quint reappears (this time, framed by a window) "with a nearness that represented a forward stride in [their] intercourse, and made [her] . . . turn cold," and not primarily because his manifestation at this abrupt juncture confirms that history returns in ghostly form to subvert the consolations of the governess's repression. Rather, it is because the ghost sustains a particular and intense familiarity with the governess, and addresses, in his very silence, her own past: "He remained but a few seconds—long enough to convince me he also saw and recognized; but it was *as if I had always been looking at him for years and had known him always*" (20; emphasis added). Despite the slipperiness of James's language, these "few seconds" represent far more than the arrest of time that attends traumatic experience in the present. What chills is the mutuality of recognition, as the "few seconds" both recede and expand into the governess's reiterated "always." The point of her grammatical redundancy is to conjoin "looking" with "knowing"; moreover, this is, I would argue, the only instance in the visual economy of *The Turn of the Screw* where James permits an immediate leap from seeing to conclusive knowledge. It seems incontrovertible that the governess has met some version of Peter Quint before, most likely in her childhood, which this passage establishes as the most recessive "story" in this labyrinth of occlusions. And it is here, too, where Jamesian gothic most fully dilates the temporality of returning: as a species of sexual predators among the vampiristic undead, the Peter Quints are a historical constant, preying on the successive generations represented by the governess and Miles. James, then, seems intent on laminating the case histories of Miles and the governess, for the moment of recognition that brings her repressed history into visible presence is also a moment of relay, or transference, by which Miles is revealed as always already the governess's double and substitute. For in the wake of her recognition, the governess experiences "the added shock of the certitude that it was not for me he had come. He had come for someone else" (20).

It is important to remember that the traumatic reopening of old wounds that suspends the difference between past and present, that indexes the anatomical congruity of Miles and the governess as precarious survivors of unspecified anterior "horror," occurs precisely to go behind, to remember by dismembering "the rose-flush of [Miles's] innocence." If James's emplotment of going behind to return the repressed is a tortuous psychoanalysis, it recalls implicitly the traumatic wound as physical torture. Emily Dickinson describes the process of extracting the origin of trauma—some indispensable scene concealed in the historical record, some essential knowledge—in an allegorical discourse that has a punctual relation to James's narrative of suffering:

> Essential oils—are wrung—
> The Attar from the Rose
> Be not expressed by Suns—alone—
> It is the gift of Screws—[36]

In Dickinson's temporal frame, the ontological residue of the present accrues coherence in the future not through natural process or the cycle of time represented by "Suns," but through the violence done to the body. This is the paradoxical "gift of Screws," and if Dickinson's emblematic Rose anticipates Miles's "rose-flush," then her physics of "wringing" figures forth the geometry of James's spiral of returns to, and around, the essence that is both a residue of the anterior and the persistent sign of injury. To put this another way, the governess's psychoanalytics are less a return to traumatic origin than a persistence of trauma.

In a theoretical argument that closely resembles this narrative perseveration, Cathy Caruth defines trauma as the temporal matrix of obsessive return, for "trauma is not locatable in the simple violent or original event in an individual's past, but rather in the way that its very unassimilated nature—the way in which it was precisely *not known* in the first instance—returns to haunt the survivor later on."[37] The epistemology of an "unassimilated" event that happens too soon and too unexpectedly is conceptualized as a matter of intrinsic belatedness: the original event "haunts" a retrospective narrative that approaches it but can never contain it. Caruth's model of the traumatized temporality of return, like my revision of Felman's model of the narrative spiral, understands historical reconstruction as, at bottom, a question of *narrative poetics*. Analytically deconstructive, it nonetheless recuperates what Caruth calls "the locus of referentiality"; while the poetics of obliquity refuses a straightforward model of historical referentiality, there remains the Jamesian solution of "permitting *history* to arise where *immediate understanding* may not."[38] Because history arises in "a language that is always somehow literary—a language that defies, even as it claims, our understanding," the analytic project is to trace "the textual itinerary of insistently recurring words or figures."[39]

Having mapped some of the discursive configuration of the problem of how the governess *approaches* the problem—of the interlinearity between her own case history and that of Miles—I would particularize Caruth's rather vague focus on language that is "somehow literary." For as we have seen, the "textual itinerary" of James's gothic narrative locates an occluded referentiality through specific and complex unfoldings of tropic connection: the governess's spiral of hermeneutic connotation is restrained when it comes too close to nomination; because nomination is simultaneously unbearable and unknowable, it is arrested by aposiopesis, the gap in explanatory syntax in which, as we have seen, the prosopopoeic figure of the ghost is generated. Prosopopoeia in turn requires interpretation, but because the governess cannot read the figure her repressions return, she is compelled to return to connotative speculation. In the perverse "gift of screws" that is *The Turn of the Screw*, language itself is traumatized, for connotation as master trope entails that the efficacy of rhetoric—figure and syntax—is suspended, its performative contract broken. From faulty similes to fractured sentences, James's narrative poetics queers the anthology of tropes; in going behind the symptomatic evidence to refer to traumatic origin, it sustains a wound from behind that refracts that origin.

Among James's many teasing comments about *The Turn of the Screw* contained in his letters, one is strikingly arresting: the tale is "a down-on-all-fours pot-boiler"—"I can only rather blush to see any real substance read into it."[40] As well he might, for his "blush"—like Miles's "rose-flush," an intermediate position between innocence and shame—arises from his already having read a "substance," accruing in his personification of the tale as not merely abject, but positioned for penetration from behind. This sexual innuendo, combined with the tale's emplotment of reiterated goings-behind, points to a substantial, however obliquely substantiated, locus of queer referentiality in an original traumatic wound, preterited because sexually proscribed. Inevitably, this locus—the origin of story, of case history, and of narrative's haunted poetics—acquires the *positionality* of a *coitus a tergo* that Freud articulates as the substance of the traumatic "primal scene" in his case history of the "Wolf Man." Freud understands the primacy of the primal scene as both etiological and historiographical imperatives: "It is indispensable to a comprehensive solution of the conundrums that are set us . . . [for] all the consequences radiate out from it, just as all the threads of analysis have led up to it."[41] The "threads" to which Freud metaphorically refers are identical, in their circularity and deflection, to the indexical spiraling, the precisely connotative "conundrum," of James's screw. Peter Brooks argues that Freud both operated under and subverted "nineteenth-century confidence in explanation," which "reposes on the postulate that a history can and should be a tracing of origins."⁴² The essential modernity of both Freud's and James's case histories turns upon the recessive nature of origin, their recuperability only as a matter of provisional analytic construction: consequently, the relation "between [traumatic] event and its significant reworking is one of suspicion and conjecture, a structure of indeterminacy which can offer only a framework of narrative possibilities rather than a clearly specifiable plot."⁴³ While both James and Freud reconstruct along the axis of the indexical, connotative sign, James's interpretant is continually arrested in the act of "going along" as it turns to "going behind"; Freud of course imposes no sanctions on his rather free associations. Putting aside the obvious differences between the medical and fictional enterprises—wherein the literal conclusiveness of the former would preclude the gothic suspenses of the other—and the equally obvious difference between the loquacious Freud and the reticent James, I shall give a final turn to the questions that have shaped my project from the outset: Why can the governess's terms not come to terms with the sodomitical scene of a *coitus a tergo*? Why is her rhetoric—the particular matrix of queerly traumatized poetics analyzed above—so reclusive and yet so resilient? What overlies what lies at bottom? What is wound about her wound?

"At bottom," Freud writes, there is "nothing extraordinary, nothing to give the impression of being the product of an extravagant imagination" in his reconstruction of the Wolf Man's primal scene, or in his location of trauma as the child's realization that his "longing for sexual satisfaction from his father" entailed "that castration is a necessary condition of it."⁴⁴ The child's observation of the parents' *coitus a tergo* confirmed the reality of castration: "he saw with his own eyes the wound," concluded that his mother had been made ill by sexual penetration, and installed himself in his mother's place, expressing this identification through the "anal zone."⁴⁵ In his essay "Seeing Things," Lee Edelman ponders the anxieties that attend Freud's speculative etiological construction of the primal scene, for the central problem of this case history is his temporalizing equivocations of the plausibility of this ultimate historical origin. Central to Edelman's interrogation is the "scandal of supposition" that implicitly installs "homosexuality" as the primary subject of negotiation in the primal scene: "What wound," he asks, "can the scene of sodomy inflict to make its staging, if only in the space of the imagination [and, I would add, inflected through heterosexuality], so dangerous to effect?"⁴⁶ For the wound is not simply a matter of the *exposition* of homosexuality's interlinearity with castration in the primal scene, but rather is a *process of wounding* that is coterminous with analysis itself, with "the direction [from which] one approaches it and in what position one chooses to engage it."⁴⁷

Because Freud's theories of trauma, like Caruth's and the governess's, are predicated axiomatically on the conviction that the constitutive, pre-historical drama "can never be viewed head on, . . . never taken in frontally, but [are to be] only approached from behind," the *coitus a tergo,* according to Edelman, "allegorizes both the retroactive understanding" whereby the primal scene will unfold its dark meaning and "the practice of psycho-analysis itself insofar as it too approaches experience from behind."[48] If the emergent point of this allegorical interimplication is that "the analytic scene and the primal scene uncontrollably collapse into one another,"[49] it occurs because the indexing motions of analysis track connotative evidence rather *too* closely, ultimately producing a traumatic origin that both arises from the "going behind" operation of tracking itself and returns to or doubles back on the "penetrations" of the indexical to reveal its imma-nent "homoerotics." Therefore, famously, Freud can conclude only with a *non liquet,* as he "tries to distance his method from the anal eroticism he identifies as characteristic of the Wolf Man by casting doubt upon the *coitus a tergo* that [he] himself had initially proposed in approaching the primal scene through analytic '(be)hindsight.'"[50]

The expository irresolution of Freud's "Wolf Man" case history, as Peter Brooks suggests, offers "a paradigm of the status of modern explanation":[51] its problematization of the historical base, the bottom line, reverberates in the analeptic circumlocutions of modernist experimental fiction. I detect an intriguing torsion (an act of twisting, or turning *spirally*) between the tortuous narrative predicaments of Freud and James's governess: following Edelman's argument that Freud's *attenuations* serve to deflect a *potential* traumatic wound—that is, the implication of psychoanalytic reconstruc-tion in the very homoerotics he has unveiled—I would suggest that the governess's *adumbrations* are generated by a *retrospective* deflection of a traumatic wound that binds her case history too proximately to Miles's. Sus-pended between blindness and insight, between repression and its insistent, uncanny return, the governess's narrative is driven by the connotative spi-ral of narrative desire that I have elaborated, a desire that, as Brooks avers, "never can quite speak its name—never can quite come to the point—but that insists on speaking over and over again its movement toward that name."[52]

Had I sufficient room to turn around in, I would double back to the several moments in *The Turn of the Screw* in which connotation approaches the point and then backs away, scenes in which the governess compulsively returns to the letter from Miles's school that is the moment of origin, the primal scene of narrative if not of story, and irresolutely probes the hor-rors behind, the precise question of Miles's "badness." I must be content with two points—critical synecdoches, really—about the operations of the narrowing spiral of focalization that constitutes "its movement toward that name." First, to really read *The Turn of the Screw,* it is necessary to understand that the spiral narrows vertically in localized speech acts, gravitating syntactically from general to more pointed connotative signs. For instance, when the governess goes behind the "superficial" explanation of Peter Quint's death—"the icy slope, the turn mistaken at night and in liquor" that officially "accounted for . . . everything"—her discourse is characterized by a progression toward nomination: "There had been matters in his life, strange passages and perils, secret disorders, vices more than suspected, that would have accounted for a good deal more" (27). *Would* have accounted, that is, if the governess had quitted the connotative lexicon of fin de siècle "homosexuality" for sharper denotation. At the same time, however, it is vitally important to note the increasingly particularized nouns in her arrested turn toward nomination, as she moves from the general "matters" to "perils," "disorders," and, ultimately, the supremely suggestive "vices."

Second, the entire structural topography of the text is constituted by an *overarching,* horizontal spiral from the governess's initial conclusion about Miles's "contaminating," "corrupt" presence to the question she poses at the spiral's, and the narrative's, apex. In the final scene, as the governess presses Miles to confess exactly what he did at school, he yields, "Well—I said things," and subsequently he adds, to "those I liked." Characteristically, this movement toward transparency is but an occasion for occlusion, for the governess "seemed to float not into clearness, but into a darker obscure" (83) as she comes up against the thing itself. The final, ironic recession of the thing itself—the wound and its traumatic fallout—occurs when the governess sharpens connotation to its ultimate point. *The Turn of the Screw* concludes with a question that, predictably, occasions the return of Peter Quint's "white face of damnation," Miles's death cry "as a creature hurled over the abyss," and the narrative's abrupt closure: "What *were* those things?" (84).

We'll never know.

Notes

1. Margaret Wente, "Vilma Climaco Was a Popular Nanny . . . ," *Globe and Mail,* January 20, 2001, A7.

2. James R. Kincaid, *Child-Loving: The Erotic Child and Victorian Culture* (New York: Routledge, 1992), 78; emphasis added.

3. Henry James, *The Turn of the Screw,* 2nd ed., ed. Deborah Esch and Jonathan Warren (New York: W. W. Norton, 1999), 1–2. Page numbers from this edition are hereafter cited in text.

4. Cathy Caruth, *Unclaimed Experience: Trauma, Narrative, and History* (Baltimore: Johns Hopkins University Press, 1996), 6, 4.

5. John Fletcher, "The Haunted Closet: Henry James's Queer Spectrality," *Textual Practice* 14 (2000): 57, 63.

6. Ibid., 65.

7. Eric Haralson, "'His Little Heart, Dispossessed': Ritual Sexorcism in *The Turn of the Screw*," in *Questioning the Master: Gender and Sexuality in Henry James's Writings*, ed. Peggy McCormack (Newark, NJ: University of Delaware Press, 2000), 138, 139.

8. Ibid., 146.

9. John Silver, "A Note on the Freudian Reading of *The Turn of the Screw*" (1957), in *A Casebook on Henry James's "The Turn of the Screw*," 2nd ed., ed. Gerald Willen (New York: Thomas Y. Crowell, 1969), 239.

10. Ned Lukacher, *Primal Scenes: Literature, Philosophy, Psychoanalysis* (Ithaca, NY: Cornell University Press, 1986), 123.

11. Henry James, "Preface to *The Turn of the Screw*," in *French Writers, Other European Writers, the Prefaces to the New York Edition*, ed. Leon Edel and Mark Wilson (New York: Literary Classics of the United States, 1984), 1188; emphasis added.

12. Ibid., 1187.

13. Ibid., 1188.

14. Ibid., 1187.

15. Ibid., 1184, emphasis added.

16. Shoshana Felman, "Turning the Screw of Interpretation," in *Literature and Psychoanalysis: The Question of Reading: Otherwise*, ed. Shoshana Felman (Baltimore: Johns Hopkins University Press, 1982), 179.

17. Ibid., 178.

18. Ibid., 172.

19. Leo Bersani, *A Future for Astyanax: Character and Desire in Literature* (Boston: Little, Brown, 1976), 132.

20. Henry James, "The Figure in the Carpet" (1896), in *The Complete Tales of Henry James*, vol. 9, *1892–1898*, ed. Leon Edel (Philadelphia: J. B. Lippincott, 1964), 282.

21. Ibid.

22. D. A. Miller, "Anal Rope," in *Inside/Out: Lesbian Theories, Gay Theories*, ed. Diana Fuss (New York: Routledge, 1991), 124–25; emphasis added.

23. Lukacher, *Primal Scenes*, 117.

24. Felman, "Turning the Screw," 140, 141, 143.

25. Ibid., 144; emphasis added.

26. Ross Posnock, *The Trial of Curiosity: Henry James, William James, and the Challenge of Modernity* (New York: Oxford University Press, 1991), 81; Michael Moon, *A Small Boy and Others: Imitation and Initiation in American Culture from Henry James to Andy Warhol* (Durham, NC: Duke University Press, 1998), 4.

27. Millicent Bell, *Meaning in Henry James* (Cambridge: Harvard University Press, 1991), 240, 230, 236.

28. Henry James, "The Pupil" (1891), in *The Complete Tales of Henry James*, vol. 7, *1888–1891*, ed. Leon Edel (Philadelphia: J. B. Lippincott, 1963), 437; emphasis added.

29. Felman, "Turning the Screw," 149.

30. Miller, "Anal Rope," 130.

31. Ibid., 129.

32. Paul de Man, *The Resistance to Theory* (Minneapolis: University of Minnesota Press, 1986), 49–50.

33. Miller, "Anal Rope," 131.

34. Ibid.

35. Edmund Wilson, "The Ambiguity of Henry James" (1934), in *A Casebook on Henry James's "The Turn of the Screw"* (see note 9), 115.

36. Emily Dickinson, poem 772 in *The Poems of Emily Dickinson,* ed. R. W. Franklin (Cambridge, MA: Belknap, 1999), 345.

37. Caruth, *Unclaimed Experience,* 3.

38. Ibid., 6, 11.

39. Ibid., 5.

40. Quoted in Leon Edel and Adeline Tintner, "The Private Life of Peter Quin[t]: Origins of *The Turn of the Screw," Henry James Review* 7 (1985): 2.

41. Sigmund Freud, "From the History of an Infantile Neurosis (The 'Wolf Man')" (1918), in *Case Histories II,* ed. Angela Richards, trans. James Strachey et al. (Harmondsworth: Penguin, 1991), 289.

42. Peter Brooks, *Reading for the Plot: Design and Intention in Narratives* (Cambridge: Harvard University Press, 1984), 275–76.

43. Ibid., 275.

44. Freud, "From the History," 269, 274.

45. Ibid., 278, 315.

46. Lee Edelman, *Homographesis: Essays in Gay Literary and Cultural Theory* (New York: Routledge, 1994), 174.

47. Ibid., 175.

48. Ibid.

49. Ibid., 182.

50. Ibid., 178.

51. Brooks, *Reading for the Plot,* 268.

52. Ibid., 61.

Growing Sideways, or Versions of the Queer Child: The Ghost, the Homosexual, the Freudian, the Innocent, and the Interval of Animal

Kathryn Bond Stockton

Fraught Depictions

Consider, to begin, depictions of the queer child ranging from the simple—but also rather funny—to the highly complex. One boy's summary of himself as "Shopped. Homework[ed]. Masturbated. Read." Another boy's tendency to call himself a "filly"—the word, he thought, for a "homosexual seagull." Another boy's story of how, "idiotic as it may seem, watching [John Huston's] *The Bible* on a lousy ['substandard'] TV during an acid trip [in college] with my best friend" brought up childhood sexual memories surrounding this film and thus enabled him to "half-acknowledge [himself] sexually" for the first time.[1] The jokes by queer comedians that they "found themselves" in the characters of Ernie (the rather odd boy in *My Three Sons*), Robin (of *Batman*), *The Beverly Hillbillies'* Miss Jane Hathaway, or Josephine the Plumber.[2] Renderings, more aesthetic, of children who are hanging, suicide-like, from flowering trees; lying children spying, Hitchcock-fashion (isolated eye, decided startle, diagonal visual plane), on their teachers, whom they claim are lovers; the specter of a six-year-old acting both mother and wife to two men.[3]

Even a highly complicated image of a ghostly woman-child—she with the charming "look of cherubs in Renaissance theatres," who "strangely aware of some lost land in herself . . . took to going out"—haunting train terminals, wandering into different parts of the country, speaking sotto voce to the animals, "straining their fur back until their eyes were narrowed and . . . teeth bare, her own teeth showing as if her hand were upon her own neck," as she heads up into girlfriend territory.[4] On a chapel bench, she suddenly awakens to the barking of a dog. The dog makes his way to her, her lover runs behind. When they arrive (lover and dog) at the chapel door, they find her at an altar, before a Madonna, in her boy's trousers, with flowers and toys. Her pose is broken. She starts going down—

> Down she went [we read in *Nightwood,* on the novel's final page], until her head swung against his; on all fours now, dragging her knees. . . .
>
> Backed into the farthest corner, the dog reared as if to avoid something that troubled him to such agony that he seemed to be rising from the floor. . . .
>
> He let loose one howl of misery and bit at her . . . . Then she began to bark also, crawling after him—barking in a fit of laughter, obscene and touching.
>
> The dog began to cry then, . . . and she grinning and crying with him . . . until she gave up . . . her face turned and weeping: and the dog too, gave up then, and lay down, his eyes bloodshot, his head flat along her knees.

Here is a woman, who is like a child, playing with and as a dog.

Queers, one observes, trail children behind them or alongside them, as if they are wedded, one to another, in unforeseen ways. This interests me. But so does the seeming flip side of this axiom. Scratch a child, you will find a queer. Virginia Woolf's Mr. Ramsay would say: if all P are Q, and R is P, then R is Q. I will contend: all children are Q. Lolita, recall, was packed off to Camp Q—a clue to the reader to realize Lolita's alignment with things that are "q"ued in the novel—Quilty, for one, Humbert Humbert's "queer mirror side."[5] A child need not twin Lolita Dolly Haze—the Dolly sexually schooled by "little lesbians"—in order to belong to Camp Q, though playing dollies is not beside the point, leading analysts to wonder whether the girl who plays dolly is playing with herself or playing the mother who plays with her child or playing with the child she would like to imagine is born from her sexual union with her mother (Irigaray famously wonders just this).[6]

In light of this knot, this haze surrounding one's pleasure with one's dollies, I offer something akin to a little glass ball of hypotheses. I am hypothesizing versions of the queer child, offering a set of initial (not exhaustive) suppositions to be pondered. Think of this ball as breakable and vulnerable, as just getting cut along the precise historical and literary lines that will refine it but also turn it to milky coloration, showing how the distinctions I will make (the ghost, the homosexual, the Freudian, the innocent) coalesce into dense configurations. Density, in fact, will be this essay's climax. I am going to move from the convenience of certain spelled-out versions of the queer child (which, even so, are fraught with complication) to the complexities of literary portraits, in which the role of metaphor helps to convey a queer take on growth. Central to my claims is the theorist's need to engage highly literary indirections and linguistic seductions (such as we find in demanding fictions) that do what children are often shown as doing: approach their destinations, delay; swerve, delay; ride on a metaphor they tend to make material and, so, imagine relations of their own—my dog is my wife; my dolly is my child.

Not uncommonly, children are shown as having a knack for metaphorical substitution, letting one object stand for another, by means of which they reconceive relations to time. Given that "the child" is often defined as a point in time, how are children depicted as conceiving their relation to the concept "growing up"?[7] Are they shown as unwittingly making strange relations ("my dog is my wife") when they anticipate how they will participate in adult time? Must they turn their relations sideways (fantasizing having a baby with their parent, or even with a playmate) in order to imagine themselves growing *up*? What if they are shown as eschewing a sense of family altogether, or as not marking their time in terms of producing generations? Especially in relation to the children our law courts don't believe in—overtly same-sex oriented children—the tendency of metaphor to reconfigure relations and time will prove why fictions (particularly those of an experimental nature) uniquely nurture ideas of queer children.

Sideways growth: We are going to see that concepts of the queer child demand that we talk in terms of growing sideways. If you think about it, metaphors, in some respects, are themselves a sideways growth. They "grow" meanings ("increase [them] in quantity, size, and degree") by putting people and things rather oddly beside themselves. A "metaphor" is an "implied comparison," the dictionary tells us. So, when the gospels say, for example, that "Christians are sheep," we compare their features. We put a sheep body next to a Christian and "find" the Christian inside of the sheep, growing, expanding the meaning of a Christian by putting "Christian" beside itself in a figure for itself (putting the concept of "sheep" by its side). Such a move is so familiar (fattening up a concept through the use of metaphor), we may not notice its reliance on both strangeness and time. That is to say, while in the act of domesticating meaning—making meaning more familiar and accessible—we often use a strangeness. When we say, "Christians are sheep," we almost seem perverse as we make a sacred point. Yet we are willing to put up with this strangeness because sheep *take us somewhere* to a more important point about Christians. This is why a metaphor is said to have a "vehicle" (a figure of speech—"sheep," in this instance) that takes us to a "tenor" (a metaphor's meaning). "Sheep," as a "vehicle," takes us for a ride. It conveys us to some new meaning as it moves us across the distance between two different concepts ("Christian" and "sheep"). And it takes time. There is an interval (sometimes it is long, sometimes it is short) between every vehicle and its tenor: the time it takes, of course, to arrive upon a meaning. This makes a metaphor a moving suspension. Meaning is moving and growing in a metaphor even while time almost seems to hang suspended.

Take the figure of the family dog. A metaphor, it seems, for all that is loyal, familiar, familial, and family-photo-perfect. Or, as Leo Bersani once said: "The family identity produced on American television is much more likely to include your dog than your homosexual brother or sister."[8] This is true—and false. Lassie was never such a simple companion as she seemed. Never just a figure oozing with the ordinariness of family life. Rather, the dog is a living, growing metaphor for the child itself, as we are going to see, and for the child's own propensities to wander into sideways growth. The dog is a vehicle to the child's strangeness. It is the child's companion in queerness. As a recipient of the child's attentions (its often bent devotions) and a living screen for the child's self-projections (its mysterious bad-dog postures of sexual expression), the dog is *a figure for the child beside itself,* engaged in a growing quite aside from growing up. Doggy style, dead dog, dog tired, a dog's life, going to the dogs, let sleeping dogs lie: the dog has a habit of taking on meanings that could not appear overtly in *Lassie.* But they emerge in other texts. The principle of Lassie is even quite abstract, as we're going to find out, making the family dog a time machine in modernist prose.

Experimental metaphors. Moving suspensions. Active pause (even animal pause) on the threshold of adulthood. Sexual kids and their sideways growth through the figures of their dogs. A same-sex lover *as* a child and a dog. I will make these matters explicit in this essay. First, four claims form the basis of my argument. My initial claim, "All children are Q," will just below open out onto versions of the queer child, showing the tangle of Anglo-American cultural logics (or at least a slice of them) surrounding "the child" throughout this century. Then, three novels with children and dogs—one the most famous "lesbian" novel ever written, two rather dense modernist gems—will be seen as working out (in the 1920s and 1930s) comminglings of these categories that are such recognizable strands in the discourse on children in the 1990s. I am going to argue (this is my third claim) that now, as then, we are in a time that does not officially recognize children as growing sideways. We are in a world not ready to receive this thought or formulation. In fact, one could say that we are in the time of the historical prematurity of the love of lateral growth. Such a love—of turning sex and growth on their sides—is ultimately antigenerational. At the very least, it questions developmental models based on one's steady progress toward genital maturity and one's "growing up" to reproductive goals. One last claim: we are likely to find that metaphors are crucial to the love of sideways growth. Supple and creative substitutionary chains (rather than established figures of speech) seem required for pointing to a kind of growing that is not a growing up.

Nightwood, for example, offers us the supple and creative metaphor of a dazzling dog. Here, as we shall see, we find a grown "homosexual" woman relentlessly metaphorized as a child. Her access to her childhood (through her female lover who acts like her mother) is reaching her on linguistic delay. Now she is a queer child when she is not a child. We seem to be watching her tunnel back in time to where she is suspended in a sideways growth. In loving her, her lover tries to grasp a wayward child. To complicate matters (in a way that almost outdoes Freud), before this queer "child" finds her lover, she becomes a mother, the process of which triggers, so it seems, her sudden desire to sleep with one. Rounding out our knotted sense of childhood, this queer child (in several senses) births a boy whose innocence (on the order of a kind of holiness) makes him fully strange—and estranged from adults.

There is something more. Even though *Nightwood*'s most central metaphor should sound familiar—lesbian lovers as mother and child—this worn trope (well worn by Freud) becomes in the hands of Djuna Barnes an intricate metaphorical skein, leading to the novel's extremely strange ending, where the one lover who is figured as a child gets down in the dirt with her lover's dog, barking, howling, and biting, as if she, too, is a canine. Stressing the relation of metaphor to children (as a means of figuring—to adults and to themselves—children's strangeness), I aim to show how Barnes's queer "child" enters into (what I call) an "interval of animal" and therefore creates a moving suspension, one both touching and active on its own behalf.

Oddly, this relation has a kind of legal precedence. I cite it not to suggest direct influence but to show the force of an animal metaphor. In what is called "the Mary Ellen affair" (1874), a New York social worker found, to her dismay, that no laws existed that made abuse of a child illegal. Based on this discovery, she took a clever tack. She convinced the Society for the Prevention of Cruelty to Animals to prosecute the parents of her abused child client according to the terms of the existing cruelty-to-animals law, armed with the logic, successfully presented, that children belong to the animal species and therefore should enjoy an animal's right not to be treated cruelly by anyone, including their parents. If, in this Mary Ellen affair, the animal comes to the aid of the child in need of safe space, it does so tellingly. It becomes a metaphor—actually, a metaphor claimed to be material—where the child can legally hide. Undercover as an animal, the child can have its day in court as something other than itself.

In the case of *Nightwood*, as I explain below, an animal metaphor (Barnes's queer child playing with and as a dog) offers a solution to a problem first announced by Woolf's *Mrs. Dalloway* (in 1925), then by Radclyffe Hall's *The Well of Loneliness* (in 1928). I speak of the historical prematurity not only of queer childhood, but also (as if they are wedded to each other) of queer love in the twenties and thirties. Both of these stand for a kind of growth that Anglo-American culture, in its mainstream, its official bodies, and most of its laws, has not yet embraced. But this is getting ahead of ourselves. We cannot fully grasp these fraught depictions from the twenties and thirties without first hypothesizing versions of the queer child that may be in play from the first and most indisputable proto-homosexual child in 1928 (in Hall's *The Well of Loneliness*) to depictions of (queer) children in the 1990s.

Species of Strangeness

To begin, then, if we call the child "queer," we lean on the almost too elastic properties of this word—so supple they seem to let everything in. "All children are Q," I claimed above. I anticipate (and understand) a reader's objection to this kind of claim. Some readers will find this claim offensive, as if I contaminate sacred ground by throwing the blanket of abnormality over the child. This objection reads me right, insofar as I think we have much to learn from parsing our investment in "the child" (and "the children" and "the future for our children") as our most agreed upon anticontaminant. Viewing the child as a species of strangeness—or, more intriguingly, as a source of endlessly disavowed danger—we may excavate, and so reveal, the layers of violence in "our" culture's most cherished ideal.[9] I speak of "the child" for whom we are asked by governments, schools, and religions to work and better the world. So much for one objection—the objection from offense. A different objection concerns me more: the objection from boredom. I share a reader's likely response to what is commonly called the "queering" of wholesale domains (all sex is queer, all people are queer . . .). Far too often, such blanket assumptions preclude any interesting finer distinctions. It is as if the faux-risqué contaminating job of queering held as its virtue this sole rebellion. But must this be the singular limit to my claiming "All children are Q"? I suggest we fashion a braided theoretical response to mainstream culture's obsession with its child. We could interlace the innocent child with its dangerous peers, who are not its opposites but its companions in human (and, even, inhuman) strangeness.

Consider this: Our figure of the child reveals our most earnest attempts to grasp time and tame its effects. Embedded in "the child" are perplexing issues surrounding the ways we speak of growth: that most enduring problem of change. "The child" also links, or so we imagine, Time to Sex. As a specter of human reproduction and the making of so-called generations, the child is the sign of parents differing from themselves (at least temporally) in the act of reproducing. All of which is why I think that the figure of the child presents the most apt domain in which to understand the broad and narrow poles of the word *queer: strange* and *homosexual*. For by any angle or measure, I will argue, the child, from the standpoint of "normal" adults, is always queer: either "homosexual" (an interesting problem in itself) or "not-yet-straight," merely approaching the official destination of straight couplehood (and therefore estranged from what it "should" approach). For this reason, I would urge that we make distinctions only among queer children. Start with four: (1) the ghostly "gay" child, (2) the grown "homosexual," (3) the child queered by Freud, and (4) the child queered by innocence.

The Ghostly "Gay" Child

The first is the ghost, the queer frontier, television's still watertight taboo: a child with clear-cut same-sex preference.[10] This queer child, whatever its conscious grasp of itself, cannot unfold itself according to the category of "the homosexual"—a category culturally deemed too adult, since it is sexual. And yet to refuse a child this designation actually reveals our culture's contradictions over childhood sexual orientation: the tendency to treat all children as straight while we culturally consider them asexual. The effect for the child who already feels queer (different, odd, out-of-sync, and attracted to same-sex peers) is an asynchronicity. Certain linguistic markers for its queerness arrive only later and ride the back of this person's recognition of a road not taken. "I am not straight": "I was a gay child." This is the only grammatical formulation allowed to gay childhood. That is to say, in one's teens or twenties, when (parental) plans for one's straight destination can be seen to have died, the designation "homosexual child," or even "gay kid," may finally, retrospectively, be applied. Often, it is raised as a tombstone to a death. The phrase "gay child" is a gravestone marker for where and when a straight person died. Straight person dead; gay child born—albeit retrospectively (even, for example, at the age of twenty-five). And yet, by the time the marker is raised ("I was a gay child"), it would seem that the "child" has died with the straight. This could be an efficient means for aborting "gay kids": allow them to appear only when they can no longer exist.

Picture for a moment a very heavy boy who is hanging from a noose. He is a teenager, named Sweet William, hung above a garden in all of its flowering. In point of fact, he is a ghost, seen by a gay man seeing his fat teen self suspended above the flowers. Hung fatness: What is this image a metaphor for? Something worn heavily that has finally died? Something big with birth (amid the ripening flowers)? Something growing sideways and, therefore, getting fat? Something still growing while being suspended? Not in any way is this a simple image of a gay man's "truth" about his young self. It's wider than that. Which could suggest that the tag "gay child" is another kind of noose—strangely, at gay-affirmative hands. When I can say, "I was a gay child," I may be in danger of putting to death all of the metaphors richly spun out before "the" word arrived. All of those vehicles sent in search of tenors, *moving* along their paths of suspension, may be lost as they're parked into "gay." Hence a straight's metaphorical death (marked, we have said, by the phrase "gay child") or a gay child's backward birth (put in motion by a straight person's "death") may be attended by the death of metaphors. Unless they are cherished alongside the words *gay* and *homosexual* as an ill fit. (The fat boy's suits cannot, for example, fit the gay man.) Here is what I mean: it is not impossible that the phrase "gay child"—as a backward birthing mechanism—can not only birth a child retrospectively form-fitted to the marker "gay" but also release, like spirits from a box, the metaphors by means of which ("seagull," "dog," or "ghost," for example) children grow themselves. The touching occulting of himself as fat ghost, which points toward but does not fully join its hands with "gay man" or "gay child," is released by the gay man's reflections on his origins. One could say that, by looking back, he births (as much as anything) metaphor's rather moving suspensions.

These webbed issues of temporal interval, retrospection, metaphorical death, and the birth or death of metaphors run through a range of gay-affirmative helping books—manuals for parents, personal stories, and academic interviews—as they search for "typical patterns" in (what they call) the proto-gay, the prehomosexual, the doomed-to-be-queer, the pre-gay neophyte, the undercover child, and the sexual minority youth. Quite intriguingly, inside the "proto-," "pre-," "undercover," as if they are harboring ghostly vehicles revving up their motors for the work of occultation, are the lurking child, the soon-to-be-roosting-chickens child, the sinister child, the shadowy child, the indirect child, the table-setting child, the best-resting child, the obedient-child-as-fearful child, the not-stopping-what-other-boys-begin child, even the not-covered-by-what-is-said child.

Amid these searches for typicality in nonnormativity, interval and metaphor make their presence felt.

Take the informational *A Stranger in the Family: How to Cope If Your Child Is Gay* (1996). Here, in the chapter "Mum, Dad, I'm Gay," we are told of a "typical pattern, expressed as a series of stages" in families' reactions: subliminal awareness, impact, adjustment, resolution, and integration.[11] The first stage picks up a hint of retrospection, implying the family's subliminal awareness of awareness: something (some child) "always lurking there in the back of our minds," says one parent—making the later discovery of gayness, says this person, moving into metaphor, "like the chickens coming home to roost."[12] Far more striking, in the discourse of the book, than lurking children (seen as soon-to-be-roosting chickens) is the frank talk of death. Under the heading "The Bereavement Effect," parents are told that "this phenomenon" of their reactions "has many symptoms in common with those experienced when someone in the family dies. The previously beloved son or daughter suddenly seems to disappear from life and is replaced by a sinister version of the same person. Parents . . . grieve for what they have lost."[13] So there is a loss (a metaphorical death) and a "sinister" replacement: the specter of "a stranger in the family," who, perhaps, was already haunting the family in shadowy form. ("Sinister": "impending or lurking danger that makes its presence felt indirectly by signs or portents.") As one parent is quoted as saying: "The Carole that I'd known for the previous twenty-four years was suddenly replaced by this woman who was saying she was a lesbian"; "I got very depressed, very much like I did when my husband died."[14]

In a different helping book, with dual retrospections foregrounded in the title, *Not Like Other Boys: Growing Up Gay: A Mother and Son Look Back* (1996), the *interval* between subliminal "awareness" and conscious "acceptance" is tapped as the source of family pain. It is as if suspension on the path to "growing up" (even "growing up gay") is itself on trial. Not the child's actual gayness, but the interval of inaccessibility to the child who was lurking all along—even though mother and son both related, secretly, separately, to the lurking child. In her preface to the book, the mother mournfully wonders out loud (but also through ellipsis): "Why didn't I ask him at eleven, or at thirteen, 'Do you think you might be . . . ?' [her ellipsis]. It was an unthinkable, out-of-the-question, horrifying inquiry to put to a boy who might, after all, be heterosexual. . . . Now, when I allow myself to imagine how that question . . . might have saved my son years of desolation, assuaged a childhood and adolescence of torment . . . I become distraught."[15] Perhaps not surprisingly, the son in his preface states as his goal in writing the book "to shorten the distance between acknowledgement and self-confidence in others like me"; he ends the preface by surfacing, it seems, from this painful interval: "I'm no longer lost."[16] But is he growing *up*?

The story is meant to be read as fairly typical (for boys, of course, who are not like other boys). The mother's subliminal awareness attaches to nothing so much as her son's enjoyment in "setting the table": "Our second son was turning into an odd little fellow." "The super-obedience, his non-cutup personality, his ability to sit quietly, the soft nature that had won him The Best Rester Award in nursery school": "I'm afraid he may grow up to be a homosexual," she confides to his kindergarten teacher, making her child the present carrier of a future narrative manifestation.[17] But he was already manifesting something (a feel-good wrongness, as we're about to see) and reacting to its manifestation. For at that time, as we learn from her son, he, at a neighbor's, "while [the mother] busied herself in the kitchen," "embarked on what I consider my first sexual experience" with her son Ted. "Even then, at age five, I knew it felt too good, and knew without being told that it was wrong."[18] Though Ted soon afterward moved away, "the phantom Ted was as close as I came to having a confidant for most of my prepubescent life."[19] Ghostly metaphors continue in his narrative: "By first grade, definable shadows appeared" and "the fear of my parents' finding out followed me like a sinister shadow through my childhood and adolescence." "This ongoing fear [moreover] propelled me into creating an obedient child persona, as if somehow that would overcome the blow that would ultimately come."[20] A child's conspicuous (and, to his mother, suspicious) goodness was the subtle sign of his ghostlike "self"—that subjectivity drawn to "taut, second-grade flesh"[21] and to the very boys he feared.

Finally, by the sixth grade, the author tells us, "words used to describe homosexuals seemed to describe my secret feelings."[22] He felt unlike other boys, who declared in reference to pervasive sleepover sex, "When we're fourteen, this has to stop."[23] (In this case, that is, he was not like other boys, since he would not stop acting like they had all acted together.) As for his mother, for whom "his secret . . . had been my secret"[24]—one recalls that elegant moment in *The Deep End* (2001) when the son's secret transfers with stunning, terrible force to occupy the mother, bodily and mentally, though their secrets are precisely not the same—this book's mother metaphorizes her "responsibility" for making her son "go sexually in the right direction" as a "black dog that kept nipping at my heels, following me wherever I went."[25] This figure is based perhaps on her belief that "wives were at home . . . to be benevolent watchdogs of their children and their neighborhood."[26] Ghost and dog: mother and son were each headed for words—some clinical, some clearly not—that would spell a mother's "crucifixion," we are told, and the "point of no return" for her son.[27] Until they could imagine him "growing up gay."

In the emerging social science studies on "sexual minorities," the interval of the child's self-ghosting, we might say (before it takes on the label "gay") is both measured (in terms of time) and explored through subjects' memories—all in the service of discovering "the typical developmental histories of gay youths."[28] For example, in a treatise titled ". . . And Then I Became Gay": Young Men's Stories (1998), researcher Ritch C. Savin-Williams, unabashedly seeking the "normative experiences" of "growing up gay," lays out a common developmental pattern, based on interviews—all to various extents retrospective—with young men (age ceiling: twenty-five). The pattern he delineates for going-to-be-gay boys goes like this: not fitting in, same-sex attractions, "the deniable" becomes "undeniable," "adoption" of "sexual identity or label"—in other words, "and then I became gay." We are given averages for each interval (an average of five years from same-sex attractions to label "homosexual" for those attractions; almost nine years from attraction-awareness to a "gay or bisexual identity").[29] Although Savin-Williams doesn't put it this way, history can be located in these intervals, since "the ages at which developmental milestones are reached . . . have been steadily declining from the 1970's to current cohorts of youth."[30] Therefore, the implied-child-in-ellipsis (whatever child predates ". . . and then I became gay") is increasingly coming closer to (or, one could say, coming in danger of, at ever earlier ages) community or clinical labels. These labels are more pointed than "strange," "weird," "odd," "queer," "clumsy," "The Artist," or even (as one boy reports being voted by grammar school classmates) "The Person Most Likely to Own a Gay Bar."[31] Or, to put it differently, gay "adoption" of their own child selves ("I was a gay child") may, in future years, appear ever earlier, sneaking ever closer to a public proclamation, "I am a gay child." What this specific labeling will mean for children's creative occulting of themselves in metaphors or narrative strings is, of course, anyone's guess. What will get lost through this way of being found?

A striking example of creative occulting appears in the film to which I alluded at the start of this section: The Hanging Garden (1996), which depicts an instance of queer-child-ghosting through the materializing metaphor of fat. In this film, out of Nova Scotia, gay man, fat teen, queer child, and haunted dog all come together to make a picture of sideways growth. The story is retrospective in that a gay man is returning to his family (after ten years away) to attend his sister's wedding. As the film unfolds, viewers see his fat teen self not only as a character in flashback (eating, being lonely, being hit by his father, having sex with a boy) but also as the film's primary ghost—since an image of him hanging dead above the garden (from the branch of a tree) keeps appearing to the viewer and to several other characters (also to himself). More intriguing, this primary ghost is made to stand for yet another ghost we glimpse only briefly: a "normal"-looking child (the gay-man-as-a-boy), who, we are told, didn't want "to play . . . sports, have any fights, [or] have a girlfriend." We see this ghost-child in the kitchen, his hand in the cookie jar, as the gay man tells his mother: "Skinny was the only thing you couldn't make me be . . . it felt good . . . I wasn't going anywhere."

Fat, we find, is a thick figuration and referent for a child (a sexual child) we cannot fully see. Fat is the visible effect, in this instance, of a child who cannot grow "up" in his family as his preferred self. So he grows sideways—literally, metaphorically. The queer child is occulted into something to be seen: a visible difference from the film's other boys (the only fat teen) that bespeaks a dead or dying growing up to the stature of straightness. The fat ghost hanging above the garden flowers (which grow and die in time-lapse photography) speaks not only a suicide threat—which the viewer is never sure occurred—but, more powerfully, moving suspension at the crossroads of adulthood. After being caught having sex with a friend (another young male), the teen is taken by his rather Catholic mother to a woman who is paid to take his virginity. Two virginities, sequentially lost, both losses leading nowhere ("I wasn't going anywhere"). Except perhaps to a hanging in the garden.

And something even stranger. When the gay man "awakens" from this flashback, he can hear his tomboy sister (whom, before this trip, he had never met) yelling at the dog: "You're dead . . . I hate you, you freaking flea bag." The dog, we realize, though he is old and has lost his sight, can always tell when a ghost is about. He fidgets and whimpers over both ghosts (child and teen) as if, though blind, he can see the unseen—the child and teen both lurking at the thresholds of everyone's consciousness. That the fifth-grade tomboy girl—along with the gay man—is herself bound up with the dog (who is the seer of sideways growth) foretells what we have next to learn. The girl is not the sibling of the now-gay man but actually his child (born of the woman he was sent to by his mother). Against his will, he has (re)produced a child—and, from all signs, she is a queer child (maybe a going-to-be-gay child, too). *The Hanging Garden* comes to an end when this parent-child duo, both named for flowers, Sweet William and Violet, who still act like siblings, head for the city. "Are we running away?" Violet asks her brother-father. "Yeah, sort of . . . no, we're just leaving," William answers.

And so *The Hanging Garden* shows the rather fraught relations of a gay man to what he may now regard, at this point in life, as his gay child self. By the terms of this film, this child is retrospective (he is hidden in time); he is occulted (he appears as a ghost); he is bound up with death—metaphorical death (in the image of a hanging)—but he gives birth to metaphors. The space of the garden where the fat ghost hangs is aesthetically moving and a treasure trove of metaphors for flowering and growth—though not a growing up as William's father had imagined.

The Grown "Homosexual"

Notice how the oddities of gay retrospection ("I was a gay child") make a second queer child seen: the grown "homosexual" who is fastened, one could say, to the figure of the child. The question of origins (When did you know? What may have been the cause?) keeps supplying so-called homosexuals with a sexual inner child. The grown homosexual has even often been metaphorically seen as a child. *Arrested development* is the official-sounding phrase that has often cropped up to describe the supposed sexual immaturity of homosexuals: their presumed status as dangerous children, who remain children in part by failing to have their own.

Who, one may ask, still uses this phrase, and where did it come from? Not surprisingly—the answer is tiring—it stays alive largely in certain political (and religious) rhetoric on the right. As a British evangelical leader states the matter (he is a former homosexual, he tells us): "I don't really believe there is such a thing as a true homosexual"; "it's a name we give to an arrested development, or an immature emotional state where we've got stuck."[32] A voice from the American religious right echoes: "Homosexuality is arrested development" and "most gays are stuck in the adolescent courtship stage, or what is called 'sexual liberation.'" Gays even spread their "symptoms of . . . arrested development" to the general population, "seen in plummeting birth rates, epidemics of adultery, divorce, out of wedlock childbirth" and so on.[33]

What is interesting—if these predictable instances are not—is the developmental history of "arrested development." It happens that contemporary users of this phrase—right-wing fundamentalists—would, if they checked, find themselves in bed with Darwin and, of course, Freud. The phrase as it develops is almost always negative, with the intriguing exception of its use at the hands of Freud, who is likely most responsible, nonetheless, for passing it on.

But to go back a little, we find that the *OED* lists example uses of the phrase by Sir Thomas Huxley (in 1859) and by Darwin in *The Descent of Man* (1871). Huxley is discussing "oceanic hydrozoa" (which are not, he says, "'arrested developments' of higher organisms"). Darwin is discussing what he calls "microcephalous idiots," who illustrate "a difference between arrested development and arrested growth, for parts in the former state continue to grow whilst still retaining their early condition."[34] By this rendering, arrested development is a certain kind of nonnormal growth, but growth nonetheless. And yet the section that follows upon "Arrests of

Development" in *Descent of Man* is one called "Reversion," where Darwin states: "When a structure is arrested in its development, but still continues growing . . . it may in one sense be considered as a case of reversion. . . . [T]he simple brain of a microcephalous idiot, in so far as it resembles that of an ape, may in this sense be said to offer a case of reversion."[35]

Famously, writers on decadent art and criminality—Max Nordau and Cesar Lombroso—picked up "reversion" and showcased it. Nordau scorned:

> He who places pleasure above discipline, and impulse above self-restraint [decadent artists like Oscar Wilde], wishes not for progress, but for retrogression to the most primitive animality. . . . They confound all the arts, and lead them back to the primitive forms they had before evolution differentiated them. Every one of their qualities is atavistic, and we know, moreover, that atavism is one of the most constant marks of degeneracy.[36]

Not just of degeneracy, but of criminality, held Lombroso (who wrote his author's preface to *Crime: Its Causes and Remedies* in the form of a letter to Nordau in 1906). Lombroso emphasized the "atavistic" origins of human criminality, the features of which corresponded to "savages," children, and/ or animals. Hence he urged that "born" "homo-sexuals," "who manifest their evil propensities from childhood," "should be confined from their youth, for they are a source of contagion and cause a great number of occasional criminals."[37]

Freud, by contrast, undercuts moralistic judgments against "homosexuality" at the same time that he uses the phrase "arrested development." In a famous letter to a young American homosexual's mother, Freud confides:

> Homosexuality is . . . no vice, no degradation, it cannot be classified as an illness; we consider it to be a variation of the sexual function produced by a certain arrest of sexual development. . . . It is a great injustice to persecute homosexuality . . . for a perverse orientation is far from being a sickness.[38]

What does Freud mean by "a certain arrest"? That "in every aberration from the normal sexual life [there is] a fragment of inhibited development and infantilism"?[39] Is homosexuality, then, a growing-sideways-only-sexually with no other psychological consequence, since "inversion is found in people who otherwise show no marked deviation from the normal"?[40] What is clear—even if the sum of Freud's phrases is not—is that a negative slant on *arrested development* was unmistakably continued by conservative, moralizing (and largely American) psychoanalysts writing after Freud. One analyst claimed that the homosexual "is ill in much the same way that a dwarf is ill—because he has never developed"; another found "petrified patterns of living" and "atrophied states" among homosexuals. Yet another stated that "most . . . homosexuals do not feel like adults. Rather

Kathryn Bond Stockton

they see themselves as children or adolescents."[41] And so we glimpse how religious fundamentalists came by their phrase—through the odd circuits of Darwin and Freud, who crafted uses that got taken up and developed by others with differing views. Strange bedfellows, Darwin and Freud, for Anglo-American fundamentalists.

How fat, then, are the senses of this phrase. And how nicely turned by queer textualities in the direction of sideways growth. *The Hanging Garden* twines its sense of nowhere-to-grow for a queer youth with its depictions of a growing sideways in among the blooms of mums—keeping mum—telling mum. The homosexual cultivates himself, even in the face of a family's arrested willingness to speak about (the ghost of) his developments.

The Child Queered by Freud

The ghostly "gay" child and the grown-"homosexual"-as-a-child. Two other children shadow these, though perhaps in seeming contrast, for up to this point we've been talking of the dangers of those queer children who will never be straight. But there is a type of dangerous child who, "if all goes well," will be straight, not gay, in a future incarnation, though this child can never be straight as a child. The child who answers to this riddle, of course, is the child queered by Freud (our third queer child): the not-yet-straight child who is, nonetheless, a sexual child with aggressive wishes. From wanting the mother to have its child, to wanting to have its father's baby, to wanting to kill its rival lover, the Freudian child (the child penned by Freud) looks remarkably, threateningly, precocious: sexual and aggressive. The Freudian parent, by contrast, looks regressive. In this sense: an oddly pedophilic fantasy emerges between "normal" husband and wife, who find they are "a phase apart psychologically."[42] Freud makes this point in his essay "Femininity," saying, "Even a marriage is not made secure until the wife has succeeded in making her husband her child."[43] And yet Freud regards this pedophilic marriage, in which the husband is metaphorized as his lover's child, as normative, marital, "genital maturity."[44] This from the man who pointed out that lesbians ("female homosexuals")—those who seemingly show a "certain arrest of development"—"play the parts of mother and baby with each other as often and as clearly as those of husband and wife."[45]

The sexually aggressive child, who is both eerily mature and infantilized, already floats in Victorian novels, reminding us that fiction queered the child before Freud—joined soon enough by the cinema's production of its odd children. Little Polly Home in Charlotte Brontë's 1853 novel *Villette* parrots, in the figure of her six-year-old person, the mother-wife conglomeration later sketched by Freud—all in relation, aggressively so, to two different men. That is, though an "infant," "a shawled bundle," "a mere doll," and one of those motherless children spawned by Victorian novels, Polly plays both mother and wife with her father and Graham (age sixteen), whom Polly comes to love (she calls him "'my dear boy,'" "adopted in imitation of his mother").[46] This precocity makes the narrator, Lucy Snowe, tell the reader, "When I say *child* I use an inappropriate and undescriptive term," for "this small stranger," this "minute thing," was "most unchild-like," praying like "some precocious fanatic," "growing old and unearthly," "lavishing her eccentricities regardlessly before me," proving "a perfect cabinet of oddities."[47] Strange for the reader—but also not—is the way in which Polly's motherly posture makes her act very much like a dog. Sitting "at [her] Papa's [Oedipal] feet" when not doting on him ("'I must hand his tea,'" she says, "as she intercepted the cup in passing, and would stir the sugar and put in the cream herself"),[48] Polly is his "pet." The young man's, too. "Bring me something particularly nice; that's a kind little woman," he tells Polly, who substitutes for his mother's close attentions but also lies "down on the carpet at his feet, her face to the floor," where Graham, "un-conscious of her proximity . . . push[es] her with his restless foot."[49] Later, he kisses "her little hot face and burning lips," having first "seduce[d] her attention" with an etching of a Blenheim spaniel, for which he demands "kisses" in "payment."[50]

The upshot of these miniature mating games is the way in which Polly—not grown up and, therefore, "queer" in Graham's vocabulary[51]—is the willing libidinal "playmate" for all three major players in these scenes. Not just for her father and Graham, that is, but for Lucy Snowe, too. At the point of greatest heartbreak (Polly's required departure from Graham), the cool Lucy Snowe (who confesses much later her own love for Graham) takes Polly to her breast:

> "Come to me," I said, wishing, yet scarcely hoping, that she would comply: for she was a most strange, capricious, little creature, and especially whimsi-cal with me. She came, however, instantly, like a small ghost gliding over the carpet. I took her in. She was chill; I warmed her in my arms. She trembled nervously; I soothed her. Thus tranquillized and cherished she at last slumbered.[52]

The homo- and autoerotic suggestions of Lucy's holding Polly, Lucy touch-ing upon her own desire through Polly's maternal, erotic aggressions, are implicit in Lucy's reference to "wishing, yet scarcely hoping" and in the sense that Miss Snowe, embracing this doll, even this pet, was warming, in part, her own chill, caressing her need to be "tranquillized and cherished."

The child's role in adult libidinized realizations, combining infantilized postures with strangely knowing gestures, is particularly intense in Henry James's fiction, as I have shown elsewhere and at length.[53] But turn for a moment to Hollywood cinema, to a moment when America was still not sexually revolutionized (or Stonewalled), to a film that notoriously helped to force the Hays Code to make newly possible "tasteful treatment[s]" of "homosexuality"—which, evidently, included the suicide at the film's end.[54] *The Children's Hour*, a 1961 film adapted from Lillian Hellman's 1934 play is the film I have in mind. In this movie with mainstream stars (Audrey Hepburn, James Garner, and Shirley MacLaine), a child with an unnamed aggressive motivation (at times it looks like jealousy, sometimes like resentment over simple discipline) and with the help of a child kleptomaniac, whom she blackmails into backing her, wrongly and willfully accuses her school's co-headmistresses (Karen and Martha) of being lovers. The school goes under; a libel suit (shades of Oscar Wilde) is lost by the two accused women; and one of these, Martha, confesses that she really did love the other, and then promptly hangs herself in her room. *The Children's Hour*, with its innocent storytime title that signals a fleeting temporality, ends with suspense as its finality. The time for possibility and clear restoration seems to run out at the end of a rope.

In fact, it appears that a sexual child (or at least a child with sexual knowledge) with aggressive wishes—aimed, it appears, at *in loco parentis*—puts a stop to sideways growth. For until this time, the hyphenated couple of Karen Wright and Martha Dobie, running the Wright-Dobie School, were not growing up to marriage and childbirth but were growing sideways in their labors for the school. Martha had no intention of marrying ("I have twenty children upstairs"), and Karen's marriage to Dr. Joe Cardin ("I delivered my hundreth baby today," he declares) was on hold. The child intervenes in this fertile delay not to straighten this bent trajectory, but to bend it further—and in public view. She gets her ideas of lesbianism from a book she's smuggled into school. She then attaches these ideas to a word she overhears describing Martha's "propensities since childhood," spoken by Martha's loudmouthed aunt. (The word is "unnatural," used in reference to Martha's possessiveness over Karen.)

What stuns viewers potentially in all of this is not the theme of "homosexuality" (at least not now) but the inversion of child/adult conventions. It is not that, in *The Children's Hour*, innocent childhood is put under threat by adult pathologies. Rather, in the film, adult legal innocence is threatened by quasi-pathological children (a compulsive liar and a kleptomaniac). Or, more intriguingly, adult *perversions* are clearly threatened by aggressive children. In addition, a pupil schools a teacher—through the clarifying act of her deception. The pupil's lie reveals to the teacher (Martha) her own latent feelings, making her pregnant, one might say, with the child's suggestion of her (retrospective) queerness: "You have something in you and you don't know it's there, and then one night a little girl . . . tells a lie and there for the first time you see it. You say to yourself, 'Did she sense it?' ... She found the lie with the ounce of truth."

In fact, one could claim that *The Children's Hour* follows the logic of most Wildean epigrams: the inverse, that is, is always true. What looks like guilt is innocence, but innocence is guilt. Before the child's lie, when they're still considered innocent, Martha and Karen look like a couple (hyphenated, partnered, Martha jealous). When accused of couplehood, they start to look innocent, since they make strong, convincing denials. However, when Karen speaks her innocence to Joe, she believes he must in some way think her guilty, so she sends him away. This act prompts the talk between the two accused teachers in which Martha claims her innocent love for her friend Karen, which, of course, suddenly blooms into rancid declarations of her guilt: "I've loved you like a friend, like thousands of other women have felt; you were a dear friend who was loved, that's all. ... But maybe I've loved you the way they said! Listen to me! ... There's always been something wrong. ... I can't keep it to myself any longer. I'm guilty. ... I feel so damn sick and dirty I can't stand it." Quite remarkably, after this scene, the lying child's grandmother comes to the women to admit their innocence (the lie now having been discovered as a lie). At the height of Martha's guilt (she is only guilty of wanting sex with Karen), their slate is wiped clean. Now, declared innocent, they have a perfect cover for what could become a full-blown affair, since their once-suspicious closeness would now function as the sign that they are now again their innocent selves. Rather than interrupt this dialectic, the film suspends it. The child slips out of the spectator's view (what becomes of her?), and the "homosexual" hangs postconfession. Hung jury on two different counts.

Of course, the most famous sexual child in Western depictions remains Lolita. What readers may not recall or notice is the crucial role of an animal metaphor in this book. *Lolita*'s queer child (in 1955) both advances and hides herself in a dog. Read for a dog (a bundle of motion each time we see one) and you will find clues to Lolita's surprising and hidden intents. In fact, we know that the dog is a clue to a Lolita mystery because Humbert tells us in an aside, "Every once in a while I have to remind the reader of my appearance much as a professional novelist, who has given a character of his some mannerism or a dog, has to go on producing that dog or that mannerism every time the character crops up in ... the book."[55] As we may notice, the dog is a sign that Quilty is lurking about Lolita and that she makes secret movements toward him. In the Enchanted Hunters Hotel, Lolita, we read, "sank down on her haunches to caress a pale-faced, blue-freckled, black-eared cocker spaniel swooning on the floral carpet under her hand—as who would not, my heart [Humbert adds]"; and yet what Lo is doing is "squatting, listening in profile, lips parted, to what the dog's mistress, [Quilty disguised as] an ancient lady swathed in violet veils, was telling her from the depths of a cretonne easy chair." "Lo [Humbert notes], leaving the dog as she would leave me some day, rose from her haunches."[56] Later, on their car trip west, Humbert panics that Lolita has escaped, only to find her cavorting with a dog:

> Oh Lolita! There she was playing with a damned dog, not me . . . but suddenly something in the pattern of her motions, as she dashed this way and that . . . struck me . . . there was an ecstasy, a madness about her frolics that was too much of a glad thing. Even the dog seemed puzzled by the extravagance of her reactions. . . . One of the bathers had left the pool and, half-concealed by the peacocked shade of trees, stood quite still . . . following Lolita with his amber eyes . . . his tight wet black bathing trunks bloated and bursting with vigor where his great fat bullybag was pulled up and back like a padded shield over his reversed beasthood. . . . And I also knew that the child, my child, was looking, enjoying the lechery of his look and was putting on a show of gambol and glee [with the dog].[57]

Indeed, Humbert comes to describe Lolita's disobedience to his wishes in doglike terms: not only is she "my reluctant pet," but "she would be, figuratively speaking, wagging her tiny tail, her whole behind in fact as little bitches do—while some grinning stranger accosted us and began a . . . conversation."[58]

For all of Humbert's obvious animus against Lolita's canine connections ("I loathe dogs," Humbert says in passing), we must recall that the dog (as both animal and metaphor) enters the story as Humbert's ally. It is a dog who chases the car that swerves and kills Lolita's mother, thus enabling Humbert's abduction, also by car, of his "car pet" from her Camp Q. Yet, though the dog seems to offer a Freudian wish fulfillment (bringing fake father and daughter together), the dog is clearly a motion without motive. Or, put more precisely, the dog is like Lolita on her bike, in a car, or just on a sex drive, *a body in motion with its motive force obscured*. The answer to the question that is chasing Humbert's tale—What drives Lolita?—is not so much Quilty as it is something hazier. The answer to the detective mystery is the motion of childhood sexuality.

Humbert, in fact, may drive Lolita hither and yon, but as the novel in a thousand ways indicates, metaphorically and quite literally, Dolly is always driving Humbert from behind. Communicating constantly with Quilty, who follows their every move a few lengths back, she is wrapped up in Quilty in the car that's chasing Humbert. For it's the great joke of the plot to have Humbert's "pet" be in league with Mr. Quilty, her preferred pedophile, who, with Lolita's knowledge and help, steers sad Humbert to a predetermined terminus in the state of Utah where both Dolly and her Quilty disappear. The queer child's agency in *Lolita* is, by definition, a detective fiction that defeats Humbert, since he forgets the simplest law of his own plot—*dogs chase cars.*

This way of answering a mystery with a mystery (children's motives appear in the hieroglyphics of their motions) makes the more compelling twin of Humbert Humbert not Clare Quilty but the law itself. Like Nabokov's pedophile—who is himself shockingly incurious about Lolita's wishes—American legal protections of the child rob children of their motives. In order to protect itself against a mystery, the law, like Humbert, can see only an innocence. To the motions of the child's body, and the wish of children to move in certain ways, the law is blind.[59]

The Child Queered by Innocence

These three models of dangerous children—the ghostly "gay" child, the grown "homosexual," and the child queered by Freud—present us with what for at least two centuries have often been viewed as antithetical to childhood: sex, crime, secrets, closets, or, indeed, any sense of what the police like to call, in common parlance, "a past." The child is the specter of who we were when there was nothing yet behind us. Which brings us to the fourth queer child we must consider—the one made famous by so many landmark studies of childhood and by the romantic poets, who, along with Euro-American legal systems, have nurtured it.[60] This would be the seemingly normative child—or the child who, on its path to normativity, seems safe to us and whom we, consequently, seek to safeguard at all cost. I am speaking, of course, of the child made strange (though appealing) to us by its all-important "innocence." This is a form of normative strangeness, one might say; from the standpoint of adults, innocence is alien, since it is "lost" to the very adults who assign it to children. Adults retrospect it through the gauzy lens of (what they attribute to) the child. This is the child for whom, we imagine, sex itself seems shockingly queer.

Volumes may be spoken of the child queered by innocence over several centuries. Philippe Ariès, in a groundbreaking book that appeared in French two years before *The Children's Hour* hit film screens (the book appeared in English as *Centuries of Childhood* in 1962) was the pioneering voice in historicizing "innocence." Exploring the family not as a reality but as "an idea," Ariès explained why there was "no place for [the concept of] childhood" in the Middle Ages and thus how childhood-as-an-idea evolved "from immodesty to innocence" only in the middle of the seventeenth century.[61] Ariès's thesis (and those of writers who later extended it) turns on the axes of literacy, education, legislation, and shame. The story goes—I imagine most know it—for the child to be born as a cultural idea, adulthood must be seen as a wholly different state, as something that the child to begin does not possess and therefore must acquire in the place of innocence. Adulthood must be something a child approaches gradually, legally, as it takes on, by degrees, the secrets of adult linguistic codes. With the changing conditions of literacy (the appearance of the printing press dividing children from literate adults), with the changing conditions of education (the increasing emergence, first in Scotland, of a graduated curriculum), and with the changing conditions of censorship (what is thought essential to withhold from children—sexual knowledge heading the list), "the child," as we like to imagine we know it, began to take shape. It is a creature (quite different from adults) of gradual growth and managed delay, bolstered by laws that ideally will protect it from its own participation in its pleasure and its pain.[62] For if the child is innocent it is also weak. "Weakness" and "innocence," Ariès claims, are the twin pillars of the child's "reflection of divine purity,"[63] requiring of its keepers both safeguarding measures and strengthening help. Adults must walk the difficult line of keeping the child at once what it is (what adults are not) and leading it toward what it cannot (at least, as itself) ever be (what adults are).

What, then, do children queered by innocence share? They all share estrangement from what they approach: the adulthood against which they must be defined. This is why "innocent" children are strange. They are seen as normative but also not like us, at the same time. The contours of this normative strangeness may explain why children, as an idea, are likely to be both white and middle-class. It is a privilege to need to be protected—and, indeed, to be sheltered—and thus to have a childhood. Not in spite of privilege, then, but because of it, the all-important feature of weakness sticks to these markers (white and middle-class) and helps to signal innocence.

The complex poem "The Little Black Boy" (1789) in William Blake's *Songs of Innocence* turns upon this point.[64] It hits the wall of interpretive dilemmas precisely because it gives us children of two different colors. The narrating black boy announces, at the start, his rather mixed relation to central terms: "My mother bore me in the southern wild, / And I am black, but O! my soul is white; / White as an angel is the English child: / But I am black as if bereav'd of light." Strange to say, what he, the little black boy, is really bereaved of, come to find out, is the *weakness* of whiteness, which is so central to the sign of innocence (and, by extension, to privilege and childhood). The black boy, quite simply, is not weak enough to come across as innocent. He is a paragon of strength and experience. How do we know? What signals this experience? His black skin. Or so his mother tells him. He has experienced, intensely on his skin, the burning rays of God's own love. He's burned black. And so his blackened skin is the sign of "bearing" God,

▼ Growing Sideways

which of course requires (and also fashions) strength. Or, as his also blackened mother narrates: "We are put on earth a little space. / That we may learn to bear the beams of love, / And these black bodies and this sun-burnt face / Is but a cloud and like a shady grove. / For when our souls have learn'd the heat to bear, / The cloud will vanish." If the angel metaphor excludes the little black boy ("White as an angel is the English child")—or just eludes him—the blackened boy participates in tropes of cloud and shade.

No wonder this poem has no companion in *Songs of Experience*. (There is no need. It is about experience.) No wonder the critics who war with each other over the poem's ultimate meaning largely agree that the poem is too complex for *Songs of Innocence,* that these ambiguities are deepened, not resolved, by the illustrations, and that the poem is so elaborately about learning through suffering that the black boy seems oddly superior to the white boy.[65] What he actually is, is stronger, and thus less privileged. "And thus I say to little English boy: / When I from black and he from white cloud free, / And round the tent of God like lambs we joy, / I'll shade him from the heat till he can bear / To lean in joy upon our father's knee." Freed from their color clouds—though as they meet in the metaphor of lamb, we likely sense a dominant color—one boy still seems too advanced for innocence.

In the 1990s there are historically specific echoes of this problem. Experience is still hard to square with innocence, making depictions of streetwise children (who are often neither white nor middle-class) hard to square with "children." The ingenious solution to this problem (of children lacking the privilege of both weakness and innocence) is to endow these children with abuse. For as odd as it may seem, suffering certain kinds of abuse, from which they need protection and to which they don't consent, working-class children or children of color may come to seem more "innocent."

To take just one example, in the feminist film production of Dorothy Allison's 1993 book *Bastard Out of Carolina* (1996, directed by Anjelica Huston), the working-class protagonist, a child named Bone, is raped on-screen, at agonizing length, as she is made to sit against her will on her stepfather's lap. Why was this scene allowed to be shown? (Remember that the 1997 Adrian Lyne film of *Lolita* was nearly banned from American theaters due to its depictions of a sexual child.) Perhaps because its unquestioned brutality (showing the child's need for protection and her weakness in this instance) confirms the child's innocence. But innocence of what? Not sexual knowledge; the child sadly knows what is being done to her, and she is bearing it. Rather, she is innocent of any consent. Unlike Lyne's and Nabokov's Lolita, there is no counter sexual motion on her part. No pleasure in her own world. And no mystery. Knowingly, and fully unambiguously, Bone *does not* consent. Evidently, this equal-opportunity innocence (for the underprivileged) is worthy of our sight.

The Interval of Animal

One more turn remains in this essay. As fraught as they are, the versions of the queer child I have been discussing up to this point are on some level easily seen, even if their twists are not always understood. Now I want to show how even the peculiar densities of certain modernist novels—especially their sly experiments with metaphor—shed their light on the many issues, aesthetic and political, surrounding my project called "The Queer Child." In fact, I have claimed that three famous novels from the twenties and thirties are already braiding versions of the queer child—*Nightwood* most complexly— as they enter the interval of animal as a central marker of queer child time. *Nightwood* is only the most lavish rendering of problems shared by Virginia Woolf and Radclyffe Hall in shaping plots of sideways growth.

A woman like a child playing with and as a dog. I left this image hanging at the start of my essay. Now it's time to say that this is not a species of political invective ("lesbians are dogs"). Nor is it simply a story of revenge: Djuna Barnes's "life with Thelma [Wood]," as she liked to put it (in dog terms: my girlfriend was a bitch). This is a large literary tale. A modernist fantasia. For Barnes's end to *Nightwood, Nightwood*'s freakish close, an-nounces a problem known so well to Virginia Woolf and Radclyffe Hall (also to Stein, H.D., and Nabokov): the way in which a dog saves a girl from crippling metaphors by himself becoming a figure she can play with. This makes the dog a political animal, as we shall see, one who intervenes in his-torical prematurity and in the modernist abstraction of Time, granting to children a precious kind of shelter for their feelings and their growth.

Nightwood's readers may be forgiven if the novel's final scene over-runs their sympathies, for the critics themselves are a study in how to skirt around a dog. Some imply that *Nightwood* does not really end here (has already ended with the scene before, making the dog scene merely an "epilogue"). Others substitute juicy author gossip for a reading of the end, stressing that Barnes, though she *did* intend revenge against her former lover, Thelma Wood, did not intend the ending to seem crassly sexual. Still others say that attempts to make meaning from the ending reveal a reader too attached to meaning making (a reader with a bone?).[66] Brave strategies all. And yet any reader of *Nightwood* I have known still wants to know what to do with the dog.

Obviously, something in *Nightwood* perplexes us. Barnes's fantastic mu-seum of metaphor, moving us forward "in recoil," along "rococo halls, giddy with plush . . . designs," is busy dazzling some estrangement.[67] No won-der we as readers feel dazzled and estranged. We realize, as well, that time in *Nightwood*—that modernist obsession—emerges as a problem wound around women who are loving women. Time is what separates same-sex lovers metaphorized as mother and child; exiled, as it were, to separate generations, even though, by dint of age, they are each other's peers:

> [Nora] . . . should have had a thousand children and Robin . . . should have been all of them.[68]

> In Nora's heart lay the fossil of Robin, intaglio of her identity, and about it for its maintenance ran Nora's blood.[69]

> "Sometimes," Nora said, "[Robin] would sit at home all day looking out of the window or playing with her toys, trains, and animals. . . . Sometimes, if she got tight by evening, I would find her standing in the middle of the room in boy's clothes, rocking from foot to foot . . ."[70]

> There goes [Nora] mother of mischief, running about, trying to get the world home.[71]

This figurative mother-child relation (Nora-mother, Robin-child) dooms these lovers to separate temporalities, dooms them to a time that by definition can never arrive: the time when mother and child will inhabit the same generation, an impossibility akin to waiting for night to be day, an impassability akin to the historical prematurity of queer love in the 1930s (in a world so clearly not ready to receive it). Simply, time is out of joint for the woman who loves other women, and so cannot "grow up" in this relation. Generational time is a choke hold wound around her neck that the dog must undo. This is what the dog is doing when we see him. The dog is undoing the effects of a metaphor (women lovers as "mother" and "child") when he and Robin lie down, side by side; when she herself is like a dog. That is to say, in the place of one metaphor, the dog seems to offer his body for another, addressing, as he does so, a problem of time. The dog's time machine turns vertical impasse (the "child's" impossible reach for its "mother" as its lover) into a new horizontal relay: a lateral movement of lovers toward each other—if one consents for a time to *being dog.*

This is a dynamic that French philosopher Gilles Deleuze and psychoanalyst Félix Guattari might appreciate, given their reflections on being-and-becoming animal in *Mille Plateaux* (1980; *A Thousand Plateaus*). For these theorists, a "plateau" (a sort of sideways growth?) is a state of "intensity," leading to "irreducible dynamisms . . . and implying other forms of expression." One such plateau is what they call "becoming-animal": an "alliance" between human and animal that "traverse[s] human beings and sweep[s] them away."[72] Such an alliance is "anti-Oedipal"—has "nothing to do with a sentimental or domestic relation" or "filiation"; rather, it is "an unnatural participation" of the human with the animal.[73] Quite importantly, this becoming-animal is "a question . . . not of development or differentiation but of movement and rest, speed and slowness."[74] (Deleuze and Guattari speak of "transport" in this context.) Children are particularly "moved" by animals in this way, and "continually undergo becomings of this kind," leading Deleuze and Guattari to note (in rather general terms) "the assemblages a child can mount in order to solve a problem from which all exits are barred him."[75]

Given these suggestive terms, one might wonder how Deleuze and Guattari would read the dog in *Nightwood*, along with Robin's linkage (as the queer child) to becoming-animal. It is likely they would see the dog as largely anti-Oedipal, since he interrupts the Oedipal metaphor that keeps Robin and Nora stranded in their temporalities of mother and child. They would surely read "unnatural participation" and "alliance" between the dog and Robin in the novel's final scene, leading to an obvious state of "intensity" and to "dynamisms" of a strange sort. But would these theorists trip up on metaphor? Would they be too tempted to dismiss it as "resemblance" (just as they might be tempted to dismiss the dogs in *Mrs. Dalloway* and *The Well of Loneliness* as sentimental pets)? They strongly claim: "This [becoming-animal] will not involve imitating a dog, nor an analogy of relations. I must succeed in endowing the parts of my body with relations of speed and slowness that will make it become dog, in an original assemblage proceeding neither by resemblance nor by analogy."[76] Would Deleuze and Guattari be able to see in metaphor a crucial kind of "transport" and therefore relations of movement and rest, slowness and speed?

Commonly, metaphor and simile appear in terms of translation: a metaphor translating one thing as another (a lover as a child), making something "like" something else, pictured "as if" it were something else, the unfamiliar made to seem like something we know, even though likeness must hail from difference (Christians are not sheep). But what if metaphor, I have been suggesting, were grasped not solely in terms of translation, but in terms of transport and time, *a transport across a chasm of time*? Two kinds of time travel would then emerge, both of which surface in *Nightwood*'s dog: (1) the time it takes a metaphor's "vehicle" literally to travel to its tenor, making us wait for or hurry through the "carryover" (metaphor from the Greek *metapherein*, "carry over") from one sense to the other (the time it takes to get from "dog" to the meaning it make possible); (2) the time relations that get rearranged in a metaphor's vehicle (in the novel's chief example, the way in which women are temporally torn asunder if they are figured as mother and child).

Nightwood offers both time travels. As to the first, we know that metaphors can offer shortcuts in what are often rapid carryovers from vehicle to tenor, making something grasped more quickly, because made more familiar, by comparison. And yet metaphors can also take time. In Barnes they do, and generally the most estranging ones, taking no small time to construe, cause the most delay in plot advance. Indeed, though the novel might not seem to move at all, or so it has seemed to many readers, it actually *moves by suspensions* largely made up of metaphors. Barnes at times even offers metaphors that seem to figure this aspect of her metaphors: "as if privacy . . . by the very sustaining power of its withdrawal kept the body eternally moving downward, but in one place, and perpetually before the eye."[77] But can a metaphoric suspension address a dilemma posed dramatically as a political and historical impasse? In the case of *Nightwood*, the dilemma of two lovers ("mother" and "child") who cannot share their own historical light of day? Can the estranging metaphor of dog cause us to encounter the potential for time travel held suspended in a metaphor's vehicle? Where can the queer child in "dog" go?

Woolf, it appears, contemplates these matters in her brief portrait of queer child with dog, coming to these issues, so crucial to Barnes, a decade ahead. I am thinking, of course, of *Mrs. Dalloway* (1925). One formal project of that novel is delay. Mrs. Dalloway, if she could, would make time hang. She works to create suspended states that make one's flow with time less terrifying. Pause, exquisite in itself, prepares a woman for exquisite transport—though what we often see is the pause.

> So [Mrs. Dalloway] . . . felt often as she stood hesitating one moment on the threshold of her drawing-room, an exquisite suspense, such as might stay a diver before plunging while the sea darkens and brightens beneath him, and the waves which threaten to break, but only gently split their surface, roll and conceal and encrust as they just turn over the weeds with pearl.[78]

Dalloway-as-diver. The action of her dive may be hung upon the threshold, but, while it hangs, the ongoing threatening motion of the waves, given to us in metaphoric suspension, continues to roll toward its climax in "pearl." The metaphor, in this way, actually moves the diver to safety (and to pleasure) before there is any literal plunge.

The novel's sapphic material also comes in on a pause, first with Clarissa's rendering of orgasm, in a rush of metaphors, as a suspension that is also a flowing, a moving pause. ("Only for a moment . . . a tinge like a blush which . . . , as it spread, one yielded to its expansion, and rushed to the farthest verge and there quivered . . . swollen with some astonishing significance . . . which split its thin skin and gushed and poured. . . . Then, for that moment . . . a match burning in a crocus."[79] Then the pleasures of moving suspensions, if anything, intensify with her extended memories of herself (at age eighteen) with Sally Seton—her most erotic pause before her plunge into marriage: "She felt that she had been given a present [by Sally], wrapped up, and told just to keep it, not to look at it—a diamond, something infinitely precious, wrapped up."[80] (Again she rides a "vehicle" that takes her to jewels: a diamond that is pointing away from her engagement to a male suitor.) More striking yet, Woolf lets Clarissa see herself repeated in another generation, as she watches her daughter's relations (at age seventeen) with a female history tutor ("the woman who crept in to steal and defile," according to Clarissa; a woman old enough to be, like Clarissa, her daughter's mother). What is so intriguing is the mother's upset over her daughter's participation in a kind of love—she hopes it is "a phase"—that the mother still worships as an interval (that magical sideways time-out-of-time with Sally Seton). The worry is not "my child is queer," but "is my child being queer in my way?" Evidently, what matters is the kind of sapphic relation that ushers one's daughter into womanhood. And yet, Woolf insists, an obvious interval separates a mother from her child; the mother cannot deliver her daughter into a future that is her own past. The child cannot be in mother-time.

Which is how the dog comes into play. The dog is a sign of playful rebellion, a sign that Clarissa's daughter, Elizabeth, will not assimilate completely into her mother's sense of future—a growing up to knowing the right shoes and gloves. Elizabeth, we are told, "cared not a straw for either of them [shoes or gloves]. . . . [She] really cared for her dog most of all. . . . Still, better poor Grizzle [the dog]," thinks Clarissa, "than Miss Kilman ['Elizabeth's seducer']."[81] One gets a sense of the dog as pause—the dog as marking Elizabeth's own space for suspension and lateral movement on the threshold of adulthood, which makes the dog a safer choice than Miss Kilman (at least in Clarissa's eyes) but also an ally in schemes of resistance. The dog may specifically defend the child from metaphors of a particular, damaging sort. These are the kinds of figures of speech that carry (truly, hand over) the girl to conventional plots: metaphors culturally shared and repeated in a kind of fixed chain.

> It was beginning. . . . People were beginning to compare [Elizabeth] to poplar trees, early dawn, hyacinths, fawns, running water and garden lilies; and it made her life a burden to her . . . and she had to go to parties, and London was so dreary compared to being alone in the country with her father and the dogs.[82]

And later:

> (She was like a poplar, she was like a river, she was like a hyacinth, Willie Titcomb was thinking. Oh how much nicer to be in the country and do what she liked! She could hear her poor dog howling, Elizabeth was certain.)[83]

In at least three passages, mention of Elizabeth's loveliness by others is set beside her own attention to her dog. Even, at last, on the novel's final page, amid a father's delight at seeing his daughter "come out" as a lovely young woman, the dog appears to undercut the daughter's disappearance into Oedipal pride:

> Richard [Dalloway] was proud of his daughter. . . . He had looked at her, he said, and he had wondered, Who is that lovely girl? and it was his daughter! That did make her happy. But her poor dog was howling.[84]

Dalloway's hints of the dog-as-pause, as a tie to horizontal relations that resist the talk of "growing up," swell to almost absurd proportions in Radclyffe Hall. For in *The Well of Loneliness* (1928) animals and "inverts" talk to one another in "a quiet language" outside of English.[85] They exchange vows. They pledge devotion. They create a contemplative space in which the invert rehearses her exclusion from a world that is not yet ready to receive her. (The female servant with whom she, at the tender age of seven, falls in love calls her a "queer kid" and a "queer fish.")[86] In short, the world of horses and dogs offers what young-women-who-are-not-seeking-men cannot so easily or otherwise discover: a lateral community that understands, affirms, and, perhaps most crucially, offers sorrow for unsupported choices:

> David [the dog] sat watching with luminous eyes in which were reflected [Mary's] secret troubles. . . . He nearly broke his own heart. . . . He wanted to lay back his ears and howl with despair to see her unhappy. He wanted to make an enormous noise, the kind of noise wild folk make in the jungle— lions and tigers and other wild folk that David had heard about from his mother. . . . But instead he abruptly licked Mary's cheek—it tasted peculiar, he thought, like sea water.[87]

With this young woman's troubles in his eyes, and with the lateral breaking of his heart, the dog (inseparable from his howling) is truly a figure for what it means to be beside oneself with sorrow. Yet as a figure for Mary-beside-herself, the dog is, in some respects, a metaphor that licks her, tasting her tears. He even thinks in similes ("it tasted peculiar, he thought, like sea water").

The dog, to be sure, renders not only someone-beside-herself. Because he himself cannot grow generationally in human time (though he has a mother), the dog is a figure for lateral growth. Like the child who will never be straight (who puts the goal of approved couplehood on perpetual delay), he grows sideways in relation to his mistress. Further, if the dog marks a space for the child the women between them cannot produce, he is at least compensation for a sorrow: sorrow for the historical prematurity of the love of lateral growth:

And this sadness mingling with that of the house, widened into a flood that compassed Mary and through her David, and they both went and sat very close to Stephen [the novel's heroine] on the study divan. As the twilight gradually merged into dusk, these three must huddle even closer together— David with his head upon Mary's lap, Mary with her head against Stephen's shoulder.[88]

The queer lovers' dog (the messianic David) finally stands as witness to the novel's overarching lament over interval: "How long? How long?" (This is the novel's economical phrase for historical impasse.) And so in a very strange close of its own, Hall's novel ends with its invert, Stephen, just having permanently parted from Mary, being watched by David, their beloved dog. As it happens, he is watching his mistress being haunted by historical prematurity: haunted by the ghosts of unborn going-to-be-unacknowledged children, along with the ghosts of dead queer friends, pleading for their right to existence:

Oh, but they were many, these unbidden guests. . . . The quick, the dead, and the yet unborn. . . . In their madness to become articulate through her, they were tearing her to pieces. . . . They were everywhere now, cutting off her retreat. . . . [A]t the cry of their suffering the walls fell and crumbled: "We are coming Stephen . . . and our name is legion—you dare not disown us!" . . . They possessed her. Her barren womb became fruitful—it ached with its fearful and sterile burden. It ached with the fierce yet helpless children who would clamour in vain for their right to salvation.[89]

So Hall's novel, rooted in nineteenth-century realist and sentimental fiction, ends with an almost gothic depiction of the impossibilities of queer love and childhood in Hall's time. Stephen is now the metaphorical mother of melodramatically occulted queer children ("they possessed her," "her barren womb became fruitful"). And though the dog sees her suffering from these ghosts—"they were tearing her to pieces"—David, the dog, as a savior still to come, can only crouch and tremble with eyes of amber, struck by anguish.

Nightwood, too, ends with "The Possessed" (the final chapter title). It seems as if a lover has been suddenly possessed by the spirit of a dog. But can the figure of the dog this time serve not just as witness to historical impasse but also as a vehicle (a metaphor's vehicle) by which two women are transported to each other? Can the dog facilitate a moving delay? As it happens, Barnes's dense opening echoes Hall's: the birth of a child, "heavy with impermissible blood," who is ejected into a life that won't receive it.[90] However, this is not a queer kid of Hall's sort (not yet, that is) but the child of a Jew, who feels "that the great past might mend a little if he bowed low enough."[91] Barnes, we recall, in a much-discussed move, makes her novel's Jews and homosexuals windows onto each other's pain.[92] And it is this child—generationally burdened, to put it mildly, given that he carries four centuries of memories—who, when he is grown, attempts to "dazzle his own estrangement."[93] Indeed, it is this child—and this very phrase, "dazzle . . . estrangement"—that links the novel's political allegory (its commentary on historical prematurity) to the literary inventions that feed it, which themselves may be fed by revenge. In other words, being inventive in her grudge against her former lover, Djuna Barnes—wittingly?—fashions a stunning political swipe against what blocks a lateral growth.

Importantly, the strategy of "dazzl[ing] . . . estrangement" is shared by members of the Berlin circus, who enter the novel as characters connected to *Nightwood*'s Jew. One, in particular, known as Frau Mann, holds a key to understanding Barnes's range of metaphors: how the novel begins with suspensions that look much more like limbo than like movement. Frau Mann's occupation, for instance, *is* suspension. She works the trapeze: "Her legs had the specialized tension common to aerial workers; something of the bar was in her wrists, the tan bark in her walk."[94] If, from this description, she seems to have embodied her aerial occupation—such that it is hard to distinguish metaphor from physical description ("something of the bar was in her wrists"), it is because Frau Mann *becomes* the vehicle to her tenor, metaphor turning strangely material:

> She seemed to have a skin that was the pattern of her costume: a bodice of lozenges, red and yellow, low in the back and ruffled over and under the arms . . . one somehow felt they ran through her as the design runs through hard holiday candies, and the bulge in the groin where she took the bar, one foot caught in the flex of the calf, was as solid, specialized and as polished as oak. The stuff of her tights was no longer a covering, it was herself; the span of the tightly stitched crotch was so much her own flesh that she was as unsexed as a doll.[95]

Candied by her costume (costume as anatomy, and anatomy still destiny), the trapeze artist, whose job is suspension, seems remarkably sewn up in metaphor, going nowhere.

Believe it or not, this is precisely the kind of sewing up that the dog will undo, when the queer child enters *into* him. But we are still a ways off from this possession. Indeed, as we now roll her onto the stage, asleep on her bed, she, the queer child, hardly seems a candidate for breaking out of anything—never mind that her name is Robin, promising material or metaphoric flight. She seems enclosed (even entombed) by Barnesian metaphors, offering the kind of portrait you will not likely see at the cinema or on *Will & Grace*:

> *On a bed,* surrounded by a confusion of potted plants, exotic palms and
> cut flowers, faintly over-sung by the notes of unseen birds, which seemed
> to have been forgotten—left without the usual silencing cover, which,
> like cloaks on funeral urns, are cast over their cages at night by good
> housewives—half flung off the support of the cushions from which, in
> a moment of threatened consciousness she had turned her head, *lay the*
> *young woman,* heavy and dishevelled.[96]

This is our queer child. And this is a sentence that Woolf might have written. We notice how the sentence base is promised but suspended until the
last line ("On a bed . . . lay the young woman"). The figure on the bed, surrounded by plants that are over-sung by birds who should have been covered by something "like cloaks on funeral urns," begins to hint at the queer
child's peculiar inaccessiblity to others or herself.

But I believe the paragraph that follows this suspension demonstrates
Barnes's own mad metaphorics, taking us to a remarkable portrait of the
queer child's hung-up growth:

> The perfume that her body exhaled was of the quality of that earth-flesh,
> fungi, which smells of captured dampness and yet is so dry, overcast with
> the odour of oil of amber, which is an inner malady of the sea, making her
> seem as if she had invaded a sleep incautious and entire. Her flesh was the
> texture of plant life, and beneath it one sensed a frame, broad, porous and
> sleep-worn, as if sleep were a decay fishing her beneath the visible surface.
> About her head there was an effulgence as of phosphorous glowing about
> the circumference of a body of water—as if her life lay through her in
> ungainly luminous deteriorations—the troubling structure of the born
> somnambule, who lives in two worlds—meet of child and desperado.[97]

This, evidently, is how you bury a queer child under metaphor, making
her seem dramatically submerged and held down under her culture's consciousness—even her own. Metaphor entirely covers over her body ("her
flesh was the texture of plant life"). And yet, though these descriptions
make the figure described seem unavailable to any kind of motion (even
the back-and-forth sort that comes with Frau Mann's trapeze), Robin's costume is at least more alive (more vegetable than mineral, if not yet animal).
Hers is more organic than polished oak; and *"life* lay through her," we are
told, not designs of hard holiday candies (though this is a life, importantly
so, of "ungainly luminous deteriorations"). Indeed, there may be more
hope for life in her decay (not to mention in her phosphoric glow) than in
Frau Mann's stitchings. The woman/child/desperado may awake, since we
learn she has "invaded" a sleep.

Whose sleep does she, the queer child, "invade"? Perhaps not hers alone.

If this is so, her sleep suspension may stand for something—may at least imply a waiting that is actively signaling its delay, like a car with motor running that is not yet put in motion. And now we must recall that Robin, figured by *Nightwood* as a child, is also the novel's sign of an invert (in this case, a girlboy). Intriguingly, *Nightwood* imagines the invert as the poster child of fairy tales: "It was they [inverts] who were spoken of in every romance that we ever read. The girl lost, what is she but the Prince found? . . . We were impaled in our childhood upon them as they rode through our primers. . . . They go far back in our lost distance where what we never had stands waiting."[98] Robin, the invert, is where the future has not arrived, where something from our childhood—our love of the invert—has never grown up into culture's day. This "thin blown edge of our reverie," along which edge what is waiting may awaken, summons two feelings: "terror and joy," which are themselves "wedded somewhere back again into a formless sea where a swan (would it be ourselves, or her or him, or a mystery of all) sinks crying."[99] This is a wonderfully dense image of queer child ghosting.

Indeed, this sinking beauty is befitting of *Nightwood*'s sleeping beauty, "where what we never had stands waiting." Nora, in fact, the metaphorical mother, can touch on her "child" only from the place of its parting (where the swan sinks crying?). No wonder the trauma of *Nightwood*'s lesbians suggests the metaphorics of amputation:

> Robin's absence, as the night drew on, became a physical removal, insupportable and irreparable. As an amputated hand cannot be disowned because it is experiencing *a futurity*, of which the victim is its forebear, so Robin was an amputation that Nora could not renounce. As the wrist longs, so her heart longed, and dressing she would go out into the night that she might be "beside herself," skirting the cafe in which she could catch a glimpse of Robin.[100]

"Amputation" begins to tip the vertical mother/child metaphor on its side. Robin, according to the terms of this metaphor, no longer issues from Nora as a child but as a lopped-off hand, something that has a more lateral existence, postamputation, than a generational one. Amputation, then, importantly differs from abortion. It imagines not a wholesale destruction of "the child" (or "the mother," for that matter), but the kind of separation from these terms that puts one beside oneself. More complexly, by virtue of the amputation metaphor, the lover-mother is forced to sever herself from a futurity, which she cannot renounce but in which she, at the moment, has no hand. Left empty-handed, the metaphor of mother shows its trauma to the reader.

This, incidentally, is the brilliance of *Nightwood*. Unlike Hall's more public tale, caught up by the censors, *Nightwood*'s sense of historical impasse (and thus of prematurity) is not worn on its sleeve but on its missing limb, to be recognized by those who themselves are severed from the too-easy promise of procession and attachment. *Nightwood* knows that if your lover-as-lost-child is approaching you, her destination may well be your dog.

Strikingly, the novel's philosophy of the night is tied to a theology of the lost child, who finds its own destination in a beast. This philosophy is delivered to us by the quack abortionist—the novel's parody of Sigmund Freud—Dr. Matthew O'Connor:[101]

> They [the French] think of the two [night and day] as one continually and keep it before their mind as the monks who repeat, "Lord Jesus Christ, Son of God, have mercy upon me!" Bowing down from the waist, the world over they go, that they may revolve about the Great Enigma—as a relative about a cradle—... [using the back of the head] when looking at the beloved in a dark place, and she is a long time coming from a great way. We swoon with the thickness of our own tongue when we say, "I love you," as in the eye of a child lost a long while will be found the contraction of that distance—a child going small in the claws of a beast, coming furiously up the furlongs of the iris.[102]

It is fascinating that a temporal quandary—the enigmatic coupling of night and day—gets turned, by the doctor, toward a stranded beloved who "is a long time coming from a great way." As if it naturally would explain such a strandedness, the figure of the child suddenly appears. More pointedly, a simple declaration of love ("I love you") takes a detour through a distance: one held in the eye of a child. According to this metaphor, the child holds in its eye an image of the distance it would have to travel in order not to be lost to its beloved (an issue as intriguingly historical and political as it is erotic). Layered onto this "contracted distance" is the image of a child (attacked? embraced? or just "kept small"?) in the claws of a beast. This puzzling image storms up the eye—flowers, even, in the image of the iris—as if to insist itself as an image that must be seen.

Here may be why: Early in the novel when Robin and Nora meet at the circus, Robin flees the gaze of a beast: the "powerful lioness ... with its yellow eyes afire ... [who] thrust [her paws] through the bars."[103] This animal, importantly, has keen links to both sorrow and suspension, since "her eyes flowed in tears that never reached the surface ... as if a river were falling behind impassable heat." Here might be a Barnesian block to certain forms of sentimentality—think of Hall's tearful lamentations. The Barnesian interval of animal, however, is moving in its own right. It is a beautiful moving suspension, embedding subtle movement (here a flowing) inside an emotion: these hung tears. In fact, what looks like suspension-as-limbo may be a canny gloss on transport. Animals, in their sorrowful engagement with our world, according to *Nightwood*, harbor secret forms of travel—forms of time travel. At the start of the novel, Dr. O'Connor mentions the cow he encountered in a cellar (in the midst of a bombing raid), a cow with "tears soused all over her great black eyes." "And I thought," says O'Connor, "there are directions and speeds that no one has calculated, for believe it or not that cow had gone somewhere very fast that we didn't know of, and yet was still standing there."[104]

For these reasons, I have to believe that the demon possession at the conclusion to *The Well of Loneliness*—the grown "homosexual" haunted by children who may "tear her to pieces"—gets revised at the end of *Nightwood*. For what better way for *Nightwood*'s "child" (who is simultaneously the grown "homosexual") to get into her lover's presence and her *present* than to enter the spirit of her dog: one not removed by generations from its mistress, one who openly cries in pain and pleasure, and one who, past the censors, can freely get into a woman's lap. Robin has taken her status as a child into her body all along, with "the face of an incurable yet to be stricken with its malady," who "yet carried the quality of the 'way back' as animals do," whose "attention . . . had already been taken by something not yet in history," who like "a figurehead in a museum, which though static . . . seemed yet to be going against the wind" "as if this girl were the converging halves of a broken fate, setting face, in sleep, toward itself in time, as an image and its reflection in a lake seem parted only by the hesitation in the hour."[105] At the end, she shifts metaphorical schemes, and in such a way as to lateralize relations and literalize what might seem metaphorical. She, again, revising Frau Mann ("as unsexed as a doll"), becomes a vehicle to her tenor, crawling back to Nora through the body of a metaphor. She becomes as sexed as a dog.

There is nothing simple about the queer child. I began this essay and, indeed, have proceeded with the pretext of building from simplicity to density, rather than supplying a historical survey that would appear in chronological time. I have offered some hypotheses: certain supposedly accessible strands of what the phrase *queer child* might mean. And yet each strand that I have proposed—each version of the queer child—has ended up showing how even familiar categories of the queer child are not so simple when we examine them.

First of all, they start to braid, one with another, leading quickly to commingling portraits of the queer child. The first film I cite, *The Hanging Garden*, simultaneously illustrates the ghostly gay child and the grown homosexual, though Freud's child and the child queered by innocence (in this case, invoked by the gay child's abuse at the hands of his father) could also be found. So, too, *The Children's Hour* and *Lolita* both demand com-mingling models of the queer child in order to account for their depictions of not exclusively homosexual childhood sexuality. Even the question of innocence proves to be remarkably layered, oxymoronic, requiring the pretzel logic of what I call normative strangeness, not to mention the logic of abuse, to account for its appearance as a queer child strand. This is to say that each category in itself offers tangles. The first one alone, involving the gay child (which would be the meaning most people would associate with "the queer child"), is entirely tangled up with retrospection, linguistic delay, the metaphorical deaths of certain children and the births and deaths of metaphors. In fact, from self-help books to *Nightwood*, we cannot grasp the queer child's multiple manifestations in twentieth-century culture without getting formal and also abstract—taking on the formal dimen-sions of metaphor and the abstractions of queer child time.

This might be the most surprising and challenging aspect of my essay: Some of the densest, most commingled, most experimental, most intertex-tual, and most telling portraits of the queer child appear in the first half or the first third of the twentieth century. And they involve dogs. The family pet swerves from the Oedipal path it treads in order to offer an interval of animal and thus a figure of sideways growth. In the guise of metaphor (one the child can actively touch), the child, for a time, can hang suspended in an intensity that is a motion, an emotion, and a growth, even though, from certain conventional angles, it may look like a way of going nowhere.

Notes

1. Ritch C. Savin-Williams, "*. . . And Then I Became Gay*": *Young Men's Stories* (New York: Routledge, 1998), 30; Matthew Stadler, "Homo Sex Story," in *Boys Like Us: Gay Writers Tell Their Coming Out Stories*, ed. Patrick Merla (New York: Avon, 1996), 168; Ed Sikov, "Chemistry," in *Boys Like Us*, 230–31.

2. See Funny Gay Males (Jaffe Cohen, Danny McWilliams, and Bob Smith), *Growing Up Gay: From Left Out to Coming Out* (New York: Hyperion, 1995), 127–28.

3. I am referring to scenes from the films *The Hanging Garden* (1997) and *The Children's Hour* (1961), and from Charlotte Brontë's novel *Villette* (1853).

4. Djuna Barnes, *Nightwood* (New York: New Directions, 1961), 41, 45, 168.

5. Vladimir Nabokov, *Lolita* (1955; repr., New York: Vintage, 1991), 306. Quilty, remember, is nicknamed "Cue."

6. Luce Irigaray, *Speculum of the Other Woman*, trans. Gillian C. Gill (Ithaca, NY: Cornell University Press, 1985), 36, 42, 77–78.

7. *Webster's New World Dictionary* defines the child as "1) an infant; baby 2) an unborn offspring; fetus 3) a boy or girl in the period before puberty 4) a son or daughter; offspring 5) a descendent 6) a person like a child in interests, judgment, etc, or one regarded as immature and childish." All of these meanings will appear in this essay.

8. Leo Bersani, "Is the Rectum a Grave?" in *AIDS: Cultural Analysis/Cultural Activism,* ed. Douglas Crimp (Cambridge: MIT Press, 1988), 203.

9. On the linkage of "children" as a concept to the concept of a "future," see Lee Edelman's important essay "The Future Is Kid Stuff: Queer Theory, Disidentification, and the Death Drive," *Narrative* 6, no. 1 (1998): 18–30. On the violence embedded in ideals, see Georges Bataille, "Rotten Sun" and "The Language of Flowers," both in *Visions of Excess: Selected Writings, 1927–1939,* ed. and trans. Allan Stoekl (Minneapolis: University of Minnesota Press, 1985).

10. All of television's flirtations with this category have involved gay or experimenting teens and gender-identity issues for children—never (to my knowledge) an explicitly same-sex-oriented child.

11. Terry Sanderson, *A Stranger in the Family: How to Cope If Your Child Is Gay* (London: Other Way , 1996), 8.

12. Ibid., 5.

13. Ibid., 21.

14. Ibid., 20.

15. Marlene Fanta Shyer and Christopher Shyer, *Not Like Other Boys: Growing Up Gay: A Mother and Son Look Back* (Boston: Houghton Mifflin, 1996), viii.

16. Ibid., ix, x.

17. Ibid., 2.

18. Ibid., 10.

19. Ibid., 11.

20. Ibid., 13, 12.

21. Ibid., 15.

22. Ibid., 54.

23. Ibid.

24. Ibid., 114.

25. Ibid., 20.

26. Ibid.

27. Ibid.

28. Savin-Williams makes it clear whom he is excluding in order to find his normative patterns. He refers to earlier studies on gay youth "composed primarily of 'marginal' teenagers such as male hustlers, streetwalkers, homeless youths, and draft dodgers" and then remarks, "Only at great peril could anyone attempt to generalize findings from these studies to current cohorts of sexual-minority youths." *"And Then I Became Gay,"* 11.

29. Ibid., 15.

30. Ibid., 16.

31. Ibid., 31.

32. Cole Moreton, "Christian Centre 'Turns Gays Straight,'" *Independent,* November 20, 1994, 6.

33. Henry Makow, "We're Being Brainwashed to Be Gay," *Toogood Reports,* December 12, 2001, 3.

34. Charles Darwin, *The Descent of Man* (New York: Modern Library, 1936), 421.

35. Ibid., 421.

36. Max Nordau, *Degeneration*, 8th ed. (New York: Appleton, 1896), 554–55.

37. Cesar Lombroso, *Crime: Its Causes and Remedies*, trans. Henry P. Norton (Boston: Little, Brown, 1918), 418.

38. Sigmund Freud, "A Letter from Freud," *American Journal of Psychiatry* 107 (April 1951): 786.

39. Quoted in Kenneth Lewes, *The Psychoanalytic Theory of Male Homosexuality* (New York: Simon & Schuster, 1988), 30.

40. Sigmund Freud, *Three Essays on the Theory of Sexuality,* in *Standard Edition of the Complete Psychological Works of Sigmund Freud,* vol. 7, ed. and trans. James Strachey (London: Hogarth, 1966), 138.

41. Quoted in Lewes, *The Psychoanalytic Theory,* 149.

42. Sigmund Freud, "Femininity," in *New Introductory Letters on Psychoanalysis,* ed. and trans. James Strachey (London: Hogarth, 1974), 134.

43. Ibid., 133–34.

44. Ibid.

45. Ibid., 130.

46. Charlotte Brontë, *Villette* (1853; repr., New York: Penguin, 1979), 64, 81.

47. Ibid., 73, 64, 72, 66, 69, 90, 85.

48. Ibid., 72.

49. Ibid., 80, 90.

50. Ibid., 91, 76–77.

51. Ibid., 75.

52. Ibid., 92.

53. See Kathryn Bond Stockton, "Eve's Queer Child," in *Regarding Sedgwick: Essays in Queer Culture and Critical Theory,* ed. Stephen Barber and David L. Clark (New York: Routledge, 2002), 181–99.

54. See Vito Russo's discussion in *The Celluloid Closet: Homosexuality in the Movies,* rev. ed. (New York: Harper & Row, 1987), 121.

55. Nabokov, *Lolita,* 104.

56. Ibid., 117, 118.

57. Ibid., 237.

58. Ibid., 164.

59. For an essay-length treatment of these issues, see Kathryn Bond Stockton, "Motive's Mysterious Motions: Narrative Trials for the Queer Child," in *The Queer Child* (unpublished manuscript). Here I discuss two famous murders in the 1950s and two trials by narrative thirty years apart: the murder of the Clutter family (1957) as depicted by Truman Capote in *In Cold Blood* (1966) as well as in a 1967 film based on the book and the murder (in 1954) of a New Zealand mother by her daughter and her daughter's "special" friend as represented by Peter Jackson's film *Heavenly Creatures* in 1994.

60. What I am calling "landmark studies" are particularly helpful for understanding the stunning contradictions (especially with reference to class) surrounding the historical invention of Western childhood innocence. James R. Kincaid has most recently explored the Victorian versions of these contradictions in his indispensable *Child-Loving: The Erotic Child and Victorian Culture* (New York: Routledge,

1992). See also the earlier, famous studies by Philippe Ariès, *Centuries of Childhood: A Social History of Family Life,* trans. Robert Baldick (New York: Vintage, 1962); Lloyd deMause, ed., *The History of Childhood* (New York: Psychohistory, 1974); Ivy Pinchbeck and Margaret Hewitt, *Children in English Society,* vol. 2, *From the Eighteenth Century to the Children Act of 1948* (Toronto: University of Toronto Press, 1973); Laurence Stone, *The Family, Sex, and Marriage in England, 1500–1800* (New York: Harper & Row,1977).

    61. Ariès, *Centuries of Childhood,* 33, 110.

    62. See, in these respects, Neil Postman's laments in *The Disappearance of Childhood* (New York: Vintage, 1982).

    63. Ariès, *Centuries of Childhood,* 113.

    64. William Blake, "The Little Black Boy" (1789), in *The Norton Anthology of Poetry,* rev. ed., ed. Alexander W. Allison et al. (New York: W. W. Norton, 1975), 547.

    65. See, for example, Harold Bloom, "Introduction," in *William Blake's Songs of Innocence and of Experience,* ed. Harold Bloom (New York: Chelsea House, 1987), 1–28; David V. Erdman, "Blake's Vision of Slavery," in *Blake: A Collection of Critical Essays,* ed. Northrop Frye (Englewood Cliffs, NJ: Prentice Hall, 1966), 88–103; Myra Glazer, "Blake's Little Black Boys: On the Dynamics of Blake's Composite Art," in *Blake's Songs,* 85–100; Robert F. Gleckner, "The Strange Odyssey of Blake's 'The Voice of the Ancient Bard,'" in *Blake's Songs,* 101–21; E. D. Hirsch Jr., *Innocence and Experience: An Introduction to Blake* (New Haven, CT: Yale University Press, 1964); Nicolas M. Williams, *Ideology and Utopia in the Poetry of William Blake* (Cambridge: Cambridge University Press, 1998).

    66. One could consult Charles Baxter, "A Self-Consuming Light: *Nightwood* and the Crisis of Modernism," *Journal of Modern Literature* 3 (1974): 1175–87; Elizabeth Pochoda, "Style's Hoax: A Reading of Djuna Barnes' *Nightwood,*" *Twentieth-Century Literature* 22 (1976): 179–91; Cheryl Plumb, "Introduction," in Djuna Barnes, *Nightwood: The Original Version and Related Drafts* (Normal, IL: Dalkey Archive Press, 1995): vii–xxvi; Phillip Herring, *Djuna: The Life and Work of Djuna Barnes* (New York: Penguin, 1995); Donna Gerstenberger, "Modern (Post)Modern: Djuna Barnes among the Others," *Review of Contemporary Fiction* 13, no. 3 (1993): 33–40.

    67. Barnes, *Nightwood,* 3, 5.

    68. Ibid., 101.

    69. Ibid., 56.

    70. Ibid., 28.

    71. Ibid., 61.

    72. Gilles Deleuze and Félix Guattari, *A Thousand Plateaus: Capitalism and Schizophrenia,* trans. Brian Massumi (Minneapolis: University of Minnesota Press, 1987), 237.

    73. Ibid., 244, 240.

    74. Ibid., 255.

    75. Ibid., 257, 259, 260.

    76. Ibid., 258.

    77. Barnes, *Nightwood,* 51.

78. Virginia Woolf, *Mrs. Dalloway* (1925; repr., New York: Harvest, 1981), 30.

79. Ibid., 32.

80. Ibid., 35.

81. Ibid., 11.

82. Ibid., 204.

83. Ibid., 287.

84. Ibid., 296.

85. Radclyffe Hall, *The Well of Loneliness* (1928; repr., New York: Anchor, 1990), 59.

86. For a detailed discussion of this queer child's remarkable attempt to court her servant, see Kathryn Bond Stockton, "Cloth Wounds, or When Queers Are Martyred to Clothes: The Value of Clothing's Complex Debasements," *Women: A Cultural Review* 13, no. 3 (2002): 289–321.

87. Hall, *The Well of Loneliness*, 336.

88. Ibid., 394.

89. Ibid., 436–37.

90. Barnes, *Nightwood*, 3.

91. Ibid., 9.

92. The best index to this issue is Jane Marcus's essay "Laughing at Leviticus: *Nightwood* as Woman's Circus Epic," in *Silence and Power: A Reevaluation of Djuna Barnes*, ed. Mary Lynn Broe (Carbondale: Southern Illinois University Press, 1991), 221–50.

93. Barnes, *Nightwood*, 11.

94. Ibid., 12.

95. Ibid., 13.

96. Ibid., 34.

97. Ibid., 34–35.

98. Ibid., 136–37.

99. Ibid., 137.

100. Ibid., 59.

101. Jane Marcus examines Dr. O'Connor as a parody of Freud in "Laughing at Leviticus."

102. Barnes, *Nightwood*, 82–83.

103. Ibid., 54.

104. Ibid., 23.

105. Ibid., 41, 40, 44, 38.

Contributors

Lauren Berlant is professor of English at the University of Chicago. She is completing a national sentimentality trilogy, *The Anatomy of National Fantasy*, *The Queen of America Goes to Washington City: Essays on Sex and Citizenship*, and the forthcoming *The Female Complaint: The Unfinished Business of Sentimentality in American Culture*. She is editor of several volumes, including *Intimacy*, *Venus Inferred* (with Laura Letinsky), and *Our Monica, Ourselves* (with Lisa Duggan), as well as coeditor of *Critical Inquiry*, contributing editor of *Public Culture*, and an active editorial board member of *Modern Fiction Studies*, *Cultural Values*, and *Topia*.

Steven Bruhm is associate professor of English at Mount St. Vincent University, Halifax, Canada. He is author of *Gothic Bodies: The Politics of Pain in Romantic Fiction*, *Reflecting Narcissus: A Queer Aesthetic* (Minnesota, 2001), and numerous articles on the contemporary gothic. He is now working on the project "Only the Dead Can Dance: Gothic Choreographies of Mortality," which analyzes the intersections between dance and death in gothic aesthetics.

Andre Furlani is associate professor of English at Concordia University in Montreal. His recent publications include essays on collage, postmodernist fiction, rhetoric in Henry James, and historiographical drama. His book *Guy Davenport: Before and After Postmodernism* is forthcoming.

Judith Halberstam is professor of literary and cultural studies at the University of California, San Diego. She is author of *Skin Shows: Gothic Horror and the Technology of Monsters* and *Female Masculinity*, and coauthor with Del LaGrace Volcano of *The Drag King Book*. She is working on a book on queer subcultures.

Ellis Hanson teaches in the English department and is chair of the Lesbian, Bisexual, and Gay Studies Program at Cornell University. He is author of *Decadence and Catholicism* and editor of *Out Takes: Essays on Queer Theory and Film.*

Natasha Hurley teaches children's literature and queer theory at Mount St. Vincent University and St. Mary's University in Halifax, Canada. She is completing a dissertation on the rise of the gay and lesbian novel in nineteenth-century America.

Paul Kelleher recently received his Ph.D. in English at Princeton University. His dissertation, "Men of Feeling: Sentimentalism, Sexuality, and the Conduct of Life in Eighteenth-Century British Literature," rereads the history of sexuality through the literature and philosophy of sentimentalism. He is the author of essays on the work of Eve Kosofsky Sedgwick and on queer forms of affect and social relation in Enlightenment and twentieth-century philosophy.

Kathryn R. Kent is associate professor of English at Williams College. She is the author of *Making Girls into Women: American Women's Writing and the Rise of Lesbian Identity.*

James R. Kincaid, Aerol Arnold Professor of English at the University of Southern California, is author of *Erotic Innocence: The Culture of Child Molesting, Annoying the Victorians,* and *Child-Loving: The Erotic Child and Victorian Culture.* He has written on Victorian literature, cultural and literary theory, and various cultural issues.

Richard D. Mohr is professor of philosophy at the University of Illinois–Urbana.

Michael Moon, professor of English at Johns Hopkins University, is author of *Disseminating Whitman: Revision and Corporeality in "Leaves of Grass"* and *A Small Boy and Others: Imitation and Initiation in American Culture from Henry James to Andy Warhol.*

Kevin Ohi is assistant professor of English at Boston College. He has just completed a book manuscript on children and aestheticism and is beginning a new project on Henry James. He has recently published articles on James Baldwin, Charles Dickens, Vladimir Nabokov, Oscar Wilde, and the films *Suddenly, Last Summer* and *The Boys of St. Vincent.*

Eric Savoy is associate professor of English at the University of Montreal. He has published many articles on Henry James and homotextuality, and is coeditor (with Robert K. Martin) of *American Gothic: New Interventions in a National Narrative.* He is working on a book on James's queer formalism.

Eve Kosofsky Sedgwick is Distinguished Professor of English at CUNY Graduate Center. Her books include *Between Men: English Literature and Male Homosocial Desire, Epistemology of the Closet, Tendencies, A Dialogue on Love,* and *Touching Feeling.*

Kathryn Bond Stockton, associate professor of English and the director of gender studies at the University of Utah, is author of *God between Their Lips: Desire between Women in Irigaray, Bronte, and Eliot, Beautiful Bottom, Beautiful Shame: Where "Black" Meets "Queer,"* and *The Queer Child.*

Michael Warner is professor of English at Rutgers University. His most recent works include *Publics and Counterpublics, The Trouble with Normal: Sex, Politics, and the Ethics of Queer Life,* and *American Sermons: The Pilgrims to Martin Luther King.* He is editor of *Fear of a Queer Planet: Queer Politics and Social Theory* (Minnesota, 1993) and coeditor (with Myra Jehlen) of *The English Literatures of America, 1500–1800* and (with Gerald Graff) of *The Origins of Literary Studies in America: A Documentary Anthology.* His essays and journalism have appeared in the *Village Voice, VLS, The Nation, The Advocate, POZ, In These Times,* and other magazines. He lives in Brooklyn.

Publication History

"Oh Bondage Up Yours! Female Masculinity and the Tomboy," by Judith Halberstam, was originally published in *Sissies and Tomboys: Gender Nonconformity and Homosexual Childhood,* edited by Matthew Rottnek (New York: New York University Press, 1999), 153–79. Reprinted with permission of New York University Press.

"Tongues Untied: Memoirs of a Pentecostal Boyhood," by Michael Warner, was originally published in the *Village Voice Literary Supplement,* February 1993. Reprinted by permission of the author.

"Oh Bondage Up Yours!" words and music by Marian Elliott. Copyright 1977 Westminster Music Ltd., London, England. TRO–Essex Music International, Inc., New York, controls all publication rights for the United States and Canada. Reprinted by permission.

"Wild Thing," by Sapphire, from *American Dreams* (London: Serpent's Tail, 1994). Reprinted with permission from Serpent's Tail.

Index

Firestarter (film), 111
Fitzhugh, Louise, 189n27
Fletcher, John, 248–49
Forrest Gump (film), 11
Foster, Jodie, 8, 207
Foucault, Michel: and criminality, 152,
    160–62; and discourses of sex, x,
    xiv, 180; perverse implantation, 20;
    "Repressive Hypothesis," xv
Fourier, Charles, 227, 232; calculus
    of the passions, 226; on sexuality,
    229–30, 233, 235, 238, 240
Fourteenth Amendment, 64, 66
Foxes (film), 207
"Fragments of an Analysis of a Case of
    Hysteria" (Freud), 135n8
Fraser, Nancy, 176
Free Willy (film), 210
Fresh Air Fund, 25, 27
Freud, Sigmund, xix–xx, xxi, xxvi,
    xxviii, xxix, xxxii, xxxvin26, 13, 50,
    110, 114–17 *passim*, 121, 125, 127,
    128, 135n8, 140, 152–59, 160–65,
    168n8, 169n16, 170n33, 170n39,
    171n52, 171n60, 223, 227, 230,
    235–36, 247–48, 253, 270–71, 272,
    279, 281, 283, 289, 290–91, 295, 296,
    309, 310, 315n101; and Bersani,
    xx, xxvii, 155; and Brown, 50; and
    James, 271, 272; and Klein, 162–68.
    See also crime; heterosexual(ity);
    homosexuality; narcissism; Oedipal
    conflict; perversion; psychoanalysis;
    sexuality
*Freudian Body: Psychoanalysis and Art,
    The* (Bersani), xxvii, 155
Friedman, Richard C., 140–45, 148n5,
    148n10
Frohnmayer, John, 60, 52–65
"From the History of an Infantile Neu-
    rosis (The Wolf Man)," 115, 116, 165,
    171n60, 247–48, 253, 270–71, 272
Fun (film), 206
Furlani, Andre, xxxiii, 225–44
Fury, The (film), 111
Fuss, Diana, 171n65, 189n31

future: as heteronormative, xiii–x,
    xviii–xix, xxx, xxiv, xxxvnn10–11,
    84, 89–90, 159, 202, 205, 208, 291,
    312n9; national, 58, 60, 65–66,
    72, 243n56; as queer, 89–90, 192,
    196–97, 205, 211, 308; utopian, xiii,
    xiv, 45

Gainsborough, Thomas, 228
Gans, Herbert J., 117–18
Garber, Jenny, 193
Gay Ideas (Mohr), xxxiii, 30
gay youth. *See under* queer
Gender Shock (Burke), 212n3
Gentleman in Trollope (Letwin), 55n15
Gilmour, Robhi, 55n15
girls, xi, xiii, xvii, xxxiii, 11, 19, 24, 29,
    120, 173–87, 182, 188n21, 191–214,
    226, 232; androgyny, 197–206; and
    class, 40–41, 173–87, 191–214; dead
    girls, xvii; as erotic figures, xvii,
    66–71, 186; and female masculinity,
    191–214; and femininity, 191, 192,
    194, 205, 206, 207, 208, 212n3; and
    feminism, 61–69, 191; and gender
    crossing, 11, 51, 40–41, 141, 191–214;
    Girl Scouts, 183–87, 188n21; hetero-
    sexuality, 205, 208, 211; lesbianism/
    homosexuality of, 141, 174, 177,
    185, 202, 204, 207, 208, 209, 210;
    and medicine, xxxivn1, 201–2, 211,
    212n3, 213n28; as minor citizens,
    66–71; and motherhood, xi, 120,
    121, 175; as objects of the gaze, xvii,
    19, 24, 51, 66–71, 186, 206; parent-
    ing of, 197; and pornography, 69–71;
    proper gender roles, 19, 24, 51, 120,
    121, 141, 182, 186, 191, 192, 193, 194,
    195, 197, 198, 199, 200, 201, 204, 204,
    205–6, 207, 208, 210, 211, 212n3,
    226, 232; queerness of, xiii, 179, 192,
    196, 209; rebellion of, 192, 196, 206,
    207, 208, 210, 211; sexuality of, xvii,
    xxxiii, xxxivn1, 29, 115, 121, 174,
    176, 177, 185, 192, 186, 202, 204, 207,
    208, 209, 210, 228

▼ Index

331

65, 112, 117, 120, 209; and Oedipal narrative, 162, 164–65, 209, 291, 301; and phallic mother, 115, 124; and primal scene, 248, 271 (*see also* "Case of the Wolf Man"); self-mothering, 49; substitute, 45, 181, 184–85, 292, 300, 305

Mrs. Dalloway (Woolf), 282, 301–2

Mystères de Paris, Les (Sue), 36

Mysteries and Miseries of New York (Buntline), 36

Mysteries of London (Reynolds), 36

"Mysteries of the Joy Rio, The" (Williams), xxxviii

Mystic Chords of Memory (Kammen), 78n2

My Three Sons (TV), 277

Nabokov, Vladimir, 296, 298, 299

narcissism, 120; and Freud, xix–xx, xxxvin26, 163

narrative, xxviii, xxx, xxxvi, 5, 6, 7, 15, 34, 42, 45, 49, 63, 72, 83, 85, 87, 92, 94, 95, 113, 114, 116, 142, 155, 168n9, 175, 181, 194, 211, 223, 226, 239, 246, 247–48, 249, 250, 251, 252, 253, 255, 256, 257, 259, 261, 263, 264, 266, 267, 268, 269, 270, 271, 272, 273, 256, 287, 313n59; and adults, xxi, xxix, 194, 246; antifeminist, 175; antinarrative, xxi, 155; apocalyptic, 129; authority, 15, 246; and/about children/child sexuality, ix–xiv, xviiin60, 6, 8, 11, 15, 85, 113, 114, 118, 121, 132, 194, 209, 211, 239, 247, 253, 255, 257, 273, 286, 287, 313n59; and closure, 45, 273; constraints, ix–xiv, xxxiv, 226; continuity, 248; conversion, 223, 237; didactic, 38; domestic, 56n22; emancipatory/redemptive, 132, 134, 226; of enlightenment, 92; forms, 14; gothic, 5, 13, 15, 85, 101, 110, 113, 114, 121, 134, 181, 146, 248, 249, 261, 264, 270; of hermaphrodit-

ism, 209; and homosexuality, xiv, xxviii, 155; incomplete, xxi, 155; and innocence, 5, 98; intensity, 42; interest, xxii; irony, 85; and law, 73; life, xxiii, xxxiv; and lyric, 73; master, 56n22; and memory, xxviii, xxiv; nationalist, 57–80, 175; and normativity, ix–xiv, xvii, xxi; and panic, 246, 248; and pastoral, 226; and pleasure, xi, 8, 57, 85, 135, 246, 249, 253, 302; popular, 50, 113; and psychoanalysis, xxi, xxix–xxx, 83, 118, 132, 143, 149n10, 155, 168n9, 253, 272; of resistance, 175; scandalous, 15, 113; of sexuality, ix–xxxviii, 8, 12, 15, 155, 118, 245–46, 249, 251; of simplification, ix–xiv, xxiv, xxxiv, 15; and storytelling, theories of, ix–xiv; suspense, 264, 266; time, xix, xviii–xix, xxxii, 7, 218, 250, 251, 255, 286; tomboy, 194, 209, 211; and trauma, xxi, xxiii, xxv, xxvi, xxviii, xxx, xxviiin60, 72, 110, 132, 146–57, 267, 269, 270, 308; unconscious of, xxi; of upward mobility, xxi, 56n22; victim, xxix; voice, 84, 95; and wish-fulfillment, 155; woman's, 220

National Child Labor Committee (NCLC), 51–52

National Endowment for the Arts, 62–65

National Velvet (film), 207

Nesler, Elli, 4–5, 8, 15n2, 16n5

Nesler, Willie, 4–5

New Introductory Lectures on Psycho-analysis (Freud), 156–57, 159, 235

Newman, Lesléa, xxxvn8

New York Times, 17, 20, 23–24, 27–29

New York v. Ferber, 71

niche marketing, institutions of, 48–49

Nietzsche, Friedrich, 166, 218, 223, 242n35

Nightwood (Barnes), 278, 281–82, 299–302, 305–11

Nordau, Max Simon, 290